COLUMBIA COLLEGE

Black Communities and Urban Development in America 1720–1990

A Ten-Volume Collection of Articles Surveying the Social, Political, Economic, and Cultural Development of Black Urban Communities

Edited by
**Kenneth L. Kusmer
Temple University**

A GARLAND SERIES

Volume 6

Depression, War, and the New Migration, 1930–1960

Edited with an Introduction by
Kenneth L. Kusmer

GARLAND PUBLISHING, INC.
NEW YORK & LONDON
1991

973.0496073 D424k

Black communities and urban
development in America 1720

Introduction © 1991 Kenneth L. Kusmer
All rights reserved.

Library of Congress Cataloging-in-Publication Data

Black communities and urban race relations in American history / edited with an introduction by Kenneth L. Kusmer.
    p.   cm.
   Includes bibliographical references.
   Contents: v. 1. The Colonial and early national period — v. 2. Antebellum America — v. 3. The Civil War and Reconstruction era, 1861–1877 — v. 4. From Reconstruction to the Great Migration, 1877–1917 (2 v.) — v. 5. The Great Migration and after, 1917–1930 — v. 6. Depression, war, and the new migration, 1930–1960 — v. 7. The ghetto crisis of the 1960s — v. 8. Progress versus poverty, 1970 to the present — v. 9. Overviews, theory, and historiography.

   ISBN 0-8153-0430-7 (v. 6 : alk. paper)

   1. Afro-Americans—History. 2. Afro-Americans—Social conditions. 3. United States—Race relations. I. Kusmer, Kenneth L., 1945–
E185.5.B515   1991   91-3756
973'.0496073—dc20   CIP

Printed on acid-free, 250-year-life paper.
Manufactured in the United States of America.

Volume 6

Depression, War, and the New Migration, 1930–1960

The optimism and sense of progress that suffused many black communities in the 1920s collapsed abruptly as the nation slid into economic depression in the fall of 1929. Traditionally, blacks were the first to be fired during economic downturns, and the 1930s were no exception. High levels of black unemployment had a disastrous effect on black businesses, and poverty conditions increased dramatically in the ghettos as the depression deepened.

The impact of the New Deal on black communities was complex and sometimes contradictory. The New Deal's relief and employment programs benefitted urban blacks greatly, but in hiring blacks, federal agencies made no effort to overcome the pattern of job discrimination that had limited black mobility in the 1920s. Likewise, the New Deal provided public housing for blacks as well as whites, but the construction of black housing projects in ghetto areas frequently displaced poor blacks while reinforcing residential segregation. The problem, as Raymond Mohl has pointed out in his article on Miami, was not the federal programs themselves, which were often progressive, but the way in which they were implemented by local power brokers.

World War II brought a renewal of hope for black urbanites, as well an era of intensified racial conflict. As industry began to revive in 1940–1941, blacks at first were excluded or restricted to menial employment. Black protest and a vast expansion of industrial demand in 1942 to meet the war effort, however, finally opened up factory work in the North for blacks.[1] Blacks benefitted as well from the policy of interracial solidarity of the new Congress of Industrial Organizations. As Christopher Wye has indicated in his previously unpublished essay in this volume, the shift in racial attitude from the discriminatory American Federation of Labor unions to the more racially inclusive CIO marked an important turning point in labor relations in the industrial cities.

Black migration to northern centers had declined sharply during the 1930s, but the wartime need for industrial labor promoted a new exodus from the South. The migration of World War II was every bit as intense as that of World War I, and it led to a similarly hostile response from many whites. A series of race riots broke out in 1943, including a violent encounter in Detroit that year that left twenty-five blacks and nine whites dead.[2]

Politically, the 1930s and 1940s led to a sea change in the voting patterns of blacks in the northern cities. Despite the failure of the federal government to confront segregation, millions of African-Americans received jobs, training, and relief as a result of New Deal programs. As a result, blacks deserted the Republican party *en masse* in 1936 to help give Franklin D. Roosevelt his landslide victory of that year.³ At the local level, however, blacks often remained committed to the Republican party much longer, primarily because of distrust of local white Democrats and commitment to entrenched black Republican politicos. Beginning in the late 1930s, then accelerating during World War II and afterward, urban blacks in the North began to extend their support to the Democratic party at the local level as well, and gradually a new group of black Democratic political leaders emerged in cities across the North.

The postwar era brought a continuation of the wartime migration of blacks from the South. Although it has been little studied, the migration of the 1940s, 1950s, and 1960s was actually far greater than the "Great Migration" of the World War I period. The influx of blacks into cities of the North and West sometimes led to an expansion of the ghettos formed in the 1920s, but more importantly it often promoted the creation of new, much larger "second ghettos" as well—such as the West Side ghetto in Chicago.⁴ By 1960 residential segregation had reached an all-time high in American cities, and the level of segregation in southern and western cities was aproaching that of the North. Federal housing and urban renewal programs, as Kenneth Jackson and others have pointed out, often reinforced the racist policies of real estate dealers.⁵ At the same time, overt discrimination in public accommodations in northern cities declined during the postwar era. Exclusion of African Americans from restaurants or hotels and segregation of blacks in theaters and recreation facilities had all but disappeared from the North by 1960.

The issues of voting rights and segregation in public facilities, which energized the civil rights movement and convulsed the South between 1955 and 1965, played only a small role in northern cities during this period. The much enlarged black populations of northern cities led to an increase in the number of black elected officials, now almost always Democrats. Black representation in city councils grew steadily. In 1944, Harlem's Adam Clayton Powell became the second northern black to win election to Congress; by 1964 there were six blacks in Congress, five from northern cities and one from Los Angeles. For the most part, however, the new black political leaders of the postwar era continued to play a subsidiary role within white-dominated political machines. As Paul Kleppner has shown in a case study of Chicago, black votes became increasingly important to the machine in the 1950s and early 1960s. In spite of this, blacks did not receive a fair share of political patronage, and Mayor Richard J. Daley consistently ignored the demands of reformers for more black police and better schools and services in black neighborhoods.⁶ It was issues like these, rather than the fundamental struggle for basic civil rights, that would turn cities like Chicago into an urban battleground in the late 1960s.

Kenneth L. Kusmer

Notes

1. See Joe William Trotter, Jr., *Black Milwaukee: The Making of an Industrial Proletariat* (Urbana: University of Illinois Press, 1985), 147–95.
2. The conflict over black access to a New Deal housing project in Detroit in 1942 was in many ways a prelude to the riot the following year. See the excellent study by Dominic Capeci, *Race Relations in Wartime Detroit: The Sojourner Truth Housing Controversy of 1942* (Philadelphia: Temple University Press, 1984).
3. On the New Deal, see Harvard Sitkoff, *A New Deal for Blacks: The Emergence of Civil Rights as a National Issue* (New York: Oxford University Press, 1978), and Nancy Weiss, *Farewell to the Party of Lincoln: Black Politics in the Age of F.D.R.* (Princeton: Princeton University Press, 1983).
4. Arnold Hirsch, *The Making of the Second Ghetto: Race and Housing in Chicago, 1940–1960* (Cambridge, Eng.: Cambridge University Press, 1983).
5. Kenneth T. Jackson, "Race, Ethnicity, and Real Estate Appraisal: The Home Owners Loan Corportation and the Federal Housing Administration," *Journal of Urban History* 6 (1980), 419–52.
6. Paul Kleppner, *Chicago Divided: The Making of a Black Mayor* (DeKalb, Ill.: Northern Illinois University Press, 1985).

Further Reading

Capeci, Dominic, Jr. *The Harlem Riot of 1935.* Philadelphia: Temple University Press, 1977.
———, *Race Relations in Wartime Detroit: The Sojourner Truth Housing Controversy of 1942.* Philadelphia: Temple University Press, 1984.
Cayton, Horace R., and George S. Mitchell. *Black Workers and the New Unions.* Chapel Hill: University of North Carolina Press, 1939.
Drake, St. Clair, and Horace R. Cayton. *Black Metropolis: A Study of Negro Life in a Northern City.* New York: Harper and Row, 1945.
Harris, Abram L. *The Negro as Capitalist.* New York: Negro Universities Press, 1969 [originally published 1936].
Hirsch, Arnold. *The Making of the Second Ghetto: Race and Housing in Chicago, 1940–1960.* Cambridge, Eng.: Cambridge University Press, 1983.
Jackson, Kenneth T. "Race, Ethnicity, and Real Estate Appraisal: The Home Owners Loan Corportation and the Federal Housing Administration." *Journal of Urban History* 6 (1980), 419–52.
Naison, Mark. *Communists in Harlem during the Depression.* Urbana: University of Illinois Press, 1983.
Thomas, Richard W. *Life Is What We Make It: Building a Black Community in Industrial Detroit, 1915–1945.* Indianapolis: University of Indiana Press,

Trotter, Joe W. *Black Milwaukee: The Making of an Industrial Proletariat, 1915–1945.* Urbana: University of Illinois Press, 1985.

Weisbrot, Robert. *Father Divine and the Struggle for Racial Equality.* Urbana: University of Illinois Press, 1983.

CONTENTS

Raymond A. Mohl, "Trouble in Paradise: Race and Housing in Miami During the New Deal Era," *Prologue* 19 (1987), 7-21 1

E. Franklin Frazier, "Some Effects of the Depression on the Negro in Northern Cities," *Science and Society* 2:4 (1938), 489-99 17

Christopher G. Wye, "The New Deal and the Negro Community: Toward a Broader Conceptualization," *Journal of American History* 59:3 (1972), 621-39 29

Mark D. Naison, "Communism and Black Nationalism in the Depression: The Case of Harlem," *Journal of Ethnic Studies* 2:2 (1974), 24-36 48

Joel Schwartz, "The Consolidated Tenants League of Harlem: Black Self-Help vs. White, Liberal Intervention in Ghetto Housing, 1934-1944," *Afro-Americans in New York Life and History* 10:1 (1986), 31-51 61

Christopher Robert Reed, "Black Chicago Political Realignment During the Great Depression and New Deal," *Illinois Historical Journal* 78:4 (1985) 242-56 82

Harvard Sitkoff, "The Detroit Race Riot of 1943," *Michigan History* 53:3 (1969), 183-206 97

Janet L. Langlois, "The Belle Isle Bridge Incident: Legend Dialectic and Semiotic System in the 1943 Detroit Race Riots," *Journal of American Folklore* 96:380 (1983), 183-99 121

L. Alex Swan, "The Harlem and Detroit Riots of 1943: A Comparative Analysis," *Berkeley Journal of Sociology* 16 (1971-72), 75-93 139

Alonzo N. Smith, "Blacks and the Los Angeles Municipal Transit System, 1941-1945," *Urbanism Past and Present* 6:1 (1980-81), 25-31 159

Christopher G. Wye, "The Black Worker and the Labor Movement in Cleveland, 1930-1945: Forging a New Relationship." Previously unpublished 166

Monroe Billington, "Public School Integration in Missouri, 1954-64," *Journal of Negro Education*, 35:3 (1966), 252-62 192

Lewis Killian and Charles Grigg, "Race Relations in an Urbanized South," *Journal of Social Issues* 22:1 (1966), 20-29 204

E. H. Beardsley, "Good-bye to Jim Crow: The Desegregation of Southern Hospitals, 1945-70," *Bulletin of the History of Medicine* 60:3 (1986), 367-86 215

Ronald H. Bayor, "Urban Renewal, Public Housing and the Racial Shaping of Atlanta," *Journal of Policy History* 1:4 (1989), 419-39 .... **235**

Emma Lou Thornbrough, "Breaking Racial Barriers to Public Accommodations in Indiana, 1935-1963," *Indiana Magazine of History* 83:4 (1987), 301-43 .... **257**

E. James Davis, "The Effects of a Freeway Displacement on Racial Housing Segregation in a Northern City," *Phylon* 26:3 (1965), 209-15 .... **301**

William J. McKenna, "The Negro Vote in Philadelphia Elections," *Pennsylvania History* 32:4 (1965), 406-15 .... **308**

Allan Pred, "Business Thoroughfares as Expressions of Urban Negro Culture," *Economic Geography* 39:3 (1963), 217-33 .... **319**

Leo F. Schnore, "Social Class Segregation Among Nonwhites in Metropolitan Centers," *Demography* 2 (1965), 126-33 .... **336**

ACKNOWLEDGMENTS

Raymond A. Mohl, "Trouble in Paradise: Race and Housing in Miami During the New Deal Era," *Prologue* 19 (1987), 7–21. Reprinted with the permission of the author and "Prologue". Courtesy of Yale University Seeley G. Mudd Library.

E. Franklin Frazier, "Some Effects of the Depression on the Negro in Northern Cities," *Science and Society* 2:4 (1938), 489–99. Reprinted with the permission of John Jay College. Courtesy of Yale University Sterling Memorial Library.

Christopher G. Wye, "The New Deal and the Negro Community: Toward a Broader Conceptualization," *Journal of American History* 59:3 (1972), 621–39. Reprinted with the permission of the Journal of American History. Courtesy of Yale University Sterling Memorial Library.

Mark Naison, "Communism and Black Nationalism in the Depression: The Case of Harlem," *Journal of Ethnic Studies* 2:2 (1974), 24–36. Reprinted with the permission of Western Washington University. Courtesy of Yale University Sterling Memorial Library.

Joel Schwartz, "The Consolidated Tenants League of Harlem: Black Self-Help vs. White, Liberal Intervention in Ghetto Housing, 1934–1944," *Afro-Americans in New York Life and History* 10:1 (1986), 31–51. Reprinted with the permission of the Afro-American Historical Association. Courtesy of *Afro-American New York Life and History*.

Christopher Robert Reed, "Black Chicago Political Realignment During the Great Depression and New Deal," *Illinois Historical Journal* 78:4 (1985), 242–56. Reprinted with the permission of the Illinois Historic Preservation Agency. Courtesy of the *Illinois Historical Journal*.

Harvard Sitkoff, "The Detroit Race Riot of 1943," *Michigan History* 53:3 (1969), 183–206. Reprinted with the permission of the Michigan Department of State Bureau of History. Courtesy of Yale University Sterling Memorial Library.

Janet L. Langlois, "The Belle Isle Bridge Incident: Legend Dialectic and Semiotic System in the 1943 Detroit Race Riots," *Journal of American Folklore* 96:380 (1983), 183–99. Reproduced with permission of the American Folklore Society. Not for reproduction. Courtesy of Yale University Sterling Memorial Library.

L. Alex Swan, "The Harlem and Detroit Riots of 1943: A Comparative Analysis," *Berkeley Journal of Sociology* 16 (1971–72), 75–93. Reprinted with the permission of the University of California Berkeley. Courtesy of *Berkeley Journal of Sociology*.

Alonzo N. Smith, "Blacks and the Los Angeles Municipal Transit System, 1941–1945," *Urbanism Past and Present* 6:1 (1980–81), 25–31. Reprinted with the permission of the University of Wisconsin-Milwaukee. Courtesy of Yale University Sterling Memorial Library.

Christopher G. Wye, "The Black Worker and the Labor Movement in Cleveland, 1930–1945: Forging a New Relationship." Previously unpublished. Reprinted with the permission of the author. Courtesy of Christopher Wye.

Monroe Billington, "The Public ool Integration in Missouri, 1954–64," *Journal of Negro Education*, 35:3 (1966), 252–62. Reprinted with the permission of Howard University. Courtesy of Yale University Seeley G. Mudd Library.

Lewis Killian and Charles Grigg, "Race Relations in an Urbanized South," *Journal of Social Issues* 22:1 (1966), 20–29. Reprinted with the permission of The Society for the Psychological Study of Social Issues. Courtesy of *Journal of Social Issues*.

E. H. Beardsley, "Good-bye to Jim Crow: The Desegregation of Southern Hospitals, 1945–70," *Bulletin of the History of Medicine* 60:3 (1986), 367–86. Reprinted with the permission of Johns Hopkins University Press. Courtesy of *Bulletin of the History of Medicine*.

Ronald H. Bayor, "Urban Renewal, Public Housing and the Racial Shaping of Atlanta," *Journal of Policy History* 1:4 (1989), 419–39. Reprinted with the permission of the Pennsylvania State University. Courtesy of *Journal of Policy History*.

Emma Lou Thornbrough, "Breaking Racial Barriers to Public Accommodations in Indiana, 1935–1963," *Indiana Magazine of History* 83:4 (1987), 301–43. Reprinted with the permission of Indiana University. Courtesy of *Indiana Magazine of History*.

F. James Davis, "The Effects of a Freeway Displacement on Racial Housing Segregation in a Northern City," *Phylon* 26:3 (1965), 209–15. Reprinted with the permission of Clark Atlanta University. Courtesy of Yale University Sterling Memorial Library.

William J. McKenna, "The Negro Vote in Philadelphia Elections," *Pennsylvania History* 32:4 (1965), 406–15. Reprinted with the permission of the Pennsylvania Historical Society. Courtesy of Yale University Sterling Memorial Library.

Allan Pred, "Business Thoroughfares as Expressions of Urban Negro Culture," *Economic Geography* 39:3 (1963), 217–33. Reprinted with the permission of Clark University. Courtesy of Yale University Seeley G. Mudd Library.

Leo F. Schnore, "Social Class Segregation Among Nonwhites in Metropolitan Centers," *Demography* 2 (1965), 126–33. Reprinted with the permission of the author and the Population Association of America. Courtesy of Yale University Sterling Memorial Library.

Trouble in Paradise: Race and Housing in Miami During the New Deal Era

By Raymond A. Mohl

It is one of the axioms of twentieth-century urban history that the New Deal forged a new relationship between the federal government and the cities. Before the 1930s city governments generally had been limited in their powers and functions by state legislative control over city charters. The lack of sufficient home rule often prevented municipal governments from embarking on necessary programs of physical development or social reform. The New Deal, however, created myriad new federal agencies and provided vast sums for relief, recovery, and reform. Although the Roosevelt administration had little in the way of a systematic urban policy, much of the new federal activism was directed to the cities and their problems. One study in 1936 noted some "500 points of contact between the federal bureaucracy and the cities in the fields of planning, zoning, education, health, internal improvements, relief, and housing." Another study has pointed out that the Roosevelt administration was the first to become "intimately concerned with urban life and city problems."[1]

Traditional interpretations of the New Deal era generally asserted the salutary effect of the new programs on urban America. Recent historical research, however, has begun to sketch out a somewhat different analysis, one that suggests that New Deal urban programs had negative as well as positive consequences. Some urban historians have demonstrated that New Deal work and welfare programs actually strengthened rather than dismantled the old political machines.[2] Others have concluded that New Deal city planners relentlessly promoted the automobile culture, while simultaneously undermining mass transit systems.[3] Still other historians have noted the New Deal's mixed record in the area of housing. Slum clearance and public housing projects were promoted only in lukewarm fashion so as not to offend powerful advocates of the free-market economy. At the same time, federal mortgage programs and highway construction encouraged middle-class and working-class whites to flee the central cities for the lily-white suburbs, leaving urban blacks and the poor behind.[4] Thus, while it is clear that the New Deal initiated a new era of federal-municipal cooperation and activism, it is also evident that this new relationship entailed unanticipated costs.

This was clearly the case in Miami during the New Deal era, particularly with respect to housing. New Dealers, with help from local political and business leaders, implemented federal public housing and mortgage programs in Miami by the mid-1930s. A succession of federal housing agencies financed several public housing projects, first for blacks and then for whites. The Home Owners Loan Corporation (HOLC), another new federal agency, conducted an extensive real estate appraisal of the Miami housing market in order to systematize the HOLC mortgage program. Both efforts stemmed from the liberal reformist impulse of the New Deal, but both had long-term and not altogether positive consequences in shaping Miami's future growth and development.

New Deal housing reform began in 1933, when Franklin D. Roosevelt's new Public Works Administration (PWA) launched a slum clearance and public housing program. The PWA's Housing Division first supported limited-dividend housing corporations in a number of cities, but it soon went on to direct federal housing construction. Both methods, generally, were slow in producing results. By 1937 the PWA had initiated only seven limited-dividend projects and forty-nine public housing projects. In 1937 the United States Housing Authority (later reorganized as the Public Housing Administration) replaced the PWA as a provider of public housing, working through state and local housing agencies.[5]

Public Housing in Miami

Action on public housing in Miami began in late 1933, when the limited-dividend Southern Housing Corporation submitted an application to the PWA Housing Division. Organized by several leading members of the city's downtown white business elite, the Southern Housing Corporation wanted both slum clearance and low-cost housing for Miami's blacks. The project soon foundered for lack of private investment, but in

A view of alley life in the black ghetto of "Overtown" in Miami during the 1930s. Most shacks lacked electricity and indoor plumbing facilities, and streets remained unpaved and unlit. Contagious diseases were common in the community.

PROLOGUE

John Gramling represented the civic elite in Miami and helped secure federal support for Liberty Square.

1934 the PWA decided to go ahead with a federally financed housing project.[6]

The need for such action on housing for blacks was compelling. By the early 1930s, most of Miami's black population of over twenty-five thousand was crowded into a 350-acre section just northwest of the central business district known at the time as "Colored Town." Today it is called Overtown. The area was covered with tiny, dilapidated shacks, sometimes as many as fifteen on a single fifty-by-one hundred-foot lot. Most buildings lacked electricity, toilets, bathing facilities, and hot water. Municipal services were noticeable by their absence, streets were unpaved and unlit, and contagious diseases were rampant. This "deplorable slum district," the *Miami Herald* editorialized in 1934, had become the "plague spot" of Miami.[7] In its application to the PWA, the Southern Housing Corporation contended that "the sanitary conditions are a menace to the whole city . . . and a shame and disgrace to the respectable citizens of Miami." But obviously the situation was worse for the blacks who lived there.[8]

Blacks were heavily concentrated in this shacktown because there were few other places for them to live in Miami at the time. A small black community had been established in Coconut Grove, mainly by Bahamian blacks who came to Miami early in the twentieth century. Farther north, two small black subdivisions emerged in the 1920s. At first a sparsely settled but integrated area, Brownsville, was located between Northwest 41st Street and Northwest 53d Street and west of 27th Avenue. Developed by a white real estate man named Floyd W. Davis, the Liberty City subdivision was home to a few hundred blacks in the neighborhood of Northwest 62d Street and 17th Avenue (see Davis subdivision on map 1). The New Deal housing program provided Miami's civic elite with an opportunity to do something about black housing conditions in the central Negro district, but it also had important implications for the future development of Liberty City.[9]

Support for the PWA housing program was widespread among Miami's business and political leaders. If the correspondence in the PWA records in the National Archives is any guide, Miami attorney John C. Gramling served as the point man for the civic elite in securing federal housing in Miami. Arriving in Miami from Alabama as a young man in 1898, Gramling became active in public affairs, serving first as a justice of the peace, then as city judge, county judge, and state's attorney. By the 1920s Gramling had emerged as an important city booster. He had established his own law firm and had become involved in local Democratic politics, real estate development, and extensive sugar cane production near Lake Okeechobee. As one writer put it in 1921, Gramling was "deeply interested in everything that tends to build up the city and community."[10] When the limited-dividend Southern Housing Corporation was organized in 1933, Gramling provided the chief motivating energy. That project failed, but Gramling remained undeterred. In a barrage of correspondence with federal officials in 1934 and 1935, Gramling argued the case for the black public housing project and, once it was approved, guided federal officials through the thickets of state and local politics.[11]

Gramling was not the only supporter of public housing for blacks in Miami. By early 1934 the PWA project had been endorsed by the *Miami Herald* and by the *Miami Daily News*, as well as by the Miami City Commission and a long list of civic and business leaders, some of whom were appointed to the Miami Advisory Committee on Housing.[12] The black community was supportive, too. The *Miami Times*, the city's black newspaper, editorialized in favor of the project. Through such groups as the Miami Colored Chamber of Commerce and the Negro Civic League, Miami's black leaders endorsed the housing plan.[13] As Gramling put it in a letter to Eugene H. Klaber of the PWA Housing Division, "all of our papers and best citizens are in favor of the

PROLOGUE

This startling poster dramatized the social problems that plagued Miami's slum areas in the 1930s.

project."[14]

The story laid out here in its essential outlines conforms to a traditional view of the federal-local relationship during the New Deal era. The New Dealers wanted to help with urban problems, and Miami's local leaders took advantage of federal largesse to bring housing reform to their town. But there are other and better explanations for what happened. One aspect of the story is partially hidden in the PWA records and other sources in Washington. These materials address the crucial question of motivation. The evidence clearly suggests that the Miami civic elite sought to eliminate the downtown black community entirely to make way for further expansion of the business district. Liberty Square, the proposed black public housing project, was to be located on Northwest 62d Street between 12th and 14th Avenues and was envisioned as the nucleus of a new and distant black community five to six miles from the city core (map 1).

Another part of the story lies in the hidden links among some members of the Miami business leadership. In particular, John Gramling served as the personal attorney of Floyd W. Davis, the developer of the small black subdivision near the proposed PWA housing project. Gramling and Davis had worked together in organizing the limited-dividend Southern Housing Corporation. Davis owned much of the unoccupied land surrounding his Liberty City subdivision, including the land ultimately purchased by the federal government for the black housing project. Davis stood to profit enormously if the PWA project stimulated the private housing market for blacks in the neighborhood. The connection between Gramling and Davis was not widely known at the time, but it helps to explain Gramling's active role in promoting the federal housing project, and especially his support for the 62d Street location. Gramling appeared to federal housing officials to be a disinterested local leader, but it is obvious that he had a personal stake in housing decisions for Miami blacks.[15] Thus, questions of land, profit, business expansion, and white racism appear more significant than any publicly stated interest in housing reform in the development of public housing for blacks in New Deal Miami.

The Miami civic elite was not noticeably altruistic when it came to the black community. John Gramling's hostile attitude toward blacks, for instance, was well known. While serving as a city judge, Gramling often praised the police for clamping down on Bahamian blacks who preached or practiced racial equality.[16] Similarly, A. B. Small, a county judge, civic leader, and active promoter of the black housing project, expressed a fairly typical kind of paternalism toward blacks. In a 1935 letter to PWA Housing Director A. R. Clas, Small wrote: "I am one of those, being a true-bred Southern man and a descendant of slave owners, who feel that the negroes are the wards of the white people and that we ought to be very scrupulous in trying to see to it that they are given proper living conditions, and I am one of those who would do anything I can to bring this about." It was in "the best interests of the city," Small argued in his benevolent way, to build the PWA project not downtown, where most of the blacks lived, but at the 62d Street location.[17]

Gramling and other white promoters of federal housing for blacks in Miami consistently used a public health argument as the primary justification for the black project more than five miles north of the city. In their correspondence with federal officials, Gramling and others repeatedly depicted the black shack-town near the business district as "a constant and deadly menace to the health of the community." Syphillis, tuberculosis, and influenza were widespread in the area,

10 SPRING 1987

PROLOGUE

Gramling noted on numerous occasions, but it was the whites, not the blacks, that he was worried about. "From this cess-pool of disease the white people of Greater Miami draw their servants," Gramling wrote to Klaber of the PWA in February 1934. Again in October, Gramling used a similar argument: "This project will be one of the greatest blessings that Miami ever had. It will not only eliminate the possibility of fatal epidemics here, but fix it so that we can get a servant freed from disease."[18]

Miami's white leaders worried about the oft-stated health "menace" in the black community, but they also used this argument to mask another motive. Indeed, PWA and other records clearly reveal this underlying purpose of the Miami business and political leadership—that of completely displacing the downtown black neighborhood. Writing to Klaber in February 1934, Gramling tipped his hand about the true purpose of the new project: "The people of Miami realize that something must be done and the newspapers agree with me that it ought to be done in the manner so that we could eventually remove the entire colored population from the dump in which they are now living."[19] Opponents of the Liberty Square project—including white "Colored Town" slum lords and whites who lived near the 62d Street location—also recognized the hidden agenda of the downtown civic elite. For example, a newly organized citizens' group called the Nor'west League deluged Washington with protests over the location of the new black housing project. According to the league, the housing program was "a secret project instigated by self-interested businessmen, real estate developers or officials . . . anxious to shove its negroes anywhere to get rid of them." As Isabelle Sanderson, secretary of the Nor'west League bluntly put it in a letter to the PWA, "everybody thinks this model negro settlement idea is lovely—for somebody else's neighborhood."[20]

The removal of blacks from "Colored Town"

In Miami's tourist-oriented economy, blacks were relegated to low-paying service jobs and domestic industries like this back-yard laundry. This photo taken from the Romer Collection of the Miami-Dade Public Library.

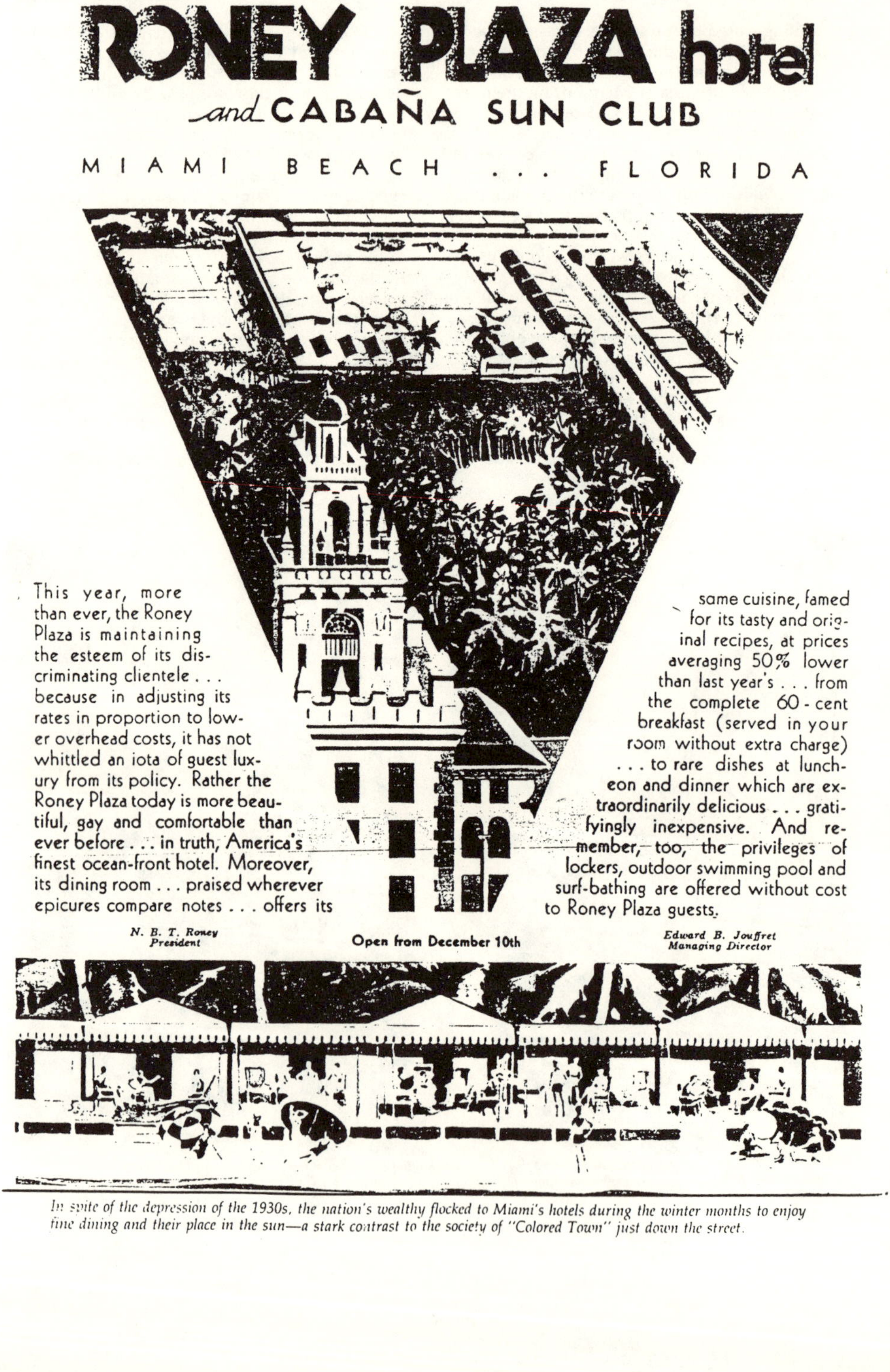

RONEY PLAZA hotel
and CABAÑA SUN CLUB
MIAMI BEACH ... FLORIDA

This year, more than ever, the Roney Plaza is maintaining the esteem of its discriminating clientele... because in adjusting its rates in proportion to lower overhead costs, it has not whittled an iota of guest luxury from its policy. Rather the Roney Plaza today is more beautiful, gay and comfortable than ever before... in truth, America's finest ocean-front hotel. Moreover, its dining room... praised wherever epicures compare notes... offers its same cuisine, famed for its tasty and original recipes, at prices averaging 50% lower than last year's... from the complete 60-cent breakfast (served in your room without extra charge) ... to rare dishes at luncheon and dinner which are extraordinarily delicious... gratifyingly inexpensive. And remember, too, the privileges of lockers, outdoor swimming pool and surf-bathing are offered without cost to Roney Plaza guests.

N. B. T. Roney
President

Open from December 10th

Edward B. Jouffret
Managing Director

In spite of the depression of the 1930s, the nation's wealthy flocked to Miami's hotels during the winter months to enjoy fine dining and their place in the sun—a stark contrast to the society of "Colored Town" just down the street.

PROLOGUE

would pave the way for slum clearance and the expansion of the Miami business district. Despite the depression, the city was growing rapidly in the 1930s. Miami, the *Herald* asserted in 1934, was "enjoying a boom that is greater in many respects than the dizzy, swaggering days of 1925." The city's population rose by 64 percent, from 110,637 in 1930 to 172,172 in 1940. Dade County population increased by over 87 percent during the decade. The bust was over, and Miami tourism, real estate, business, and building construction all were looking good. Clearly, the business community perceived the arrival of federal slum clearance and housing programs as an opportunity to eliminate the eyesore of "Colored Town" and to push out the boundaries of the central business area.[21]

Gramling was not alone in his approach. Other Miami civic leaders were thinking along the same lines. George E. Merrick, for instance, the Coral Gables developer who had lost his fortune in the collapse of the 1920s boom, was back in the thick of Miami real estate activities by the mid-1930s. In a speech to the Miami Realty Board in May 1937 Merrick proposed "a complete slum clearance . . . effectively removing every negro family from the present city limits." This black removal, Merrick asserted, was "a most essential fundamental" for the achievement of Miami's ambitious planning goals.[22]

About the same time, the Dade County Planning Council, of which Merrick was chairman, announced its "negro resettlement plan." This plan, the council asserted, was "based upon very intensive research through the best national authorities and experience, as well as upon the consensus of the best thought on the subject here in South Florida." The idea was to cooperate with the city of Miami "in removing [the] entire Central Negro town to three Negro Park locations, and establishment there of three model negro towns." One of the planned communities was to be located on distant agricultural land on the Tamiami Trail west of the city limits. The plan envisioned other black communities west of Perrine to the south and west of Opa-locka to the north. Distance was not a problem, the planning report noted, since "an exclusive negro bus line service directly from these negro areas to the heart of Miami" would be established. The Dade County Commission unanimously adopted the planning report, and it was enthusiastically endorsed by the *Miami Herald*.[23]

Thus, the forces unleashed by the New Deal housing program had a dramatic and shaping impact on Miami. The availability of federal housing funds mobilized the civic elite, who saw in slum clearance a golden opportunity to push

Blacks continued to get the runaround in 1950 from a city commission opposed to federally funded housing projects.

the blacks out of the downtown area. The Liberty Square project drew upon an undisguised racism among the city's decision-makers. It also generated several decades of racial tension in the northwest area where the 243-unit project ultimately was completed in 1937.[24]

The seemingly simple decision to provide housing for blacks had other consequences, too. As Floyd Davis and John Gramling had anticipated, the Liberty Square housing project became the nucleus of a new and rapidly growing black ghetto—the enormous fifteen square mile area now known as Liberty City. A tacit agreement among city officials, black leaders, and real estate developers designated the northwest area of Miami for future black settlement. Previously confined to the limited territory of Overtown, blacks rapidly pushed out the boundaries of Liberty City, sweeping into undeveloped land as well as white working-class neighborhoods on the northern fringes of Miami. As in such cities as Chicago and Detroit, the racial turnover of existing neighborhoods in Miami was a process filled with tension, conflict, and violence.[25]

Although smaller in population, the black central district remained, obviously frustrating the ambitious segregation plans of Gramling, Mer-

PROLOGUE

The original caption on this photograph from the Romer Collection at the Miami-Dade Public Library reads, "Father in jail, mother gone." These children, and others like them, faced dim prospects for a better life in Miami's slums.

rick, and others. But the black-removal goals of the downtown business leaders have never completely disappeared from the scene. The highway building mania of the late 1950s and early 1960s accomplished some of the black removal program. The construction of interstate highways 95 and 395 gouged wide swaths through the center of Overtown. A single interchange on the North-South Expressway (I-95), for instance, destroyed the housing of twenty-five hundred Overtown families in the early 1960s. Urban renewal programs in the 1960s provided new opportunities to achieve the same end. In a 1964 study, geographer Harold M. Rose noted that "a recently proposed urban renewal project, if instituted, would result in the elimination of this historic center of Negro settlement, which has been blamed for stifling the economic growth of the central business district."[26] More recently, Metro-Dade County and City of Miami office buildings and parking lots have gobbled up most of southeast Overtown. The so-called Park West Project will bring upscale townhouses, trendy retail shops, and perhaps a sports arena to the eastern fringes of Overtown. Close observers of the Miami political scene know that the idea of pushing the business district into what remains of Overtown is fully alive in the mid-1980s.[27]

It would, moreover, be difficult to describe Miami's early experience with public housing as a roaring success. From 1937, when Liberty Square was completed, until 1949, only three public housing projects with 1,515 units had been completed, one for blacks and two for whites. An aggressive antislum campaign in 1949 led to a successful referendum permitting the Miami Housing Authority to construct an additional fifteen hundred public housing units, but ten years later only half that number had been completed. Not until the 1960s and the creation of the Metro-Dade County Department of Housing and Urban Development—"Little HUD," as it was called—did public housing in the area get serious attention. But despite the relatively meager results in terms of housing units actually completed, it should be clear that federal intervention beginning in the New Deal years shaped Miami's urban physical and spatial development.[28]

The Home Owners Loan Corporation

Another New Deal federal agency—The Home Owners Loan Corporation (HOLC)—had an equally pernicious influence on the development of segregated housing patterns in Miami, as well as in other cities. Established in 1933, the HOLC was designed to grant long-term, low-interest mortgages to homeowners who were unable to secure regular mortgages, who were in danger of losing their homes through default or foreclosure, or who sought to recover homes

(Left) While many blacks faced one hardship after another, the country's rich revelled in Miami. (Above) George Merrick chaired the Dade County Planning Council in the 1930s and advocated the removal of every black family from residential areas within Miami city limits.

already lost by foreclosure. The HOLC developed an elaborate appraisal and rating system by which to evaluate neighborhoods in every city. HOLC appraisers—usually local bankers and real estate men—assigned each neighborhood to one of four categories, beginning with the most desirable (*A* sections) through the least desirable (*D* areas). These appraisal decisions were plotted on "residential security maps," on which the four categories were color-coded—green for those areas designated *A*, blue for the *B*, yellow for the *C*, and red for the *D*. These maps, the HOLC noted, "graphically reflect the trend of desirability in neighborhoods from a residential viewpoint." As one urban historian has suggested, the HOLC appraisal system actually initiated "redlining," the practice by banks and other lending institutions of refusing to grant mortgages or other loans in older, poorer, and black neighborhoods.[29]

How did redlining work in actual practice? The HOLC "residential security maps" were accompanied by detailed area descriptions compiled by the local appraisers. The area descriptions listed the characteristics of Miami neighborhoods; the economic and occupational status of residents; positive and detrimental influences in the neighborhood; and the type, age, and price of buildings. In addition, the appraisers noted any "restrictions set up to protect the neighborhood"—an obvious reference to discriminatory deed restrictions.[30] The HOLC made two such residential surveys in Miami during the 1930s, one in 1936 and another in 1938.

In the surveys of Miami, as well as of other cities, the HOLC began with a general statement describing the four different neighborhood categories. The *A* areas were new and well planned, with a homogeneous population and well-built, high-priced homes; these sections of Miami, HOLC appraisers wrote in 1938, were "synonymous with the area where good mortgage lenders with available funds are willing to make their maximum loans." The *B* neighborhoods were slightly less good, although "still desirable." The houses were older, the residents less wealthy, the areas less uniform in architecture and building style, and the availability of mortgage money "slightly limited."[31] The *C* category was assigned to sparsely developed sections on the metropolitan fringe and to areas of transition characterized by age, obsolescence, poor building or maintenance, inadequate transportation and utilities, lack of zoning or building restrictions, and closeness to black neighborhoods. They were, HOLC appraisers said in 1936, "definitely declining." The least desirable *D* rating went to so-called "hazardous" areas—"neighborhoods in which the things that are now taking place in the *C* neighborhoods have already happened." Specifically, the *D* sections were inhabited by blacks and "low grade white population" and characterized by such "detrimental influences" as a low percentage of home ownership, dilapidated housing, poor sanitation, industrial land uses, and nearness to trash dumps, incinerators, and railroads.[32]

Although the HOLC was a federal agency, its appraisal decisions were made by local mortgage bankers and real estate men. The 1936 survey, for instance, was prepared by a HOLC official

PROLOGUE

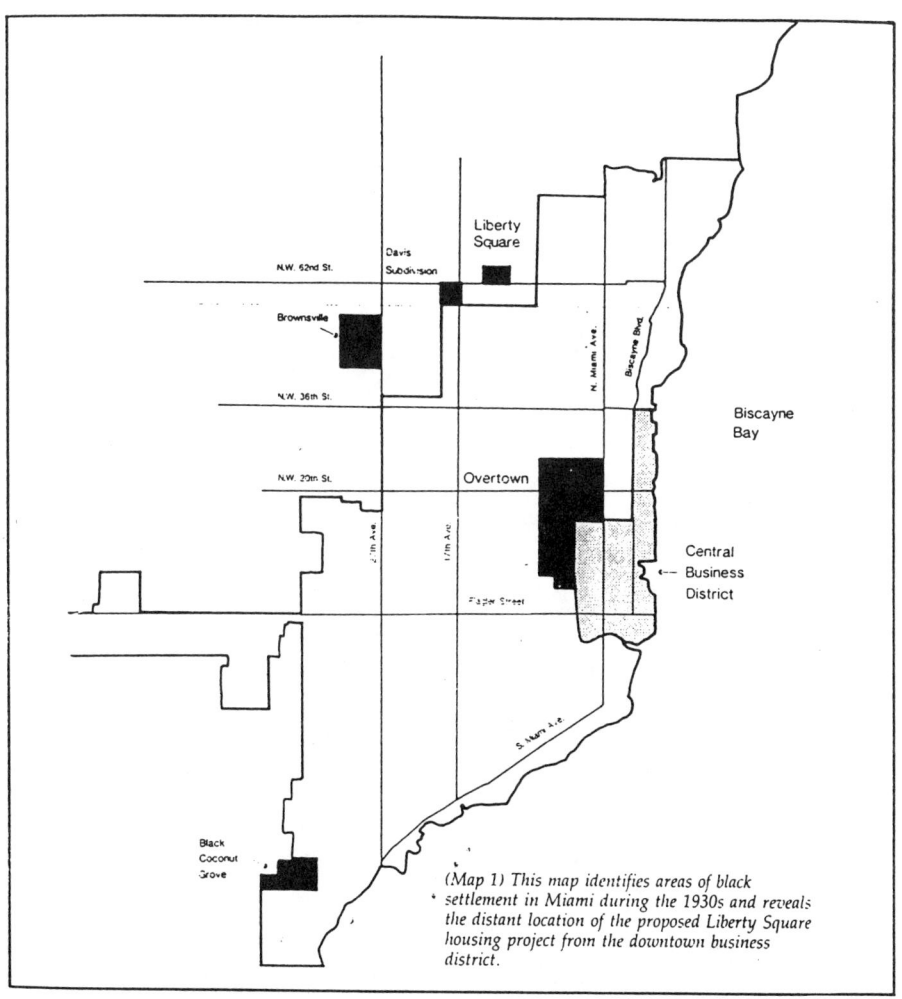

(Map 1) This map identifies areas of black settlement in Miami during the 1930s and reveals the distant location of the proposed Liberty Square housing project from the downtown business district.

and four Miami realtors. The 1938 survey was made by a HOLC man and seven local realtors and mortgage bankers. The participation of Miami realtor and savings and loan president Lon Worth Crow on both surveys typified the involvement of the city's civic elite in the local workings of the HOLC. Arriving in Miami in 1913 from west Florida, where he had operated a lumber and sawmill business, Crow quickly became an inveterate city booster. He served for twenty-seven years as a director of the Miami Realty Board and for several years in the 1920s as president of the Miami Chamber of Commerce. As one admirer put it, Crow "concerned himself with practically every kind of vital problem connected with his city and its life. He had a keen sense of civic pride and loyalty to Miami and worked tirelessly for its welfare and growth." Similarly, a 1936 biographical sketch of Crow noted that he "has always been alert in fostering any project beneficial to the Greater Miami area." Like John Gramling, Lon Worth Crow found in the new federal housing programs an opportunity to shape Miami to his own liking.[33]

TROUBLE IN PARADISE 17

PROLOGUE

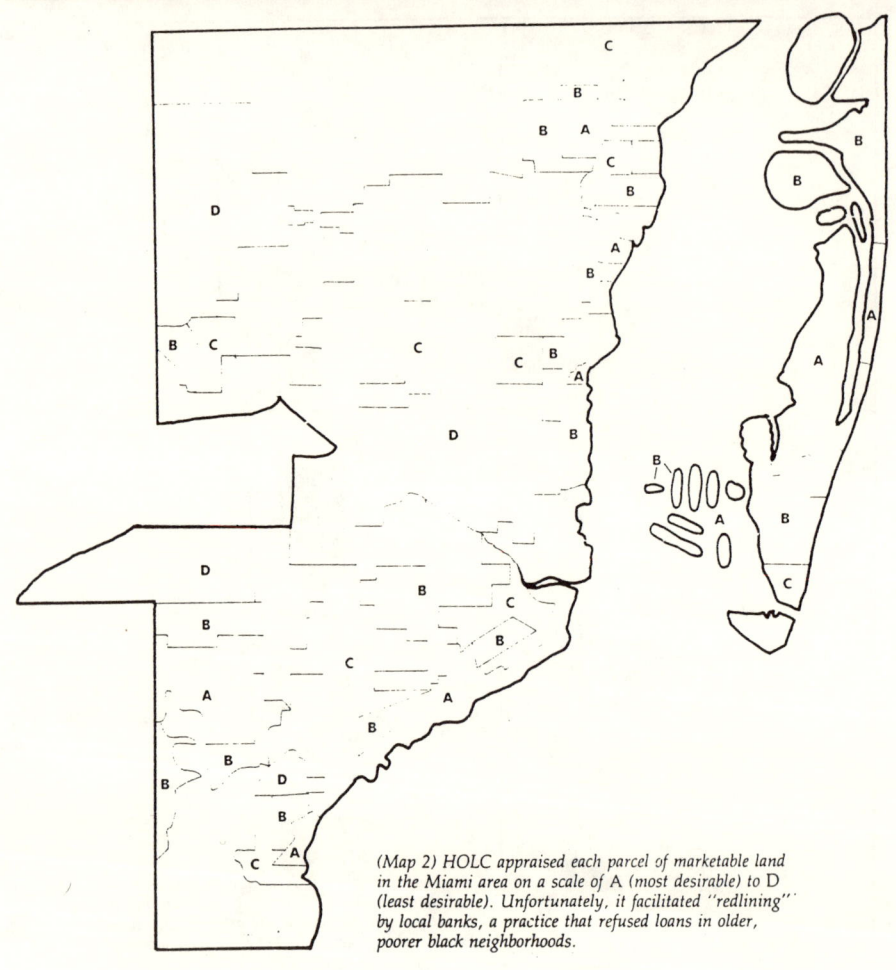

(Map 2) HOLC appraised each parcel of marketable land in the Miami area on a scale of A (most desirable) to D (least desirable). Unfortunately, it facilitated "redlining" by local banks, a practice that refused loans in older, poorer black neighborhoods.

As might be suspected, the HOLC appraisals of Miami neighborhoods reflected the bias of the local appraisers. The 1936 survey assigned the A designation to only a few small sections of the metropolitan area. These included a portion of Miami Beach north of Lincoln Road, sections of Coral Gables and Miami Shores, a few bayshore neighborhoods north and south of the business district, and the Biscayne Bay islands between Miami and Miami Beach. These were neighborhoods of larger and more expensive homes on sizable lots; their residents were "native-born whites" who ranged from "the extremely wealthy" to professionals, "salaried executives," and retired businessmen. It is not surprising to learn that the HOLC appraisers themselves lived in these same neighborhoods. Of the Miami Beach section, the appraisers noted with approval that "the northward movement of Jews from the southern part of the island . . . is limited in most cases by deed restrictions." The 1938 survey was even more parsimonious with the A rating, some of the north bayshore neighborhoods being downgraded to the B category.[34]

The appraisers were relatively generous in the assignment of the B rating in 1936. A few Miami Beach, Coral Gables, and Miami bay-front areas received this second-grade rating, as did a few older Miami neighborhoods (Riverside, Lawrence, Shenandoah, Shadowlawn, and Biltmore). However, the 1938 appraisal downgraded some of these areas to the C category because of the encroachment of businesses, tourist homes, and boarding houses, as well as the "infiltration of Cubans." (There is a sense of déjà vu here in this reference to exiles from the Cuban revolution of 1933).[35]

There were no C designations in 1936, but virtually the entire remainder of the metropolitan area received the lowest D rating. As might be expected, the downtown black section near the central business district was assigned to the D category. So also were "some of the outlying southwest sections of Miami and practically all of the northwest sections, including Hialeah." The brand-new Liberty Square housing project of the PWA was also assigned the lowest rating, even though it was not yet completed.[36] The 1938 appraisers were even tougher in their real estate evaluations. Many A and B neighborhoods were downgraded, and a large number of new C and D areas were designated. The 1938 HOLC map reveals a smattering of green and blue and a vast expanse of yellow and red covering the entire metropolitan area.[37] By 1938 Miami for all practical purposes had been redlined by the local real estate and banking community (map 2).

The Miami appraisers of the HOLC noted the hesitancy of banks and mortgage lenders to invest in the C and D neighborhoods. Mortgage money for home purchase or home building generally was described as "ample" in A and even some B areas. But in the C areas mortgage money was "limited." In the white, working-class Shadowlawn section, for instance, mortgage money was "limited," even though the area was "close to good transportation and schools and shopping centers" and despite the fact that portions of the area were "being improved with houses too good for the area." In the judgment of the HOLC appraisers, the "trend of desirability" of Shadowlawn over the next ten to fifteen years was "down."[38] Banks and other lending institutions were reluctant to invest in these C neighborhoods, even though their populations were entirely white. According to the HOLC these areas were in the process of "transition"—a code word which meant that they were near black neighborhoods and that they might soon be less white and more black. For the D neighborhoods, a single word described the availability of mortgage money from local institutions—"None."[39]

The impact of the HOLC in Miami, it should be clear, was to consign the city's black sections, as well as adjacent white areas, to a future of physical decay and intensified racial segregation. Some HOLC mortgage loans were made in C and D neighborhoods, but local financial institutions strengthened their earlier discriminatory loan practices. As urban historian Kenneth T. Jackson has written, "the damage caused by the HOLC came not through its own actions, but through the influence of its appraisal system on the financial decisions of other institutions."[40] HOLC "residential security maps" were available to local bankers (after all, they had an important role in drawing them up), and the HOLC appraisal categories were used in evaluating mortgage and loan applicants.

The Federal Housing Administration (FHA), which insured private mortgages for home construction, also used the HOLC appraisal categories and probably the HOLC residential security maps. In fact, housing scholar Charles Abrams has written, the FHA "set itself up as the protector of the all-white neighborhood" and "became the vanguard of white supremacy and racial purity—in the North as well as the South." It is also clear that the FHA had a discriminatory loan record in Miami. According to Elizabeth Virrick, author of a 1960 study of Miami housing, it was "well-known locally that Negroes in Dade County were refused FHA commitments until recently."[41] Thus, the Home Owners Loan Corporation, a federal agency originally designed to help poor homeowners combat the depression, was effectively turned against the people who most needed it.

The effect of federal redlining was to hasten the physical decay of the city and strengthen the process of residential segregation. Several studies have demonstrated that of more than one hundred large American cities, Miami had the highest degree of residential segregation by race in 1940, 1950, and 1960.[42] This was not a racial pattern that happened by accident. Residential segregation and the rapid physical deterioration of the black inner city, moreover, has had devastating human and social consequences in Miami. Race riots in 1968, 1980, and 1982 revealed the extent of black anger and frustration. A succession of studies has singled out housing as one of the most pervasive and serious grievances of Miami's blacks.[43] The redlining of urban America, initiated in the New Deal era by the

Home Owners Loan Corporation and carried through by the Federal Housing Administration, has had devastating and long-term consequences for Miami.

This Miami research conforms to several recent studies elaborating the shaping impact of federal intervention on urban development and change since the 1930s.[44] The New Dealers put together a new Democratic coalition—one largely held together by a vast federal investment in urban employment programs and new urban construction. But although the funding came from Washington, the implementation and direction of these various urban programs were left to local governments and local leaders. The much-vaunted liberalism of the New Deal was often tempered in cities like Miami by segregation and the opportunism of local entrepreneurs.

NOTES

© 1987 by Raymond A. Mohl

Raymond A. Mohl is professor of history and chairman of the department at Florida Atlantic University, Boca Raton, Florida. He is the author most recently of *Steel City: Urban and Ethnic Patterns in Gary, Indiana, 1906–1950*. Research for this article was supported by grants from the National Endowment for the Humanities, the American Association for State and Local History, the Florida Atlantic University Division of Sponsored Research, and the Florida International University/Florida International University Joint Center for Environmental and Urban Problems.

[1] Zane L. Miller, *The Urbanization of Modern America: A Brief History* (1973), p. 161; George E. Mowry and Blaine A. Brownell, *The Urban Nation, 1920–1980* (1981), p. 79. For a general overview of the subject, see William H. Wilson, "A Great Impact, A Gingerly Investigation: Historians and the Federal Effect on Urban Development," in Jerome Finster, ed., *The National Archives and Urban Research* (1974), pp. 113–123.

[2] Bruce M. Stave, *The New Deal and the Last Hurrah: Pittsburgh Machine Politics* (1970); Lyle W. Dorsett, *The Pendergast Machine* (1968); Lyle W. Dorsett, *Franklin D. Roosevelt and the City Bosses* (1977); Charles H. Trout, *Boston, The Great Depression, and the New Deal* (1977). See also the essays by Stave and Dorsett in John Braeman, et al., eds., *The New Deal: The State and Local Levels* (1975), pp. 376–419.

[3] Marks S. Foster, *From Streetcar to Superhighway: American City Planners and Urban Transportation, 1900–1940* (1981).

[4] Charles Abrams, *Forbidden Neighbors: A Study of Prejudice in Housing* (1955), pp. 229–230; Stephen J. Diner and Helen Young, eds., *Housing Washington's People: Public Policy in Retrospect* (1983), pp. 169–175; Kenneth T. Jackson, *Crabgrass Frontier: The Suburbanization of the United States* (1985), pp. 190–230; Joseph L. Arnold, *The New Deal in the Suburbs: A History of the Greenbelt Town Program, 1935–1954* (1971).

[5] Public Works Administration, *America Builds: The Record of the PWA* (1939), pp. 207–217; Timothy L. McDonnell, *The Wagner Housing Act: A Case Study of the Legislative Process* (1957), pp. 29–50; Mark I. Gelfand, *A Nation of Cities: The Federal Government and Urban America, 1933–1965* (1975), pp. 59–65.

[6] "Application of the Southern Housing Corporation, Miami, Florida, to the Administration of Public Works, Division of Housing, Washington, D.C., for Financing Low Cost Housing Project at Miami, Florida," Dec. 19, 1933, Records of the Public Housing Administration, Record Group 196, National Archives, Washington, D.C., (hereafter cited as PHA, RG 196, NA), Box 299; Horatio B. Hackett to Harold L. Ickes, Oct. 18, 1934, ibid., Box 297; A. R. Clas to M. J. Orr, July 15, 1935, ibid., Box 299.

[7] *Miami Herald*, Jan. 28, Aug. 29, 1934; Chas. S. Thompson, "The Growth of Colored Miami, *The Crisis*, 49 (Mar. 1942), 83–84; Paul S. George, "Colored Town: Miami's Black Community, 1896–1930," *Florida Historical Quarterly*, 56 (Apr. 1978): 432–447.

[8] "Application of the Southern Housing Corporation," PHA, RG 196, NA, Box 299.

[9] Raymond A. Mohl, "Black Immigrants: Bahamians in Early Twentieth-Century Miami," *Florida Historical Quarterly*, 65 (Jan. 1987): 271–297; Reinhold P. Wolff and David K. Gillogly, *Negro Housing in the Miami Area: Effects of the Postwar Building Boom* (1951); Elizabeth L. Virrick, "New Housing for Negroes in Dade County, Florida," in Nathan Glazer and Davis McEntire, eds., *Studies in Housing and Minority Groups* (1960), pp. 135–143; Harold M. Rose, "Metropolitan Miami's Changing Negro Population, 1950–1960," *Economic Geography*, 40 (July 1964): 221–238. On blacks in Miami, the following are also useful: Warren M. Banner, *An Appraisal of Progress, 1943–1953* (1953) and James W. Morrison, *The Negro in Greater Miami* (1962). For an interpretation of the thought and activities of the "civic elite" in the urban South, see Blaine A. Brownell, *The Urban Ethos in the South, 1920–1930* (1975).

[10] E. V. Blackman, *Miami and Dade County, Florida: Its Settlement, Progress and Achievement* (1921), pp. 104–105; Tracy Hollingsworth, *History of Dade County, Florida* (1936), p. 146.

[11] Dozens of Gramling letters to federal housing officials can be found in PHA, RG 196, NA, Boxes 297–301.

[12] *Miami Herald*, Aug. 9, 1934; John L. Gramling to Eugene H. Klaber, Jan. 22, 1934, PHA, RG 196, NA, Box 301; A. R. Clas to M. J. Orr, July 15, 1935, ibid., Box 299.

[13] *Miami Times*, Jan. 20, 1934, clipping, PHA, RG 196, NA, Box 301; R.E.S. Toomey to Robert D. Kohn, Jan. 15, 1934, ibid., Box 299; Miami Colored Chamber of Commerce, "To Whom It May Concern," May 17, 1935, ibid., Box 301.

[14] Gramling to Klaber, Jan. 24, 1934, PHA, RG 196, NA, Box 301.

[15] Floyd W. Davis to A. R. Clas, July 28, Aug. 13, 1935, PHA, RG 196, NA, Box 301; Tom Petersen, "Reaching for Utopia: The Origins of the Liberty Square Housing Project," unpublished manuscript, p. 12.

[16] Paul S. George, "Criminal Justice in Miami, 1896–1930" (unpublished Ph.D. diss., Florida State University, 1975), pp. 158–159.

[17] A. B. Small to A. R. Clas, May 31, 1935, PHA, RG 196, NA, Box 298.

[18] [Miami] *Friday Night*, Jan. 12, 1934, clipping, PHA, RG 196, NA, Box 301; Gramling to Klaber, Feb. 19, 1934, ibid., Box 299; Gramling to Horatio B. Hackett, Oct. 17, 1934, ibid., Box 301.

PROLOGUE

[19] "Gramling to Klaber, Feb. 19, 1934, PHA, RG 196, NA, Box 299.
[20] "Isabelle Sanderson to Hackett, Apr. 19, 1935, PHA, RG 196, NA, Box 297; Sanderson to Clas, May 17, 1935, ibid., Box 297.
[21] *Miami Herald*, Feb. 21, 1934. On Miami's growth during this period, see Raymond A. Mohl, "Miami: The Ethnic Cauldron," in Richard M. Bernard and Bradley R. Rice, eds., *Sunbelt Cities: Politics and Growth Since World War II* (1983), pp. 58–99.
[22] George E. Merrick, *Planning the Greater Miami for Tomorrow* (1937), p. 11.
[23] Dade County Planning Board Minutes, Aug. 27, 1936, George E. Merrick Papers, Box 2, Historical Association of Southern Florida, Miami, typescript; Dade County Planning Council, "Negro Resettlement Plan," 1937, National Urban League Papers, Part I, Series VI, Box 56, Library of Congress, mimeo.
[24] Abrams, *Forbidden Neighbors*, pp. 120–136; Stetson Kennedy, "Miami: Anteroom to Fascism," *The Nation*, 173 (Dec. 1951):546–547.
[25] Recent studies confirming this pattern for other cities include: Arnold R. Hirsch, *Making the Second Ghetto: Race and Housing in Chicago, 1940–1960* (1983) and Dominic J. Capeci, Jr., *Race Relations in Wartime Detroit: The Sojourner Truth Housing Controversy, 1937–1942* (1984).
[26] *Miami Negroes: A Study in Depth* (1968), p. 23; Rose, "Metropolitan Miami's Changing Negro Population," p. 224. For the negative consequences of highway urban renewal programs generally, consult: Martin Anderson, *The Federal Bulldozer: A Critical Analysis of Urban Renewal, 1949–1962* (1964); Scott Greer, *Urban Renewal and American Cities: The Dilemma of Democratic Intervention* (1965); and Sam Bass Warner, Jr., *The Urban Wilderness: A History of the American City* (1972), pp. 37–52.
[27] Robert M. Press, "Miami's Overtown: Blacks Fight Inequality to Revive Community," *Christian Science Monitor*, Mar. 20, 1984: 5; *Miami Herald*, Nov. 30, Dec. 28, 1981, Jan. 5, 1982, Dec. 2, 1983, May 19, June 26, Aug. 12, 1984, Aug. 10, and Sept. 7, 1986; *Miami Times*, Dec. 16, 1982, June 5, 1986; *Miami News*, Oct. 6, 1983, May 1, 1984.
[28] *Better Housing: [First] Report of the Housing Authority of the City of Miami* (Miami, 1940); Haley Sofge, "Public Housing in Miami," *Florida Planning and Development*, 19 (Mar. 1968): 1–4; Aileen Lotz, "The Birth of 'Little Hud,'" ibid., 19 (Jan. 1968): 1–3, 6, and (Feb. 1968):1–3, 12. See also Richard O. Davies, "One-third of a Nation: The Dilemmas of America's Housing, 1607–1970," in Finster, ed., *The National Archives and Urban Research*, pp. 41–55.

[29] "Security Area Map, Miami, Florida," and "Analysis of Realty Area Map of Miami, Florida," both 1936, Records of the Home Owners Loan Corporation, Record Group 195, National Archives, Washington, D.C. (hereafter cited as HOLC, RG 195, NA); "Security Area Descriptions: Metropolitan Miami, Florida," Sept. 24, 1938, ibid. See also Jackson, *Crabgrass Frontier*, pp. 190–218; Lowell C. Harriss, *History and Policies of the Home Owners' Loan Corporation* (1951).
[30] "Security Area Descriptions: Metropolitan Miami," 1938, HOLC, RG 195, NA.
[31] Ibid.
[32] "Security Area Map" and "Analysis of Realty Area Map of Miami," 1936, HOLC, RG 195, NA.
[33] Hollingsworth, *History of Dade County*, pp. 118–120; *The East Coast of Florida*, 3 vols. (1962), 3:532.
[34] "Analysis of Realty Area Map of Miami," 1936, HOLC, RG 195, NA; "Security Area Descriptions: Metropolitan Miami," 1938, ibid.
[35] Ibid.
[36] "Analysis of Realty Area Map of Miami," 1936, HOLC, RG 195, NA.
[37] "Security Area Map, Miami, Florida," 1938, HOLC, RG 195, NA.
[38] "Security Area Descriptions: Metropolitan Miami," 1938, HOLC, RG 195, NA.
[39] Ibid.
[40] Jackson, *Crabgrass Frontier*, p. 203.
[41] Ibid., pp. 203, 213–215; Abrams, *Forbidden Neighbors*, pp. 229–230; Virrick, "New Housing for Negroes in Dade County," p. 140.
[42] Donald O. Cowgill, "Trends in Residential Segregation of Non-Whites in American Cities, 1940–1950," *American Sociological Review*, 21 (Feb. 1956):43–47; Karl E. Taeuber and Alma F. Taeuber, *Negroes in Cities: Residential Segregation and Neighborhood Change* (1965), pp. 40–41; Annemette Sorenson, et al., "Indexes of Racial Residential Segregation for 109 Cities in the United States, 1940–1970," *Sociological Focus*, 8 (1975):125–142.
[43] National Commission on the Causes and Prevention of Violence, *Miami Report: The Report of the Miami Study Team on Civil Disturbances in Miami, Florida, during the Week of August 5, 1968* (1969); U.S. Commission on Civil Rights, *Confronting Racial Isolation in Miami* (1982); Bruce Porter and Marvin Dunn, *The Miami Riot of 1980: Crossing the Bounds* (1984).
[44] John H. Mollenkopf, *The Contested City* (1983); Roger W. Lotchin, ed., *The Martial Metropolis: U.S. Cities in War and Peace* (1984).

TROUBLE IN PARADISE 21

SOME EFFECTS OF THE DEPRESSION ON THE NEGRO IN NORTHERN CITIES[1]

E. FRANKLIN FRAZIER

SINCE the migration of thousands of Negroes to the metropolitan areas of the North during and following the World War, there has been a growing tendency to view the problems of the Negro in relationship to the dominant social and economic currents in American life. As an example of this shift in viewpoint, one might mention Professor Frank A. Ross's study of the urbanization of the Negro population which views the cityward movement of the Negro as a part of the whole process of urbanization in America.[2] Viewed from this standpoint, the Negro migrations to northern industrial centers are seen in their relation to changes in southern agriculture and the cessation of European immigration coupled with a demand for cheap unskilled labor. Consequently, it was not by accident, but because of certain fundamental economic forces in American life that New York, Chicago, Philadelphia, and Detroit became the chief goals of the migrating black masses. Within the metropolitan districts of these four cities, there were, in 1930, 1,185,530 Negroes or about a half of the entire Negro population in the North. The remainder of the Negro population in the North, excluding less than 300,000 rural dwellers, was concentrated in smaller industrial centers where there was a demand for cheap labor. The social consequences of the shift of these peasant folk to the industrial centers of the North has been the subject of a vast literature.[3]

---

[1] Paper read before the annual meeting of the Eastern Sociological Society, Vassar College, April 16, 1938.

[2] Frank A. Ross, "Urbanization and the Negro," *Publication of the American Sociological Society*, XXVI, 115-128.

[3] See Louise V. Kennedy, *The Negro Peasant Turns Cityward* (New York, 1930) and E. Franklin Frazier, "The Impact of Urban Civilization Upon Negro Family Life," *American Sociological Review*, II, 609-618.

But concerning the effects of the depression on these newcomers to modern industrial society very little systematic information is available. In this paper, an attempt will be made to bring together and interpret the available information which we have been able to secure from various sources.

Concerning the volume of unemployment and relief in the Negro population in northern cities, our information is about as reliable as that for the whites. In fourteen of the sixteen northern and western cities included in the unemployment census of 1931, the percentage of Negroes unemployed was higher than that of either native or foreign-born whites. This was true for women as well as men. For example, in Chicago, 40.3 per cent of the employable Negro men and 55.4 of the women were reported unemployed, whereas only 24.6 per cent of the foreign-born white men and 12.0 per cent of the foreign-born white women; and 23.4 per cent of the native white men and 16.9 per cent of native white women were reported unemployed.[4] Klein, in his recent survey of Pittsburgh, reported that in February 1934, "48 per cent of the employable Negroes were entirely without employment . . . while only 31.1 per cent of the potential white workers were unemployed."[5] That this situation was generally true in regard to Negro women was indicated in a study of fluctuations in the employment of women from 1928 to 1931 in Bridgeport, Buffalo, Syracuse, and Philadelphia. According to this study, "the proportion of Negro women unemployed ordinarily was greater than their share in the total woman population or among those in gainful employment."[6]

Although there is a rather general but uncritical acceptance of the belief that the "Negro is the last to be hired and the first to be fired," it is difficult to make any generalization concerning practices during the depression in northern cities. In a paper read before the Conference on the Economic Status of the Negro held in Washington, D.C., in May 1933, it was reported that in the meat packing industry, "Reductions in the working force due to the depression have in general left these Negro workers in relatively larger proportions than other

---

[4] *Fifteenth Census of the United States: 1930. Unemployment*, II, 370-373.

[5] Phillip Klein, *A Social Study of Pittsburgh. Community Problems and Social Services of Allegheny County* (New York, 1938), p. 279.

[6] *Employment Fluctuations and Unemployment of Women. Certain Indications from Various Sources, 1928-31.* By Mary Elizabeth Pidgeon, U. S. Department of Labor, Bulletin of the Women's Bureau, Washington: 1933. p. 43.

workers."[7] On the other hand, Dr. Joseph H. Willits of the University of Pennsylvania, in a study of unemployment among several groups in Philadelphia, found the following situation during the years 1929 to 1933. "In 1929 when 9.0 per cent of all white employables were unemployed, 15.7 per cent of the Negroes were unemployed. In 1930 it was 13.8 per cent for whites and 19.4 per cent for Negroes; in 1931 it was 24.1 per cent for whites and 35.0 per cent for Negroes; and in 1932 it was 39.7 per cent for whites and 56.0 per cent for Negroes."[8] It is likely that these figures are typical of northern cities since the vast majority of Negro workers are employed on jobs which are generally susceptible to fluctuations in industry.

We are on much surer ground when we consider the incidence of relief. When the unemployment relief census was taken in 1933, there was in New York, Chicago, Philadelphia, and Detroit, a total of 78,027 Negro families on relief or 32.5 per cent of the Negro families in these four cities. Measured in terms of population, New York with 23.9 per cent and Detroit with 27.6 per cent had smaller percentages of Negroes on relief than Chicago and Philadelphia in each of which cities 34 per cent of the Negro population was on relief.[9] The situation was even worse in Pittsburgh and Cleveland each with 43 per cent and Akron, Ohio, with 67 per cent of the Negro population on relief. After the census of 1933 was taken, the situation in these cities undoubtedly became worse. For example, by February 1935, "practically three out of every five Negroes in Allegheny County," where Pittsburgh is located, were on the relief rolls.[10] A study of the situation in the Harlem area of New York City in 1935 revealed that 24,293 or 43.2 per cent of 56,157 Negro families were receiving relief.[11] In addition to these relief families, 7,560 unattached Negro men had registered with the Emergency Relief Bureau over a period of four years.

---

[7] *The Economic Status of Negroes.* Summary and Analysis of the Materials Presented at the Conference on the Economic Status of the Negro, held in Washington, D. C., May 11-13, 1933, under the Sponsorship of the Julius Rosenwald Fund. Prepared by Charles S. Johnson. Fisk University Press, 1933. p. 10.

[8] *Ibid.,* p. 19.

[9] *Federal Emergency Relief Administration. Unemployment Relief Census,* October 1933. Report No. 1. Washington: 1934. p. 78, 8.

[10] Klein, *op. cit.,* p. 279.

[11] From an unpublished *Social and Economic Survey of the Harlem Negro Community* made by the writer for The Mayor's Commission on Conditions in Harlem.

There is good reason for believing that as the depression lifted momentarily, Negroes were not reabsorbed into industry to the same extent as white workers. According to a report of the F.E.R.A. on Baltimore, Bridgeport, Connecticut, Chicago, Detroit, Omaha, St. Louis, Mo., and Paterson, N.J., as late as May 1935, Negroes were "being added to the relief population in greater proportions of total intake than they existed in the general population (1930 Census)." The report ventured the explanation that it reflected in part "a tendency for employers to favor unemployed white persons as compared with Negro workers."[12] In Pittsburgh, two of the largest employers of Negroes in the steel industry who claimed that they had brought hundreds of Negroes north would not guarantee the reemployment of Negroes because, in their opinion, Negro workers had been demoralized by relief and had become radical.[13] Although there is some evidence that Negroes have been displaced by white workers in northern cities, the question has not been studied systematically. The 1930 census indicated that for the country as a whole the Negro was being pushed back into domestic and personal service. However, in an analysis of the occupational statistics for individual cities, it was found that this was true in southern rather than in northern cities. But, it appears from statistics on relief that Negro domestic workers in northern cities have become unemployed as the depression has become worse. In New York State, there were 26,359 unemployed Negro domestic workers on relief in 1935.

Negro workers who have not lost their jobs have suffered a reduction in earning power. In Kiser's study of 2,061 Negro households in a section of Harlem in New York City, it was found that the median income of skilled workers had declined from $1,955 in 1929 to $1,003 in 1932 or 48.7 per cent. The decline in the incomes of semi-skilled and unskilled workers was slightly less or 43 per cent.[14] This study also gave information on the effect of the depression on the earning power of the Negro middle class which had rapidly emerged in response to the varied demands of large Negro communities in northern cities. It was found that among the white collar workers, who comprised 16 per

[12] *Federal Emergency Relief Administration. Research Bulletin. Current Changes in the Urban Relief Population.* May 1935. Series I, Number 12, p. 3.
[13] Klein, *op. cit.*, p. 280.
[14] Clyde V. Kiser, "Diminishing Family Income in Harlem," *Opportunity*, XIII, 173-174.

cent of the households studied, "the income decreases were 35 per cent in the professional class, 44 per cent in the proprietary class and 37 per cent among clerical and kindred workers." First hand observations and reports of college students indicate that this was representative of the Negro middle class throughout the North. Their savings and incomes, and investments from business, which gave this class a favored position in the Negro community, were largely wiped out and even Negro doctors were forced to seek relief.

Concerning the effects of the depression upon the Negro family in the northern city, the void in our knowledge is not illumined even by one shining exception such as Cavan and Ranck have provided in their study of one hundred white families.[15] However, it appears that among Negroes, just as these authors found among white families, "well organized families met the depression with less catastrophic consequences than families that were already disorganized."[16] That this was true of upper-class Negro families was revealed in the documents furnished by college students who come from the more stabilized elements in the Negro population. Although in many cases, savings were lost or consumed, homes were mortgaged or lost, and the children had to delay their college education for one to three years, these families maintained their solidarity and by pooling their resources were able to achieve some of their major family objectives. But since family disorganization among the masses has been one of the main problems resulting from the migration of the Negro to the northern city, it is not unreasonable to assume that family disorganization increased as a result of the depression.[17] First, among the consequences of reduction or loss of income was the seeking of cheaper living quarters or the crowding of families and relatives in a single household. We have a record of a case of mass housing in Chicago, where 67 families were permitted to move into an old apartment building that had been partially destroyed by fire and was without heat and light. For heat, they used coal stoves such as are used in the rural districts, and for light, they burned kerosene lamps. The owners of the building operated the house through a committee of Negroes and collected rents from

---

[15] Ruth Shonle Cavan and Katherine Howland Ranck, *The Family and the Depression, A Study of One Hundred Chicago Families* (Chicago, 1938). See Introduction.
[16] *Ibid.*, Introduction, p. viii.
[17] See E. Franklin Frazier, *The Negro Family in Chicago* (Chicago, 1932).

those families who were able to pay. In some cases, the men in the families made payments in terms of various services. Although thousands of Negro families in northern cities, who had constantly lived close to the margin of existence, had been crowded into slum areas, the depression made their condition worse and reduced thousands of others to their level. An analysis of deserted "under care" families of the Charity Organization Society of New York City revealed that the number of families with one or more relatives had increased significantly during the depression. Although even under normal conditions from 10 to 30 per cent of Negro families in northern cities have women heads, it is probable that the number increased during the depression. Among the relief families in Chicago, Detroit, New York, and Philadelphia, we find that only from 29 per cent (in Chicago) to 50 per cent (in New York City), were normal family groups; i.e., man, wife, and children. Among the relief families in these same cities, a fifth to a fourth of the families had a woman head. Moreover, it is also significant that a relatively larger number of Negro dependents than white dependents were unattached women. It is because of this fact that the F.E.R.A. views the rehabilitation of Negroes as less a problem of the aged than a problem of female dependency often involving children.[18]

The next question to which an answer has been sought is: What effect has the depression had on the health and survival of the Negro in the northern city? The studies of Thompson and Whelpton indicate that prior to the depression Negroes in large cities, including New York and Chicago "were not maintaining their numbers on a permanent basis in either 1920 or 1928."[19] For the period subsequent to the depression, we might draw some conclusions from the preliminary data released by the National Health Survey.[20] These data indicate that illnesses disabling for one week or longer in a twelve month period occurred among families on relief at a rate 57 per cent higher than among families with annual incomes of $3,000 and over. Since Negroes were included among such families, and as a matter of fact a larger

[18] *Federal Emergency Relief Administration. Unemployment Relief Census*, October 1933. Report No. 3. Washington: 1934. pp. 90-91, 32-33.
[19] Warren S. Thompson and P. K. Whelpton, *Population Trends in the United States* (New York, 1933), p. 280.
[20] *Preliminary Reports. The National Health Survey Sickness and Medical Care Series*, Bulletin No. 2. United States Public Health Service, Washington, 1938.

proportion of the Negro families enumerated were on relief than white families, it is reasonable to conclude that Negro relief families have been subject to disabling illnesses more than those not on relief.[21]

In this connection, we can cite the results of a statistical study, growing out of our social and economic survey of Harlem, which deals with the relation between dependency and birth and death rates.[22] In this study, a graduate student at Columbia University worked out correlations between the percentage of families on relief and the changes in the birth and death rates and infant mortality in eleven health areas, each with a population of 5,000 or more Negroes. A high positive correlation (.89 for birth rates and .83 for death rates) was found between the dependency rate and the percentage of change in birth and death rates. The author of this closely thought-out study presented cogent reasons for believing that the correlation between increases in birth rates and dependency was due to a shifting of the population, which tended to segregate the relief families, that normally had a relatively higher birth rate in certain areas. But, he also presented good reasons for his belief that the changes in the death rates were due to the depression which resulted in a lack of adequate food, changes in habits of living, and vicious behaviour often associated with idle adults on relief. On the other hand, there was a relatively high negative correlation (—.60) between changes in infant mortality and dependency. His explanation of the tendency of the infant mortality to decrease as the dependency rate mounted was as follows:

The Home Relief Bureau made available medical services to the recipients of relief which they had been unable to afford previously out of their own earnings; the fact that a trained investigator visited the home periodically, was able to advise and instruct the families in the proper care of their children, refer them to the community pre and post natal clinics, arrange for their hospitalization, and distribute and explain literature on the proper care of mother and infant before and after birth proved to be a very helpful factor in overcoming some of the above mentioned things which contributed to the very high rate of infant mortality. There is also the factor that the mother, if employed prior to the family's going on relief,

---

[21] The proportion of white and Negro relief families among those enumerated in three cities was as follows: Chicago—white, 11.3 per cent; Negro, 34.9 per cent; Philadelphia—white, 12.2 per cent; Negro, 47.0 per cent; Detroit—white, 10.1 per cent; Negro, 32.8.

[22] Herbert L. Bryan, "Birth Rates and Death Rates in Relation to Dependency in Selected Health Areas in Harlem." (M.A. Thesis) Columbia University, 1936.

worked several months during pregnancy and returned to work within a minimum time after the birth of the child whereas the mother on relief remains at home and is thus able to take greater precautions in regard to her own health during pregnancy, and devote more care to her child after its birth. . . . It is much easier to get an expectant mother to visit the clinics regularly and exercise the proper precautions to insure the good health of her offspring, but the problem becomes more difficult when persuading an adult to exercise proper care about his own health, visit clinics regularly, take preventive measures, and seek medical attention and advice.[23]

If the author's explanation of these correlations may be taken as valid, and if the situation in Harlem is typical of other northern cities, then it appears that the Negro child has been afforded a better chance of survival because of relief measures than if he had been born into a family existing upon the sub-standards of living of the great body of Negro workers who make their own livelihood.

We turn, finally, to those changes in the Negro's philosophy and outlook on life which may reasonably be attributed to the depression. First, among these changes, one might mention the disillusionment of the Negro middle class. Probably no section of the middle class in America had such high hopes as the Negro middle class during the years of prosperity. Their dream of reaping the rewards of individual thrift and foresight which had had only a partial fulfillment in the South seemed to have come true in the northern city. The Negro professional and business man had prospered upon the earnings of the black masses in northern cities. Moreover, the political power of the Negro had opened the way to political patronage and the civil service held out a substantial living for many educated Negroes. Then, suddenly, the purchasing power and savings of the masses began to melt. Doctors' and lawyers' fees dwindled and finally ceased, and the hothouse growth of Negro business behind the walls of segregation shrivelled and died, often swallowing up the savings of the black masses. Fine homes and cars and other forms of conspicuous consumption were given up. In their disillusionment, some of the very professional men in New York who had laughed at the small group of radical intellectuals now formed a class to study Marx. But disillusionment did not breed radicalism among a very large group. It appears that more often,

---

[23] *Ibid.*, p. 39-40.

they turned to racial chauvinism as a way of realizing their dreams. In Chicago, those of the middle class who had laughed at Garvey's grandiose ideas of a back to Africa movement began to talk of a Forty-ninth State which according to their specifications would be a Black Utopia where the black middle class could exploit the black workers without white competition. In New York City, small Negro business men pointed to the Jewish merchant as the cause of their failures and began to demand that Harlem be reserved as their field of exploitation.

Closely associated with the chauvinistic aims of many members of the middle class have been the efforts of Negroes in a number of northern cities to organize cooperatives as a solution of the Nergo's economic problems. However, little or no success has attended these efforts which tended in some instances to nurture if not encourage racial chauvinism. Another movement of greater significance so far as it reflects the growth of militancy directed toward immediate economic ends, has been the picketing and boycotting of stores in order to enforce the employment of Negro workers, usually as clerks. In Columbus, Ohio, the Housewives League assumed the leadership in this movement.[24] Although in some cities white storekeepers have made concessions to the demands of the Negroes, they secured relief for a time through court injunctions. But the recent ruling of the United States Supreme Court on a case in the District of Columbia has removed legal barriers against this type of picketing. Inasmuch as the demands for employment in stores where Negroes were the chief customers involved the employment of Negroes as clerks and salesmen, it implied a demand for status, which redounded also to the economic advantage of the middle class.

Although the middle class Negro intellectuals and business men tried to arouse the Negro masses to support their chauvinistic aims, the militancy of the Negro masses did not flow in a single channel. Much of the militancy was unorganized and without an ideology. There were rent strikes to force lowering of rentals. When tenants were evicted for non-payment of rent, crowds often gathered and returned the belongings of the evicted family to the house. In one of these battles in Chicago, several were killed. It has often been charged that white radicals were responsible for the militancy on the part of

[24] Richard Clyde Minor, "The Negro in Columbus, Ohio" (Ph.D. Dissertation), The Ohio State University, 1936, p. 67.

the Negroes. It seems nearer to the truth to say that white radicals attempted to give direction to these more or less spontaneous outbursts and to provide Negroes with the ideology of the class struggle. This was undoubtedly true of the spontaneous outburst in Harlem in March 1935. This riot, which began during a time of severe economic stress and when there was much complaint against the Home Relief Bureau, flared up when a flimsy rumor was circulated that a boy had been murdered in a five and ten cent store for stealing a pocket knife. Although the riot at first had a racial character, under the stimulation, if not the direction of white radicals, it became a riot against property rather than persons. The influence of radical white leadership was probably most effective in the various unemployed councils in which Negroes participated on a basis of equality. Perhaps, one of the chief effects of the depression in northern cities upon the thinking of the Negro has been the spread of radical ideas among working class Negroes through cooperation with white workers. Probably at no time in the past have the Negro masses had so many white allies as in their present struggle for work and relief. This newly developed sympathy and cooperation between the two races has even extended to white collar workers especially in the relief agencies.

In summing up the effects of the depression on the Negro in northern cities, one can say, first, that the depression has laid bare the general economic insecurity of the Negro masses. It has tended to destroy the high hopes that were kindled during the War period when it appeared that the Negro, though at the bottom of the industrial ladder, had secured a firm foothold in the industries of the North. From a position of increased earning power, unequalled during his career in America, the Negro has become the ward of the community with from a third to a half of his numbers dependent upon relief. His family life, which had been shattered by the impact of the modern metropolis upon his simple folk life, had scarcely had time to recover and reorganize itself before the shock of the depression shattered it once again. The struggle for survival, always precarious and in doubt, became even more uncertain, though relief has probably enabled children to survive who otherwise would have died. Naturally, the crisis produced a tremendous change in the Negro's evaluation of his position in American life. Many conflicting currents of thought were set in motion. Though the fatuous philosophy of racial chauvinism supported by a segregated black economy, advocated by many of the middle class, did not succeed in winning the masses, they, as a whole, have not accepted a radical definition of their problems. But, at least, it seems certain that the Negro in the northern city with his back to the wall and cut off from retreat because of the collapse of southern agriculture will fight rather than starve and that he has found allies among whites, especially those who find themselves in similar circumstances.

The New Deal and the Negro Community: Toward a Broader Conceptualization

CHRISTOPHER G. WYE

WITH rare exceptions, research that evaluates the significance of the New Deal public housing and emergency work programs for Negroes has been conceptualized around certain well-defined questions. Most scholars who have approached the subject have focused their attention on the extent to which Negroes were included in these programs in an effort to assess the degree to which the New Deal was successful in alleviating the problems which Negroes faced as a result of the Depression, especially unemployment and the need for low cost housing. These studies have noted that, although Negroes received less assistance than their relatively greater needs warranted, they also received more than their proportionate share. Largely on this basis scholars concluded that the New Deal symbolized a salutary turning point in the attitude of the federal government toward Negroes.[1]

However, if research is conceptualized on a broader basis to include not only questions relating to the extent of Negro participation in the New Deal programs but also questions concerning the impact of these programs on the anatomy of the Negro community, notable qualifications are added to this conclusion and new insight is gained into the problems which the government faced at the local level. If the experience of Cleveland Negroes is representative, it is apparent that the New Deal's inclusion of Negroes in programs designed to relieve the special problems created by the Depression must be balanced against certain adverse side effects which these programs had on the social structure of

---

This essay received the Organization of American Historians' Pelzer Award for 1971. Christopher G. Wye is a graduate student in Kent State University. The author acknowledges the financial assistance of the Ford Foundation.

[1] Richard Sterner and others, *The Negro's Share: A Study of Income, Consumption, Housing and Public Assistance* (New York, 1943); Gunnar Myrdal and others, *An American Dilemma: The Negro Problem and Modern Democracy* (New York, 1944); Leslie H. Fishel, Jr., "The Negro in the New Deal Era," *Wisconsin Magazine of History*, XLVIII (Winter 1964-1965), 111-26; Raymond Wolters, *Negroes and the Great Depression: The Problem of Economic Recovery* (Westport, Conn., 1970); St. Clair Drake and Horace R. Cayton, *Black Metropolis: A Study of Negro Life in a Northern City* (New York, 1945); Robert C. Weaver, *The Negro Ghetto* (New York, 1948); Robert C. Weaver, *Negro Labor: A National Problem* (New York, 1946); Robert C. Weaver, "Negro Labor since 1929," *Journal of Negro History*, XXXV (Jan. 1950), 20-28. These sources occasionally note that the New Deal housing program encouraged segregation and that the emergency work program employed Negroes below their level of ability or training.

621

TABLE I

Distribution of Negro and White Families in New Deal Public Housing Projects in Cleveland

	Outhwaite Homes	Outhwaite Extension	Carver Park	Cedar Central Homes	Woodhill Homes	Lake Shore Village	Berea Homes
Negroes	574	1,217	1,226	9	0	1	72
Whites	14	4	21	645	568	800	1,644

Compiled from Cleveland *Call and Post*, Oct. 14, 1937, Aug. 31, 1940, March 8, 1941; and Robert C. Weaver, *The Negro Ghetto* (New York, 1948), 171-72, 197-98.

the black community, especially on patterns of residential and occupational distribution.

On the one hand, the housing projects provided many Negroes with inexpensive and well-maintained living accommodations and the public work programs furnished jobs for a large number of Negroes who would otherwise have been unemployed. On the other hand, the housing projects encouraged residential segregation, contributed to the disruption of the normal pattern of socioeconomic differentiation within ghetto neighborhoods, and played a crucial role in spreading slum conditions to new areas of the city, while the public work program appears to have depressed the Negro job structure to lower levels by employing Negroes in occupational categories below those which had been open to them in the private sector of the economy.

In Cleveland, there is evidence to substantiate the familiar conclusion that the New Deal low cost housing program provided Negroes with more than their share of new dwelling units. First through the Public Works Administration (PWA) and later through its successor, the United States Housing Authority (USHA), the federal government sponsored the construction in Cleveland of seven housing projects comprising 7,192 apartments. Three of these projects totaling 3,223 units were eventually occupied by Negroes. Since these 3,223 dwellings represented nearly 50 percent of the total number of units erected and since Negroes made up just under 10 percent of the city's population,[2] this meant that Negroes received approximately five times their share of public housing (see Table I).

At the same time, the experience of Cleveland Negroes also confirms the conclusion that the public housing provided for Negroes fell far short of meeting their need. The 3,223 slum clearance units made available to Negroes replaced only one third of the nearly 10,000 homes located within the ghetto

[2] Howard Whipple Green, *Census Facts and Trends by Tracts* (Cleveland, 1954), 5.

which the city's Real Property Inventory classified as "unfit for human habitation."[3] Nevertheless, the fact that the housing projects did not entirely solve the problem of substandard housing in the Negro community should not obscure the fact that they did provide a substantial number of modern and relatively inexpensive homes in an area which had become notorious for its poor condition.

Yet, while the housing projects rejuvenated certain slum sections, their distribution also encouraged residential segregation. Before the advent of the New Deal, more than 90 percent of Cleveland's 72,469 Negroes were concentrated in twenty-nine contiguous census tracts, comprising a compact ghetto on the city's east side.[4] Generally referred to as the Central Avenue district, the ghetto was bordered on the north by Euclid Avenue, an important shopping thoroughfare which marked the fringe of white settlements; on the east by the city's exclusive Shaker Heights suburb; on the south by the New York Central railroad tracks and the industrial zone beyond; and on the west by Cleveland's downtown shopping area. By constructing three projects—Outhwaite Homes, Outhwaite Extension, and Carver Park—in the very heart of the ghetto, designating them as "Negro projects," and then failing to ensure Negroes free access to "white projects" located outside the Central Avenue district, the federal government lent its considerable influence toward preserving the local pattern of segregated housing (see Map I).[5]

Moreover, several of the "white projects" actually had the effect of intensifying residential segregation. Cedar Central Homes, which was erected just inside the northwest border of the ghetto, and Woodhill Homes, which was constructed on the southeast boundary of the Negro district, were located in racially mixed neighborhoods. In both locations Negroes had constituted approximately 50 percent of the residents. However, when these projects were rented, only nine Negroes were admitted to the Cedar Central projects and none were accepted at the Woodhill complex.[6] Cartographic data indicating the final residence of each family who moved to make way for the construction of Cedar Central Homes makes it possible to establish with certainty that Negroes were pushed inward toward the center of the ghetto (see Map II). And, although similar data is lacking for the families who moved from the Woodhill Homes site, the absence of a significant increase in the number of Negroes in adjoining

[3] Howard Whipple Green, *Substandard Housing as Determined by the Low Income Housing Area Survey* (Cleveland, 1940), 5-6.
[4] Green, *Census Facts and Trends by Tracts*, 108-10.
[5] For reports of official references to the housing units as either "Negro projects" or "white projects," see *Cleveland Press*, Jan. 19, 21, 23, 1935; L. P. Mitchell to Harold L. Ickes [1935], National Association for the Advancement of Colored People Branch Files (NAACP Branch Files) (Library of Congress).
[6] Howard Whipple Green, "Cedar Central Apartments are 100 Per Cent Leased," *Shut A Week*, Nov. 26, 1937; Cleveland *Plain Dealer*, Jan. 22, 1935; Cleveland *Call and Post*, April 23, Oct. 21, Nov. 23, 30, 1937, Dec. 7, 1940; Cleveland *Gazette*, Oct. 30, 1937.

31

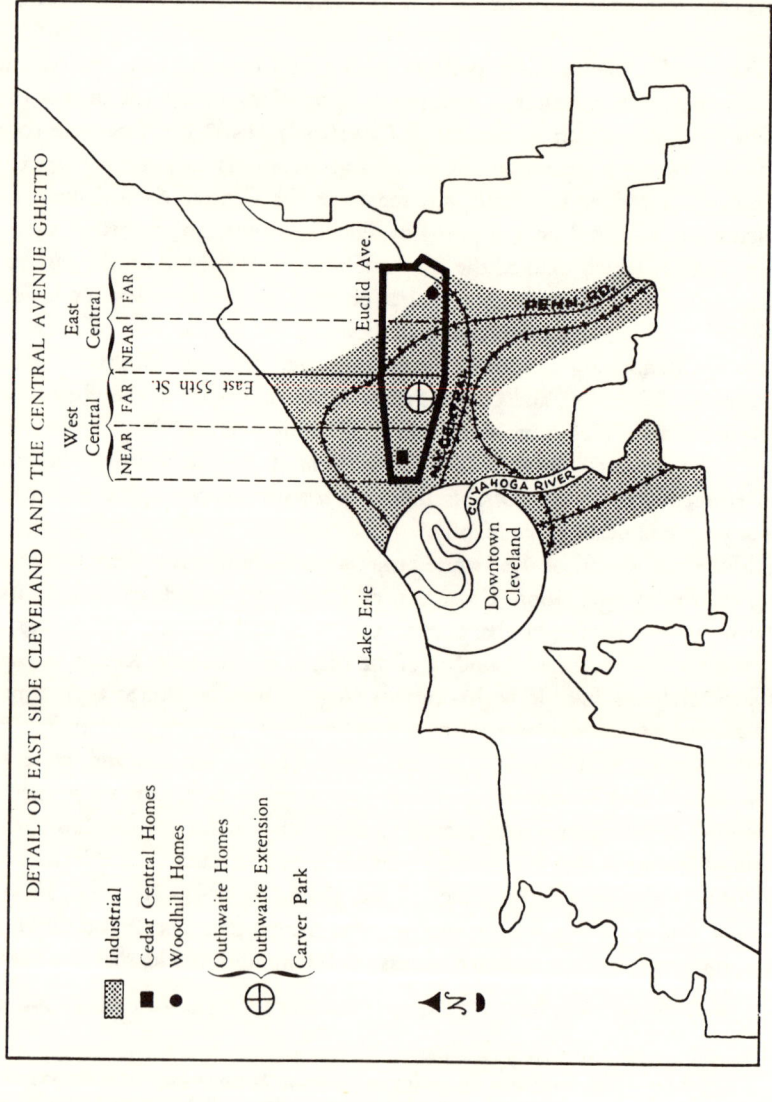

census tracts outside the Central Avenue district suggests that they too were forced deeper into the Negro section.⁷ The influence of the two projects was reflected in the decline in the number of census tracts in which 90 percent of the Negro population lived from twenty-nine in 1930 to twenty-four in 1940.⁸ Thus, as a result of the New Deal's housing program, ghetto borders were pushed inward, Negroes were even more heavily concentrated in the Central Avenue area, and segregation was increased.

Negroes were not silent. Protests made by the local National Association for the Advancement of Colored People (NAACP), the Urban League, and Negro politicians eventually resulted in a delegation that was sent to Washington to seek an end to the discrimination in the projects.⁹ The director of PWA, Secretary of the Interior Harold L. Ickes, personally sought to assure the group that he was in sympathy with their cause. He pointed to his record as a former president of the Chicago NAACP and indicated that he was "in hearty accord that all groups must work together in the housing program." Moreover, at the conclusion of the meeting, Ickes made it clear that "PWA never had any intention of adopting a race segregation policy."¹⁰ Yet, despite these assurances, Negroes never gained more than token representation in any of the projects located outside the Central Avenue ghetto (see Table I).

If PWA was in fact committed to opposing segregated housing, its practice of handling the actual construction and rental of the project units through local personnel sometimes worked at cross purposes to this policy. In Cleveland the man chosen to oversee PWA housing program, Warren C. Campbell, was a local businessman whose career in real estate offered very little to suggest that he was in sympathy with the principle of integrated housing.¹¹ As a past president of the Cleveland Real Estate Association, Campbell represented an organization which made it a policy not to rent or sell homes to Negroes in neighborhoods outside the ghetto.¹² Moreover, during World War II, the same organization was primarily responsible for the fact that needed defense housing units were not built for Negroes because it refused to approve the construction site selected by Washington officials.¹³ At the same time, as a trustee of the

---

⁷ Green, *Census Facts and Trends by Tracts*, 108-10.
⁸ *Ibid.*
⁹ Cleveland *Gazette*, Feb. 2, 1935; Cleveland *Call and Post*, Jan. 26, 1935; Cleveland *Eagle*, Jan. 17, 1936; Cleveland *Press*, Jan. 22, 1935; Cleveland *Plain Dealer*, Jan. 22, 1935. See also Mitchell to Walter White, Oct. 6, 1937, H. A. Gray to White, Sept. 28, 1937, C. K. Gillespie to White [1935], NAACP Branch Files.
¹⁰ Cleveland *Gazette*, Feb. 2, 1935.
¹¹ *Ibid.*, July 25, 1936.
¹² Cleveland *Eagle*, April 3, 1936; Cleveland *NAACP Branch Quarterly*, NAACP Branch Files.
¹³ The Federal Housing Administration was ready to construct war housing for Negroes in Cleveland. A local financial institution was ready to finance the projects if the Cleveland Real Estate Board would approve the construction site. The board, however, failed to approve the location and the local source of finance then

Apartment House Owners Association, Campbell represented an organization which had opposed the slum clearance projects and had proposed to solve the problem of congestion in the Central Avenue district by sending recently arrived southern Negro migrants back to the South.[14]

Although the evidence concerning both Campbell's attitudes and the influence which they had on the housing program in Cleveland is circumstantial, it was under his administration that a variety of techniques were employed with the apparent purpose of ensuring that Negroes and whites were separated.[15] One such strategy was to open two units simultaneously, permitting Negroes to enter only one. This practice had the advantage of making it appear as though Negroes were being equitably included in the public housing program. When Cleveland's first two projects, Cedar Central and Outhwaite Homes, were made available in 1937, a special dedication ceremony featuring prominent Negro leaders was held at the Outhwaite complex, and a Negro project manager was appointed who conducted a special campaign to sell the units to the Negro community; no such activities attended the opening of Cedar Central Homes.[16]

For Negroes who persisted in seeking apartments at Cedar Central, other methods were used. Those who made their race evident by applying in person encountered the suggestion that apartments could be obtained more quickly at Outhwaite.[17] Those who applied by mail were compelled to answer a question asking for their "race or nationality" and found that their applications were transferred to the Negro project.[18] Moreover, as it became evident that Negroes were not being accepted at certain projects, a psychology of avoidance seemed to develop within the Negro community. Many Negroes refused even to apply at projects located outside the ghetto, feeling that "What's the use when we know they don't let Negroes live there anyway."[19]

The housing projects not only encouraged residential segregation but also disrupted the normal pattern of socio-economic differentiation within the ghetto neighborhoods, a process which eventually led to the spread of slum conditions into new sections of the city. Prior to the construction of the units, Negroes were distributed according to a definite pattern of socio-economic gradation

withdrew its offer. As a result, no units were built in Cleveland for Negroes. For details of this episode, see Weaver, *Negro Ghetto*, 216.

[14] Cleveland *Gazette*, Sept. 24, 1932.

[15] In 1940 when the Cleveland Metropolitan Housing Authority took over the management of the housing projects from the United States Housing Authority, Warren C. Campbell was replaced by Marc J. Grossman, a civic leader well known for his interest in philanthropic movements. But, the policy of segregating Negroes and whites did not change under his administration before 1944.

[16] Cleveland *Call and Post*, July 12, 1937, Feb. 1, 1941.

[17] Cleveland *Gazette*, Oct. 16, 1937; Cleveland *Call and Post*, Nov. 30, 1940. See also Gillespie to Ickes, Sept. 23, 1937, Campbell to Gray, Oct. 4, 1937, Mitchell to White, Oct. 22, 1937, NAACP Branch Files.

[18] Cleveland *Gazette*, March 20, 1937; Cleveland *Call and Post*, Aug. 25, 1937.

[19] Cleveland *Call and Post*, Feb. 15, 1941.

MAP II

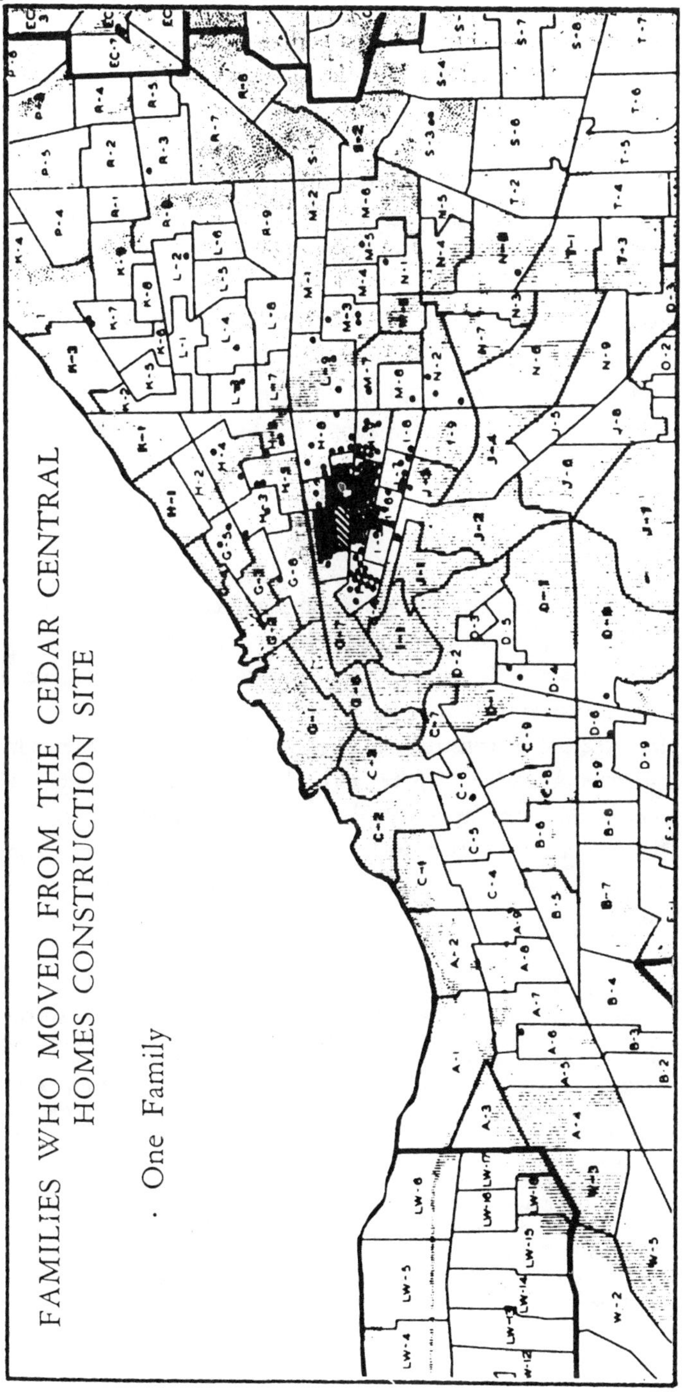

FAMILIES WHO MOVED FROM THE CEDAR CENTRAL HOMES CONSTRUCTION SITE

· One Family

Source: Howard Whipple Green, *Shant A Veak*, Dec. 9, 1937

within the Central Avenue ghetto. East 55th Street, a main thoroughfare which bisected the Negro community on a north-south axis, represented the dividing line between a lower-status area on the west and a higher-status area on the east. The West Central Avenue district was predominantly a slum and vice area. It was here that Negroes were most heavily congested, that educational and occupational levels were lowest, that disease and death rates were highest, that housing and sanitation conditions were worst, and that prostitution, bootlegging, and other forms of vice and crime flourished.[20] In contrast, most of the Negro community's affluent families, those whose incomes permitted them to afford the more expensive homes and apartments located closer to Cleveland's suburbs, lived in the East Central Avenue district. The social characteristics of the two sections were aptly summarized in the phrases that the city's Negroes used to refer to them.[21] The western half of the ghetto was called "the jungle"; the eastern half was termed the "Blue Stocking District."[22]

The three Negro projects were built in a tight cluster close to East 55th Street in the heart of the West Central slum and were intended to provide inexpensive lodgings for low-income groups in that neighborhood (see Map I).[23] Yet, as a result of a ruling by the United States comptroller general that the returns from PWA units had to be sufficient to repay the federal government's total investment, only an estimated 10 percent of those Negroes who moved from the project construction sites were able to afford the rents in the completed apartments.[24] When USHA succeeded PWA and an attempt was made to remedy this problem by providing a government subsidy, the rental figures were still too high for the most bereft elements of the Negro community.[25] Negro and white leaders, as well as local housing officials, all agreed that the low cost housing projects had failed to reach the lowest income groups.[26] Instead, most of

[20] Robert Bernard Navin, *Analysis of a Slum Area* (Washington, 1934), 24-56; Howard Whipple Green, "Slums—A City's Most Expensive Luxury," *Sheet A Week*, Sept. 22, 1934; Gordon H. Simpson, "Economic Survey of Housing in Districts of the City of Cleveland Occupied Largely by Colored People" [mimeographed report of the Cleveland Chamber of Commerce, 1931], 20-50; "The Central Area Social Study" [mimeographed report of the Welfare Federation of Cleveland, 1944], 42-53, 124-46.
[21] Simpson, "Economic Survey of Housing," 51-135; "Central Area Social Study," 42-53, 124-46; Wellington G. Fordyce, "Immigrant Colonies in Cleveland," *The Ohio State Archaeological and Historical Quarterly*, XLV (Oct. 1936), 320-40.
[22] "Central Area Social Study," 124; Cleveland *Call and Post*, March 16, 1939.
[23] Cleveland *Gazette*, May 16, 1931; Cleveland *Call and Post*, Feb. 6, 1936.
[24] Cleveland *Gazette*, Feb. 1, 1936; Sterner, *Negro's Share*, 317; Cleveland *Call and Post*, Feb. 1, 1941.
[25] Cleveland *Gazette*, Nov. 23, 1935; Cleveland *Call and Post*, March 21, 1940; Howard Whipple Green, "The Families That Moved to Make Way for the Outhwaite Housing Project," *Sheet A Week*, June 11, 1936.
[26] Cleveland *Gazette*, May 28, 1938; Cleveland *Press*, Aug. 8, 1932. Grossman, who became head of the Cleveland Metropolitan Housing Authority on January 1, 1940, remarked in answer to a query from local Negro leaders: "The Housing projects built and to be built in the city of Cleveland do not and will not permit members of the lowest income group for whom they were first ... [intended] to become tenants ... " Cleveland *Gazette*, Nov. 25, 1939.

the new apartments went to middle-class Negroes whose incomes required them to seek more modest accommodations."

It was the failure of the slum clearance projects to provide homes for the lower-class Negroes whom they displaced that provided the impetus for a shift in the pattern of socio-economic differentiation within the ghetto. Cartographic data available for the Outhwaite Homes complex disclose that most of the middle-class Negroes who were eventually housed in the new units came from the upper-status East Central district and that most of the lower-class Negroes who moved from the construction site were forced across East 55th Street into the same higher-status section (see Maps III and IV). This meant that the housing projects pulled middle-class Negroes from the upper-status East Central area into the lower-status West Central district, while they pushed lower-status Negroes from the lower-status West Central section into the upper-status East Central area. In effect, the construction of Outhwaite Homes led to a reversal of residential zones.

Other statistics add weight to this conclusion and suggest that the effects of Outhwaite Extension and Carver Park were similar. Data calculated for two socio-economic indices—education as measured by illiteracy rates and income as measured by median rental figures—reveal that before the projects were constructed there was a pattern of upward gradation from lower levels in the near West Central area through to higher levels in the far East Central area. However, in 1940 when all the three Negro units were completed, this pattern was no longer the same. Statistics for three socio-economic indices—education as measured by years of school completed, income as measured by median rental figures, and occupations as measured by percent of white collar workers—demonstrate that, while in all cases except occupations the near West Central area was still lower than the far East Central area, the two middle areas located on either side of East 55th Street were now reversed with the far West Central area higher than the near East Central area (see Table II).

The slum clearance housing projects, therefore, actually succeeded only in moving the slum area from one neighborhood to another. Both black and white observers agreed that the penetration of lower-class Negroes into the upper-status East Central section was attended by a marked deterioration in neighborhood conditions.[*] One and two family homes were converted into "kitchenette apartments," which usually consisted of one room with modest cooking facilities and which generally violated all of the city's building, safety, and sanitation codes." In an area to which Negroes had once pointed with pride as "our

⁷⁷ Cleveland *Press*, Nov. 23, 1932, June 2, 1933.
²⁸ Cleveland *Gazette*, May 15, 1937; Cleveland *Press*, June 2, 1933.
²⁹ Cleveland *Call and Post*, Nov. 8, 1941; Cleveland *Press*, Aug. 22, 1935, Dec. 1, 2, 3, 4, 1941.

MAP III

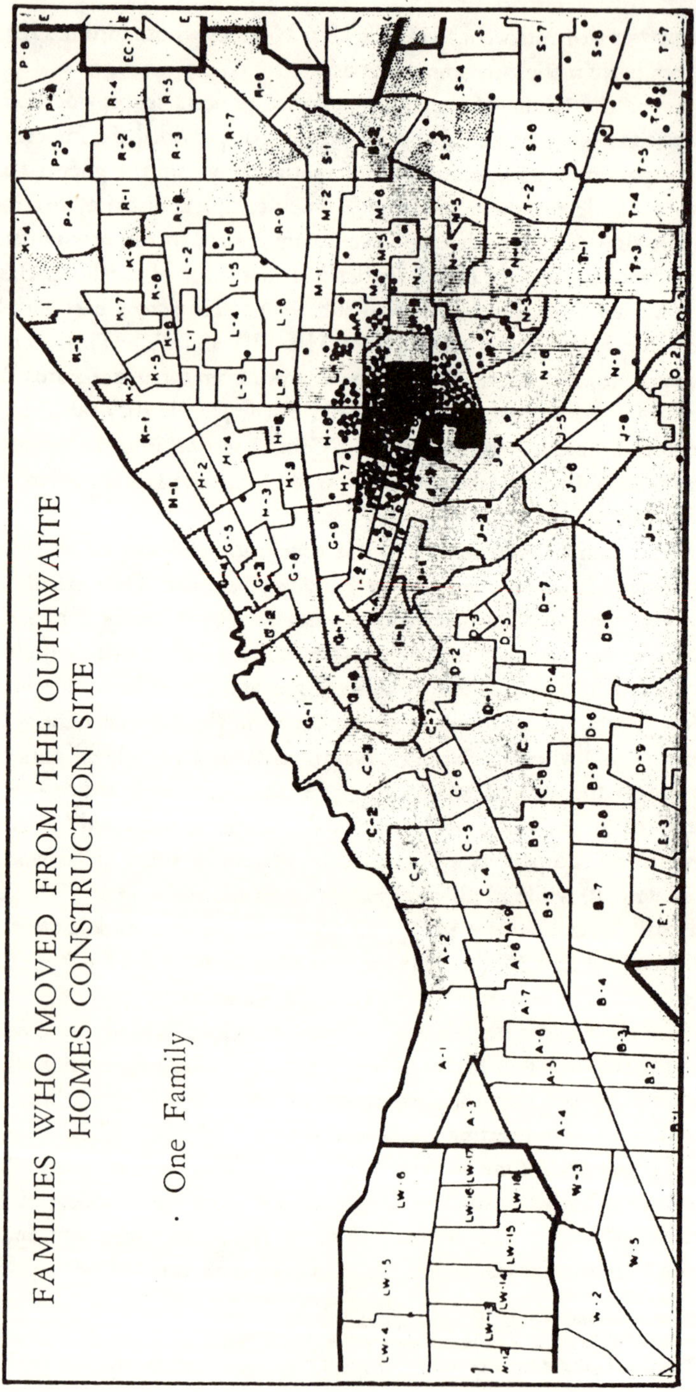

FAMILIES WHO MOVED FROM THE OUTHWAITE HOMES CONSTRUCTION SITE

· One Family

Source: Howard Whipple Green, *Cleveland Real Property Inventory*, 1936.

New Deal and the Negro Community 631

showcase of progress ... [where] many of our outstanding businesses [as well as] several of our outstanding churches ... and fine homes add their dignity to the landscape ... " surveys conducted by social agencies and the white press now found "shacks that even in the most vivid imagination never again can be termed houses ... " with "holes in the walls and floors, paper falling off, lights out of order, plumbing faulty ... [and] rats 'so big they look like cats.' "[30] Negro leaders commented bitterly that for those Negroes who had been forced to move by the housing projects, the notice posted on the construction sites which read "Property of the ... United States Housing Authority" had become an "emblem of despair, desperation and disease."[31] Others went so far as to call USHA the "greatest menace to the Negro ... in Cleveland today."[32]

Moreover, as lower-class Negroes moved into the East Central section, the "sporting element" appeared with greater frequency east of East 55th Street. Prostitutes, both Negro and white, plied their trade as far east as East 80th Street in a district referred to as "Little Hollywood."[33] Speakeasies dispensing liquor obtained from Cleveland's Italian bootleggers, the Mayfield Road Gang, which was itself centered on the eastern fringe of the ghetto, became numerous along the Pennsylvania railroad tracks which cut across the area.[34] And, policy, a form of nickle-and-dime gambling, was ubiquitous.[35]

While the New Deal low cost housing projects had both positive and negative effects on ghetto residential patterns, the public work program had a similarly mixed impact on the structure of Negro employment. Because Negroes were concentrated in jobs that were particularly vulnerable to dislocation in a contracting economy—primarily in unskilled labor and domestic service— the Depression hit Negroes with unusual severity. Although they made up only 10 percent of the available workers, they constituted 27 percent of the unemployed.[36] Within the Central Avenue ghetto unemployment averaged 50 percent and in some sections was as high as 90 percent.[37] Moreover, the effects of the Depression on Negroes were not relieved to any appreciable extent by the

[30] Cleveland *Press*, March 12, 1934, Dec. 1, 2, 1941.
[31] Cleveland *Call and Post*, Feb. 1, 1941.
[32] *Ibid.*, Sept. 13, 1941.
[33] Gordon H. Simpson to White, June 24, 1932, NAACP Branch Files; Cleveland *Press*, Aug. 12, 1930; Cleveland *Call and Post*, Oct. 24, 1935.
[34] Cleveland *Press*, June 2, 1932.
[35] *Ibid.*, March 14, 1935; David H. Pierce to Roy Wilkins, July 9, 1932, NAACP Branch Files; Cleveland *Gazette*, June 1, 1935; Cleveland *Call and Post*, Oct. 24, 1935.
[36] *Fifteenth Census of the United States: 1930. Population: Occupations, by States: Reports by States, Giving Statistics for Cities of 25,000 or More* (Washington, 1933), 1269.
[37] Weaver, "Negro Labor since 1929," 22; "Press Release," Cleveland NAACP, April 15, 1942, NAACP Branch Files.

39

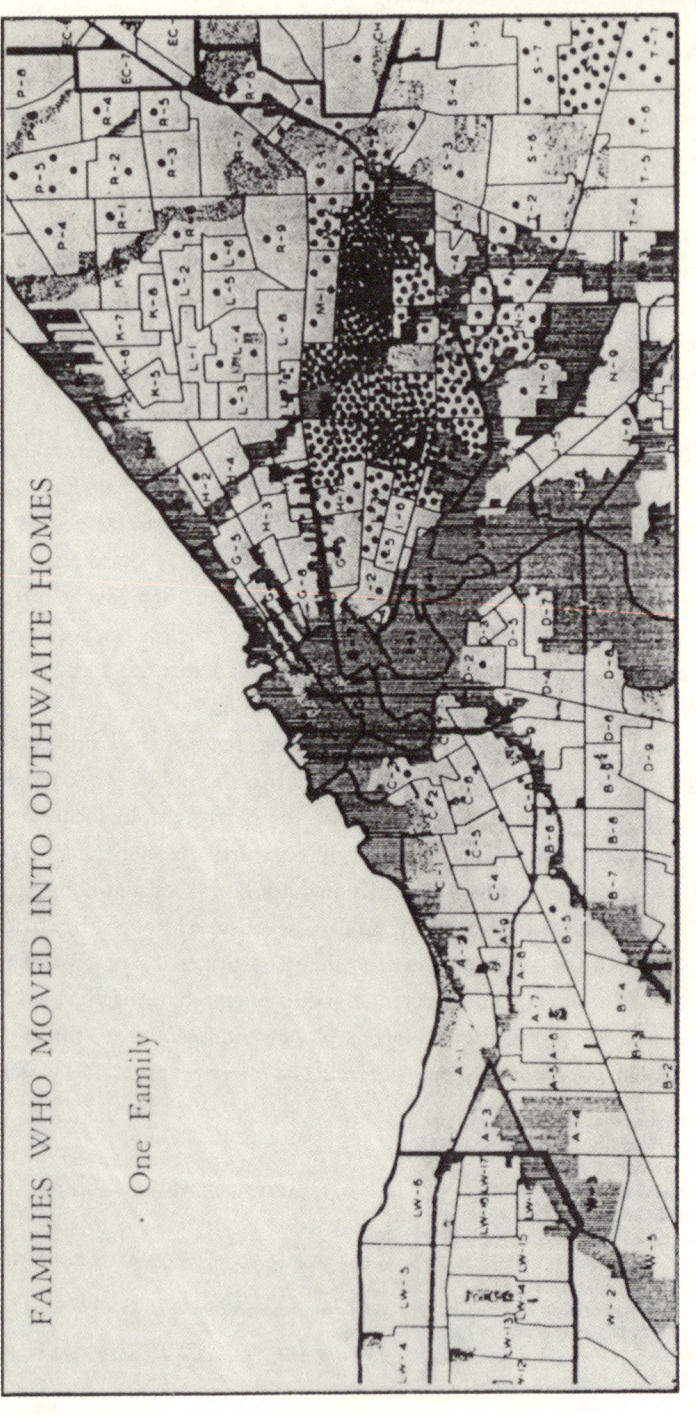

TABLE II

SOCIO-ECONOMIC AREAS IN CENSUS TRACTS OVER 50 PERCENT
NEGRO WITHIN THE CENTRAL AVENUE GHETTO, 1930–1940

	1930			
	Near West Central Area	Far West Central Area	Near East Central Area	Far East Central Area
Education by percent illiterate	7.5	5.5	5.0	2.0
Income by rent per month	23.0	27.5	29.7	34.2
	1940			
Education by years completed	7.2	8.5	7.7	8.7
Income by rent per month	16.3	20.3	16.3	21.6
Occupation by percent white collar	32.2	28.0	20.5	24.6

Both illiteracy and rental data for 1930 were derived from census tract statistics presented in Howard Whipple Green, *Population by Census Tract*, Cleveland Health Council, 1931. There were no data for occupations for 1930.

Of the data for 1940, those for education were derived from figures in Howard Whipple Green, *Sheet A Week*, February 11, 1943; those for rentals from Howard Whipple Green, *Cleveland Real Property Inventory, 1941*; and those occupations from *16th Census of the United States: 1940. Population and Housing: Statistics for Census Tracts: Cleveland, Ohio and Adjacent Areas* (Washington, 1943).

To correlate the statistical areas indicated here with ghetto neighborhoods see Map I.

limited relief and emergency work projects sponsored by local agencies.[28] The seriousness of the Negroes' plight was summed up in reports made by the Negro community's two leading social welfare agencies. A survey conducted by the Phyllis Wheatley Association expressed the belief that "the race is standing on a precipice of economic disaster," while the Annual Report of the Cleveland Urban League for 1933 indicated that conditions among Negroes had "reached a state approaching chaos."[29]

[28] Lucia Johnson Bing, *Social Work in Greater Cleveland: How Public and Private Agencies Are Serving Human Needs* (Cleveland, 1938), 14-26; Joanna C. Colcord, *Cash Relief* (New York, 1936), 59-63.
[29] Cleveland *Call and Post*, Jan. 12, 1935; "Annual Report of the Negro Welfare Association, 1933,"

Although the New Deal public work programs did not entirely meet the needs of the Negro community, Negroes received more than their share of the jobs which were provided.[40] The result was a substantial reduction in the high unemployment rate within the ghetto. Negroes generally constituted more than 10 percent of all workers assigned to the Civilian Conservation Corps from Cuyahoga County.[41] Central High School, which was located within the ghetto and was attended almost entirely by Negroes, regularly received larger grants from the National Youth Administration than any other single school in the city.[42] PWA—the same agency which built the low cost housing units—operated under a percentage formula which assured Negroes at least the number of jobs equal to their proportion of the total labor force.[43] And in the Works Projects Administration (WPA) activities, which accounted for the largest share of emergency work in Cleveland, Negroes averaged approximately 30 percent of the work force.[44] Moreover, Negroes held nearly 40 percent, or about four times their proportionate share, of all the jobs that were created by emergency work programs.[45] By at least the mid-1930s, New Deal public work projects had succeeded in reducing unemployment among Negroes from about 50 percent to 30 percent and the federal government had become the largest single employer of Cleveland Negroes as well as the most important new influence on the Negro job structure.[46]

However, while the federal government's emergency work programs significantly reduced the high rate of unemployment within the Negro community, they also appear to have depressed the Negro job structure by engaging many workers in job categories below those which they had filled in the private sector of the economy before the Depression began. A comparison of the occupational distribution of Negro workers with that of whites indicates that on eve of the Depression Negroes were underrepresented by from 30 percent to 80 percent in occupations above the skilled level, while they were overrepresented by from 20

Cleveland Urban League Papers (Western Reserve Historical Society). The Negro Welfare Association was the Cleveland affiliate of the National Urban League.

[40] Interview with Russell W. Jelliffe, Oct. 20, 1969.

[41] "Minutes of the Board of Trustees of the Negro Welfare Association, June 1, 1936," Cleveland Urban League Papers; Cleveland *Call and Post*, July 14, 1936; C. V. Colwill to Clayborne George, June 11, 1933, NAACP Branch Files.

[42] Cleveland *Call and Post*, July 6, 1939.

[43] "Minutes of the Board of Trustees of the Negro Welfare Association, May 3, 1935," Cleveland Urban League Papers.

[44] Cleveland *Press*, April 18, 1941.

[45] Statistics derived from data in *Sixteenth Census of the United States: 1940. Population*. Vol. III, *The Labor Force: Occupation, Industry, Employment, and Income*. Part 4: *Nebraska-Oregon* (Washington, 1943), 639.

[46] *Census of Partial Employment, Unemployment, and Occupations: 1937: States from North Carolina to Wyoming, Alaska, and Hawaii*. Part 4: *Nebraska-Oregon* (Washington, 1938), 71-75. "Annual Report of the Negro Welfare Association, 1938," Cleveland Urban League Papers.

percent to 300 percent in occupations below this category. As a result, 79 percent of all Negro males and 93 percent of all Negro females were employed below the skilled level, primarily in Cleveland's iron and steel mills and as servants in white homes.[47]

Yet, there is evidence to suggest that Negroes may have sunk to lower occupational levels. On public work projects the experience of Cleveland Negroes with PWA illustrates this point. PWA was especially important to Negro skilled workers in the building trades since, during the Depression-engendered lull in private building, it held a virtual monopoly over the available jobs in the construction industry. But at best the policies of PWA could have accomplished no more than to maintain the occupational color line.[48] This was evident from the terms of an agreement worked out between the Cleveland Urban League and the Department of the Interior that provided only that "the percentage of Negroes in each skilled craft shall equal the ratio that the number of Negro skilled workers bore to the number of white workers in each skilled craft as shown by the census of 1930."[49] Even this minimum standard, however, was widely disregarded.[50] The Negro press reported that "only four to five lonely Negroes are polka dotted among the hundreds of skilled workers" and concluded that "the percentage agreement from Washington ... is apparently not being followed."[51] A survey conducted by the Cleveland Urban League confirmed this conclusion when it found that only five Negro carpenters, two cement finishers, six bricklayers, and one engineer were employed on all of PWA projects.[52]

More detailed information regarding the concentration of Negroes in unskilled occupations on the New Deal projects is available for WPA. The

[47] These statistics were obtained by reclassifying all of the occupations of blacks and whites in the 1930 census according to the ranking system developed by Alba M. Edwards. This system involves a six category classification from unskilled labor at the bottom, through semiskilled, skilled, clerical, business, and finally to professional workers at the top. But for the purpose of brevity the procedure followed here has been to refer to all jobs in the skilled, clerical, business, and professional categories as simply skilled labor. The advantage of Edwards' system is that it permits an orderly ranking of jobs according to desirability and, therefore, provides a good basis for comparing the structure of Negro and white employment. The concept of a proportionate share, on which the figures concerning underrepresentation and overrepresentation are based, assumes that all other things being equal Negro workers might be expected to approximate the percentage which they represent of the total labor force in each occupational category. Drake and Cayton, *Black Metropolis*, 223-32; Alba M. Edwards, *A Social-Economic Grouping of the Gainful Workers of the United States: Gainful Workers of 1930 in social-economic groups, by color nativity, age, and sex, and by industry, with comparative statistics for 1920 and 1910* (Washington, 1938).
[48] Wolters, *Negroes and the Great Depression*, 203-12.
[49] "Minutes of the Board of Trustees of the Negro Welfare Association, May 3, 1935," Cleveland Urban League Papers.
[50] Interview with George W. Hanzly, Sept. 15, 1971.
[51] *Cleveland Eagle*, Nov. 22, 1935.
[52] "Minutes of the Organization of Building Trades Craftsmen [an organization sponsored by the Negro Welfare Association], Oct. 13, 1936," Cleveland Urban League Papers.

Cleveland Urban League in 1936 made a survey to determine what jobs Negroes held on eight sample public work projects, and the national *Census of Unemployment* in 1937 obtained information relative to the *former* occupations of Negroes temporarily employed on the government projects.³³ A comparison of these data shows that, while the former occupations of Negroes on emergency work constituted a representative cross section of the total Negro labor force, the jobs which Negroes held on government projects were disproportionately unskilled labor. Among Negro males, 819, or 16.7 percent, of those on public work had been formerly employed in skilled jobs, yet of these, only thirty-four, or .6 percent, held similar jobs on the emergency work projects. Similarly, among Negro females, 213, or 20.4 percent, of those in the public work programs had been formerly occupied in skilled jobs, but of these only, five, or .3 percent, held comparable jobs on federal projects. Thus, in the private sector of the economy 79 percent of all Negro males and 93 percent of all Negro females were employed in unskilled labor, on eight WPA projects sampled by the Urban League these percentages increased to 99.4 percent for men and to 99.7 percent for women.³⁴

The tendency for Negroes to be employed at lower job levels on the New Deal projects than those which they had occupied in private industry was the result of several factors. Of primary importance was the occupational design of the relief effort. Despite the attempts of government administrators to provide employment for skilled, white collar, and professional workers, the greatest number of federally sponsored jobs were in manual labor. For this reason occupational depression on the work projects was a characteristic of the white as well as the Negro labor force. The problems of black workers, however, were intensified by an apparently widespread pattern of discrimination in job classification at the local level. A survey by the Negro press both summed up this pattern and revealed the resentment Negroes felt toward it:

Not a single Negro has a job on the state WPA staff. Not a single Negro ... has an executive position on the WPA county staff. Out of the hundreds of clerks employed by the WPA headquarters not one is a Negro. Of the hundreds of foremen on the scores of projects that are being operated by the WPA here there are only two Negroes. Practically all of the jobs the WPA has to offer above the role of menial labor are given to whites. We have good ground for the charge that there is widespread and deliberate discrimination against our people. There are practically no promotions of Negroes on projects. When Negro workers reach the point where they are eligible for promotion their jobs are abolished or some trumpted up charge against them brings their dismissal. When Negroes are fortunate enough to be placed on a project where the work is

³³ Cleveland *Eagle*, Jan. 3, 1936; *Census of Partial Employment*, 83.
³⁴ These data were obtained by using the Edwards classification.

pleasant they are mysteriously laid off.... All of our men are not ditchdiggers, neither are all of our women domestics.... The administration of WPA in Ohio and especially in Cuyahoga County has about reached the point of scandal."

Although a continuous stream of protest from Negro leaders prompted Washington administrators to action on several occasions, very little improvement was effected. A conference in 1935 of the Cleveland Urban League and WPA officials resulted in the employment of a "few Negro supervisors and foremen," mostly on Negro projects." Negroes continued to complain, however, and three years later representatives of the national administration conducted an investigation of WPA operations in Cleveland which confirmed the existence of discrimination but which resulted only in a promise to employ Negroes in "several white collar jobs" and to appoint "at least three [Negroes] in a supervisory capacity."" A similar investigation made in 1939 ended with the dismissal of several local white executives on charges of discriminating against Negro skilled workers. But it appears that none of these actions achieved more than temporary improvement. A Negro leader observed, "When there is a rumor of an investigation they seem to find [skilled] Negroes from somewhere, but as soon as the heat is off the Negroes ... on the projects begin to disappear. It is about as difficult for a skilled Negro operator to be assigned to a power machine as it is for him to find a job in private industry.""

The failure of the federal government to curb discrimination on the public work projects was due largely to its ineffectiveness in dealing with lower echelon personnel. Washington officials might attempt to eliminate the discrimination exhibited by administrators in executive positions at county headquarters, but only rarely did they make a determined effort to curtail the discriminatory practices of project leaders in the field, especially among foremen and supervisors. Yet it was the project leaders who controlled the allocation of jobs on the emergency work programs. Effectively, it was they who determined the final job classification for most workers; it was they who determined who was to be laid off when cutbacks were made; it was they who administered discipline (which could result in dismissal); and it was they who recommended promotions and demotions.

The variety of techniques employed by foremen and supervisors to restrict Negroes to unskilled occupations were frequently documented in the Negro press. Sometimes a project leader would refuse altogether to accept a skilled Negro. In one such instance, WPA county headquarters assigned two Negro

" Cleveland *Call and Post*, Feb. 24, 1938.
" "Minutes of the Board of Trustees of the Negro Welfare Association, Dec. 13, 1935," Cleveland Urban League Papers; *ibid.*, Jan. 10, 1936; Cleveland *Call and Post*, June 16, 1938.
" Cleveland *Call and Post*, June 2, 1938.
" *Ibid.*, Sept. 14, 1939.

typists to an indexing project, but the project supervisor wrote on the back of their assignment slips, "This project cannot use colored typists" and then sent them back to the county office."⁹ More frequent was the practice of accepting a skilled Negro worker on a project and later demoting him to an unskilled job. This was the experience of a Negro electrician who was reclassified as a common laborer and put to work washing light bulbs.⁴⁰ Moreover, when Negro skilled workers who had been demoted to unskilled positions applied for reclassification their application forms were frequently lost between the office of the project foremen and the office of county headquarters.⁴¹ And, Negroes who sought to register a complaint about their failure to be reclassified were threatened with dismissal, demotion, or a disciplinary reduction in pay.⁴²

That lower echelon personnel in the field rather than executives at county headquarters were primarily responsible for the discrimination against Negro skilled workers on the public work projects was widely recognized by Negro leaders who considered them to be "czars" in the matter of job classification.⁴³ By the late 1930s comments of Negro leaders reflected a respect for the efforts of the county officials to secure a fair distribution of work for Negroes, while at the same time they displayed a certain resignation to the role of prejudiced foremen. In 1939 the Cleveland *Call and Post*, which had been one of the leaders in the campaign conducted by the Negro press to secure skilled jobs for Negroes, concluded that, "Despite the obvious efforts of departmental heads to do something about the violation of orders with reference to the classification ... of workers ... [their] efforts to secure a square deal for Negro skilled ... workers ... has continued to be obstructed by prejudiced foremen and office underlings."⁴⁴ A year later the same paper remarked that "while the central office WPA is innocent of responsibility for discrimination against Negro applicants, it is known that under officials at that office have turned their heads in the opposite direction while some underling supervisor or project foreman did the dirty work."⁴⁵

These findings suggest that new perspectives on the relationship between Negroes and the New Deal are revealed if research is conceptualized on a basis broad enough to embrace both questions concerning the extent of Negro participation in government programs as well as questions relating to the impact of these programs on the social structure of the Negro community.

³⁹ *Ibid.*, June 23, July 7, 28, 1938, Feb. 1, 1940.
⁴⁰ *Ibid.*, June 16, 1938.
⁴¹ *Ibid.*, July 14, 1938.
⁴² *Ibid.*, July 28, 1938.
⁴³ *Ibid.*, April 27, 1939.
⁴⁴ *Ibid.*, July 14, 1938.
⁴⁵ *Ibid.*, Feb. 1, 1940.

Specifically, the Cleveland experience demonstrates that although the New Deal public housing and emergency work programs played an important part in alleviating the problems generated by the Depression, they also contributed to the preservation of perhaps the two salient components which combine to produce a caste-like Negro social structure—residential segregation and a distinctly racial occupational pattern.

COMMUNISM AND BLACK NATIONALISM IN THE DEPRESSION: THE CASE OF HARLEM

by Mark D. Naison*

During the Depression years, the Communist Party carried on a determined campaign to win ideological and political leadership of the Black population in the United States. While this campaign involved the recruiting of Black members for the Party, its major impact on the Black community came in the form of mass struggles against unemployment, lynching, and racial discrimination, and Party work in the labor movement. Unlike previous groups on the American Left, the Communists viewed the Negro question as a national question, and defined their role as fighting for "proletarian and Communist hegemony" within a broad Negro liberation movement that included other political tendencies.[1] The Party believed that it could attain influence over the Negro masses only by proving that it had eliminated racism in its own ranks and could deal more effectively than any other organization with the Black community's day to day problems.

One of the most interesting, and largely unexplored aspects of the Party's Negro work during the Depression is its relationship with the Garvey movement and the numerous neo-Garveyites groups that arose in urban Black communities throughout the period. These nationalist organizations, some of which had a genuine mass base, developed strategies for dealing with Black unemployment that emphasized control of the ghetto economy and opposed strategies of economic advancement or campaigns against discrimination that were based upon alliances with the labor movement and the White working class. The Party fought these organizations politically and sometimes physically, but never assumed it could make them disappear. The Communists viewed Negro nationalism as a fundamentally revolutionary impulse which was given reactionary form by leaders who hoped to rise to power in traditional capitalist terms (business or electoral politics). Their strategy was to ally with the nationalist organizations whenever possible, or else isolate them, and at all times to try to win over their rank and file to the Party's positions.

The Party's conflict with Negro nationalists took place in almost every urban center where Communist Negro work met with some success (e.g., New York, Chicago, Cleveland, Detroit, Buffalo, Philadelphia) and remained intense throughout the Depression. Although the specific content of the conflicts varied from city to city, some of the issues raised seem to have been important everywhere--Who were the Negro community's allies? Should Black people think in class or race terms? What is the proper strategy to deal with mass unemployment in the Black community? Should the Negro ghetto be seen as the basis for a positive struggle for "group autonomy" or a negative manifestation of Jim Crow? Where does power lie in capitalist society and how should Black people organize to use it in their own interest?

---

*Mark D. Naison is in the Institute of Afro-American Studies at Fordham University.

MARK D. NAISON

The Communists were able to build broad united fronts in the late Depression years based upon their perspectives on these questions, but were never able to undercut the mass base of the nationalist groups. The struggle was continuous, and in somewhat attenuated form, it persists even today.

One well documented example of the nature and scope of the struggle is Harlem. Harlem was a national concentration point for the Communist Party during much of the Depression[2] and its struggle with Harlem nationalists was a regular subject in the Party press and in Negro newspapers. However, it is important to remember that Harlem was not representative of all of Black America, and that the struggle may have taken another form in Black communities with a different class composition and economic base. Before general conclusions are drawn, similar investigations need to be made in cities like Chicago and Detroit where the Black industrial working class was larger, more unified and more accessible to unionization.

Harlem

The political struggle between nationalists and communists in Harlem had its roots in the Twenties. Communists in the African Blood Brotherhood had waged a bitter ideological struggle with Marcus Garvey in the post-war period over questions of race loyalty vs. class loyalty, the significance of the Russian Revolution to African peoples, the viability of an alliance between Blacks and the working class movement. But the specific form of Communists-nationalist conflicts in the Depression was shaped by mass unemployment. Harlem's Black population was devastated by the Depression (an Urban League spokesman estimated unemployment at 80% at the time of the 1935 Harlem Riot)[3] and the fundamental issues were physical survival and the regaining of a foothold in the economy. Both nationalists and Communists recognized this issue, but developed completely different strategies to deal with them--for the nationalists there were the "Don't Buy Where You Can't Work" campaigns and the encouragement of Black business; for the Communists, the trade union movement and the struggle for adequate relief.

The Communists' emphasis on the government as the target for economic action enabled them to develop a coherent strategy to organize the unemployed from almost the moment the Depression struck. In January 1930, the Party mandated the Trade Union Unity League to organize unemployed councils which would try to force local, state, and federal authorities to provide immediate cash relief to the unemployed and pass unemployment insurance legislation. While mass demonstrations were being organized at city halls and state capitals, the neighborhood councils would conduct rent strikes to lower rents, move furniture back after evictions, and march on private and public charities to demand relief for unemployed individuals. Through 1931, the unemployed councils were effective in Harlem primarily as an organization to resist evictions. But after December of 1931, when the city began to establish Home Relief Bureaus for the distribution of cash relief, the councils became "unions of the unemployed" which made sure that members got on the relief rolls and used picketing,

COMMUNISM AND BLACK NATIONALISM IN THE DEPRESSION:

sit-ins and mass demonstrations at the Relief Bureaus to achieve their ends. In addition, the Harlem unemployed council protested discrimination and segregation in city relief programs and demanded additional funds and facilities for Harlem.[4] Throughout the entire Depression period, this movement was one of the major sources of Communist influence in Harlem, a concrete demonstration of the Party's ability to gain access to resources through mass interracial action. It became particularly effective in 1934 and 1935 when the Party began to organize employees of the Home Relief Bureaus and built cells in almost every Bureau in Harlem.[5]

The nationalist organizations were much slower in mobilizing to meet the impact of the crisis. The Garvey movement and its spinoffs were business oriented and tended to look for a solution to Black unemployment in the development of a tradition of Negro entrepeneurship. They had a difficult time adjusting their outlook to a Depression when poorly capitalized Black businesses were failing, and new ones were difficult to form.[6] In addition, factional conflicts in the Universal Negro Improvement Association hindered the nationalists' capacity to act. Competing groups fought for control of the UNIA's headquarters in the courts and in the streets,[7] and the membership increasingly fell prey to the religious cults that proliferated in the community. In 1933, Negro World columnist Samuel Haynes complained: "Our organization has disintegrated into a vicious network of private clubs and societies, where the principles of the movement have been subordinated to new "isms," creeds, cults and mysticism. Former Garveyites are now enrolled in the Moorish-American Society; in various African movements, most of them founded by ex-Garveyites themselves, who had filched the constitution of the UNIA to fool the people in new religious movements claiming to be associated with Garveyism."[8]

Nevertheless, if the nationalists were too internally divided to develop a coherent economic strategy in the early Depression years, they were strong enough to present a serious problem for the Party when it organized interracial rallies and demonstrations in the streets of Harlem. St. William Wellington Wellwood Grant, head of the UNIA's Tiger Division, led several assaults on Communist street rallies in 1930 and 1931, one of which led indirectly to a Party member's death.[9] As late as September 1933, a Party Scottsboro meeting was attacked by Garveyites when the speaker made a pejorative reference to Garvey, but the Party was by that time strong enough to easily subdue the attackers.[10]

More serious than this intermittent physical harassment, in the Party's view, were efforts to organize a "Don't Buy Where You Can't Work" movement in Harlem. Several Harlem newspapers had openly called for such a campaign even before the Depression, inspired by a successful boycott in Chicago,[11] but the Depression intensified its appeal among both the nationalists and Harlem's middle class. During the spring of 1931, the Harlem Business Men's Club organized a "race loyalty parade," and a group of housewives associated with the Abyssinian Baptist Church led a march through the community advocating a boycott of merchants who refused to hire Blacks.[12] The Harlem Communists, actively organizing unemployment councils in the community, publicly attacked

26

this movement as an effort to arouse sentiment against the foreign-born and sabotage the growing unity of Negro and White workers in the struggle for "unemployment insurance and real relief."[13] Party theoretician Cyril Briggs assessed the movement as a campaign by the economically crippled Negro middle class to "divert the Negro masses . . . from revolutionary struggle":

> These fakers are attempting to narrow down the struggle against unemployment to a boycott movement against white merchants in Harlem, which would obtain at best a few thousand jobs for the tens of thousands of unemployed workers in Harlem. The boycott movement is offered as a complete solution for the tragic situation of the Negro unemployed and as a substitute for joint revolutionary mass action of Negro and white workers in the struggle for unemployment relief. It is in reality an attempt to utilize the misery of the masses for the strengthening of the Negro petty bourgeoisie under the old fake slogan of race loyalty. . . .[14]

Briggs' analysis tended to underplay the broad appeal that a jobs campaign had too many segments of Harlem's population, not all of whom were nationalists or would-be businessmen. But some of the boycott movement's most vocal advocates fit Briggs' description perfectly. Harlem Business Men's Club president Ralph Gothard wrote regularly in the Negro World that the boycott and the encouragement of Negro business would solve Harlem's unemployment problem: "I believe that EFFICIENCY on the part of the Negro business man . . . coupled with RACE LOYALTY on the part of the public. . . will in a few years CREATE sufficient jobs to ABSORB our unemployed group."[15]

The "Don't Buy Where You Can't Work" agitation, to the Party's great relief, failed to crystalize into an effective movement in 1931. But the issue was kept alive by nationalist street speakers, Harlem business leaders, and editors and clergymen, and in the spring of 1933, a Garveyite who called himself Sufi Abdul Hamid began a picket campaign against White storeowners in the 135 Street area.[16] By the end of that summer, his activities had attracted enough community support to persuade both the Party and middle class community leaders that they had to enter the jobs movement to maintain their credibility.

The Party's manner of entry into the campaign was awkward and hesitant, reflecting its commitment to fight discrimination in Harlem without pitting White against Black or reinforcing the anti-foreign and anti-semitic sentiments that Sufi sometimes evoked. In August of 1933, the Party formed a "Committee Against Discrimination of Negro Workers on Jobs" which demanded that a majority of workers in 125 Street stores must be Negro, but that no White workers be fired to replace them.[17] The Committee decided to direct its activities exclusively at chain stores, large establishments and public utilities, so that the small Jewish or Italian "mom and pop" stores would not be the targets of attack. It asked that White workers in the large establishments be switched to other stores of the chain or be given shorter hours without reduction in pay so that Negro workers might be hired.

The Committees' first major target was the Fifth Avenue Coach Company, which had long been notorious for its failure to hire Negro drivers. After an unsuccessful meeting with the company's president, the Party began picketing the Bus Company's 125 Street terminal and urging Harlem residents not to ride its buses. The campaign, which began in February 1934, was enthusiastically supported by trade unions sympathetic to the Party and resulted in several arrests.[18]

The Party's approach to the jobs campaign provoked some opposition in its own ranks. Harlem Party leader Richard B. Moore argued that White workers in Harlem were "living on the backs of the Negro masses," and had no claim to the Party's protection.[19] A jobs campaign which asked that no Whites be fired, Moore asserted, would be completely ineffective and regarded as dishonest by the Harlem community.[20] Moore's objections, however, were overruled by the Section Committee and his supporters were forced to accept the Party line.[21] The Harlem section's position on the matter was forcefully expressed by William Patterson in a March 17, 1933 article in the Liberator:

> The revolutionary struggle of the Negro masses must be built along the line of indissoluble struggle with the white working class. There can be no wavering on this point, there can be no concessions to petty-bourgeois nationalism. The Negro masses cannot carry on a successful emancipation struggle alone. . . . It must be recognized that every tendency which to the slightest degree disrupts the growing unity of Negro and white workers strengthens the forces of the enemy. Concessions are not won by Negroes at the expense of white workers. Concessions must and can only be won at the expense of the ruling class.[22]

This iron determination to maintain Black-White working class unity in the jobs campaign isolated the Party, for the time being, from other Harlem organizations active on this issue. The Party's boycott of the bus company, carried on throughout the spring and summer of 1934, was not supported by an important non-Party organization and failed to open up any jobs.

At about the same time the Party began picketing the bus company, leading Harlem ministers put together a Black united front organization called the Citizens League for Fair Play aimed at opening jobs for Blacks in stores on 125 Street. Under the leadership of Rev. John H. Johnson, the group began picketing Blumstein's department store in June of 1934 to try to open up positions for Negro sales personnel. The Citizens League was dominated by middle-class leaders and presented itself as a "reasonable alternative to the agitation of Sufi.[23] The organization had a nationalist component, the African Patriotic League, but the basic direction of the campaign lay in the hands of the ministers and the editorial staff of the New York Age.[24]

28

MARK D. NAISON

The success of the Citizen's League in uniting diverse organizations and arousing broad-based community support caused the Party to shift its strategy in the jobs struggle. In July of 1934, just before the Citizen's League signed an agreement with Blumstein's, the Party decided to try to join the picket line outside the store with an interracial delegation to inject a note of Black-White unity. Their delegation was handled roughly by leaders of the African Patriotic League who were organizing the picketing: Bonita Williams had a League of Struggle for Negro Rights sign taken from her and a White Party member was escorted from the line and told "this is a Negro's fight."[25] The Party subsequently praised the boycott movement, but demanded that Whites be allowed to participate:

> The boycott movement is very good, because it is essentially a mass movement, which when properly conducted will bring many rights to the oppressed Negro people. We denounce the present method of barring those sympathetic whites--workers, intellectuals, and professionals--who have manifested a desire to sincerely fight for the rights of the Negro people by picketing stores where whites are only employed at the present time.... The cry of "We are going to run Harlem by driving the white people out" can do nothing but harm to the poor Negro people of Harlem, ninety percent of whom must go outside of Harlem to work. Therefore, we appeal to the Negro people to unite with all sincere whites who are willing to fight with us side by side for Negro rights.[26]

In order to demonstrate the practicality of Black-White unity in the jobs movement, the Party and the Young Liberators, the youth wing of the League of Struggle for Negro Rights, began picketing the Empire Cafeteria on 125 St. and Lenox Avenue to demand that Black workers be hired as countermen. After a week long picketing campaign, the Cafeteria agreed to hire four Negro countermen. without firing any Whites.[27] The Party hailed this victory as an example of "The Right Way to Boycott" and pointed proudly to the fact that rank and file Garveyites and Sufites participated in the picketing without objecting to the campaign's objectives or the presence of whites on the picket lines.[28]

The success of the Empire struggle was magnified in the Party's eyes by the factional bickering that followed the Citizen's League's settlement with Blumsteins. After a number of Negro women were hired by the store, the middle-class leaders of the Citizens League found themselves under attack from nationalists on the "picket committee" of their group for allegedly giving preference to light skinned women. Ira Kemp and Arthur Reid, African Patriotic League representatives on the group, led renewed picketing of the store with the demand that "dark-skinned" women who had participated in the picketing be hired in place of the women who had been referred to Blumstein by the Citizens League.[29] In addition, the League found itself under attack from Sufi for having taken credit for a campaign that he had initiated. Sufi also continued picketing,

29

demanding that his followers be given the jobs.

When this additional picketing failed to yield results, both Sufi and the African Patriots took their campaign to the smaller stores on 125 Street. Each group held to its special ideological trade-mark--Sufi's was that the "Jews be driven out of Harlem" and Kemp and Reid that darker Negroes be given preference in the hiring. Both groups maintained considerable grass-roots support, but were decisively isolated from the middle-class leaders of the Blumstein boycott who were horrified by their injection of the color issue, their antiforeign rhetoric, and their use of physical intimidation. Both major Harlem newspapers denounced the nationalists as "racketeers" and called upon lawenforcement agencies to halt their agitation. The two groups were both restrained by court injunction from "racial picketing"; Reid and Kemp's organization in November of 1934, and Sufi's in June of 1935.[30]

The growing division between the nationalists and mainstream community leaders helped prepare the way for the Party to take the initiative in the jobs movement. After the Empire Cafeteria boycott succeeded, the Harlem section began to set the stage for a broad united front against discrimination in Harlem that would link the issue of jobs in Harlem to the question of employment discrimination throughout the city and bring in the issue of discriminatory distribution of relief around which the Party had been organizing for years. "The line of the section," Party spokesmen declared, "was not to confine this movement to Harlem, but to make it a starting point for the development of a real drive throughout the city for the right of Negroes to work on all jobs, in all trades and professions, against all forms of discrimination, in connection with relief work and the issuance of unemployment relief."[31]

The Party's ability to build such a coalition was significantly improved by the role that its organizers played in the March 19, 1935 Harlem Uprising and the investigations which followed. During the afternoon and evening rioting, Black and White party members circulated through the crowds with leaflets which denounced the "police brutality" in Kress Department store, allegedly setting off the violence, and which urged people not to turn it into a race riot which pitted Black against White! Although the Police Commissioner, the Manhattan District Attorney, and the Hearst papers initially tried to blame the Party for instigating the rioting, the Commission that LaGuardia picked to investigate the disturbances came to a totally different conclusion:

> While one...would hesitate to give the Communists full credit for preventing the outbreak from becoming a race riot, they deserve more credit than any other element in Harlem for preventing a physical conflict between whites and blacks. The young white men who mounted the ladder and lamp post on 125 Street and were beaten and arrested because they took the part of the indignant Negro crowds certainly changed the complexion of the outbreak. It was probably due in some measure to the activities of these racial leaders, both white and black, that the crowds attacked property rather than persons.[32]

In the hearings that followed the uprising, Party activists joined with a wide range of community leaders to help turn the investigation from a search for "villains" into a thorough exposure of social conditions in the community. Party activists in Harlem and lawyers from the International Labor Defense were present at every open hearing held by the committee and helped to shape the discussion in a manner which prevented polarization along racial lines. The Committee concluded:

> ...the main role which the Communists played at the public hearings was by no means that of professional agitators and propogandists, they only defined and gave direction to the often vague dissatisfaction of the people, and attempted to interpret injustices which were regarded as racial persecution as a phase of the general expression of submerged classes. Although it is difficult to say how far they succeeded in accomplishing this end, they certainly played a part in preventing these hearings from becoming purely the resentment of blacks against whites.[33]

The Party emerged from this experience with greatly increased credibility in the community--it had "won its spurs" one organizer was to say.[34] The Party's ability to maintain interracial unity under fire and take the offensive in the face of a concerted propaganda attack against it gave it what amounted to ideological hegemony in the economic struggles of the community. From 1935 through 1939, there was not a single broad coalition around a significant social issue in Harlem in which the Party did not play an important role--whether it was housing, employment, police brutality, or the defense of Ethiopia.[35] Moreover, such coalitions were always explicitly interracial and contained White representatives from the Party and the labor movement.

One of the first united fronts to emerge was the "Joint Conference Against Discriminatory Practices" whose goal was to "fight discrimination in the administration of relief," to "boycott establishments in Harlem where Negroes are systematically discriminated against, and to open up jobs for Blacks in the public utilities."[36] Headed by a Black Cuban named Arnold Johnson, who was a member of the Rome Relief Employees Association (organized by the Party) it included a broad range of organizations from the African Patriotic League, to the Elks, to the NAACP. Its first campaign was to organize a boycott of Weisbeckers market to demand that Blacks be hired (with Whites transferred to other stores of the chain) and to demand the dismissal of Home Relief Bureau officials in Harlem who were accused of practicing discrimination. In line with Party perspectives, it attempted to "obtain the support of labor unions and other white and Negro organizations."[37]

This broad interracial coalition, in somewhat different form (the Greater New York Coordinating Committee on Employment) would be responsible for some important breakthroughs against job discrimination in New York City. In the late 1930's and the early 40's, under Adam Clayton Powell's leadership, the coalition opened jobs in the Fifth Avenue Coach Company, the New York Telephone Company, the IRT lines (as motormen) and Macy's.[38] All these campaigns were organized in alliance with the unions who were organizing or who had contracts at the companies in question. Nationalists participated in the coalition, but had little influence on its basic policies—the coalition presented its fight as a struggle against discrimination and segregation rather than a campaign to control Harlem's economy. In 1938, Party leader Abner Berry assessed the history of the Harlem job's movement as a victory for the Party's program and analysis:

> In 1932, we witnessed a number of movements throughout the country sponsoring the slogan "Don't Buy Where You Can't Work."
>
> The content of that slogan is quite different from the present content....In 1932 when we had not big trade union movement and when there was a petty bourgeois element among the Negroes which did not see the role of the trade unions and the necessity of unity between Negro and white workers, that slogan meant the bringing about of a division in the ranks of the working class and keeping the Negroes away from the trade union movement and its progressive sector....But today, the growth of the CIO movement, the organization of some ten thousand Negroes into the trade union movement have changed the content of that slogan. Today, the slogan "Don't Buy Where You Can't Work" is a progressive slogan and is being realized in the interest of working class and trade union unity and is overcoming some of the antagonisms which existed against the Negro people in the trade unions.[39]

Throughout the entire period of the "Popular Front" (1935-1939), the Party functioned freely within almost all areas of Harlem community life. But its political "victory" over Negro nationalism was never really secure. Nationalist politics retained an impressive degree of grass-roots support within the community and the Party was required to wage continual ideological warfare against the most extreme manifestation of this—pro-Japanese sentiment, waves of anti-Jewish or anti-Italian feeling, hostility to the labor movement. Ira Kemp and Arthur Reid, leaders of the African Patriotic League and the dissident "picket committee" of the Citizens League for Fair Play were particular Party hindrances. During the Ethiopian War, they opposed White participation in the Ethiopian support rallies, advocated a boycott of Italian store owners, and tried to drive Italian icemen out of Harlem and replace them with Blacks.[40] After their picket committee had been enjoined from "racial picketing" by court action, they organized a group called the Harlem Labor Union which attempted to force smaller Harlem stores to hire black employees from its ranks and to recruit employees of the large establishments into their group and require owners to sign a contract with it. The Harlem Labor Union took an antagonistic attitude toward both AFL and CIO organizing drives in Harlem--it accused them of protecting the jobs of White workers which should rightfully belong to Negroes. Kemp and Reid opposed the Amsterdam News strike (which the Party supported) and tried to undermine AFL and CIO organizing drives on 125 street by underbidding their wage levels. Its justification for such actions, which were opposed by most community leaders, were that trade unions refused to fight for the advancement of Negro workers within the workplace and kept Harlem jobs in the hands of Whites.

The Harlem Labor Union's appeal was strong among the large segment of Harlem's population that was still unemployed.[42] The organization recruited unemployed people into its ranks and promised them jobs if they participated in the group's picketing campaigns and paid their dues. The Union's success in opening up jobs in Harlem's smaller establishments was substantial,[43] and assured it of a significant following in a community which resented the sight of Whites working while masses of Negroes were unemployed.

The ideology of the Harlem Labor Union was an updated Garveyism which saw the organization of Negro trade unions as a vehicle to achieve Black control of Harlem's economy. Kemp and Reid used the Garveyite rhetoric of "race loyalty" and "economic independence" and viewed trade union advocates of class solidarity as their enemy.[44] In Reid's final statement as president of the organization, after a lawsuit curtailed the group's activities, he asserted that "his primary purpose in the movement was to force White firms to hire Negroes, and thus train them to enter business for themselves, to the end that all business in Harlem should be owned and operated as well as patronized by Negroes."[45]

The appeal of Reid's vision within many segments of the Harlem community remained immune to the Party's criticism and attacks. While the Party could persuade many church, fraternal and political leaders that the real solution to unemployment lay outside Harlem, and that the power of the government and the large corporations could only be reached through broad alliances with Labor and the Left, it could not project that "understanding" to thousands of Harlemites who remained unemployed during the height of the jobs campaigns and the organizing drive of the CIO. The one interracial movement which impinged on their daily lives, the unemployed movement, helped them survive in the crisis, but failed to stir their imaginations or evoke dreams of a better day. The gains it won at the welfare bureau and in government public works programs were at bare subsistence levels, and involved a degree of dependency which many of them found humiliating.[46]

The Garveyite dream of "Black independence" thus remained alive and well at the height of Communist influence in Harlem. Although it had little place in the coalition politics of the Left or the anti-discrimination struggles waged by prominent community leaders, it remained a powerful undercurrent among the unemployed, among marginal Black businessmen, and among race-conscious intellectuals who envisioned a black economic empire built on the consuming power of the Negro masses.

In Communist terms, this was a vision that lacked realism--there could

COMMUNISM AND BLACK NATIONALISM IN THE DEPRESSION

be no economic independence in a monopoly capitalist economy sustained by the state. But the striving for Black autonomy that the nationalists expressed transcended the entrepeneurial schemes they put forth as solutions, and the Party's inability to provide an outlet for it (other than the Black Belt nation) limited its appeal among those Harlemites that the Depression hit the hardest.

NOTES

[1] "Resolution of the Communist International, October 26, 1928, in The Communist Position on the Negro Question (New York: Workers Library Publishers, 1934), pp. 57-63.

[2] Bonita Williams, "Work Among Negro Jobless, Struggle for Negro Rights," The Daily Worker, July 22, 1935.

[3] "Dodge on Trail of 'Red Menace' in Harlem Riot," The New York Post, March 21, 1935.

[4] "Workers Delegates Smash Jim-Crow on New York CWA Jobs, Negroes Were Forced to Register Only in Harlem," The Daily Worker, January 27, 1934, p. 4.; "Harlem Council Win," The Daily Worker, June 16, 1934, p. 4.

[5] Interview with Abner Berry, November 20, 1973, United Nations, New York City.

[6] An example of the incredible naivete of many nationalists about the economic impact of the Depression is the following quote from an editorial of the Negro World dated January 18, 1930; "Judging from...the announcement of those who are close to the world of business and who are thoroughly informed along economic lines, the year 1930 promises to be a banner year for the Negro business man."

[7] Ebeneezer Ray, "Alleged Gunmen of UNIA Battle Held for Grand Jury," The New York Age, October 1, 1932, p. 1.

[8] Samuel Haynes, "Through Black Spectacles," The Negro World, April 15, 1933, p. 6.

[9] "Cops Kill Negro Delegate to July 4-5 Conference, Garveyite Leaders Join N.Y. Police in Murderous Attack," The Daily Worker, June 30, 1930, p. 1.; "Negro Masses Repudiate Misleader, Garvey Misleaders Allied With Police in Attack on Workers, The Harlem Liberator, April 25, 1931, p. 2; "Garvey Traitors Attack Meet on Scottsboro Defense," The Harlem Liberator, July 4, 1931, p. 7.

[10] "Garvey Misleaders Feel Fists of Harlem Crowd," The Harlem Liberator, September 2, 1933, p. 1.

[11] Samuel I. Brooks, "What Inducements Do Chain Stores Offer Us," The New York Interstate Tatler, September 6, 1929, p. 3, and September 13,

1929, p. 3; "You Can Do It Too," The New York Amsterdam News, October 16, 1929, p. 20.

[12] "Women Stage Protest Parade, Urge Boycott of White's Stores," The Negro World, May 2, 1931, p. 2; "Observe Race Loyalty Week and Emancipate Yourself," The Negro World, May 16, 1931, p. 1.

[13] Solomon Harper, "Attacks on Foreign Born Under Cover of Job Getting," The Daily Worker, March 13, 1931, p. 4.

[14] Cyril Briggs, "Negro Reformists, Faking Fight on Unemployment, Plan Parade," The Daily Worker, April 7, 1931, p. 2.

[15] Ralph Gothard, "It Can Be Done," The Negro World, August 22, 1931, p. 4.

[16] Melville Weiss, "Don't Buy Where You Can't Work," Columbia Thesis, 1941, pp. 56-57.

[17] The Daily Worker, August 24, 1933, p. 2.

[18] "7 Negro and White Workers Arrested Picketing Bus Co." The Daily Worker, March 9, 1934, p. 2.

[19] "Leader Quits, Flays Soviets," New York Amsterdam News, August 17, 1935, p. 2; A. W. Berry and L. Sass, "Facts Show Mackawain Lies About the Communist Party," The Daily Worker, August 23, 1935; Interview with Theodore Basset, November 15, 1973, New York City.

[20] Interview with Richard B. Moore, Patchogue, N.Y., November 14, 1973.

[21] Ibid.

[22] The Harlem Liberator, March 17, 1934, p. 5.

[23] Weiss, "Don't Buy Where You Can't Work," pp. 58-66.

[24] William Murashkin, "The Harlem Boycott of 1934, Black Nationalism and the Rise of Labor-Union Consciousness," Labor History XIII, 3 (Summer, 1972), p. 363.

[25] Williana Burroughs, "League Leaders Reject Aid from White Workers," The Harlem Liberator, August 4, 1934, p. 3.

[26] "Understanding the Boycott Movement," The Harlem Liberator, August 4, 1934, p. 4.

[27] "How the Empire Cafeteria Boycott Was Won," The Harlem Liberator, September 15, 1934, pp. 4-5.

[28] "Communist Candidates Lead Fight for Negro Jobs in Harlem," The Harlem Liberator, September 15, 1924, p. 1.

[29] Murashkin, "The Harlem Boycott of 1934," pp. 365-367.

COMMUNISM AND BLACK NATIONALISM IN THE DEPRESSION

[30] Charles Lionel Franklin, The Negro Labor Unionist of New York (1936, rpt. 1968, New York, AMS Press), pp. 130-140.

[31] A. W. Berry and L. Sass, "Facts Show Mackawain Lies about the Communist Party."

[32] "Report of the Mayor's Commission on Conditions in Harlem," reprinted in the New York Amsterdam News, July 18, 1936, xerox copy in the Schomburg Collection, New York City, p. 3.

[33] Ibid., p. 6.

[34] Interview with Abner Berry, United Nations, New York City, November 20, 1973.

[35] See James W. Ford, The Negro and the Democratic Front (New York: International Publisher, 1938); Interview with Abner Berry, November 20, 1973.

[36] "Map Struggle to End Job Discrimination of Harlem Merchants," The Harlem Liberator, April 15, 1935, p. 8.

[37] Ibid.

[38] George Charney, A Long Journey (New York: Quadrangle, 1968), pp. 99-100; Adam Clayton Powell, Marching Blacks (New York: Dial Press, 1945).

[39] Proceedings, 10th Convention, Communist Party, New York State (New York: International Publishers, 1938), pp. 103-104.

[40] Weiss, "Don't Buy Where You Can't Work," pp. 86-88; "Halt Near Riot Between Negroes-Italians," New York Amsterdam News, September 5, 1935.

[41] Weiss, "Don't Buy Where You Can't Work," p. 86.

[42] In a 1937 Federal Census of Unemployment, 11.64% of the whole working population in New York City was unemployed, whereas 30.47% of the Black work force was unemployed. An additional 3.46% of the White and 7.13% of the Negroes were partially unemployed. Census of Unemployment, 1937, Vol. 2, p. 645.

[43] Weiss, "Don't Buy Where You Can't Work," pp. 88-100.

[44] William Murashkin's conclusion that the Harlem Labor Union "provided publicity for the idea of trade unionism," and "made Harlemites more responsive to the appeal of progressive unionism" seems to be highly questionable. The Harlem Labor Union's ideology was more entrepreneurial than trade unionist and it saw organized labor and the Left as an enemy and a competitor.

[45] Weiss, "Don't Buy Where You Can't Work," p. 113.

[46] At many points in the job campaigns, nationalist carried signs which read, "We Want Jobs, Not Relief," "Women Stage Protest Parade, Urge Boycott of White Stores," The Negro World, May 2, 1931, p. 2; Williana Burroughs, "League Leaders Reject Aid from White Workers," The Harlem Liberator, August 4, 1934, p. 3.

THE CONSOLIDATED TENANTS LEAGUE OF HARLEM: BLACK SELF-HELP VS. WHITE, LIBERAL INTERVENTION IN GHETTO HOUSING, 1934-1944[1]

Joel Schwartz

Harlem community groups, particularly those inspired by Marcus Garvey's economic nationalism, often dreamed of black-run housing ventures that would incorporate ghetto realtors, apartment managers, and building tradesmen. But bold dreams usually ran up against the power of white realtors and white-controlled government agencies, not to mention the intentions of white liberals awakening to the Harlem "problem." Harlem's Consolidated Tenants League, which flourished during the 1930s, illustrates the limits of black ventures in a field that whites were not ready to penetrate.
Operating as a protection service for dues-paying members, the Consolidated would confront landlords and bargain for lower rents in the city courts. Although liberals regarded such efforts as faintly extortionate, they still chose to patronize the League, along with other Harlem groups, as instruments of their own housing and city planning agenda. Their recognition brought the Consolidated to periphery of New York's housing-reform circles, only to shut it out with their redevelopment programs in the 1940s. A product of the Jim Crow, Depression ghetto, the Tenants League never survived the full embrace of benevolent interracialism.
In August, 1934, a few weeks after the Harlem West Indies Federation had celebrated the centennial of island emancipation, the event's temporary chairman, Donelan J. Phillips, a young accountant and graduate of New York University, led some neighbors on a rent strike. His landlord, the Central Hanover Bank, had done what property owners often did on the West Harlem race frontier known as "Sugar Hill"—curtailed elevator and doorman service and hiked the rents for the new black tenants. At the same time, a few blocks north on Edgecombe Avenue, an acquaintance of Phillips, Vernal J.

Joel Schwartz is a faculty member of the History Department at Montclair State College (Upper Montclair, New Jersey).

Afro-Americans in New York Life and History (January 1986)
P.O. Box 1663
Buffalo, New York 14216

Williams, had also organized a rent-witholding action, complete with tenant pickets, against another arrogant landlord. A thirty-eight year old Jamaican, Williams had graduated from NYU Law School, was an ex-counsel to Marcus Garvey's Universal Negro Improvement Association, and was still prominent in Garveyite quarters. He had been a founder of the Harlem Lawyer's Association and was known as one of Harlem's most adroit trial lawyers.[2] But like many Harlemites, Phillips and Williams had been driven to extra-legal acts. With hard times, tenants had doubled-up, sheltered extra boarders, and tried to force landlords to accept rent "concessions." Because landlords rarely gave written leases, however, they could post arbitrary rent hikes or thirty-day vacate notices and rely on the courts' "summary proceedings" to evict "trouble-makers." In Central Harlem, pitiful sidewalk evictions were exploited by the Communists' Unemployed Council into occasional intimidation of the courts and eviction marshalls. But middle-class Sugar Hill searched for respectable protection and found a model in the summer, 1934, boycotts against Jim Crow practices in the stores along 125th Street. Black indignation, white-collar professionalism, and consumer agitation—all these ingredients were present when Phillips and Williams incorporated their Consolidated Tenants League and on October 5, 1934, elected Julius A. Archibald, a thirty-four year old Trinidad-born graduate of NYU Law School as president. While the letterhead boasted "Moderate Rent and Better Housing Conditions," the immediate goal was "mutual protection" against landlord reprisals.[3]

At first the Consolidated had little more than a letterhead, Phillips' apartment, and a small group of former Garveyite professionals who were attracted to its speculative possibilities. The League advertised that modest fees could retain its skilled "legal staff," along with its collective strength. But that winter, only a score, mostly women, regularly attended the bi-monthly meetings at the 135th Street YMCA, to hear an opening prayer and Phillips' harangues against landlords. With only seven active buildings by March, 1935, the League was clearly struggling to "sell" mutual protection to a Harlem wary of paid, self-improvement schemes. The officers toyed with getting insurance agents to canvass for recruits while on their collection rounds. They scouted among West Indies lodges and local churches, and sought out political endorsements. But membership continued to lag and finance remained scanty. In February, 1935, the treasurer suggested that $15 might be raised each month if men contributed $.50 and women $.25. Fearing the half-dollar might drive some away, they eventually agreed on collecting a nickle a week from each.[4]

The League might have remained frustrated on this narrow stage were it not for the Harlem Riot of March 19, 1935, which gave the

Consolidated's rent bargaining at Graham Court unexpected significance. The Graham Court Apartments (1925 Seventh Avenue at 117th Street) was a square-block, multi-elevator landmark known for its large interior court and spacious apartments. With hard times, Edbro Realty had subdivided the apartments, shut down services, and in 1933, opened the building to blacks with the customary rent increases. One demand in September, 1934, touched off a tenant protest led by Dr. Cyril H. Dolly, a Trinidad-born opthamologist at Harlem Hospital. Dolly managed to arrange a meeting with Tenement House Commissioner Langdon W. Post, who "commended their action and told them that only by bringing mass pressure to bear, could housing be made a live political issue—which . . . would force the appointment of an arbitration committee."[5] These tactics convinced Edbro to cancel the increase, but it soon reneged and handed thirty-day notices to the leaders. The Consolidated responded with pickets and dispatched fifty tenants to support Dolly at his eviction trial on March 20. By then, the Seventh District Court on West 151st Street was in utter chaos, jammed with police, reporters, and blacks being booked on charges from the riot the day before. Amid the uproar, the case was thrown out on a technicality, and the Consolidated made the downtown newspapers. Phillips warned reporters that if landlords did not end their blacklists, he would call tenants out on general strike and camp 10,000 in the streets.[6]

The next day, the Consolidated voted that one of its officers should rightly be part of the city's urgent post-riot inquiry, the Mayor's Committee on Conditions in Harlem. Convinced that Fiorello H. LaGuardia's nominees—upper class whites with a handful of Urban League blacks—could not grasp the "deeply rooted" socio-economic causes behind the upheaval, the Tenants League called for the addition of Socialist Frank R. Crosswaith, activist minister Reverend Adam Clayton Powell, Jr., Dr. Dolly, and Tenants League vice-president Mrs. Minnie L. Green. The Mayor's Office politely rebuffed them, but still invited "J. Phillip Donelan" and his associates to submit their views.[7] They soon dominated hearings held by the sub-committee on housing, chaired by white attorney Morris L. Ernst. They supplied victimized tenants, whose lurid details of rent extortion had an indelible impact on the sympathetic Ernst and the Mayor's Committee's venture into the taboo area of Harlem real estate exploitation. A draft report predictably found "great complaint and considerable distress in practices surrounding evictions" and proposed giving statutory power to judges to issue stays and to require marshalls to post "decent notice" of their intent. But virtually borrowing Williams' testimony on the subject, it also called for laws that would have enabled tenants to offer the "proof of landlord's promise to repair," and to allow rents to be paid into court-administered accounts until violations had been corrected.[8]

With understandable exaggeration, Phillips described the League's progress to an admiring young interviewer from the Mayor's Committee. He was the only paid officer, he said, of a voluntary "clearing house" for five-thousand members in Harlem and the Bronx.

He claimed that the League had already organized one hundred buildings in Harlem alone. Dollar-a-month fees bought an imposing array of services provided by standing committees. Vernal Williams' "Legal Section" took care of a continuing stream of dispossesses and thirty-day notices. The "Labor Section" kept a file of unemployed union men in the building trades, although Phillips conceded that it had found jobs for very few. Mrs. Green's "Social Service Section" provided emergency aid for the evicted and claimed that it had helped some families secure Home Relief and new lodgings. All this may have been plausible to the Mayor's Committee, particularly to Ernst, an old Socialist familiar with Harlem Communists' diatribes and perhaps anxious to recognize the Tenants League as a conservative rival.[9]

Certainly, black Communists had heated up Harlem's politics, forcing many organizations, including the Consolidated, to the left. As a veteran Garveyite, Williams was suspicious of such radicals, but like many Harlemites, he could not remain immune to their blandishments. As he admitted at a League meeting, "If the doctrine of the Communists is equal housing and good housing it is our doctrine . . . go to 6 Negro lawyers and ask them the name of the Scottsboro boys . . . try it some time and see if you can find one who knows . . . ask any I.L.D. or communist. They can tell you."[10] While the Unemployed Council had effectively exploited the evictions crisis, the Consolidated's stilted handbill tried to harvest mass excitement:

TENANTS: STOP! LISTEN! THINK!!!

Join the Consolidated Tenants' League, some of whose objects are:
(a) To take steps as soon as possible to reduce rents by calling a MASS RENT STRIKE
(b) To effect better housing conditions by compelling landlords to make their houses fit for human beings to live in.[11]

Practical cooperation made sense, as arranged by Robert T. Bess, the Consolidated's general organizer, who had been ejected from a Mayor's Committee hearing in June for heckling a Home Relief bureaucrat. While the Tenants League bitterly denounced Bess' treatment as proof of LaGuardia's indifference to "the common problems of the masses," Harlem Communists exploited the attempt to "gag" Bess and organized a Conference Against Discriminatory Practices at the Abyssinian Baptist Church.[12] They embarked on joint demonstrations. When the Consolidated learned that the Kinghaven Apartments (441 West 153rd Street) had opened to blacks but with jacked-up rents, it threw pickets around the entrance. The Communists' League of Struggle for Negro Rights took places in the jeering line, establishing a united front against what Phillips called "the traitorous deeds of the strike breakers." Williams later reciprocated, lending his legal skills to several Communist eviction contests. The *Daily Worker* published appreciative notices of the Consolidated's work and the Unemployed Council continued to reinforce Tenants League pickets that summer.[13]

Despite these flirtations, the Consolidated remained bourgeois and Garveyite. Some even branded its dues and protection a "racket," pointing to the alleged paid boycotts staged by ultra-nationalist Sufi Abdul Hamid the previous autumn. Obviously stung, Phillips collected endorsements from the Baptist Ministerial Conference, including one from a pastor who lauded "a fine experiment in self-determination."[14] But his vindication was a May 23, 1935, rally that became an outpouring of community support. League leaflets helped to assure a good turnout, as some 1,500 crowded into a nearby school auditorium, ushered by teenage girls wearing blue armbands stamped with a gold "C.T.L." Phillips held center stage, describing the League's campaign against landlord greed. Then Williams recounted his struggles in the courts against "landlord judges" and asked the crowd to bring him their dispossesses. He told them not to worry; the League would "take care" of legal fees.[15] Organizer Bess also proved more an impetuous black nationalist than a left ideologue. At a Tenants League meeting during the Ethiopian crisis, members had argued that blacks should harass Italian shopkeepers out of Harlem. Merril C. Work of the Unemployed Council attacked this "incorrect" proposition:

> We must not fall into this [race divisive] trap set by Capitalists... got to unite all Negroes and then all exploited and working people so the Wall Streeters will never live to enjoy the fruits of the next war... at the last meeting of the League Against War and Fascism, the Italian ice men gave Twenty five ($25) dollars.[16]

Bess retorted: "Where did they get it? Where do they make their living? In Harlem!!!" While some outsiders feared the Tenants League's ideological alignment with the Unemployed Council, others knew better. Harlem Assemblyman LaMar Perkins, who had succeed Vernal Williams as UNIA general counsel, amiably warned his League friends to continue to steer clear of "politics and rackets."[17]

Fierce professional and social resentments, which contemporaries only partly identified as West Indian "pushiness," kept the Consolidated going. Racism had pent up men like Phillips and Williams on Sugar Hill and forced them to make a living on divorces and custody suits, debt collection, and fraternal accounts. Law partners like Julius A. Archibald and Hutson L. Lovell found with the Consolidated another means to scrounge some income and perhaps gain some leverage on the city's political, and patronage, system. The League also won the support of Dr. Lucien M. Brown, a prominent West Indian who was among the first blacks to integrate the medical staff of Harlem Hospital and a persistent gadfly against its discriminatory practices. (His younger colleague, Dr. Dolly, had also spoken out against the hospital's racism.)[18] Two-thirds of the Consolidated's building "units" came from Harlem's bourgeois periphery along St. Nicholas and Edgecombe Avenues, particularly facing Colonial Park, and within a one-block radius of Graham Court. Both neighborhoods had undergone dizzying racial turnover in the previous years, encouraged by landlords who slashed services to remove whites and then greatly increased rents for apartments shown to blacks on a take-it-or-leave-it basis.[19]

A Mayor's Committee observer caught some of their anger at a League meeting in August, 1935.[20] Earl Miller, a World War I veteran who "walked across the desert four years for the British government to kill Germans," advised his friends:

> Keep all you know to yourself. Don't tell the landlord nothing; tell the Consolidated Tenant's League everything, that's cooperation. . . . What do you do? When the Rent is due you tell the landlord I got mine, but my partner didn't get her part. . . . If you got 100 people in your apartment it's none of his business. And look out, pretty soon he is going to put on the screws. . . if you live up to the C.T.L you have plenty jobs. Why don't you go down to 125th Street and ask Mr. Porter for jobs? When you give him Forty dollars rent, certain amount of it goes for salaries? Ask him why he doesn't hire a colored office girl and Negro lawyers on his legal staff.

Another, Earl Williams, recalled that the "Belclair Market, a colored organization, almost closed its doors last year . . . shameful . . . did not receive the cooperation of Negro housewives . . . C.T.L. will soon be able to bargain with landlords in an unprecedented manner." Vernal Williams, splendid in a borsolino and spats, gestured with his silver-tipped cane and admitted, "I guess I'm married to the League."[21] He had only intended to collect some dispossesses, but he went on to recount his day in court and a judge who reprimanded him about a landlord's complaint:

> I asked what the Court proposed to do? He said: "Investigate." I said, "I'm going to write a letter to the chief justice." I'm going to put it into the records of the C.T.L. later . . . pardon the first person, But I am one of the Negro lawyers in Harlem who fights on facts, don't go to friends on the bench or hang around Court. I go into the courts and fights on the merits of a case like a gentleman. I said, I am not impressed by the complaint, but that it comes from your office. I am one black man who will fight . . . unless a Negro is a Buffoon, a comedian or a tap dancer to entertain white people, they are after him to kill him . . . hereafter, complaints will not be coming about me but from me about the Justice who interprets the law for the landlords and disregards the tenants . . . As long as I can keep a Lawyer's license you will find me in court fighting in the future as in the past. . . . The Justice is going to make an investigation (scornfully). Well, I am going to ask the Appellate Division of the Supreme Court to make an investigation . . . I said to him, I get a large number of these cases because I am

regarded as a specialist in this kind of work and people know it and they further know that no landlord can bother with me.

Race pride set the Consolidated on a collision course with the city's housing liberals who proceeded at their own pace with plans for Harlem. Tenement House Commissioner Langdon W. Post was a zealous technocrat, who pledged scientific management of the city's vast slums and took this gospel personally into the neighborhoods.[22] By mid-1935, the Tenants League had requested that the Tenement House Department inspect its members' buildings for Multiple Dwelling Law violations and thus provide affidavits for Williams' legal defenses based on neglect of services. In 1936, League requests had become routine, indeed, part of its organizational plan. It could provide tenants who feared their landlords with a cloak of anonymity when they made complaints and could forward these by the hundreds. But League practice soon ran up against Post's own preference for systematic inspection. As he petulantly complained to Mayor LaGuardia regarding one request to check a firetrap on West 133rd Street ("in no worse condition than thousands of others," he snapped), "We are covering the City as rapidly as possible with our cycle inspection, but I do not feel that it would be desirable to disrupt this cycle in order to make wholesale inspections in particular localities which happen to be complained of."[23] It was one thing for the Tenement House Department to reach out for Harlem to confirm its initiative; it was quite another for Harlemites to presume to redirect priorities predetermined by professional city managers.

Not surprisingly, the Tenants League and city housing officials took sharply divergent views over credit for Harlem's first public housing project. In 1934, the New York City Housing Authority under Commissioner Post's chairmanship had begun to pick over sites for slum clearance. In Harlem, as elsewhere, the task went to the Authority's survey staff, which used unemployed whites on loan from federal work-relief agencies, thus shutting out blacks from any substantial contribution.[24] Yet to pry construction subsidies from the New Deal, the Housing Authority needed to politicize local support, which the Consolidated, fresh from Graham Court and the Mayor's Committee, was eager to supply. Counting on this citizens' pressure. Chairman Post during spring, 1935, presented a $150,000,000 city-housing package to the Public Works Authority. But Harlemites became exasperated when Post talked only about a *single* Manhattan project vaguely slated for "midtown." The Consolidated sent off a flurry of letters to the Authority, the Mayor, and President Roosevelt demanding that Harlem be given top priority for new public housing. In mid-May, when Chairman Post still failed to make a commitment, the League announced a neighborhood rally at which Chairman Post, Reverend Powell, and other local leaders were expected to speak and Phillips was to unveil plans for a rent strike by 30,000! While some 1,500 attended, most of the guests, including Chairman Post, never appeared, perhaps unnerved by the strike talk. The evening's resolutions stopped far short of the apocalypse, with modest demands for improved tenement inspections and the appointment of more black inspectors. But a few days later, the League boasted its new influence, when Mayor LaGuardia pointedly made a commitment to a West Harlem site, then in talks with federal officials proclaimed that the project would "take preference over all others in New York City." [25]

The League was enraged a few weeks later, however, when Interior Secretary Harold L. Ickes made the PWA subsidy for the housing site, determined for Macombs Place and 151st Street, contingent on fair value for the acreage. But the owner, the Rockefeller Estate, was demanding too much for the Macombs site and wanted to unload with it the financially-troubled Paul Lawrence Dunbar Houses. While the League helped organize a "joint community protest" against the LaGuardia Administration's alleged complicity in Ickes' decision, it also took the quarrel into the streets. "TENANTS OF HARLEM, WAKE UP!!!" read its leaflets. "$7,000,000 from the Federal Government is knocking at your door to build houses to rent from $5 to $7 a room, per month, but the monied interests won't sell the land."[26] At a July 11 League meeting, Phillips called for "mass" action against the Housing Authority, then urged members to march with the Unemployed Council at City Hall. At the same time, Bess was busy with the Unemployed Council, haranguing and leafletting, trying to focus community resentment against evictions, the meager rent allowances from the Home Relief Bureau and the shortage of low-rent housing.[27] The mood was far less patient at the Consolidated's mass rally later in July to demand that the city force the Rockefellers to relinquish their land. Phillips and Williams had aroused the crowd, as did Bess who pointed to what his pickets had won at Kinghaven and at other League "fights." This time Chairman Post was present, and on the defensive: "Said he was afraid the League had heard him promise action so many times and he had not been to Harlem for such a long time, perhaps they felt he was stalling." He promised that the project would go through. "We won't get the land without a fight," he said, "but we'll get it." Then he ended with a pledge that left the crowd on its feet: "The Macomb's project would be for the 1,800,000 people who have always had to take leavings." The League later boasted how its Harlem mobilization had forced the city to proceed with site condemnation and Secretary Ickes to release PWA funds for the new Harlem River Houses.[28]

Phillips' interest in the project became virtually proprietary when he and Mrs. Minnie Green were appointed to the Housing Authority's Harlem Advisory Committee on tenant selection. He promised that the League would "insure that only people of the low income group would be eligible for renting."[29] Phillips may also have anticipated an arrangement in Harlem similar to the First Houses project on the Lower East Side, where the Authority asked settlement house leaders on the advisory committee to go through the financial and moral credentials of some 9,000 applicants. But the Housing Authority had foreclosed that possibility by appointing a Cooperating Committee on Management dominated by the city's social work establishment. The most prominent black appointee, Roscoe C. Bruce, had managed the Dunbar Houses (and his martinet policies had already been contested by Vernal Williams in court).[30] The Cooperating Committee referred technical questions, including tenant-selection criteria, to its staff of white social workers, headed by the Housing Authority's Catherine F. Lansing, who also chaired the Harlem Advisory Committee.[31] Sensing his limited role, Phillips announced a week after his appointment that the Harlem Advisory Committee "was not up to requirements." At a League meeting, he bitterly reviewed the members, starting with the kindergarten worker who ran the Utopia Children's House and the executive secretary of the Brooklyn Urban League: "Mrs. Daisy Reed—we can't count on her; Mr. Robert Elzy, who knows anything about him?" Merrill Work of the Unemployed Council said Elzy spoke for the "business men of Brooklyn . . . he's a tool of the Rockefeller Fund." Mrs. Harriet Shadd Butcher of the Russell Sage Foundation, according to Phillips, "doesn't contribute a thing to community life . . . probably not known to ten people in this room." Another cracked that the New York Urban League's secretary, James Hubert, "has done nothing but suggest that we return to Bermuda or to the South. It is a known fact that the Urban League is segregated." The meeting was in no mood to disagree with Merrill Work's shrewd comment: "It must be publically recognized that the Consolidated Tenants League is responsible for New Low Cost Housing . . . Mayor at a meeting 2 nights ago said: 'we gave . . . we . . . we . . .' you want to let the entire world know that the C.T.L. did.'"[32] The meeting demanded that the Housing Authority accept their nominees for the committee, but Chairman Post responded with a "sharp" dismissal.[33]

They may also have resented the ineluctable institutional necessities which downtown experts could so glibly cite. Pressed by the Housing Authority—and haunted by the financial difficulties at Dunbar—the Harlem Advisory Committee felt compelled to reserve the Macombs project for blacks with proven records of rent payment. In late November, 1935, Mrs. Green agreed with the Tenant Selection Committee's adoption of a "point" system which, according to historian Larry A. Greene, provided 63 out of a possible 100 points to applicants presenting middle-class income and social traits. Citing the need to maintain project "morale," the Committee allocated extra points to those without records in the Domestic Relations or Criminal Courts. But Mrs. Green surprisingly acceded to a provision that awarded applicants who had never been involved in summary proceedings for non-payment of rent. Institutional rationales also frustrated attempts to integrate the project's construction force. A Tenants League rally in October resolved that at least 75 per cent of the work gangs, skilled and unskilled, be made up of Harlem blacks. Backed by this mass prodding, the Harlem Advisory Committee demanded that a black be appointed to the Housing Authority executive staff to coordinate a program of open-housing opportunity and fair employment. But as historian Larry Greene found, the Tenants League's resolution was dismissed by the project manager, who "refused" to hire additional blacks. He reminded the League how on his personal recommendation, skilled blacks on the site had increased from 3 to 10 percent.[34]

The Consolidated's resentments could apparently be mollified with another welcome into the vestibule of downtown decision-making. On August 28, 1935, in response to prodding from the Mayor's Committee, a new Mayor's Committee on City Planning claimed that it "has not had in view any specific investigation of conditions in Harlem," although it had already embarked on neighborhood surveys in other areas of the city.[35] In an about-face a week later, the Mayor's Committee sent the Consolidated a letter asking for recommendations of individuals to advise on a proposed study of Harlem. Phillips ultimatley chaired an advisory committee that oversaw preparation of the *West Harlem Community Study* (completed in 1937), although Phillips' group had little impact on the Columbia University-run squad of WPA investigators. While aiming for "a range of possibilities within which its [Harlem's] future may be worked out," the *Community Study* concluded that "No solution seems possible short of wide demolition . . . and complete reconstruction of whole sections." Compared to the Planning Committee's grand visions for white, middle-class Forest Hills, or even its modest hopes white, working-class East Harlem, the West Harlem survey eminently signaled the Mayor's Office's inclination to let the black ghetto fend for itself.[36]

Still, the political currents of the late 1930s had sent the Consolidated in conservative directions. The liberals' meager patronage served to encourage this tendency, as did the Communists' new Popular Front "line" which eschewed disruptive confrontation. In March, 1936, the Consolidated decisively shrank back from mass action when a strike by Local 32-B, Building Service Employees Union, paralyzed large, elevator apartments in midtown Manhattan and inspired white, middle-class radicals to withhold rent via a new City-Wide Tenants Council. When 32-B extended its strike to Harlem, effecting several Tenants League units, some firebrands saw the chance to send around organizers and wring rent concessions. "This is the psychological moment to tie up the rents," exclaimed an eager Phillips. But Vernal Williams smothered the fervor by warning members "not to loose ourselves" in the CWTC's enthusiasm.[37] His anti-Communism aroused, the veteran Garveyite absolutely refused to "accept outside domination," least of all by the white, middle-class "progressives" who controlled the CWTC.[38]

This retreat reinforced Williams' preference for litigation, even in the unreceptive environs of the city courts. When evicted for non-payment, Harlemites naturally argued that they should not be charged high rents for uninhabitable rooms, an argument that judges regularly denied. Decisions usually cited the property-law doctrine of "constructive eviction," which held that a tenant's only way to avoid his contracted rent was to quit the premises that a lack of services had made uninhabitable, or the more venerable dogma that rent payment was an obligation entirely separate from the landlord's obligation to provide services. Most judges refused to countenance a collective withholding, following the City Corporation Counsel's disdain of "such thing known to law as a 'Rent Strike.'"[39] Nevertheless, Williams constantly pursued the legal route, particularly on his home grounds, Manhattan's Seventh and Tenth District Courts (the latter created in 1930 by Assemblyman LaMar Perkins), veritable "people's courts" never immune to ghetto realities.[40] While the Consolidated's attorneys often complained about "landlord judges," they could name a sympathetic few and recall better days in court, as on June 4, 1936, when Phillips reviewed how "the judges of the Seventh District Court changed their attitudes towards the League's attorneys".[41] Furthermore, in 1930 Assemblyman Perkins had added some new statutory weapons. One defined a Multiple Dwelling Law or Health Department citation as a possible constructive eviction on which judges might stay non-payment proceedings. Another provided a six-month "hardship" stay where tenants faced evictions for failure to pay a rent *increase*. Both required tenants to deposit their usual rents into court escrow accounts, and, of course, were often sabotaged by conservative or indifferent judges.[42] Understandably, Williams pursued a more sweeping goal of laws that would have granted tenants in non-payment proceedings the right to cite landlords' breach of promise to make repairs or their failure to remove Tenement House violations. He wanted laws that would have legitimized "partial" constructive evictions—Harlem's slum reality—into practical rent-bargaining.[43]

Phillips and his associates yearned for the kind of bargaining with large institutional landlords that would have established their reputation as responsible mediators for a reliable Harlem clientele. They projected a business-like mien, even when they held in reserve threats to picket and seek jury trials.[44] Their first struggles had provided some basis for this hope. They had successfully used publicity against Graham Court and Kinghaven, in each case holding out the olive branch of compromise. At Kinghaven, Phillips played the magnanimous broker, willing to treat with management to settle mutual differences. But such approaches remained an illusion. When embarrassing publicity faded, Graham Court's management again pursued evictions, and the judge agreed. The League, it turned out, had no way to reach Edbro Realty, as evidenced by frustrated members who proposed picketing the judge's home. The Kinghaven campaign dragged on through October, 1935, as the League's strength ebbed. Nevertheless, Phillips and his friends kept up their pretence, sustained by the few instances when their offers to negotiate were taken seriously. During a July, 1937, rent strike at 312 Manhattan Avenue, the tenant committee had brought in Phillips to bargain with the owner, the Greenwood Cemetery Association. With both sides adamant, Phillips sought out local churches who had influence with the cemetery trustees. When the landlords persisted with plans to evict, the Seventh District judge mediated a compromise which stayed rent increases as long as Tenement House violations still remained. Later, when the building was sold, Phillips "extended the hand of greeting to the new landlord and said he hoped we could count on the new landlord's cooperation in developing a friendlier spirit in the house." [45]

With few real clientage relationships, the Consolidated's legal staff necessarily slogged on in the Harlem courts, fashioning Fabian defenses out of the intricacies of summary proceedings. Williams usually began by challenging defective precepts, and constantly admonished his clients to "know how to calculate the days of a notice of dispossess" or the legal ways that it had to be served.[46] Much of the time he tried to hold the judge's attention on Harlem's grim tenements, "the social circumstances, and the high rents faced by Harlemites."[47] Williams also tried to apply to Harlem's non-payment cases the argument that Depression conditions could bring about the *de facto* modification of terms of a lease where there was "consideration," i.e., corroborative evidence. While judges looked for witnessed oral agreements or receipted payments for lower rent, Williams tried to present the "evidence" of reduced services like broken elevators, peeling plaster, no hot water, for "agreements" to reduce rent.[48] Whether Williams had any more success with this ploy than with any other remains unclear. In November, 1937, the League claimed to have saved its members $30,000 rent for that month alone. Associates estimated that the Consolidated's attorneys handled 7,000 tenant cases in the courts (and settled another 4,000 outside) between 1936-1941.[49] The League certainly had an impact on Harlem's standard leases, as landlords began to phase out monthly tenancies for written agreements, which contained waivers of tenant rights to jury trials in non-payment proceedings. This new militancy inevitably entered the courts. Judge James S. Watson, the first black elected to the Seventh District Court, testified at 1936 Housing Authority hearings that while 90 percent of dispossess cases were for non-payment, most stemmed from "dissatisfaction with the condition of the premises or with services rather than by inability to pay."[50] By 1939, complaints to the Tenement House Department had become a palpable force. As a department clerk explained to a Charity Organization Society researcher:

> there is a very strong tenants' union, with thousands of members, who had taken their complaints directly to the Mayor. He intimated that there was the reason why pressure had been brought to bear on these landlords with the result that many of the buildings in Harlem had already been fire-retarded and had legal fire-escapes.[51]

For a brief time, such accomplishments brought the Consolidated on the threshold of the city's reform establishment. Invited to join the new Citizen's Housing Council, Phillips sat on sub-committees dealing with Old Law housing and tenant relationships beside realtors like James Felt, the millionaire property owner in West Harlem. Such encounters must have held a certain poignance for the Harlem accountant: in the board room of a major philanthropic agency thrashing out policy with a benvolent realtor, who had never granted the Tenants League recognition where it counted—in West Harlem apartments. The Consolidated was also summoned whenever the views of black leaders were needed to fill out a housing-reform campaign. In late 1936, Phillips and Williams appeared before Housing Authority hearings investigating high rents, where they advocated changes in the statutory six-month stays to make Harlem's overcrowding presumptive evidence of hardship. They appeared before the 1937 Temporary State Commission on the Condition of the Colored Population to demand a special rent-control zone in Harlem and struck a responsive chord among housing liberals. Later in 1938, the Consolidated joined with the City-Wide Tenants Council, settlement headworkers, and liberal reformers to lobby for the Minkoff Rent Control Law. It was Williams' favorite kind of legislation, allowing judges to stay summary proceedings for non-payment of a rent increase in any Old Law tenement that failed to conform to the MDL; and Williams, backed by the CWTC, successfully pursued the law's constitutionality all the way to the U.S. Circuit Court.[52]

Yet real recognition continued to elude the League. Although the League constantly admonished the Housing Authority for a second low-rent project in Harlem, one larger than the Harlem River Houses which it deemed "entirely inadequate" to meet the ghetto's dire needs, the Housing Authority staff chalked up such interest to its own public-relations efforts in black neighborhoods. When the League in conjunction with the CWTC planned an October 7, 1939,

"Tenants Day Parade" and mass rally and needed a speaker from the Authority, a staff member commented that she considered this organization "the most militant in Harlem—but are a representative group, and helpful in our relations with tenants, and not objectionable in any way."[53] If the Housing Authority maintained any ambiguity about the Tenants League's function, it was dispelled during a half-hour interview which James H. Hubert of the Urban League, Roy Wilkins, and Donelan Phillips had with Monsignor E. Roberts Moore and Mary K. Simkhovitch on November 6, 1939. Time and again the visitors attempted to obtain hard statements about Housing Authority decisions on racial quotas and assignments in projects, and repeatedly and firmly the steely lady bountiful from Greenwich House, Mrs. Simkhovitch, turned them aside. Appointed to advise on policy, Phillips and the others were given the chance to appear to advise on decisions already carried out in their names.[54]

Ironically, World War II would provide the Consolidated with its ultimate prominence and ensured its eventual decline. In late 1941, liberal stewards of black welfare formed the City-Wide Citizens Committee on Harlem, which viewed the impending "People's War" as the moral force that would compel broad improvements in black lives. Phillips and Williams were invited on the CWCCH housing sub-committee, although whites like Charles Abrams, James Felt, and Algernon D. Black of the Ethical Culture Society steered its emphasis to outside intervention for building-code enforcement, new public housing, and zoned rent control.[55] But the Consolidated also joined the mass Harlem agitation led by the Communist-dominated National Negro Congress and Rev. Powell's Abyssinian Baptist Church, who vowed to collect 100,000 signatures on petitions for mandatory rent controls in the ghetto. Both campaigns, however, were abruptly superceded by the November, 1942, order from the federal Office of Price Administration to hold down *city-wide* rents through voluntary means. This policy was to be carried out chiefly by "fair rent" committees of prominent realtors, including that for North Manhattan (and Harlem) organized by Felt. Phillips bitterly complained to a *New York Times* reporter that the OPA's "discriminatory order," which handed controls enforcement to landlords, had "snatched" rent relief from a suffering community.[56]

The OPA order merely intensified the campaign for Harlem controls waged by two separate camps, and the Consolidated was lured into both. Behind the scenes, Phillips worked with the CWCCH sub-committee's lobby with OPA officials, guided by Abrams' tactical assessment that "pressure should come principally from Harlem and that our Committee should urge it."[57] The sub-committee urged immediate OPA controls for the entire city, focusing on the low-rent category, and an OPA Harlem office as convenient to residents as the Seventh District Court. But the Consolidated also participated in the streeet-corner rallies of Reverend Powell's Citizens' Committee for Lower Rent in Harlem. Making his Consolidated an arm of OPA voluntarism, Phillips had never been busier. Using his CWCCH connections, he conferred with OPA attorneys. Citing these OPA briefings, he negotiated with landlords and referred examples of rent-gouging to the OPA as well as to Powell's group.[58] His work in the liberal camp reached a high point with a May, 1943, radio symposium with Charles Abrams, where Phillips pleaded that Harlem needed special, mandatory controls. But such appeals could not dent the OPA's staunch reliance on voluntarism or rally faint-hearted liberals to overcome that reliance, as divisions on the Citizens' Housing Council indicated. In July, 1943, Phillips argued heatedly that 11,000 Harlem tenants were at the mercy of wanton rent increases. Felt blandly replied that he had done his own checking "with an agent in Harlem who represents about 3,000 buildings," and was satisfied that rents had not been raised.[59]

This complacency was finally shattered on 125th Street, with the August 1, 1943, looting known as the Harlem Riot. The OPA rushed in extra attorneys, opened a 135th Street office, and tried to reassure local consumer leagues and the Harlem Civil Defense Council. But its voluntary efforts were undermined, and subsequent rumors that rents would spiral with the October renewal of leases gave voluntarism the coup de grace. On November 1, 1943, New York City became a "War Rental Area." The OPA "froze" rents at the March 1, 1943, level and required landlords to obtain OPA certificates of eviction before trying to dispossess. OPA registrars recorded March 1 rents and services of hundreds of thousands of apartments, while tenants were exhorted to be vigilant about their rights.[60]

At first the new regime proved a boon for the Consolidated, trying to familiarize Harlemites with the strange new argot of "prevailing" rents, "comparable" services, and the landlord's appeal for a "hardship increase." As the OPA's self-appointed mediator and propagandist, the League never handled so many cases or enrolled so many new units: 12 in December, and 21 in January, each with 8 to 10 tenants. Harlemites quickly swamped the 135th Street office with desperate pleas about rents, but also about hot water and building repairs, regarding the OPA as a one-stop housing office. The sheer scope of its operation soon undercut the Consolidated's efforts. The narrow grounds for OPA certificates of eviction reduced fears of thirty-day notices and much of the work of the Magistrates' Courts. Harlem was deluged with OPA leaflet advice: "WHEN IN DOUBT ASK THE RENT DIRECTOR," which the Tenants League, along with other groups, feverishly distributed.[61] The League also discovered that unlike the accessible district court judges, OPA rent decisions involved a remote administrative process. Proximity to the 135th Street OPA office counted for little. Phillips found that to expedite his cases he needed the intervention of Abrams and other liberals with the OPA downtown.[62]

By then, liberals, satisfied with Harlem's rent amelioration, had turned to other concerns, like new public housing and ventures in philanthropy proposed by James Felt. Based on his experience in West Harlem, Felt brought to the CWCCH an idea for a non-profit housing corporation that would operate Harlem tenements on progressive principles reminiscent of the English, Octavia Hill Association. Economies of scale would cut maintenance costs of the adjoining buildings without sacrificing operating standards. An interracial board of trustees would oversee an all-black staff of rent-collectors and social visitors. The Abrams sub-committee solicited the interest of Phillips and Williams in the scheme for an "Urban Housing Management Association, Inc.," which Felt readied in the weeks following the riot. But he intended it as an Urban League operation, with a board of directors chosen from Urban League officials and Harlem's social-work establishment. The plan had no place for the tenant advocates.[63]

All around Harlem, the Consolidated had become overshadowed by large downtown institutions which had awakened to Harlem's housing problems. In 1943, the Metropolitan Life Insurance Company, shaken by outcries against its all-white, 8,755-unit Stuyvesant Town planned for the Lower East Side, tried to make amends with "interracial" Riverton, planned for 135th Street and Fifth Avenue. Although affronted by Metropolitan's arrogance, Phillips broke with white liberals and welcomed Riverton's much-needed 1,232 middle-income units. As for Jim Crowism, Phillips characteristically remarked, "Negroes have their own insurance policies and can make demands on" the Metropolitan. Nevertheless, Riverton would soon render passe the Consolidated's traditional housing services. Its rent schedules were fixed and well-publicized, its waiting list was subcontracted to a Metropolitan subsidiary, and Riverton management went to Felt's protege at the UHMA, Clifford L. Alexander, Sr.[64] While busy tending the three UHMA tenements on West 136th Street, Felt was also collaborating with city planner William Lescaze on a Harlem redevelopment idea that envisioned the wholesale removal of existing slums and their replacement by monolith "superbuildings" on superblocks surrounded by arterial highways.[65] Much the same grandiosity would characterize the postwar resumption of Housing Authority slum clearance, but with the Consolidated cut loose from any special relationship with the Authority. Now politically entrenched and having systematized tenant-selection as a city-wide process with hundreds of thousands of names on IBM punch cards, the Authority could let the Harlem Advisory Committee lapse and dispense with any further citizen involvement for the next ghetto project, the James Weldon Johnson Houses. The Consolidated became one among many community groups scrambling to do the Authority's bidding, lucky enough if it could distribute project brochures and otherwise extend the Authority's "story" to the neighborhood. Little wonder that Tenants League units soon drifted away, its membership shrunk, and the few remaining members began to question what special services their League dues really bought.[66]

The Consolidated was a product of the Jim Crow ghetto which had imprisoned an extraordinary array of ambitious professionals and turned many to the logic of Garveyite self-help. It could never overcome the suspicions by outside whites that such assertive action was a "racket," and remained vulnerable to their intrusive rationales, whether the Communist-organized "united front from below," or the liberals' city-wide commissions and housing renewal authorities. Neither had much patience for young black professionals forced to play their trades on limited ghetto resources.[67] Years later, of course, the Tenants League might have found a more legitimate function in the housing field. In the 1960s, the heyday of Jesse Gray's Harlem rent strikes, the War on Poverty's Community Action Program, and the emerging fascination with Black Power, the Consolidated might have served as the prototype for a local community corporation that rehabilitated or managed housing. It might have found sponsorship and funding from the Ford Foundation or the New York Episcopal Archdiocese. Its accountants and lawyers might have been hailed as the cadre for Harlem's economic bootstraps, for Black Capitalism, or a ghetto housing venture. But much would have depended upon those outside judgments of "legitimacy."

NOTES

1 Research for this article began, in part, in conjunction with the Tenants Movement Research Project (TMRP) of the Center for Policy Research in New York, funded by the Research Foundation of the City University of New York and the Center for Metropolitan Studies, National Institute of Mental Health. The author expresses appreciation to TMRP director Dr. Ronald Lawson. The conclusions expressed here do not necessarily reflect the views of the TMRP or its director.

2 Clipping, (Kingston) **Daily Gleaner**, August 17, 1934, Vertical File, "West Indians in U.S.," Schomburg Center for Research in Black Culture (Schomburg); "Brief Outline of Consolidated Tenants League," Works Progress Administration, Federal Writer's Project, Box 5, Schomburg; John McLoughlin interview with Donelan J. Phillips, April 10, 1976; **Amsterdam News**, May 18, 1935, p. 3; **New York Times**, March 21, 1935, p. 2; February 9, 1952, p. 13; Vernal J. Williams to C. Cardoze, December 15, 1940; and to Alfred L. King, January 15, 1941, Universal Negro Improvement Association Papers, Box 10, Schomburg.

3 New York State Temporary Commission on the Condition of the Urban Colored Population (NYSTCCUCP), Hearings, (9 vols., typescript, 1937), VII, 1245, Schomburg; Betty Friedman, "A Brief Survey of Blacklisting" (typscript, 1938), in Citizens' Housing Council, Committee on Housing Management, Minutes, Citizens' Housing and Planning Council Library; **New York Times**, January 30, 1932, p. 32; February 9, 1932, p. 2; September 18, 1932, p. 16; January 15, 1933, p. 22; May 28, 1933, XI, p. 2; Larry A. Greene, "Harlem in the Great Depression, 1928-1936" (unpublished Ph. D. dissertation, Columbia University, 1979), p.252; Consolidated Tenants League, Minutes (CTL Minutes), April 4, 1935, TMRP files. See also Margaret Reynolds' interviews and reports for the Mayor's Committee on Conditions in Harlem in Fiorello H. LaGuardia Papers (FHLP), Municipal Archives and Records Center.

4 CTL Minutes, February 21, March 14, 25, April 11, 18, May 9, 16, and December 5, 1935.

5 Lassalle Best, "Brief History of Graham Court," WPA Writer's Project, Box 5; Reynolds interview with Dr. Cyril H. Dolly, no date, FHLP, Box 668.

6 CTL Minutes, March 7, 14, and 21, 1935; **New York Times**, March 21, 1935, p. 2.

7 CTL Minutes, March 20, 1935; Resolutions of the Consolidated Tenants League, March 22, 1935, and Eunice H. Carter to J. Phillip Donelan, April 4, 1935, FHLP, Box 667; Mark D. Naison, "The Communist Party in Harlem" (unpublished Ph. D. dissertation, Columbia University, 1976), pp. 324-325.

8 Handwritten history of housing subcommittee, no date, and "Preliminary Report on the Subject of Housing," April 8, 1935, both in FHLP, Box 667; **New York Age**, May 25, 1935, p. 2.

9 Margaret Reynolds interview with Donelan J. Phillips, no date, FHLP, Box 668.

10 Margaret Reynolds, Report of CTL Meeting, August 15, 1935, **ibid**. For the Communists' tenant work, see James W. Ford and Louis Sass, "Development of Work in Harlem Section," **Communist**, XIV (April, 1935), pp. 313, 319; and Naison, "The Communist Party in Harlem," pp. 23-24, 31-38, 71-72, 119.

11 Handbill, FHLP, Box 667.

12 Ethelbert D. Anderson to Dr. Charles Roberts, June 21, 1935, and to LaGuardia, June 20, 1935; handbill, "Monster Mass Meeting, July 1st," all in FHLP, Box 667.

13 CTL Minutes, July 25, 1935; clippings, **Daily Worker**, October 9 and 27, 1935; clippings, **Negro Liberator**, August 1 and 8, 1935, FHLP, Box 667.

14 CTL Minutes, May 2 and 9, 1935; Naison, "The Communist Party in Harlem," p. 247.

15 Margaret Reynolds, Report of CTL Meeting, May 23, 1935, FHLP, Box 668; **Amsterdam News**, June 1, 1935, p. 14.

16 Margaret Reynolds, Report of CTL Meeting, August 22, 1935, FHLP, Box 668.

17 **Ibid**; CTL Minutes, August 29, 1935.

18 Greene, "Harlem in the Great Depression," pp. 93-96, 317-318, 338, 343-345; and Harlem directories and guides in Vertical Files, Schomburg. Tenants League leaders fit the classic socio-economic profiles of Carter G. Woodson, Jr., **The Negro Professional Man and the Community** (Association for the Study of Negro Life and History, Inc., 1934), Chaps. VI-VIII, XIII-XVI; and E. Franklin Frazier, "Negro Harlem: An Ecological Study," **American Journal of Sociology**, XLIII (July, 1937), 72-88.

19 These conclusions are based on CTL building units and members' addresses plotted on maps of the **Landbook of the Borough of Manhattan, City of New York** (Philadelphia: G.W. Bromley & Co., 1934) and **Maps and Charts Prepared by the Slum Clearance Committee of New York** (New York: Slum Clearance Committee of New York, 1934).

The Consolidated Tenants League

20 Margaret Reynolds, Report of CTL Meeting, August 15, 1935, FHLP, Box 668.
21 Joel Schwartz interview with Hope R. Stevens, August 3, 1981.
22 Joel Schwartz interview with Arthur C. Holden, March 3, 1981; Langdon W. Post to Ralph Walker, February 9, 1934, Arthur C. Holden Papers (ACHP), Box 66, Cornell University Library.
23 CTL Minutes, 1935-1936, passim; Louis B. Bryan, "Housing Conditions," p. 24, WPA Writer's Project, Box 4; Post to LaGuardia, April 2, 1937, FHLP, Box 668.
24 Holden to Julian Levi, December 12, 1932, ACHP, Box 58; Schwartz interview with Holden, March 3, 1981; **New York Times,** May 5, 1935, p. 1. The Housing Authority's Technical Division had blueprints well underway on the Harlem River Houses long before it thought to take on a black technician in an advisory capacity. **New York Times,** July 4, 1935, p. 17; August 21, 1935, p. 38. As black architect Vertner Tandy complained to the Consolidated Tenants League, the project's white architects have "worked on plans 18 months . . . practically completed . . . if a Negro came in now, it would be only the tail end of the work as plans are finished and approved . . . can you imagine it, not even a single Negro draughtsman on a ($) 4,000,000 project." Margaret Reynolds, Report of CTL Meeting, August 15, 1935, FHLP, Box 668.
25 **New York Times,** February 12, 1935, p. 1; May 2, p. 7; May 5, 1935, p. 1; Langdon W. Post, **The Challenge of Housing** (New York: Farrar & Rinehart, 1938), pp. 157-159; **Amsterdam News,** May 18, 1935, p. 1, and June 1, 1935, p. 14; **New York Times,** May 23, 1935, p. 27, and June 11, 1935, p. 33.
26 Post to LaGuardia, June 27, 1935, FHLP, Box 761; CTL President to James Allen, July 6, 1935; Handbills, "Tenants of Harlem;" "Tenants! City Hall Rally, July 13, 1935"; clipping, **Amsterdam News,** July 27, 1935; all in FHLP, Box 667.
27 Margaret Reynolds, Report of CTL Meeting, July 11, 1935, FHLP, Box 668, Handbill, "Joint Manifesto," FHLP, Box 667.
28 Clipping, **Amsterdam News,** July 27, 1935, FHLP, Box 667; Margaret Reynolds, Report of CTL Mass Meeting, July 18, 1935, FHLP, Box 668.
29 **New York Times,** August 21, 1935, p. 38; CTL Minutes, August 8 and 15, 1935.
30 Post, **Challenge of Housing,** pp. 187-188; May Lumsden, "First Families," **Survey Graphic,** XXV (February, 1936), 103-105; New York City Housing Authority, **Community Facilities and Activities in New York City Public Housing Projects** (New York City Housing Authority, January, 1946). Williams had successfully defended a Dunbar tenant who had been evicted for owing back rent and was then hounded by Bruce at his place of work. Williams' victory made the front page of the **Amsterdam News** on March 31, 1935.
31 Harriet Townsend to Edith E. Wood, no date, Edith Elmer Wood Papers, Box 63, Avery Library, Columbia University; May Lumsden, "Procedures for Selection of Tenants, Harlem River Houses," February 1, 1937, FHLP, Box 761.
32 CTL Minutes, August 22, 1935; Margaret Reynolds, Report of CTL Meeting, August 22, 1935,: FHLP, box 668
33 CTL Minutes, August 22, September 5, 1935.
34 **Amsterdam News,** October 12, 1935, p. 1; "Recommendations of the Harlem Housing Committee," in binder marked "Management Training Course," Box 45, New York City Housing Authority Records, Williamsburg (NYCHA Records); Greene, "Harlem in the Great Depression," pp. 281-284.
35 Lawrence M. Orton to Charles H. Roberts, August 28, 1935, FHLP, Box 667.
36 CTL Minutes, September 5, November 14, 1935; Mayor's Committee on City Planning, **West Harlem Community Study** (Mayor's Committee on City Planning as a Partial Report on Project No. 165-197-6037 Conducted Under the Auspices of the Works Project Administration, 1937), pp. 29-31, 39.
37 **New York Times,** March 3, 1936, p. 2; March 9, 1936, p. 12; March 10, 1936,

p. 20; CTL Minutes, March 5, 12, and 19, 1936.

38 Bryan, "Housing Conditions," p. 24.

39 **Real Estate News**, December, 1931, pp. 410, 422; March, 1933, p. 83; Naison, "The Communist Party in Harlem," pp. 255-256; Thomas F. Keogh, **Landlord and Tenant and others in Summary Proceedings for the Recovery of the possession of real property** (New York: Baker, Voorhis & Co., 1932), pp. 302-309, 384-412.

40 Committee for the Centralization of Magistrates' Courts in Manhattan, **Brief in Support of Centralizing the Magistrates' Courts in Manhattan** (February 11, 1929).

41 CTL Minutes, December 19, 1935, and June 4, 1936.

42 For Section 1436a of the Civil Practice Act, see William B. Rudell, "Concerted Rent-Withholding on the New York City Housing Front," (unpublished paper, Yale Law School, 1965), p. 37, copy in TMRP; and for Section 1436a, sub 2, see **J.E. & A. Realty Corp.** v. **Coulter** (Mun. Ct., Bronx, 1938), 169 Misc. 871, 3 NYS 2nd 811.

43 CTL Minutes, February 28, 1935; **Report to His Honor, Fiorello H. LaGuardia, Mayor of the City of New York, by the New York City Housing Authority, Pursuant to Article Five of the State Housing Law, on its Investigation and Public Hearings on Living and Housing Conditions in the City of New York, January 25th, 1937** [NYCHA Report], pp. 76-78; NYSTCCUCP, Hearings, VII, 1247-1249.

44 NUSTCCUCP, Hearings, VII, 1246.

45 Clippings, **Negro Liberator**, August 1 and 15, 1935, FHLP Box 667; CTL Minutes, June 13, July 25, and August 15, 1935; NYSTCCUCP, Hearings, VII, 1275.

46 CTL Minutes, March 7, April 4, October 3, 1935.

47 **ibid.**, June 6, 1935.

48 Schwartz interview with Stevens, August 3, 1981; R.A.Lockwood, "Necessity and Nature of Consideration Supporting Landlord's Reduction of Rent," **American Law Review**, 3rd Series, XXX, 1259-1298.

49 Bryan, "Housing Conditions," p. 23; Schwartz interview with Stevens, August 3, 1981; Rudell, "Concerted Rent Withholding," p. 63.

50 NYSTCCUCP, Hearings, VII, 1245; **NYCHA Report**, pp. 51-52.

51 Hortense Goldstone, "A Study of Fifty Municipal Term Court Cases of the Division of Housing of the Department of Housing and Buildings," (unpublished M.A. essay, New York School of Social Work, 1939), p. 15.

52 Citizens' Housing Council, Executive Committee, Minutes, 1937-1939, **passim**; CHC Committee on Housing Management, Minutes, 1937-1939, **passim**, CHPC Library; **NYCHA Report**, pp. 76-78; correspondence in United Neighborhood Houses Papers (UNHP), Folder 110, Social Welfare History Archives, University of Minnesota; Rudell, "Concerted Rent Withholding," pp. 72-75.

53 Resolution adopted at Mass Meeting of CTL, June 13, 1938; Earl Miller to Alfred Rheinstein, July 20, 1938; Richard Barclay to same, September 12, 1939, with unsigned Housing Authority Memo, September 15, 1939; all in NYCHA Records, Box 31.

54 Transcript of meeting, November 6, 1939, in Binder marked "Management Training Course," NYCHA Records, Box 31.

55 Draft Statement by Functional Committee: Housing (early 1942), and Ruth Farbman to Charles Abrams, December 5, 1941, both in Reel 11, Charles Abrams Papers (CAP), Cornell University Library.

56 **New York Times**, May 3, 1942, IV, p. 1; May 17, 1942, IX, p. 1; June 17, 1942, p. 17.

57 **Ibid.**, September 3, 1942, p. 17; September 7, 1942, p. 21; September 20, 1942, IX, p. 1; October 4, 1942, IX, p. 1; October 13, 1942, p. 25; CWCCH, Board of Directors, Minutes, November 2, 1942, Reel 11, CAP.

58 Report on Rent Control Issued as a Supplement to the Housing Report of the City-Wide Citizens' Committee on Harlem, December, 1942, Reel 11, CAP; CTL Minutes, July 1, 10, 15, 24, and 29, 1943.

59 Transcript, WEO Symposium, May 26, 1943, Reel 11, CAP; CHC Minutes, July 27, 1943, ACHP, Box 68.

60 **New York Times**, August 3, 1943, p. 11; August 7, 1943, p. 13; Samuel Poses to Edward L. Coffey, August 5, 1943, Office of Price Administration, Enforcement Branch, Box 1207, Record Group 188, National Archives (OPA Enforcement); Joseph Platzker Memorandum, September 21, 1943, FHLP, Box 153.

61 CTL Minutes, September 30, October 28, December 2, 9, 1943; March 2, April 13, September 7, 1944; Leigh Athearn to Thomas I. Emerson, October 5, 1943, OPA Enforcement, Box 1207; Tom Tippett to Walter Hort, April 12, 1944, OPA Enforcement, Box 1208; Mildred A. Gutwillig, Latest Information on Rent Control Enforcement, December 20, 1943, Folder 103, UNHP; Ivan D. Carson, Memo, September 22, 1942, revised April 8, 1944, OPA Enforcement, Box 1207.

62 CWCCH, Housing Committee, Minutes, February 2, 1944, Algernon D. Black Papers (ADBP), Box 8, Columbia University Library.

63 Franklin O. Nichols to Charles Abrams, January 3, 1941; James Felt to Abrams, February 16, 1942; Goode A. Harney to Abrams, November 4, 1943, all in Reel 11, CAP; "Urban Housing Management Association, Inc." (Confidential Draft, New York Urban League, 1943), ACHP, Box 71.

64 Arthur Simon, **Stuyvesant Town** (New York: New York University Press, 1970), pp. 15-41; Informal Meeting on the Riverton Project, October 25, 1944, AGBP, Box 8; **New York Times**, July 2, 1946, p. 41; October 30, 1946, p. 35; August 31, 1947, VIII, p. 1.

65 While **boasting** a concern for "human needs," Lescaze's and Felt's work looked more like an attempt to clear human obstacles out of the way of the traffic generated by Robert Moses' Triborough Bridge. William Lescaze and James Felt, "A Plan for Harlem's Redevelopment," **Architectural Forum**, LXXX (April, 1944), 145-152.

66 New York City Housing Authority, **13th Annual Report** (New York City Housing Authority, 1947); **16th Annual Report for 1949**, p. 12; **17th Annual Report, 1950**, p. 8; CTL Minutes, July 8, 1948; March 24, 1949; McLoughlin interview with Phillips, October 1, 1975; John McLoughlin interview with Theodore Anderson, January 8, 1976.

67 Nor has there been much patience from analysts who are convinced that such assertiveness was a reactionary relic or at best a crude prerequisite for the mass collectivism of the 1930s. See, Naison, "The Communist Party in Harlem;" William Muraskin, "The Harlem Boycott of 1934; Black Nationalism and the Rise of Labor Union Consciousness," **Labor History**, XIII (Summer, 1972), 361-373; Martin Kilson, "Political Change in the Negro Ghetto, 1900-1960s," in Nathan Huggins, et al., eds., **Key Issues in the Afro-American Experience** (2 vols.; New York: Harcourt, Brace Jovanovich, 1971), II, 167-192.

Chicago street scene, 1933

Black Chicago Political Realignment During the Great Depression and New Deal

CHRISTOPHER ROBERT REED

During the 1930s, the character of politics in Chicago's Republican Black Belt began to undergo a steady transformation. The emergence of the Democratic Kelly-Nash machine and the advent of the New Deal—the twentieth century's most comprehensive, national program of social and economic reconstruction—produced a truly adversarial relationship between the two major parties.

At the start of the Great Depression, Chicago blacks predominantly held membership in a party that lacked the power, imagination, or will to offer relevant programs and policies to meet the challenge of the economic crisis. Harold F. Gosnell described the Republican organization as "completely bankrupt, financially and morally."[1] Nevertheless, black loyalty to the "Party of Lincoln" was remarkably durable, posing the last formidable threat to Democratic hegemony over all Chicago. While the Republican party was in demise throughout white neighborhoods, its decline in the

---

Christopher Robert Reed is assistant professor in the Black Studies Program at the University of Illinois–Chicago. He received the Ph.D. in American history from Kent State University. His area of specialization is twentieth-century urban history, and he is now completing a history of the Chicago branch of the NAACP.

Black Belt was slowed by economic circumstances, racial ideology, and local affiliations at the ward level.[2]

The Democratic party's movement toward dominance in Chicago, Cook County, and Illinois coincided with, and grew from, the New Deal. Roosevelt's socially ameliorative programs in the areas of relief, employment, and housing contributed significantly to the movement, along with two factors endemic to Chicago. By 1933, the Democratic party had experienced its fourth year of political success in the county and state and was in nearly complete control in Chicago.[3] Then, the death of Mayor Anton J. Cermak two days after Roosevelt's inauguration brought Edward J. Kelly into prominence as mayor. In concert with Patrick J. Nash, the Cook County Democratic Central Committee chairman, Kelly formed a part of the leadership known as the Kelly-Nash machine. That fusing of forces and events in 1933 initiated Democratic hegemony in the political life of the city not only for the Depression decade but for fifty years after that. Republicanism would live, but mainly on Chicago's black South Side, and with a constantly diminishing influence over political and economic matters in that racial enclave.

By consistent identification with the programs and funding of the New Deal—promising new services, opportunities, favors, and hope—the Kelly-Nash machine and the Democratic organization not only accumulated power but garnered prestige. The popularity of Mayor Edward Kelly was especially significant in the Black Belt and must be ranked as one of the key factors in understanding why black support for the Democratic party continually expanded, albeit slowly, throughout the decade.

Initially, Kelly's ascension to power was opposed by black political leaders in Chicago and Springfield. Staunchly Republican and reflecting the black electorate's aversion to Democrats along both political and ideological lines, black legislators from Chicago at first voted to stall the passage of a bill in the general assembly that would have enabled the Chicago City Council to bypass an election and instead choose a temporary mayor after Cermak's death. But once the power of the Democratic party prevailed in Springfield, Chicago's two black Republican aldermen, William L. Dawson and Robert R. Jackson, dropped their opposition and voted for Kelly. By the end of Kelly's first term in office, he was the recipient of praise from the voice of black Republicanism, the *Chicago Defender*. What was evolving was a relationship of frequent cooperation between two opposing powers: Democrats who controlled the city, and the only remnant of organized viable Republicanism extant in Chicago, the blacks of the Second and Third Wards.[4]

On taking office, Kelly continuously courted the black electorate—in one instance by restoring to the Civil Service lists those blacks removed by Cermak. Kelly prepared for his first elective campaign by having Louis B. Anderson, former Second Ward alderman, approach black Republicans for

---

[1]Gosnell, *Machine Politics: Chicago Model* (1937; rpt. Chicago: Phoenix Books, 1967), p. 18.

[2]*Ibid.*, pp. 97, 120–22, 158–59; Gosnell, "The Negro Vote in Northern Cities," *National Municipal Review*, 30 (1941), 264–67, 278; Elmer W. Henderson, "A Study of the Basic Factors Involved in the Change in Party Alignment of Negroes in Chicago, 1932–1938," Thesis University of Chicago 1939; Edward T. Clayton, *The Negro Politician: His Success and Failure* (Chicago: Johnson Pub. Co., 1964), pp. 52–56; Rita Werner Gordon, "The Change in the Political Alignment of Chicago's Negroes During the New Deal," *Journal of American History*, 56 (1969), 584–603; Roger Biles, "'Big Red in Bronzeville': Mayor Ed Kelly Reels in the Black Vote," *Chicago History*, n.s. 10 (1981), 99–111; Charles R. Branham, "The Transformation of Black Political Leadership in Chicago, 1865–1942," Diss. University of Chicago 1981; Christopher R. Reed, "A Study of Black Politics and Protest in Depression-decade Chicago, 1930–1939," Diss. Kent State University 1982; John M. Allswang, "The Chicago Negro Voter and the Democratic Consensus: A Case Study, 1918–1936," *Journal of the Illinois State Historical Society*, 60 (1967), 145–75.

[3]Gosnell, *Machine Politics*, p. 9.

[4]Reed, pp. 207–12, 216–20.

support. The Mayor was presented as a fair and powerful leader who was already assured victory. In that vein, Anderson told blacks, "In Edward J. Kelly as mayor you have another Bill Thompson."[5] The reference was meaningful to blacks because opportunities available to them were always minimal until their votes helped elect Republican William Hale "Big Bill" Thompson in 1915.

What black Chicagoans saw in Kelly was a fellow South Sider from the partially black Fourth Ward, a white politician who personally advanced the civil rights program of the *Chicago Defender* at the 1932 Democratic convention and a leader who was not afraid of incurring the wrath of his fellow whites when speaking out for justice. Kelly had once boldly challenged South Side blacks to disdain voluntary segregation and actively pursue their law-given rights throughout the city. He condemned racism in a Far South Side school as being against the public policy of both the city and the nation. (That act was to cost him a large number of votes in 1935 in the virtually all-white ward in which the school was located, but that loss was submerged in his landslide victory.)[6]

The skills of Kelly the politician matched those of Kelly the egalitarian. Before the aldermanic primary of 1935, sensing the effect that an overwhelming mandate would have both for himself and his party, Kelly declared that he would not slate Democrats against the Republican incumbents running in the Second and Third Wards, Dawson and Jackson. Praising their records and the support they had given in the city council, he applied a bit of simple and convincing political logic in his move: In an ostensibly nonpartisan aldermanic election, he was quite justified in allowing Republican

---

[5]*Chicago Defender*, Jan. 26, 1935, p. 3, cols. 1-2.
[6]*Defender*, March 30, 1935, p. 3, cols. 1-2, p. 4, cols. 7-8. For a report of Kelly's statement of the situation at Morgan Park High School, see *ibid.*, Oct. 6 (p. 1, col. 1, p. 3, col. 4), Oct. 13 (p. 1, cols. 1-2, 4-5, p. 3, cols. 3-4), 1934.

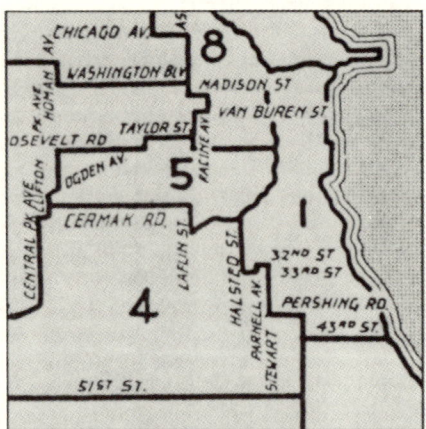

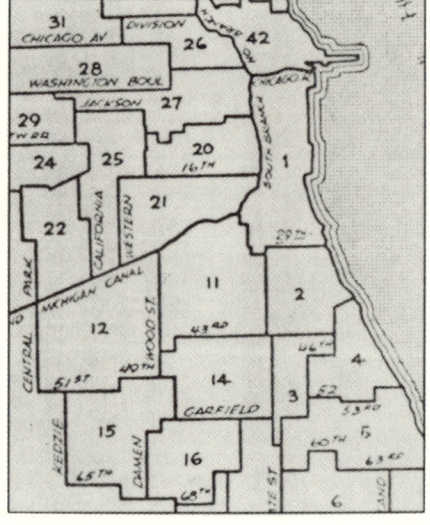

The First Congressional District of Illinois (shown above) included all of Ward One and portions of Wards Two, Four, and Eleven (shown at right).

successes if candidates had an exemplary record of public service. Dawson and Jackson, in turn, pledged to support the Mayor's bid for election irrespective of whom their party ran in the April general election. Dawson pledged more than twenty thousand votes in the Second Ward, and Jackson promised, "My Republican friends in this ward [the Third] will do for Mayor Kelly what they used to do for former Mayor Thompson." The symbol of black Chicago Republicanism, Oscar DePriest, stayed out of the city during part of the campaign, thereby avoiding the label of being a political "turncoat."[7]

The leadership of the *Defender*, always politically calculating, explained that Kelly's retention in office would "in a large sense promote our political advancement in the city of Chicago." A. N. Fields of the *Defender* noted: "You must know that the Republican party will not again come to life under its present leadership. The reasons are obvious. Those who are trying to revive the party are using the same opiate that they used in putting it to sleep. Black men and women who vote for Edward J. Kelly next Tuesday are not voting against the Republican party because there is no Republican party in Chicago.... It simply doesn't exist anymore."[8] By 1935, Republicans could not even challenge Kelly with a respectable adversary. Harold Gosnell observed that "five years earlier, a man with Kelly's record would have been regarded as an easy mark for the Republican organization."[9]

The election results demonstrated conclusively the extent of Kelly's appeal. He was a landslide victor, and the enormity of his victory would have been impressive even without the black contribution from the Second, Third, and Fourth Wards. Blacks delivered on their promises in all wards and, in effect, had indicated that they were no longer enamored with Republicanism to the detriment of their own interests. Kelly received 80.5 percent of their vote—nearly matching the 82.7 percent garnered citywide from white wards. In all, Kelly received 800,000 votes to his opponent's 167,000.[10]

There were charges that the impressive Democratic showing in black wards resulted from threats by Democratic precinct captains to remove from the relief rolls any voter who failed to cast a ballot for Kelly, a charge that was repeated with each election. "Whether these rumors are true or not," the *Defender* claimed, the frequency of straight-party Democratic tickets in municipal elections throughout the Black Belt was most suspicious.[11]

As the years progressed, Kelly's reputation among blacks grew to a point that he was credited with bestowing favors he did not, could not, or would not as long as most blacks were Republicans. In reality, his appointment of blacks to office after 1935 and until the end of the decade never matched Thompson's totals but easily exceeded Cermak's. In addition, Kelly vacillated in supporting the completion of long-overdue, federally sponsored housing such as the Ida B. Wells project. He steadfastly refused to appoint a black to the school board until late in 1939, and he did not support wholeheartedly the black aspiration to reclaim a lost judgeship.[12]

Concomitant with the rise of the Kelly-Nash machine, a few blacks began to rise within the Democratic organization.

---
[7]*Ibid.*, Feb. 23 (p. 2, cols. 1-2), March 23 (p. 3, cols. 1-2), March 30 (p. 6, col. 6), 1935; *News Bulletin of the Third Ward Republican Club*, 1936, p. 2, copy in Arthur W. Mitchell Papers, Chicago Historical Society (hereafter cited as Mitchell Papers).
[8]*Defender*, Feb. 16 (p. 3, cols. 4-5), March 30 (p. 1, cols. 1 ff.), 1935.
[9]Gosnell, *Machine Politics*, p. 18.
[10]Allswang, pp. 172-74; Gordon, p. 602.
[11]*Defender*, April 14 (p. 1, cols. 1-2, p. 10, cols. 7-8), Aug. 4 (p. 3, cols. 1-2), Sept. 8 (p. 3, cols. 1-2), 1934; *ibid.*, Nov. 12, 1938, p. 7, cols. 2-3.
[12]Henderson, p. 78. On black efforts to secure a seat on the school board, see *Defender*, Oct. 7 (p. 1, col. 5), Oct. 21 (p. 1, col. 5), 1939.

Shrewdly aware of the new political opportunities, they began to make demands upon party leaders for greater representation. The argument was always the same: If the party wanted to build a citywide organization, it could do so only by slating blacks for offices; and if it wanted to crush the Second and Third Ward Republican organizations, that could be accomplished only by attracting more blacks into the party.

The Democrats' first overtures to blacks had occurred during the Cermak administration. In 1931 Edward M. "Mike" Sneed was named Third Ward committeeman—a masterstroke that paid handsome dividends. After 1933, the benefits of New Deal patronage jobs and privileges for the underworld elements of the ward enabled Sneed to lay the foundation for a solid ward organization. Another example of the type of reward that Democrats were willing to bestow on blacks was the appointment in 1933 of Earl B. Dickerson to the post of Assistant Attorney General for the northern district of Illinois.[13] Dickerson's appointment was spurred by two factors: He had been a longtime Democratic loyalist, and he was filling a position normally held by a black man. But the Dickerson and Sneed appointments marked the limit to which Democrats would extend themselves until blacks proved their loyalty at the polls. The party stood to lose white support if blacks were rewarded too quickly without having proven decisively in attitude and substantially in electoral support that they had divested themselves of their Republican connections.

Democrats elected only two other black officials before 1939 in their efforts to win control of the Black Belt, but the two were highly significant. In 1934, Arthur W. Mitchell assumed the national mantle of black political leadership when he defeated Oscar DePriest to become the first Democratic black congressman. Throughout the decade he was the lone black man to sit in the United States House of Representatives. In 1938, William Wallace captured the Illinois Senate seat of William E. King. Yet, neither man could match the Republicans in the manner in which they used personal amiability and emphasis on racial ideology to build party loyalty.

Alabama native Mitchell, for example, an attorney and former college president who worked briefly for the Hoover administration, was unpopular among both Republicans and Democrats because of his personal eccentricities. Filled with paradoxical traits that were revealed in almost every instance of his behavior, Mitchell seemed to lack any special instinct, attribute, or strategy as he advanced politically. Yet, more than any other black politician, he symbolized the impact of the Depression on Black Belt politics.[14] With the advent of the New Deal as a remedy to the economic crisis, the emphasis on race began to subside somewhat, allowing a man such as Mitchell to rise in prominence. His politics, racial ideology, and personality were out of harmony with the racially-charged milieu of his constituents (who had traditionally not only resisted close cooperation with southern whites but also viewed the Democratic party as the incarnation of racial terrorism), but Mitchell enjoyed a successful political career because he was both an heir to and product of the New Deal.

Mitchell's three consecutive terms were directly attributable to the success of the Roosevelt victory wagon, and he drew his strongest support not from the black Republican Second Ward, but rather from the First

---

[13]*Defender*, Feb. 18, 1933, p. 5, col. 1. See also Mitchell to Dickerson, Feb. 14, 1933, and Dickerson to Mitchell, Feb. 15, 1933, both in Mitchell Papers.

[14]Reed, pp. 220–31.

[15]Mitchell to Williams, Aug. 28, 1934, Mitchell Papers.

[16]Mitchell to Pearl Silberman, March 21, 1935, and Mitchell to R. H. Folger, March 13, 1937, both *ibid*. In contrast, a typical letter to blacks displaying his caustic tone is Mitchell to Rev. W. J. G. McLin, April 11, 1935, *ibid*.

Works Progress Administration projects, such as this Chicago sewer, provided valuable city improvements as well as employment for the party faithful.

and Eleventh Wards, both of which were Democratic, pro-New Deal, and predominantly white.

Mitchell measured racial progress to a great extent by the material changes brought by the New Deal. He expressed those views in a letter to Rev. Lacey Kirk Williams, head of the most powerful black Baptist group in America: "I believe that no people have suffered as much from discrimination, injustice and prejudice as our Race. I think that I understand much that is necessary to be done to bring about better conditions, and I pledge myself to work to the end that the New Deal will mean as much, if not more, to our people than to any other group."[15]

Beyond the material promise that the New Deal held, Mitchell found inspiration, motivation, and direction in the ideology of Booker T. Washington, whom he had worked for as a youth and to whom he proved a devout follower. Mitchell's strategy for racial progress followed Washington's program to near total duplication, in that he avoided confrontations—especially verbal ones—with whites. Unlike DePriest, who had been brazen and, on occasion, belligerent when dealing with whites, Mitchell appeared to be unusually obsequious. (A major exception to that rule involved whites who would be readily identifiable as wealthy First District Republicans, whom he freely attacked as "economic royalists.")[16] Upon taking his congressional seat in 1935, Mitchell immediately disclaimed any affinity with black racial aspirations by saying: "I would work harder for my people than any other Congressman, but I would not keep thinking about the fact that I was colored.... I am not a Negro agitator, but a member of

Franklin D. Roosevelt at the October, 1937, dedication of the Outer Park Drive bridge. Built with federal money, the project was regarded as one of the outstanding accomplishments of Mayor Edward Kelly's administration.

the Congress of the United States. I am not the exclusive property of one class and race, but the agent of all the people."[17]

Ward-level politics dramatically illustrated the start of change in the Black Belt. Although the source of political power in Chicago emanated from City Hall through Roosevelt's programs, the locus of black political power—where the spoils of the New Deal were divided by black Democrats and coveted by black Republicans—was still the South Side's Second and Third Wards of Mitchell's First Congressional District. There, black Republicans held steadfastly to their party ideology, traditions, and allegiance, despite a virtual lack of patronage and privileges.

In the Second Ward, power rested in the hands of Joseph "Joe" Tittinger, a politician of German and French ancestry who since 1932 had worked in a hostile political environment to build his party from its weak, minority status to one that could operate at parity with the Republicans. By the summer of 1933, Tittinger's activities were reinforced by patronage jobs created by the new alphabet agencies, including the CWA (Civil Works Administration), FERA (Federal Emergency Relief Administration), and PWA (Public Works Administration). Under the guidelines formulated by the Kelly-Nash organization, Tittinger, as committeeman, controlled all patronage appointments in the ward. Even Congressman Mitchell, considered a protégé of Tittinger's, continually deferred to him.[18]

As the decade progressed, Tittinger's tenure became more controversial and precarious. Blacks composed ninety percent of the Second Ward's fledgling Democratic organization, and as early as 1933, the *Chicago*

---

[17]*Kansas City* (Mo.) *Times,* Dec. 7, 1934 (clipping), and Mitchell to Fred R. Moore, June 1, 1935, *ibid.;* Chicago Branch [NAACP] to Leonard Schuetz, Jan. 29, 1936, Branch Files, Papers of the National Association for the Advancement of Colored People, Library of Congress, Washington, D.C.; *Defender,* Nov. 10 (p. 1, cols. 1-2, p. 2, cols. 3-4), Nov. 17 (p. 14, col. 2), Dec. 1 (p. 14, col. 2), 1934.

[18]Mitchell to Mary Lee Colbert, Dec. 10, 1934, Mitchell to Laurine Beckwith, Jan. 8, 1935, and Tittinger to Claude Holman, Feb. 14, 1935, all in Mitchell Papers; Gene DeLon Jones, "The Local Political Significance of New Deal Relief Legislation in Chicago: 1933-1940," Diss. Northwestern University 1970, pp. 131-32, 149-52.

Defender had urged them to rid themselves of Tittinger's "mediocre white leadership" in favor of the "intelligent members of their own race" who had earned their respect and confidence. Edgar Brown, outspoken leader of the New Deal Organization, described Tittinger's power as "unbelievable." "A foreigner invades our neighborhood and starts using gang methods to inflict his will upon a defenseless people," he declared. "The bourbon South has come to 35th and Michigan."[19] Three popular black Democrats did file to run against Tittinger for the committeemanship in 1934, but two of them withdrew before the election; when the votes were in, Tittinger had won again. That challenge was the only serious one before Tittinger's removal by Kelly in 1939.[20]

Christopher C. Wimbish, a former Republican assistant state's attorney who became a New Deal Democrat, summarized the situation of blacks in Tittinger's ward:

I feel perfectly justified, regardless of politics, to address myself to the colored citizens of the Second Ward. You are bone of my bone, and flesh of my flesh. With you I must either rise or sink.... Many of you left the South because you desired to exercise the right of suffrage. The fact that you reside in the Second Ward and that your political opportunities and privileges are controlled by one not of your group should be proof positive to you that you are still being denied the proper exercise of your rights of suffrage.[21]

Opposition to Tittinger also remained strong because of his apparent negligence in rewarding loyal party workers with patronage jobs. In February, 1935, it was reported that thirty—or about one third—of his precinct captains were out of work; it was later found that one white captain was holding seven jobs while thirty-seven black captains were jobless. Rev. Junius C. Austin of the Pilgrim Baptist Church complained to Congressman Mitchell about the plight of black loyalists:

I am in quandary as to what to do right now. I am receiving the taunts and jeers, even in my congregation, from those who feel that my fight for this administration was not after all appreciated.... I shall not call attention to my service. It should be well known. I have not been able to secure any patronage for my people here; not even those of my church who have taken the civil service examination and have high ratings.[22]

There was substantial proof that Tittinger's interest in his constituents was superseded by his connections to criminal elements, both black and white. The *Defender* repeated charges that he had "insistently and continuously served certain well-known interests that are not in harmony with the program of the Democratic party . . . and [are] inimical to the progress of the majority of the voters of the Second Ward." Tittinger was accused of foregoing patronage possibilities in "return for gambling and vice privileges." Reformer Christopher Wimbish told his Second Ward neighbors, "For the most part the entire ward is farmed out for vice and racket privileges for the enrichment not of you, but of white people."[23]

Nevertheless, throughout Tittinger's tenure in office, he was supported by numerous blacks, including Congressman Mitchell. Mayor Kelly campaigned on Tittinger's behalf and extended the machine's full support throughout the 1934 election. In addition, some of Tittinger's black defenders maintained that the element of race had been injected into the elections as a substitute for political achievement by his critics. Tittinger had done as much as could be expected

---

[19]*Defender*, Sept. 2, 1933, p. 3, cols. 4-5, and March 17, 1934, p. 2, col. 5. Chicago committeemen were generally chosen from the racial or national groups of ward constituents; see Gosnell, *Machine Politics*, p. 44.
[20]*Defender*, March 10 (p. 4, cols. 1-2), March 17 (p. 2, cols. 5-6), March 26 (p. 5, cols. 1-2), 1934.
[21]Wimbish, "To the Citizens of the Second Ward," *The Truth*, March 12, 1938, p. 1, Christopher C. Wimbish Papers, Chicago Historical Society.
[22]Austin to Mitchell, Jan. 12, 1937, Mitchell Papers.
[23]*Defender*, Aug. 26, 1933, p. 2, col. 4; *ibid.*, March 26, 1934, p. 5, cols. 1-2; Wimbish, p. 3.

from a fledgling ward organization, they claimed. Although many Second Ward blacks voted Democratic in the presidential election of 1936, they did so because of federal relief and job projects. They were not, however, true Democrats with a solid party affiliation.[24]

Democrats in the Third Ward also diligently worked to build a viable political base while engaging in intense factional strife. Committeeman Edward M. Sneed, who was selected to fill an unexpired term in 1931 and ran for reelection in 1932, always faced primary challenges. Many of his other problems paralleled Tittinger's. Despite the fact that Sneed was black, he was not able to escape the charge of racial insensitivity. Critics accused him of allowing "twenty people of the opposite group [to] hold jobs which are charged to and belong to the people of the ward."[25] However, in 1938, the *Defender*, now a partisan voice of the Democratic party, hailed him as "a fighter for racial rights."[26]

Sneed was a local power when contrasted to ward Republicans, but he exercised little power in the service of his black constituents. Opponents complained that too much employment was given to whites who did not live in the ward, that too many black party workers were underemployed on city and federal jobs, and that no sizeable dent had been made in the labor woes of the ward's unemployed masses. His supporters

[24]Reed, p. 236.
[25]*Defender*, Feb. 17, 1934, p. 6, col. 3.
[26]*Ibid.*, Feb. 26, 1938, p. 4, cols. 2-3.

Subway construction, financed by the Public Works Administration

countered that "much mention [ought to be made of] the committeeman's untiring efforts in obtaining patronage jobs for some 130 deserving people of his organization; of his causing thousands in his district to receive prompt and proper aid from the various relief agencies; and his making possible the employment of over 200 others in business places of the community."[27] In 1938, Sneed took credit for recommending and placing more than four thousand persons.[28]

Throughout his terms in office, Sneed, like Tittinger, dodged accusations of associating with gambling and vice elements, black as well as white. As a city vehicle commissioner, he got into squabbles with taxi interests on the South Side and violent confrontations with competing businesses. The major opposition to his retention in office in 1938 was generated by his associations with underworld figures and the Kelly-Nash machine.[29]

Sneed did deliver the votes needed to challenge Republicans in the ward, however. Early in his tenure he remarked on the potential power that blacks had at their disposal if they voted as a unified Democratic bloc. In 1934 he pledged that he would work not only for victory but for "rolling up a record Democratic vote" in order to win "higher standing and more power with the central committee" and "greater benefits of local government for the district."[30]

Meanwhile, the black Republican organization under DePriest, King, and Dawson attempted to hold the line while the political world as they knew it was collapsing around them. Republicans found that they could sustain themselves only on the hope that the 1936 presidential election might bring a return to the halcyon milieu of pre-Depression days. But the electorate of Chicago's Second Ward gave FDR an unprecedented 47.8 percent of their votes. In contrast, the vote throughout the rest of the congressional district reached 63.7 percent and throughout the state was 67.6 percent.[31] The growing black Democratic vote clearly indicated that the New Deal was winning friends. If there was one bright spot to Republicans, it was to be found in the party's entrenched status in the Black Belt, where a preponderance of votes and not a close near-majority typified victory.

Writing in 1937, Harold Gosnell postulated that patronage was the "cement" that united the party organization. While that was true in a general sense, the ingredient that held the black Republican organization intact while the rest of the citywide organization stumbled was the element of race. Because of race consciousness, black Republican leaders had the ability to extract maximum benefits from the siege mentality that had dominated the thinking and mood of the South Side. From 1931 to 1933, blacks perceived themselves as being exploited by a hostile Mayor Cermak. Given the dire economic conditions in the Black Belt, to them it also appeared to be a program of racial debilitation.[32]

The spoils of power had all but disappeared for black Republicans, but internecine warfare based on personality marked political life throughout the 1930s. As chief *Defender* political observer A. N. Fields observed in 1934, "When there is no food for the subjects, the king must start a war."[33]

---

[27]*Ibid.*, Feb. 17 (p. 2, col. 1), March 17 (p. 3, cols. 7-8), 1934.
[28]*Ibid.*, Feb. 28, 1938, p. 4, cols. 2-3.
[29]Mitchell to Kelly, April 15, 1935, and Mitchell to George B. Weiss, Jan. 28, 1939, Mitchell Papers; "Reports on Democratic Ward Committeemen," 1936, copies in Harold F. Gosnell Papers, a part of the Robert Merriam Papers, Box XCVIII, University of Chicago Libraries.
[30]*Defender*, Feb. 26, 1938, p. 4, cols. 2-3.
[31]*Chicago Daily News*, Nov. 4, 1936, p. 6, col. 7. Not even when FDR received 56 percent of the Second Ward vote in 1940 could the Democratic party be said to be in control of the ward. In the Black Belt, a preponderance of votes cast—in the range of 80 to 90 percent—was the only indication of political hegemony.
[32]Gosnell, *Machine Politics*, p. 39.
[33]*Defender*, April 14, 1935, p. 1, cols. 1-2.

The Second Ward, Chicago's "banner Republican Ward"—alleged to be "the strongest Republican ward in the country" throughout the period of the New Deal—retained its status as the linchpin of black Republicanism into the 1940s.[34] Moreover, it was the key to the black vote of the First Congressional District, coveted prize of Democratic politicians even after the Democrats captured the congressional seat in 1934 without it.

In the days of GOP control of the city, the Second Ward committeeman had immense power, but with the New Deal the instruments of power were denied the committeeman, State Representative William E. King. Even with that disadvantage, however, King proved to be a strong leader, aggressively plotting a course attempting to substitute party loyalty and future victories for actual power in dealing with his constituents. He prevented Democrats from capturing more than two key offices, congressman in 1934 and state senator in 1938. The price that Republicans paid was warfare so intense in 1934 that King was hard-pressed to hold his committeemanship in the spring election. He did win, but only over the opposition of Alderman William L. Dawson, who had the support of DePriest. King consolidated his power by running against and defeating the only black state senator, fellow Republican Adelbert Roberts, who had run with the backing of DePriest. The *Defender* observed that King's victory meant "the reorganization of Republican politics in the Second Ward and First congressional district. . . . Congressman Oscar DePriest put his money on the wrong horse."[35]

In the Third Ward, DePriest ruled as committeeman even after his loss to Mitchell in the congressional contest of 1934. Within a year, the ward was jolted with intense factionalism. Alderman Jackson disavowed his allegiance to DePriest, allegedly over the latter's refusal to make him second in command of ward affairs. Jackson withdrew from the regular Republican organization, taking with him members of the Third Ward Republican Club, including its president, Irvin C. Mollison, and fifty precinct captains. Jackson justified his formation of a competing organization by accusing DePriest of opportunism, political inconsistency, and a tendency toward "bossism." In the committeeman election of 1936, DePriest withstood the Jackson challenge by a comfortable margin of sixteen hundred votes.[36] Still an alderman, Jackson remained active in the political field and emerged in 1938 with his political troops to help Dawson in the Second Ward.

Major changes in Republican resistance to Democratic advances in the Black Belt occurred in 1939. Democrats held the power to dictate the outcome not only of their own party's primary but also, if they chose, of the Republicans'. Second Ward Alderman Dawson sought reelection for another four-year term, and his primary challenger was Committeeman William King, the Republican leader who, as one local wag in the *Defender* put it, had "nothing to COMMIT."[37] Meanwhile, Democratic leadership at City Hall was said to be considering entering the Republican race with full support for Dawson or not running a candidate of its own. Tittinger was disposed to support Dawson; in contrast, the two key black elements in the ward, Congressman Mitchell and the precinct captains, were opposed to either strategy as a betrayal of their hard work in promoting the Democratic party.[38]

---

[34] Draft of speech, undated but evidently a version of one given by Mitchell on March 2, 1939, before the United States House of Representatives, Mitchell Papers; Barnett to John Hamilton, Dec. 1, 1937, Claude A. Barnett Papers, Chicago Historical Society (hereafter cited as Barnett Papers).

[35] *Defender*, April 14, 1934, p. 1, cols. 1-2, p. 10, cols. 7-8.

[36] *Ibid.*, Nov. 9, 1935, p. 5, col. 1, and April 18, 1936, p. 2, col. 1.

[37] *Ibid.*, March 11, 1939.

[38] Corneal Davis to Mitchell, Jan. 4, 1939, and James McLendon to Mitchell, Jan. 16, 1939, Mitchell Papers.

In the primary, Dawson campaigned on his record in the area of housing—advocating fair rents, decent housing, and an end to evictions. On the negative side, the Dawson camp engaged in ad hominem attacks, accusing King of seeking a political office simply because he lacked one.[39]

After considerable negotiation, the Democrats chose Earl B. Dickerson as their candidate. Dickerson won immediate support of precinct captains but was slow in gaining support of the machine. While an adherent to the principles of the New Deal, Dickerson was intellectually inclined, somewhat independent in behavior, and in the eyes of many, a maverick undeserving of full party support. His uncompromising commitment to civic improvement and racial advancement also made him an anomaly among the Black Belt's political leadership. Mitchell, acting as Dickerson's patron, displayed an unusual amount of political honesty when he wrote to Dickerson: "Without a doubt you are by far the ablest man running for alderman. I think there is no comparison between your ability, your statesmanship and that of the others whose names will be on the ticket."[40]

Opposing Dickerson in the primary was Corneal Davis, a black aspirant who had allied with the independent, anti-Kelly-Nash faction headed in the city at large by white States' Attorney Thomas Courtney

WILLIAM E. KING

and in the ward by Christopher C. Wimbish. When the moment of political truth came in the primary, Dickerson easily trounced Davis by a margin of 7,500 votes, and King defeated Dawson in a close race decided by a margin of only 644 votes.[41]

The stage was set for the Second Ward general election. Mitchell urged Dickerson: "You must allow no grass to grow under your feet. . . . You have made a splendid fight, and you have done a mighty fine job in eliminating Dawson. You must now finish the job by eliminating King."[42] Dickerson drew unexpected support from the Courtney-Wimbish faction and from the Dawson faction of the Republican party. The fragile nature of the new circle of unity troubled Mitchell, who was suspicious both of Dawson's ability to deliver Republican votes and of Tittinger's new willingness to support Dickerson.[43]

Farther south in the Black Belt, the political activities of the Third Ward virtually

---

[39]*Defender*, Feb. 18 (p. 2, cols. 2-3), March 4 (p. 2, col. 5), 1939; Davis to Mitchell, Jan. 4, 1939, and Edison A. Love to Mitchell, Jan. 8, 1939, Mitchell Papers.
[40]McLendon to Mitchell, Jan. 18, 1939; Henry Woods to Mitchell, Jan. 24, 1939; Mitchell to Dickerson, Feb. 22, 1939, all in Mitchell Papers. See also Footnote 38.
[41]*Defender*, Feb. 18 (p. 2, cols. 2-3), March 4 (p. 2, col. 6), 1939.
[42]Mitchell to Dickerson, March 3, 1939, Mitchell Papers.
[43]Mitchell to McLendon, March 24, 1939; Mitchell to Dickerson, March 27, 1939; Mitchell to Tittinger, March 27, 1939; Dickerson to Mitchell (telegram), March 28, 1939; Tittinger to Mitchell, March 28, 1939, all *ibid*.

duplicated the Machiavellian activities that were occurring in the Second Ward. DePriest challenged Robert Jackson for the City Council post Jackson had held for twenty-one years. Already a victim of three consecutive, major defeats in the decade, DePriest was reduced to fighting for the scraps of political recognition. Appropriately, he was an ally to another fallen Republican, William Thompson, who was making his fifth bid for the mayor's office. Jackson was another pathetic figure who desperately tried to hold on to the only trapping that gave meaning to his political life. Running on his record of having been elected to his aldermanic post without defeat since 1918, he could claim very little else in the way of major accomplishments.[44]

The Democratic primary centered around candidates supporting or opposing the Kelly-Nash organization. The Sneed camp, after considering running no candidate at all, chose an outstanding one—Benjamin A. Grant, deputy coroner and graduate of both the University of Chicago and the John Marshall Law School. Grant's support from within the party almost guaranteed success from the start as Sneed got him the support of the entire Kelly-Nash organization, including Congressman Mitchell.

Opposing him was John A. Lewis, who had been considered one of Sneed's "closest advisors and supporters" and the president of the Third Ward Regular Democratic Organization before allying with the good-government faction of Courtney and Governor Henry Horner. Grant ran on a rather bland program that avoided the issues of municipal corruption and staggering unemployment. Lewis spoke candidly on the dilemma of being "a loyal and conscientious Democratic worker" in Kelly's Chicago, summing up poignantly the impact of the Depression and New Deal on Chicago's Black Belt:

For six years I have suffered the humiliation and injury of seeing our ward given only privileges that destroy good citizenship and decent community life. I have seen the moral foundation of women and children insidiously undermined. All this under the false cry of economic necessity. I have realized that the future economic and social progress of my people and community cannot be built under a system of political exploitation such as is encouraged by the present administration.[45]

The Third Ward primaries produced a close Republican contest—DePriest defeated Jackson by 1,200 votes—but a Democratic rout. Grant trounced Lewis by 8,500 votes and went on to defeat DePriest in April by 4,000 votes.[46]

In the Second Ward, where Dickerson had pitted the successes of the New Deal against the effete rhetoric of Republican opposition, Dickerson beat King decisively by more than two thousand votes. Alderman Dickerson proved himself politically astute as he quickly attributed his success to the Roosevelt movement. "In view of the fact that my campaign was based on the New Deal, I feel that my victory was a victory for the New Deal," he said. "While my opponent was slinging mud of a vicious sort, I stuck to the issues and told the people that I would do all that I could in the event of my election to carry forth the principles of the New Deal."[47]

The elections sealed the fate of Joe Tittinger as committeeman of the Second Ward. Tittinger had always faced criticism within the ward, but there was no strong contender for his post until William L. Dawson dramatically announced his conversion to the Democratic party. Only Dawson could bridge the gap between the parties. His efficacy as a vote getter for Earl Dickerson had made a good impression on the Kelly-Nash

---
[44]*Defender*, April 8, 1939, p. 1, col. 2, p. 2, col. 1.
[45]*Ibid.*, Jan. 21, 1939, p. 1, col. 3.
[46]*Ibid.*, March 4 (p. 7, cols. 7-8), April 8 (p. 2, col. 1, p. 12, col. 1), 1939.
[47]*Ibid.*, April, 8, 1939, p. 1, col. 2; Dickerson to Mitchell, April 7, 1939, Mitchell Papers.

hierarchy. Conversely, at one point Tittinger had opposed Dickerson's nomination. The presence of Dickerson and Tittinger in the same ward generated friction. Dickerson was a product of the district, and Tittinger was not. Dickerson was a noted attorney, active civic leader, and holder of a high Democratic state post; Tittinger possessed authority without prestige.

After Dickerson's victory, an open revolt broke out among Second Ward precinct captains over the issue of unemployment within their ranks. Forty-three—or almost half—of the captains were out of work at a time when most felt that there was work available. One captain was quoted as saying, "Hungry, unfed warriors cannot win fights." He complained that too many patronage jobs went to whites who were not captains and had not contributed to the party's success and that certain trucking jobs on federal projects had been given away to white drivers from outside the Second Ward. At one meeting Tittinger was soundly booed when he attempted to explain that he had delivered as many jobs as he could.[48]

Tittinger's performance in turning out the vote was criticized by party chairman Patrick Nash. After the poor showing of Democratic judicial candidates in April, Nash warned him personally, "If you don't deliver, you had better resign."[49] Precinct captains cautioned that Tittinger's recklessness increased the likelihood that Republicans would return to power in 1940. (While that possibility was actually remote, the captains' complaints and lower-than-expected

William L. Dawson's 1939 conversion to the Democratic party was dramatic proof of political realignment in Chicago's so-called "Black Belt."

voter turnouts did seem to influence the Democratic leadership at City Hall.) Mitchell, in the meantime, tried to bolster Tittinger's standing with party leaders during the summer with letters extolling his contributions to the party and accusing Dickerson and Dawson of fomenting dissension.[50]

The reality of the situation set in as preparations began for the Mayor's Christmas Fund. Dawson and Dickerson were appointed by Kelly to head the ward effort.[51] Within days, Dawson received patronage within the Second Ward without the consent or knowledge of Tittinger.[52] Pro-Tittinger precinct captains and Mitchell rallied to the Committeeman's cause, but by November, 1939, Dawson had officially replaced him. Some captains, apprehensive about what was transpiring, refused to report to Dawson for their instructions.[53] One political critic wrote, "Some of them wanted a Negro Committeeman and they have one now and

---

[48] *Defender*, June 17, 1939, p. 1, col. 3.
[49] Thomas J. Price to Mitchell, May 27, 1939, Mitchell Papers.
[50] *Metropolitan Post* (Chicago), Nov. 11, 1939 (clipping), and James P. Durden to Mitchell, Jan. 2, 1940 (incorrectly dated 1939), Mitchell Papers.
[51] *Defender*, Oct. 28, 1939, p. 1, cols. 2–3.
[52] Mitchell to Nash (telegram), Oct. 30, 1939, Mitchell Papers.
[53] Frederick Larkins to Mitchell, Nov. 6, 1939, and Durden to Mitchell, Dec. 23, 1939, *ibid*.

still they are not satisfied."⁵⁴ What many had wanted, however, was an improvement over Tittinger's leadership. To some, the elevation of Dawson brought none, and their previous dissatisfaction and opposition to Tittinger was merely transferred to Dawson.

The conversion of William L. Dawson to the Democratic party was a significant event in Chicago politics. He developed a close identification with the masses of the Black Belt, much as DePriest had done, becoming an outspoken champion of the rights of blacks. It was during that period that W. E. B. DuBois praised him on the basis of his reported statement, "I am not playing Party politics but race politics."⁵⁵ Dawson's private and public statements along with his political actions tend to support that assertion. His highly respected Republican contemporary Claude A. Barnett called him a "fighter [for his people], but level-headed."⁵⁶ On his responsibility as a racially-oriented politician, Dawson said quite pointedly: "I believe that only a black man can speak [on] what is in the hearts of black people.... I have seen these people who are unemployed. Thousands of them live here on the south side. Anybody who says they are lazy or shiftless or don't want to work simply distorts the facts. I have hundreds of them in my organization. Why must they be insulted by every peanut politician who wants to curry favor with reaction? I have seen some of these people take jobs at 10 cents an hour in order to buy bread and feed their children."⁵⁷

Dawson's switch in party affiliation was not unusual for the times and, in fact, was quite consistent with political and economic realities. One contemporary likened his conversion to the Democratic party to that of Saul on the road to Damascus, in that it was a genuine transformation in political allegiance.⁵⁸ As the hard times of the Great Depression were relieved by the economic upswing related to the nation's involvement in the European war, Dawson's image appears to have changed. When he made his move to national prominence in 1942, he became the third in a line of complex individuals who served the Black Belt in the United States House of Representatives. Dawson the congressman differed from Dawson the local politician—at least in terms of outward appearances in his dealings with whites. He was no longer the local, selfless, activist politician, but the mature, cautious politician who instructed blacks that "party should come first and race second."⁵⁹

The realignment in political affiliation from the Republican to the Democratic party was slow in coming to Chicago's Black Belt community and was not complete until after the decade of the Great Depression. Importantly, the rate of change was directly linked to the Democratic organization that the Kelly–Nash machine produced in the Black Belt. That change also illustrates the impact of the largesse of the New Deal under the influence of the Kelly–Nash machine, which, in meeting the exigencies of the Depression, weakened the once-solid bond between racial ideology and political affiliation.

⁵⁴*Metropolitan Post*, Nov. 11, 1939 (clipping), *ibid*.
⁵⁵W. E. B. Du Bois, *Dusk of Dawn: An Essay Toward an Autobiography of the Race Concept* (1940; rpt. New York: Schocken Books, 1968), p. 203.
⁵⁶Barnett to Hamilton, May 12, 1938, Mitchell Papers; Barnett to Joseph W. Martin, June 18, 1938, Barnett Papers.
⁵⁷William L. Patterson, "Dawson for Congress: A Progressive Negro Candidate," *Midwest Daily Record*, June 18, 1938 (clipping), Mitchell Papers.
⁵⁸Author's interview with Hon. Sidney A. Jones, Jr., Chicago, Oct. 25, 1978.
⁵⁹Clayton, p. 68; James Q. Wilson, "Two Negro Politicians: An Interpretation," *Midwest Journal of Political Science*, 4 (1960), 355–56.

The Detroit Race Riot of 1943

BY HARVARD SITKOFF

For the American Negro, World War II began a quarter of a century of increasing hope and frustration. After a long decade of depression, the war promised a better deal. Negroes confidently expected a crusade against Nazi racism and for the Four Freedoms, a battle requiring the loyalty and manpower of all Americans, to be the turning point for their race. This war would be "Civil War II," a "Double V" campaign. No Negro leader urged his people to suspend grievances until victory was won, as most did during World War I. Rather, the government's need for full cooperation from the total population, the ideological character of the war, the constant preaching to square American practices with the American Creed, and the beginning of the end of the era of white supremacy in the world, intensified Negro demands for equality *now*.[1]

---

1. Louis Wirth, *Research Memorandum on the Effect of War on American Minorities* (New York: Social Science Research Council, 1942), *passim*; Carey McWilliams, "How the Negro Fared in the War," *Negro Digest*, V (January, 1946), 67-74. On Negro militancy see Horace Cayton, "Fighting for White Folks?" *The Nation*, CLV (September 26, 1942), 545-52; Roi Ottley, "Negro Morale," *New Republic*, CXCV (November 10, 1941), 613-15; Charles Williams, "Harlem at War," *The Nation*, CLVI (January 16, 1943), 86-88; Adam Clayton Powell, Jr., *Marching Blacks* (New York: Dial Press, 1945), pp. 3-5, 125-32.

Mr. Sitkoff is finishing his Ph.D. studies at Columbia University and is now in the history department at Washington University, St. Louis.

Never before in American history had Negroes been so united and militant. Led by the *Baltimore Afro-American, Chicago Defender, Pittsburgh Courier,* and Adam Clayton Powell's *People's Voice* ("The New Paper For The New Negro"), the Negro press urged civil rights leaders to be more aggressive. It publicized protest movements, headlined atrocity stories of lynched and assaulted Negroes, and developed race solidarity. Every major civil rights organization subscribed to the "Double V" campaign, demanding an end to discrimination in industry and the armed forces. The National Association for the Advancement of Colored People, National Urban League, National Negro Congress, A. Philip Randolph's March-on-Washington Movement, and the newly organized Congress of Racial Equality joined with Negro professional and fraternal organizations, labor unions, and church leaders to insist on "Democracy in Our Time!" These groups organized rallies, formed committees, supported letter and telegram mail-ins, began picketing

In 1941 this wall divided the Detroit Negroes from the whites. This section of town was near Eight Mile Road.

and boycotting, and threatened unruly demonstrations. This as well as collaboration with sympathetic whites helped exert pressure on government officials.[2]

The combined effects of exhortation and organization made the Negro man-in-the-street increasingly militant. After years of futility, there was now bitter hope. As he slowly gained economic and political power, won victories in the courts, heard his aspirations legitimized by respected whites, and identified his cause with the two-thirds of the world's colored people, the Negro became more impatient with any impediment to first-class citizenship and more determined to assert his new status. Each gain increased his expectations; each improvement in the conditions of whites increased his dissatisfaction. Still forced to fight in a segregated army supplied by a Jim Crow industrial force, still denied his basic rights in the South and imprisoned in rat-and-vermin-infested ghettos in the North, he rejected all pleas "to go slow." At the same time many whites renewed their efforts to keep the Negro in an inferior economic and social position regardless of the changes wrought by the war. Frightened by his new militancy and wartime gains, resenting his competition for jobs, housing, and power, whites sought to retain their cherished status and keep "the nigger in his place." The more Negroes demanded their due, the more white resistance stiffened.[3]

American engagement in a world war, as well as the lack of government action to relieve racial anxiety or even enforce "neutral" police control, made it likely that racial antagonism would erupt into violence. President Roosevelt, preoccupied with international diplomacy and military strategy, and still dependent on Southern support in Congress, ignored the deteriorating domestic situation. Participation in the war increased the prestige of violence and its use as an effective way to accomplish specific aims. The psychological effects of war, the new strains and uncertainty, multiplied hatred and insecurity. Many petty irritations—the rationing, shortages, overcrowding, and high prices—

---

2. "Negro Organizations and the War Effort," Report from Special Services Division, April 28, 1942, R.G. 228, Box 427, National Archives. On the Negro press see Roi Ottley, *New World A-Coming* (Boston: Houghton Mifflin Co., 1943), pp. 268-88.
3. James Davies, "Toward a Theory of Revolution," *American Sociological Review*, XXVII (February, 1962), 5-18; Everett Hughes, "Social Change and Status Protest: An Essay on the Marginal Man," *Phylon*, X (First Quarter, 1949), 58-65; Ralph Bunche, "Conceptions and Ideologies of the Negro Problem," Memorandum prepared for the Carnegie-Myrdal Study of the Negro in America, 1940, New York Public Library, p. 161; Gunnar Myrdal, *An American Dilemma* (New York: Harper & Bros., 1944), pp. 1015-16; letter from Pauli Murray to Marvin McIntyre, June 18, 1943, OF 93C, Roosevelt Papers, Franklin D. Roosevelt Library, Hyde Park, New York.

engendered short tempers; and the fatigue of long work weeks, little opportunity for recreation, the anxious scanning of casualty lists, the new job and strange city, the need for the noncombatant to prove his masculinity led to heightened tension and the desire to express it violently.[4]

For three years public officials throughout the nation watched the growth of racial strife. Fights between Negroes and whites became a daily occurence on public vehicles.[5] Nearly every issue of the Negro press reported clashes between Negro soldiers and white military or civilian police. At least seventeen Negroes were lynched between 1940 and 1943.[6] The accumulation of agitation and violence then burst into an epidemic of race riots in June, 1943. Racial gang fights, or "zoot-suit riots," broke out in several non-Southern cities. The worst of these hit Los Angeles. While the city fathers wrung their hands, white sailors and their civilian allies attacked scores of Negroes and Mexican-Americans. The only action taken by the Los Angeles City Council was to declare the wearing of a zoot suit a misdemeanor. In mid-June, a rumor of rape touched off a twenty-hour riot in Beaumont, Texas. White mobs burned and pillaged the Negro ghetto. War production stopped, businesses closed, thousands of dollars of property were damaged, two were killed, and more than seventy were injured. In Mobile, the attempt to upgrade some Negro workers as welders in the yards of the Alabama Dry Dock and Shipbuilders Company caused twenty thousand white workers to walk off their jobs and riot for four days. Only the intervention of federal troops stopped the riot. The

---

4. Arthur Waskow, *From Race Riot to Sit-In 1919 and the 1960's* (Garden City: Doubleday & Co., 1966), pp. 220-23; E. L. Quarantelli, "The Nature and Conditions of Panic," *American Journal of Sociology*, LX (November, 1954), 267-75; Louis Wirth, "Ideological Aspects of Social Disorganization," *American Sociological Review*, V (August, 1940), 474-75. War tensions in Detroit are described in two "Commentator" columns by W. K. Kelsey in the *Detroit News*, June 22, 1943, p. 18, and June 25, 1943, p. 18.

5. Robert Lee Eichorn, "Patterns of Segregation, Discrimination and Interracial Conflict" (unpublished Ph.D. dissertation, Cornell University, 1954), pp. 61-64; Allen Grimshaw, "Urban Racial Violence in the United States: Changing Ecological Considerations," *American Journal of Sociology*, LXVI (September, 1960), 117; *A Monthly News Summary of National Events and Trends in Race Relations*, I (August, 1943), 9-10, cited hereafter as *News Summary*.

6. Nancy and Dwight Macdonald, *The War's Greatest Scandal! The Story of Jim Crow in Uniform* (New York: March-on-Washington Movement, 1943), pp. 2-3; *News Summary*, I (1943), 7-9; Walter White to Roosevelt, August 13, 18, and 20, 1941, OF 25, Roosevelt Papers; minutes of the Board of Directors, September 8, 1941, NAACP Papers, Library of Congress. Wartime lynchings are listed in Florence Murray (ed.), *The Negro Handbook, 1944* (New York: Current Reference Publications, 1944), pp. 169-72.

7. On racial tensions and rumors of riots see Will Alexander, Oral History Memoir, typescript in Columbia University Oral History Center, pp. 696-99; minutes of the

President's Committee on Fair Employment Practices then backed down and agreed to let segregation continue in the shipyards.[7]

Nowhere was trouble more expected than in Detroit.[8] In the three years after 1940, more than fifty thousand southern Negroes and half a million Southern whites migrated to the "Arsenal of Democracy," seeking employment. Negroes were forced to crowd into the already teeming thirty-block ghetto of Paradise Valley, and some fifty registered "neighborhood improvement associations" and the Detroit Housing Commission kept them confined there. Although 10 per cent of the population, Negroes comprised less than 1 per cent of the city teachers and police. Over half the workers on relief in 1942 were Negro, and most of those with jobs did menial work. Only 3 per cent of the women employed in defense work were Negro, and these were mainly in custodial positions. The Negro demand for adequate housing, jobs, recreation, and transportation facilities, and the white refusal to give anything up led to violence.[9] Early in 1942, over a thousand whites armed with clubs, knives, and rifles rioted to stop Negroes from moving into the Sojourner Truth Housing Project. Fiery crosses burned throughout the city. More than a thousand state troopers had to escort two hundred Negro families into the project. Federal investigators warned Washington officials of that city's inability to keep racial peace, and the Office of Facts and Figures warned that "unless strong and quick intervention by some high official, preferably the President, is not taken at once, hell is going to be let loose." Nothing was done in Detroit or Washington. Throughout that year Negro and white students clashed in the city's high schools, and the number of outbreaks in factories multiplied.[10]

Board of Directors, May 10, and July 12, 1943, NAACP Papers. On the riots see Chester B. Himes, "Zoot Riots are Race Riots," *The Crisis*, L (July, 1943), 200-201; Thomas Sancton, "The Race Riots," *New Republic*, CIX (July 5, 1943), 9-13; "Summary of a Report on the Race Riots in the Alabama Dry Dock and Shipbuilding Company Yards in Mobile," prepared by the National Urban League, Detroit Urban League Papers, University of Michigan Historical Collections, Ann Arbor. On warnings to Roosevelt and future racial violence see Vito Marcantonio and Philip Murray letters to the President, June 16 and 18, 1943, OF 93C, Roosevelt Papers.

8. "The National Urban League Report of the Detroit Riots," and Walter White, "What Caused the Detroit Riots," both in the Detroit Urban League Papers.

9. H. Black, "Restrictive Covenants in Relation to Segregated Negro Housing in Detroit" (unpublished Master's thesis, Wayne University, 1947), *passim*; B. S. Jenkins, "The Racial Policies of the Detroit Housing Commission and Their Administration" (unpublished Master's thesis, Wayne University, 1951), *passim*; Robert Weaver, *Negro Labor: A National Problem* (New York: Harcourt, Brace, 1946), chapter six; Alfred McClungLee and Norman Humphrey, *Race Riot* (New York: Dryden Press, Inc., 1943), pp. 7, 92-93.

10. Charles S. Johnson, *To Stem This Tide* (Boston: Pilgrim Press, 1943), pp. 50-59; the administration's desire to bury racial problems is seen in a letter from McIntyre to Charles Palmer, January 19, 1942, OF 93, Roosevelt Papers.

In 1943, racial violence in Detroit increased in frequency and boldness. The forced close mingling of Negroes with Southern whites on busses and trolleys, crowded with nearly 40 per cent more passengers than at the start of the war, led to fights and stabbings. White soldiers battled Negroes in suburban Inkster. In April, a racial brawl in a city playground involved more than a hundred teenagers. Early in June, twenty-five thousand Packard employees struck in protest against the upgrading of three Negro workers.[11] More than five hundred Negroes and whites fought at parks in different parts of the city. Negro leaders openly predicted greater violence unless something was done quickly to provide jobs and housing. Walter White of the NAACP told a packed rally in Cadillac Square: "Let us drag out into the open what has been whispered throughout Detroit for months—that a race riot may break out here at any time."[12] Detroit newspapers and national magazines described the city as "a keg of powder with a short fuse." But no one in the city, state, or federal governments dared to act. Everyone watched and waited. When the riot exploded, Mayor Edward Jeffries told reporters: "I was taken by surprise only by the day it happened."[13]

The riot began, like those in 1919, with direct clashes between groups of Negroes and whites. Over 100,000 Detroiters crowded onto Belle Isle on Sunday, June 20, 1943, to seek relief from the hot, humid city streets. The temperature was over ninety. Long lines of Negroes and whites pushed and jostled to get into the bath house, rent canoes, and buy refreshments. Police continuously received reports of minor fights. Charles (Little Willie) Lyon, who had been attacked a few days earlier for trying to enter the all-white Eastwood Amusement Park, gathered a group of Negro teenagers to "take care of the Hunkies." They broke up picnics, forced whites to leave the park, beat up some

11. T. M. Newcomb, *Social Psychology* (New York: Dryden Press, 1950), p. 596. On the Packard strike see J. F. Scott and G. C. Homans, "Reflections on the Wildcat Strikes," *American Sociological Review*, XII (June, 1947), 278-79. According to the Bureau of Labor Statistics, in the three-month period from March 1 to May 31, 1943, 101,955 man-days or 2,466,920 man-hours of war production were lost by hate strikes due to the employment or upgrading of Negro workers; Naomi Friedman Goldstein, *The Roots of Prejudice Against the Negro in the United States* (Boston: Boston University Press, 1948), pp. 49-50.
12. Minutes of the Board of Directors, July 16, 1942, NAACP Papers; *Detroit Free Press*, June 4, 1943, pp. 1, 9, quotes Walter White. Also see press release of John Dancy, June 26, 1943, and memorandum of William Baldwin, July 6, 1943, in Detroit Urban League Papers.
13. A. C. Smith, "The Negro Problem in Detroit," *Detroit News*, October 5, 1942, pp. 1, 4, October 6, 1942, pp. 1, 11, October 7, 1942, pp. 1, 4, October 8, 1942, pp. 1, 4, October 9, 1942, pp. 1, 4; "Detroit is Dynamite," *Life*, XIII (August 17, 1942), 15-23, dismissed by the mayor as "scurillous" in *Detroit Free Press*, August 17, 1942, p. 13. Jeffries is quoted in *PM* (New York), June 28, 1943, p. 3.

boys, and started a melee on the bridge connecting Belle Isle with the city. Brawls broke out at the park's casino, ferry dock, playground, and bus stops. By evening rumors of a race riot swept the island. Sailors from a nearby armory, angered by a Negro assault on two sailors the previous day, hurried to the bridge to join the fray. Shortly after 11:00 P.M. more than five thousand people were fighting on the bridge. By 2:00 A.M. the police had arrested twenty-eight Negroes and nineteen whites, quelling the melee without a single gunshot.[14]

As the thousands of rioters and onlookers returned home, stories of racial violence spread to every section of Detroit. In Paradise Valley, Leo Tipton jumped on the stage of the Forrest Club, grabbed the microphone and shouted: "There's a riot at Belle Isle! The whites have killed a colored lady and her baby. Thrown them over a bridge. Everybody come on! There's free transportation outside!" Hundreds rushed out of the nightclub, only to find the bridge barricaded and all traffic approaches to the Isle blocked. Sullen, the mob returned to the ghetto, stoning passing white motorists, hurling rocks and bottles at the police, and stopping streetcars to beat up unsuspecting whites. The frustrations bottled up by the war burst. Negroes—tired of moving to find the promised land, tired of finding the North too much like the South, tired of being Jim-Crowed, scorned, despised, spat upon, tired of being called "boy"—struck out in blind fury against the white-owned ghetto. Unlike the riots of 1919, Negroes now began to destroy the hated white property and symbols of authority. By early morning every white-owned store window on Hastings Avenue in the ghetto had been smashed. There was little looting at first, but the temptation of an open store soon turned Paradise Valley into an open-air market: liquor bottles, quarters of beef, and whole sides of bacon were freely carried about, sold, and bartered.[15]

As the police hestitatingly struggled to end the rioting in the ghetto, rumors of white women being raped at Belle Isle enraged white crowds

14. The description of the riot which follows in the next fifteen paragraphs is based on Brigadier General William Guthner, "Commander's Estimate of the Situation," June 26, 1943, in Publications during the Detroit Race Riots, R.G. 389, National Archives, Alexandria, Virginia; the report of the Governor's Fact-Finding Committee, *Committee to Investigate the Riot Occurring in Deroit on June 21, 1943* (Detroit: Dowling, Oscar Olander, J. H. Witherspoon, 1943), by W. Dowling, O. Olander, H. Rushton, and J. Witherspoon, cited hereafter as *Committee to Investigate Riot*; Lee and Humphrey. *Race Riot*; Robert Shogan and Tom Craig, *The Detroit Race Riot: A Study in Violence* (Philadelphia: Chilton Books, 1964), *passim*.
15. See footnote 3 and Harold Kingsley, "Memorandum on Detroit Race Disturbance," June 23, 1943, in Detroit Urban League Papers.

103

forming along Woodward Avenue. Unhampered by the police, the mobs attacked all Negroes caught outside the ghetto. They stopped, overturned, and burned cars driven by Negroes. The mob dragged off and beat Negroes in the all-night movies along the "strip" and those riding trolleys. When a white instructor at Wayne University asked the police to help a Negro caught by a white gang, they taunted him as a "nigger lover." The police would do nothing to help.[16] Throughout the morning fresh rumors kept refueling the frenzy, and the rioting grew. The excitement of a car burning in the night, the screeching wail of a police siren, plenty of free liquor, and a feeling of being free to do whatever one wished without fear of police retaliation, all fed the appetite of a riot-ready city.[17]

At 4:00 A.M. Detroit Mayor Edward Jeffries met with the police commissioner, the FBI, State Police, and Colonel August Krech, the highest ranking Army officer stationed in Detroit. With hysteria growing, and the ability of the police to control violence diminishing, most of the meeting involved a discussion of the procedure to be used to obtain federal troops. They agreed that the Mayor should ask the Governor for troops; the Governor would telephone his request to General Henry Aurand, Commander of the Sixth Service in Chicago; and Aurand would call Krech in Detroit to order the troops into the city. Colonel Krech then alerted the 728th Military Police Battalion at River Rouge, and assured the Mayor that the Military Police would be patrolling Detroit within forty-nine minutes after receiving their orders. Nothing was done to check the plan for acquiring federal troops, and no mention was made of the need for martial law or a presidential proclamation.[18]

When the meeting ended at 7:00 A.M. the Police Commissioner prematurely declared that the situation was now under control, and

---

16. "Report of Thurgood Marshall, Special Counsel for the N.A.A.C.P., Concerning Activities of the Detroit Police During the Riots, June 21 and 22, 1943," in Jeffries Papers, Burton Historical Collection, Detroit Public Library. According to *The Nation*, CLVII (July 3, 1943), 4, the police did nothing to interfere with white mobs but were quick to use violence on Negroes attacking white property. Waskow, *Race Riot to Sit-In*, pp. 209-10, emphasizes the importance of "unneutral" police behavior in a race riot.
17. Neil J. Smelser, *Theory of Collective Behavior* (New York: Free Press, 1962), pp. 71-73, 269; G. W. Allport and L. Postman, *The Psychology of Rumor* (New York: Henry Holt & Co., 1947), pp. 33-45, 193-96; and Allen Grimshaw, "A Study in Social Violence: Urban Race Riots in the United States" (unpublished Ph.D. dissertation, University of Pennsylvania, 1959), pp. 114-15.
18. Police Commissioner Witherspoon's Report to the Common Council, June 28, 1943, in OF 93C, Roosevelt Papers.

federal troops would not be needed. The opposite was true. Negro looting became widespread, and white mobs on Woodward Avenue swelled. Two hours later Negro leaders begged the Mayor to get federal troops to stop the riot. Jeffries refused, promising only to talk with them again at a noon meeting of the Detroit Citizens Committee. The Mayor would discuss neither the grievances of the Negro community nor how Negroes could help contain the destruction in the ghetto. A half hour later Jeffries changed his mind, telling those in his City Hall office that only federal troops could restore peace to Detroit.[19]

Harry F. Kelly, the newly elected Republican Governor of Michigan, was enjoying his first session of the Conference of Governors in Ohio when shortly before 10:00 A.M. he was called to the telephone. Mayor Jeffries described the riot situation to the Governor, asserted that the city was out of control, and insisted that he needed more manpower. Kelly responded by ordering the Michigan State Police and State Troops on alert. An hour later he telephoned Sixth Service Command Headquarters in Chicago. Believing he had done all that was necessary to get federal troops into the city, Kelly hurriedly left for Detroit. But according to the Sixth Service Command, the Governor's call was only about a *possible* request for troops.[20] Thus, the twelve-hour burlesque of deploying federal troops in Detroit began. The War Department and the White House flatly refused to take the initiative. Army officials in Chicago and Washington kept passing the buck back and forth. And both Kelly and Jeffries feared doing anything that might indicate to the voters their inability to cope with the disorder.[21]

After Kelly's call to Chicago, Aurand dispatched his director of internal security, Brigadier General William Guthner, to Detroit to command federal troops "in the event" the Governor formally requested them. Military Police units surrounding Detroit were put on alert but forbidden to enter the city. In Washington the top brass remained busy with conferences on the use of the Army taking over mines in the threatened coal strike. No advice or instructions were given to Aurand. The Washington generals privately agreed that Aurand could send troops into Detroit without involving the President, or waiting for a

---

19. Lee and Humphrey, *Race Riot*, pp. 29-30.
20. "History of the Detroit Race Riot," File No. 333.5, Sixth Service Command, National Archives; and Guthner, "Commander's Estimate No. 1."
21. Robert Lovett to Roosevelt, August 19, 1943, OF 93C, Roosevelt Papers.

This lone Negro man is being chased by a crowd of white men.

formal request by the Governor, by acting on the principle of protecting defense production. But the War Department refused to give any orders to Aurand because it might "furnish him with a first class alibi if things go wrong."[22]

While the generals and politicians fiddled, the riot raged. With most of the Detroit police cordoning off the ghetto, white mobs freely roamed the city attacking Negroes. At noon, three police cars escorted the Mayor into Paradise Valley to attend a Detroit Citizen Committee meeting. The interracial committee roundly denounced the Mayor for doing too little but could not agree on what should be done. Some argued for federal troops and others for Negro auxiliary police. Exasperated, Jeffries finally agreed to appoint two hundred Negro auxiliaries. But with no power and little cooperation from the police,

22. Colonel R. G. Roamer, "Summary of Events in the Detroit Riot," Roamer-Guillon transcript, June 21, 1943, 1:45 p.m.; and Lerch-Roamer transcript, June 21, 1943, 4:45 p.m., all in R.G. 389, National Archives. On the impending coal strike see Stimson Diary, June 21, 1943, Yale University, New Haven, Connecticut.
23. Lee and Humphrey, *Race Riot*, pp. 33-34.
24. Memo from Adjutant General, "Use of Federal Troops at Request of State," July 24, 1943, A.G.O. File 370.6, National Archives; Francis Biddle to Roosevelt, July 15, 1943, and Roosevelt to Biddle and Henry Stimson, July 29, 1943, OF 93C, Roosevelt Papers.
25. *Detroit Free Press*, June 22, 1943, p. 1.

the auxiliaries accomplished nothing. Rioters on the streets continued to do as they pleased. At 1:30 P.M. high schools were closed, and many students joined the riot.[23]

Shortly after three, General Guthner arrived in Detroit to tell Kelly and Jeffries that federal martial law, which could only be proclaimed by the President, was necessary before federal troops could be called in. Dumbfounded by this new procedure, the Governor telephoned Aurand for an explanation. Aurand, more determined than ever to escape the responsibility for calling the troops, confirmed Guthner's statement. Despite Jeffries' frantic plea for more men, Kelly refused to ask for martial law: such a request would be taken as an admission of his failure.[24]

Not knowing what else to do, after almost twenty hours of rioting, Jeffries and Kelly made their first radio appeal to the people of Detroit. The Governor proclaimed a state of emergency, banning the sale of alcoholic beverages, closing amusement places, asking persons not going to or from work to stay home, prohibiting the carrying of weapons, and refusing permission for crowds to assemble. The proclamation cleared the way for the use of state troops but still did not comply with Aurand's prerequisites for the use of federal troops. Mayor Jeffries pleaded for an end to hysteria, arguing that only the Axis benefitted from the strife in Detroit.[25]

On the streets neither the proclamation nor the plea had any effect. Negro and white mobs continued their assaults and destruction. The weary police were barely able to restrain whites from entering Paradise Valley or to check the extent of Negro looting. Just as the Mayor finished pleading for sanity, four teen-agers shot an elderly Negro because they "didn't have anything to do." Tired of milling about, they agreed to "go out and kill us a nigger . . . We didn't know him. He wasn't bothering us. But other people were fighting and killing and we felt like it too."[26] As the city darkened, the violence increased. At 8:00 P.M. Jeffries called for the State Troops. The Governor had ordered the force of two thousand mobilized earlier, but now the Mayor learned that only thirty-two men were available. At the same time the Mayor was informed that a direct clash between whites and Negroes was imminent. At Cadillac Square, the police were losing their struggle to hold back a white mob heading for the ghetto. Nineteen different police precincts reported riot activity. Seventy-five per cent of the Detroit area was affected. Sixteen transportation lines had to suspend operation. The Detroit Fire Department could no longer control the more than one hundred fires. Detroiters entered Receiving Hospital at the rate of one every other minute.[27]

In Washington, Lieutenant General Brehon Somervell, Commander of all Army Service Forces, directed the Army's Provost Marshall, Major General Allen Guillon, to prepare a Presidential Proclamation. At 8:00 P.M. Guillon and Somervell took the proclamation to the home of Secretary of War Henry Stimson. Sitting in the Secretary's library, the three men laid plans for the use of federal troops; as they discussed the situation they kept in telephone contact with the President at Hyde Park, the Governor in Detroit, and General Aurand in Chicago. Stimson instructed Aurand not to issue the text of the proclamation until the President signed it. Shortly after nine, Kelly telephoned Colonel Krech to request federal troops. At nine-twenty, the Governor repeated his appeal to General Aurand. Aurand immediately ordered the Military Police units into Detroit, although federal martial law had not been declared and the President had not signed the proclamation.[28]

26. Lee and Humphrey, *Race Riot*, pp. 37-41.
27. General Guthner to Lt. Colonel F. W. Reese, August 2, 1943, Detroit Race Riot, R.G. 389, National Archives; *Detroit Free Press*, July 1, 1943, p. 1.
28. Roamer, "Summary of Events in the Detroit Riot"; Stimson Diary, June 21, 1943; "Memorandum Re Race Riots in Detroit," June 21, 1943, Stimson Papers, Yale University.

23 DEAD IN DETROIT RIOTING; FEDERAL TROOPS ENTER CITY ON THE ORDERS OF ROOSEVELT

The New York Times *carried this story on page 1 on June 22.*

As the politicians and generals wrangled over the legality of Aurand's order, three hundred and fifty men of the 701st Military Police Battalion raced into Cadillac Square to disperse a white mob of over ten thousand. In full battle gear, bayonets fixed at high port, the federal troops swept the mob away from Woodward Avenue without firing a shot. The 701st then linked up with the 728th Battalion, which had been on the alert since 4:00 A.M., to clear rioters out of the ghetto. Using tear gas grenades and rifle butts, the Military Police forced all Negroes and whites off the streets. At 11:30 the riot was over, but the Presidential Proclamation was still to be signed.[29]

After Aurand transmitted his orders to Guthner, he had called Somervell to get permission to issue the proclamation. Somervell demanded that Aurand follow Stimson's instructions to wait until Governor Kelly contacted the President and Roosevelt signed the official order. Aurand relayed this message to Guthner, but the Governor could not be located until the riot had been quelled. Not until shortly before midnight did Kelly call Hyde Park to request the troops already deployed in the city. President Roosevelt signed the proclamation at 11:55 P.M. The Detroit rioters, now pacified, were commanded "to disperse and retire peaceably to their respective abodes." Twenty-one hours had passed since Army officials in Detroit first planned to use federal troops to end the riot. More than fifteen hours had been wasted since the Mayor first asked for Army manpower. Half a day had been lost between the Governor's first call to Sixth Service Command and Aurand's decision to send the Military Police into Detroit. General Guthner sat in Detroit for six hours before deploying the troops he had been sent to command. And it was during that time that most of Detroit's riot toll was recorded: thirty-four killed, more than seven

---

29. Aurand to Guillon, July 3, 1943, Detroit Race Riot, R.G. 389, National Archives.

hundred injured, over two million dollars in property losses, and a million man-hours lost in war production.[30]

The armed peace in Detroit continued into Tuesday morning. Five thousand soldiers patrolled the streets, and military vehicles escorted busses and trolleys on their usual runs. Although racial tension remained high, firm and impartial action by the federal troops kept the city calm. Following Aurand's recommendations, Guthner instructed his troops to act with extreme restraint. Each field order ended with the admonition: "Under no circumstances will the use of firearms be resorted to unless all other measures fail to control the situation, bearing in mind that the suppression of violence, when accomplished without bloodshed, is a worthy achievement."[31]

Continued hysteria in the city caused most of Guthner's difficulties. Rumors of new violence and repeated instances of police brutality kept the Negro ghetto seething. Most Negroes feared to leave their homes to go to work or buy food. Guthner persistently urged the Commissioner to order the police to ease off in their treatment of Negroes, but Witherspoon refused. Tales of the riot inflamed Negroes in surrounding communities. A group of Negro soldiers at Fort Custer, 140 miles west of Detroit, tried to seize arms and a truck to help their families in the city. In Toledo, police turned back 1,500 Negroes trying to get rail transportation to Detroit. Muskegon, Indiana Harbor, Springfield, East St. Louis, and Chicago reported racial disturbances. Aurand changed his mind about leaving Chicago for Detroit and ordered Sixth Service Command troops in Illinois on the alert.[32]

Unrest and ill-feeling continued throughout the week. The city courts, disregarding the depths of racial hostility in Detroit, employed separate and unequal standards in sentencing Negroes and whites arrested in the riot. With little regard for due process of law, the police carried out systematic raids on Negro rooming houses and apartments. Anxiety increased, isolated racial fights continued, repeated rumors of a new riot on July Fourth poisoned the tense atmosphere. Negroes and whites prepared for "the next one." Workmen in defense plants made knives

---

30. Roamer, "Summary of Events in the Detroit Riot"; Memo from Brehon Somervell to Stimson, June 22, 1943. WDCSA-370-61 (December, 1943), National Archives; and Roosevelt's proclamation, *ibid*.
31. Guthner, "Commander's Estimate No. 2"; Field Orders No. 1 and No. 2-A; Aurand Memorandum to Guthner, "Use of Troops in Connection with the Domestic Disturbance at Detroit, Michigan," June 22, 1943, all in R.G. 389, National Archives.
32. Guthner-Aurand transcript, June 24, 1943; Aurand-Guillon transcript, June 22, 1943; Guthner, "Commander's Estimate No. 2," R.G. 389, National Archives.

Crumbling Foundations

There is no reference to the Detroit riot here, but this appeared in the Detroit Free Press *on June 23*

out of flat files and hacksaw blades. Kelly and Jeffries urged the President to keep the federal troops in Detroit.[33]

While the troops patrolled the streets, the search for answers and scapegoats to give some meaning to the outburst began. Adamant that it really "can't happen here," the same liberals and Negro leaders who had warned that white racism made Detroit ripe for a riot now attributed the violence to Axis agents. Telegrams poured into the White House asking for an FBI investigation of German agents in Detroit who aimed to disrupt war production. When the myth of an organized fifth column behind the riot was quickly shattered, liberals accused domestic reactionaries. The KKK, Gerald L. K. Smith, Father Charles Coughlin, Reverend J. Frank Norris, Southern congressmen, and antiunion demagogues were all singled out for blame.[34] The NAACP aimed its sights at reactionary Poles who led the battle against decent Negro housing. Conservatives were just as anxious to hold liberals and Japanese agents responsible for race conflict. Martin Dies, Chairman of the House Un-American Activities Committee, saw the Japanese-Americans released from internment camps behind the riot. Congressman John Rankin of Mississippi taunted his colleagues in the House who supported the anti-poll tax bill by saying "their chickens are coming home to roost" and asserted that the Detroit violence had been caused by the "crazy policies of the so-called fair employment practices committee in attempting to mix the races in all kinds of employment."[35] Many Southerners blamed Negro agitators. Some talked of "Eleanor Clubs" as the source of the riot. "It is blood on your hands, Mrs. Roosevelt," claimed the *Jackson Daily News.* "You have been personally proclaiming and practicing social equality at the White House and wherever you go, Mrs. Roosevelt. In Detroit, a city noted for the growing impudence and insolence of its Negro population, an attempt was made to put your preachments into practice, Mrs. Roosevelt. What followed is now

---

33. Guthner, "Commander's Estimate No. 3" and "Commander's Estimate No. 4," R.G. 389, National Archives; and letters from Kelly and Jeffries to the President, OF 93C, Roosevelt Papers.
34. W. J. Norton, "The Detroit Riots—And After," *Survey Graphic*, XXXI (August, 1943), 317; George Beatty, "The Background and Causes of the 1943 Detroit Race Riot," April 14, 1954 (History Department, Princeton University), especially pp. 81-87; Granger to Dancy, June 21, 1943, and National Urban League Telegram to Roosevelt, June 23, 1943, both in Detroit Urban League Papers. Also see Stimson Diary, June 22, 1943; Sancton, *New Republic*, CIX (1943), 9-13; and the Civil Rights Federation of Detroit newsletter, *Action*, June 23, 1943, Detroit Urban League Papers.
35. Walter White to Frank Murphy, June 30 and September 1, 1943, Frank Murphy Papers, University of Michigan Historical Collections; and the stories on Dies and Rankin in the *New York Times*, June 24, 1943, p. 12.

history." A Gallup Poll revealed that most Northerners believed Axis propaganda and sabotage were responsible for the violence, while most Southerners attributed it to lack of segregation in the North. An analysis of two hundred newspapers indicated that Southern editors stressed Negro militancy as the primary cause, while Northern editors accused fifth column subversives and Southern migrants new to city ways.[36]

In Detroit the causes and handling of the riot quickly became the central issue of city politics. The Congress of Industrial Organizations, Negro organizations, and many civil liberties groups formed an alliance to defeat Mayor Edward Jeffries in November, to get rid of Commissioner Witherspoon, and to demand additional housing and jobs for Negroes. Led by United Auto Worker President R. J. Thomas and City Councilman George Edwards, a former UAW organizer, the coalition gained the backing of most CIO locals, the NAACP and Urban League, the International Labor Defense, National Lawyers Guild, National Negro Congress, National Federation for Constitutional Liberties, Catholic Trade Unionists, the Socialist Party of Michigan, Inter-Racial Fellowship, Negro Council for Victory and Democracy, Metropolitan Detroit Youth Council, Union for Democratic Action, and the March-on-Washington Movement. They were supported editorially by the *Detroit Free Press, Detroit Tribune,* and the Negro *Michigan Chronicle.* Throughout the summer the coalition clamored for a special grand jury to investigate the causes of the riot and the unsolved riot deaths.[37]

Michigan's leading Republicans, the Hearst press, and most real estate and anti-union groups opposed any change in the Negro's status. The Governor, Mayor, and Police Commissioner, abetted by the obliging Common Council, squelched the pleas for better housing and jobs and a grand jury investigation. Unwilling to make any changes in the conditions underlying the riot, the Republicans made meaningless gestures. The Mayor established an interracial committee with no

---

36. Stimson Diary, June 24, 1943; Shogan and Craig, *Detroit Race Riot,* p. 98; the Gallup Poll and press analysis are reported in *News Summary,* I (1943), 19-27.
37. On the formation of the coalition see the *Detroit Free Press,* June 23, 1943, p. 19, June 28, 1943, pp. 1-2, and June 29, 1943, p. 19; Lee and Humphrey, *Race Riot,* pp. 54-55; and the scores of resolutions passed by local unions and political associations in the Detroit Urban League Papers and the 1943 Mayor's Papers. On the United Auto Worker's race policies see Benjamin McLaurin, Oral History Memoir, typescript in Columbia University Oral History Center, p. 54; and two articles in the Urban League's journal: Louis Martin, "The Negro in the Political Picture," *Opportunity,* XXI (July, 1943), 104-07, 137-39, and Albert Hamilton, "Allies of the Negro," *ibid.,* 115-17.

AN EDITOR SPEAKS OUT
Linking of Southerners to Detroit Riot Protested

By the Associated Press

ATLANTA, June 22 — Ralph McGill, editor of the Atlanta Constitution, tonight protested to Detroit authorities statements that "an influx of Southerners" into war plants contributed to race riots in the city.

"Detroit is learning what the South learned long ago that the race problem is a national problem and not a sectional problem," he said in a telegram addressed to Mayor Edward J. Jeffries and Police Commissioner John H. Witherspoon in Detroit.

McGill's telegram follows:

"According to press reports you have stated that an influx of Southerners into Detroit's war plants contributed to the riots in your city. I wish to respectfully but emphatically protest this statement. Detroit is learning what the South learned long ago that the race problem is a national problem and not a sectional problem. It grows out of injustices, maladjustments and out of economic inequalities of which Detroit and the South have each their share. The South does not criticize Detroit but shares with Detroit the hope for an early settlement.

"What I do wish to protest is the cheap and easy habit of blaming any and all racial troubles on the South even when they occur in Detroit. The fifteen-year-old youngsters who began your riot certainly were not Southern workers. Please let me call your attention to the fact that the South, with 75 per cent of the Negro troops, most of them put down by some obscure reasoning of the War Department beside small rural communities with no recreational facilities for white or Negro people, and with 76 per cent of the nation's Negroes, still has had no real trouble.

"We have a real problem, we are working at it as we have. Detroit was working at hers. Ours may be set on fire as is Detroit's. We will try, with the people of both races working, the problem, to prevent. Meanwhile we ask that you contribute to further disunity the easy and unworthy disparagement of the South in the effort to explain Detroit's troubles. Cordially, with sincere hopes for a permanent and early solution of your troubles."

Deposit your War Bonds for safekeeping at Industrial National Bank. Est. 1886, Incorporated.

During and after the riot, many groups and individuals were blamed for causing the violence.

'HITLERISM SPIRIT' FOUND VICTOR HERE

Rabbis Note 'Barbarism Creed in Detroit Riots—Avoidance of Racial Violence Sought

INVESTIGATION SUGGESTED

Social and Economic Causes of Conflict Said to Be Deep—Evils and Injustices Cited

Unite for Victory--Smash the 5th Column

Hitler's fifth-column has struck at the war effort of our arsenal of democracy. It struck against our Commander-in-Chief, President Roosevelt.

The anti-Negro riots must be publicly branded for what they are—an Axis inspired effort, organized for the purpose of wrecking the unity of the American people and helping fascism. It is timed by the fifth-column as our boys are set to invade Europe.

The Negro people are exonerated from any responsibility for these riots. The finger of accusation must be plainly pointed to those subversive forces which first showed their hand in the Sojourner Truth Housing outrage, the Inkster and Eastwood Park troubles, the Packard strike, and now the present bloody violence.

Every Detroiter must insistently demand that Attorney-General Biddle and Prosecutor Dowling once and for all act upon the great amount of information given them in the past year as to the work and activities of Detroit's fifth-column, especially the Ku Klux Klan, and demand an immediate identification, punishment of these subversive forces and disbandment of their organizations.

Smashing the fifth-column conspiracy is primarily the responsibility of the white workers, the mighty unions and progressive organizations, in closest co-operation with their Negro fellow citizens.

Defense of the rights of the Negro people is the defense of America at war. All trade union organizations, officers, committeemen, stewards should take immediate steps to plan for the full protection of their Negro brothers, guarantee their security and ability to continue producing the sinews of war in the plants.

The people of Detroit urge Mayor Jeffries and Police Commissioner Witherspoon to compel the police to perform their duties and give protection to the Negro citizenry in a democratic and impartial manner, and immediately investigate those atrocious instances where police officers delivered the brunt of their attack not against the hoodlums who have brought such shame and tragedy to our city, but against the Negro people. An immediate grand jury investigation and the meting out of all punishment to all riot organizers and their accomplices must be demanded.

Let all patriotic organizations of the people, churches, fraternal, and especially the trade union movement unite more firmly to see to it that the Negro people be given their protection that they may make their proper contribution to the war effort of our country. We urge all Negro workers to return to their jobs to produce for victory. We call upon all white people to protect their Negro brothers.

The Communist Party calls upon the people of Detroit, and especially labor, to rally behind the city, state and Federal authorities, in the discharge of their duties in restoring law and order.

The Communist Party of Michigan calls upon the people of Detroit to form solid and united ranks and show their patriotic vigilance and real devotion to their country in the face of this organized conspiracy against the unity, strength, and military victory of the United States and the United Nations. Victory over the fascist Axis and its agents, the very survival of our country and its democracy depends on the exposure and defeat of this foul conspiracy.

COMMUNIST PARTY OF MICHIGAN
2419 Grand River, Detroit

power. After a few sleepy sessions, it adjourned for a long summer vacation. Commissioner Witherspoon refused to allow changes in the regulations to make possible the hiring of more Negro policemen. Instead of a grand jury investigation, the Governor appointed his own Fact-Finding Committee of four Republican law officers involved in the handling of the riot. And the Detroit Council of Churches, non-partisan but similarly reluctant to face the issue of white racism, called upon the city to observe the following Sunday as a day of humility and penitence.[38]

A week after the riot, Witherspoon appeared before the Common Council to report on his department's actions. He blamed Negroes for starting the riot and Army authorities for prolonging it. The Commissioner pictured white mob violence as only "retaliatory action" and police behavior as a model of "rare courage and efficiency." In fact, Witherspoon concluded, the police have been so fair that "some have accused the Department of having a kid glove policy toward the Negro." No one on the Council bothered to ask the Commissioner why the police failed to give Negroes the adequate protection required by law, or how this policy accounted for seventeen of the twenty-five Negroes killed in the riot having been shot by the police.[39] Two days later, Mayor Jeffries presented his "white paper" to the Common Council. He reiterated the Commissioner's criticism of the Army and praise for the police and added an attack on "those Negro leaders who insist that their people do not and will not trust policemen and the Police Department. After what happened I am certain that some of these leaders are more vocal in their caustic criticism of the Police Department than they are in educating their own people to their responsibilities as citizens." The Common Council heartily approved the two reports. Gus Dorias and William (Billy) Rogell, two Detroit athletic heroes on the Council, advocated a bigger ghetto to solve the racial crisis. Councilman Comstock did not think this or anything

---

38. Earl Brown, "The Truth About the Detroit Race Riot," *Harper's Magazine*, CLXXXVII (November, 1943), 489; *PM* (New York), June 27, 1943, pp. 3-5; for an analysis of police activities, see the report of Thurgood Marshall, July 26, 1943, "Race Riot—Detroit, 1943," R.G. 42, Box 75, folio 1, Michigan Historical Commission Archives, Lansing.

39. "Witherspoon Report." When General Somervell read it he exclaimed: "Now what the hell do we do with a case like that"; Shogan and Craig, *Detroit Race Riot*, p. 102. Exhibit XII of the *Committee to Investigate Riot* also blamed the delay on the Army, concluding: "At the time the troops arrived there was actually no violence to suppress." On the brutality of the police see Thurgood Marshall, "The Gestapo in Detroit," *The Crisis*, L (August, 1943), 232-33, 246-47, and footnote 16.

should be done. "The racial conflict has been going on in this country since our ancestors made the first mistake of bringing the Negro to the country." The conflict would go on regardless of what was done, added Comstock, so why do anything.[40]

Throughout July the accusations and recriminations intensified. Then, as the city began to tire of the familiar arguments, a fresh controversy erupted. When three Negro leaders asked William Dowling, the Wayne County Prosecutor, to investigate the unsolved riot deaths, Dowling berated them for turning information over to the NAACP that they withheld from him. He charged the NAACP with being "the biggest instigators of the race riot. If a grand jury were called, they would be the first indicted." The NAACP threatened to sue Dowling for libel, and the county prosecutor quickly denied making the charge. "Why, I like Negroes," he said. "I know what it is to be a member of a minority group. I am an Irish Catholic myself." The next day Dowling again charged an "unnamed civil rights group" with causing the riot. Witherspoon endorsed Dowling's allegation, and the battle flared. "It was as if a bomb had been dropped," said one Negro church leader. "The situation is what it was just before June 21."[41]

In the midst of this tense situation, the Governor released the report of his Fact-Finding Committee. Parts I and II, a detailed chronology of the riot and supporting exhibits, placed the blame for the violence squarely on Negroes who had started fights at Belle Isle and spread riot rumors. Content to fix liability on the initial aggressors, the report did not connect the Sunday fights with any of the scores of incidents of violence by whites on Negroes which preceded the fights at Belle Isle. Nor did the report mention any of the elements which permitted some fights to lead to such extensive hysteria and violence, or which allowed rumors to be so instantly efficacious. No whites were accused of contributing to the riot's causes. The sailors responsible for much of the fighting on the bridge, and the nineteen other whites arrested by the police Sunday night, escaped blame. The report emphasized the culpability of the Negro-instigated rumors, especially Leo Tipton's, but let the other rumors remain "lily-white." Although many instances of

---

40. Jeffries' "White Paper" is in the 1943 Mayor's Papers; *Detroit Free Press*, July 1, 1943, p. 1; Lester Velie, "Housing: Detroit's Time Bomb," *Collier's*, CXVIII (November 23, 1946), 78; Lee and Humphrey, *Race Riot*, p. 56.
41. Stories in *Detroit Free Press*, July 27, 1943, pp. 1, 3, July 28, 1943, pp. 1-2, 22; Earl Brown, *Harper's Magazine*, CLXXXVII (1943), 497; Shogan and Craig, *Detroit Race Riot*, pp. 105-06.

police brutality were attested and documented, the committee failed to mention them. And while only a court or grand jury in Michigan had the right to classify a homicide as legally "justifiable," the committee, hearing only police testimony, took it upon itself to "justify" all police killings of Negroes.[42]

Part III, an analysis of Detroit's racial problems, completely departed from the committee's aim of avoiding "conclusions of a controversial or conjectural nature." The section on those responsible for racial tensions omitted any mention of the KKK, Black Legion, National Workers League, and the scores of anti-Negro demagogues and organizations openly preaching race hatred in Detroit. Racial tension was totally attributed to Negro agitators who "constantly beat the drums of: 'Racial prejudice, inequality, intolerance, discrimination.' " Repeatedly, the report referred to the Negro's "presumed grievances" and complaints of "alleged Jim Crowism." In the world of the Fact-Finding Committee no real Negro problems existed, or if they did, they were to be endured in silence. Publication of the obviously prejudiced report proved an immediate embarrassment to the Governor. Most newspapers and journals denounced it as a "whitewash," and Kelly's friends wisely buried it. The Common Council then declared the riot a "closed incident."[43]

In Washington, too, politics went on as usual. The administration did nothing to prevent future riots or attempt to solve the American dilemma. The problem of responding to the riots became compounded when the same combination of underlying grievances and war-bred tensions which triggered the Detroit riot led to an orgy of looting and destruction in Harlem. Henry Wallace and Wendell Wilkie delivered progressive speeches; leading radio commentators called for a new approach to racial problems; and many prominent Americans signed newspaper advertisements urging the President to condemn segregation and racial violence. But the White House remained silent.[44]

---

42. *Committee to Investigate Riot,* especially Exhibits XVIII* and XIX. For a critical analysis see Detroit Chapter of the National Lawyers Guild, "Analysis of Report of Governor's Fact Finding Committee," in 1943 Mayor's Papers.
43. *Committee to Investigate Riot* and editorial survey in *Detroit Free Press,* August 24, 1943, p. 6; *Time,* XLII (August 23, 1943), 20, denounced the report as a "broad whitewash of the city's bumbling, do-nothing administration and incompetent police force."
44. Samuel Battle, Oral History Memoir, typescript in Columbia University Oral History Center, pp. 54-55; Lee and Humphrey, *Race Riot,* pp. 64-70; Walter White, *A Man Called White* (New York: Viking Press, 1948), pp. 230-41; and pleas to the President in OF 4245-G, Roosevelt Papers.

In much the same way it had handled the question of segregation in the armed forces and discrimination in defense production, the Roosevelt administration muddled its way through a summer of violence. The four presidential aides handling race relations problems, all Southerners, determined to go slow, protect the "boss," and keep the shaky Democratic coalition together, fought all proposals for White House action. They politely buried pleas for the President to give a fireside chat on the riots and brushed aside recommendations that would force Roosevelt to acknowledge the gravity of the race problem. The Interior Department's plans for a national race relations commission, and those of Attorney General Francis Biddle for an interdepartmental committee were shelved in favor of Jonathan Daniels' inoffensive suggestion to correlate personally all information on racial problems. Even Marshall Field's proposal to circulate pledges asking people not to spread rumors and to help "win the war at home by combating racial discrimination wherever I meet it," which appealed to Roosevelt, went ignored. The federal government took only two actions: clarification of the procedure by which federal troops could be called, and approval of J. Edgar Hoover's recommendation to defer from the draft members of city police forces. Like the Republicans in Michigan, the Democrats in the capital occupied themselves with the efficient handling of a future riot rather than its prevention.[45]

With a war to win, Detroit and the nation resumed "business as usual." Negroes continued to be brutalized by the police and to be the "first fired, last hired." In the Senate, the administration killed a proposal to have Congress investigate the riots, and Michigan's Homer Ferguson and Arthur Vandenberg stymied every proposal for Negro housing in Detroit's suburbs. Their constituents continued boasting "the sun never sets on a nigger in Dearborn." Governor Kelly appropriated a million dollars to equip and train special riot troops. Mayor Jeffries, running as a defender of "white supremacy," easily won reelection in 1943 and 1945. The lesson learned from the riot? In the Mayor's words: "We'll

---

45. The four Southern aides were James Byrnes, Jonathan Daniels, Stephen Early, and Marvin McIntyre. On a fireside chat see Daniels to Roosevelt, June 22, 1943, PPF 1820, and John H. Sengstacke to the President, June 29, 1943, OF 93C, both in Roosevelt Papers. Interior Department plans are in Saul Padover to Harold Ickes, June 29, 1943, PSF Ickes, and Ickes to the President, July 15, 16, and 26, 1943, OF 6, Roosevelt Papers. Also see Biddle to Roosevelt, July 15, 1943, OF 93C; Daniels to Roosevelt, July 23, 1943, Daniels to George Haas, July 28, 1943, and Daniels to Howard Odum, September 1, 1943, in OF 4245-G; and Marshall Field to Roosevelt, July 24, 1943, OF 93C, all in Roosevelt Papers

know what to do next time." Yet Southern Negroes continued to pour into Detroit looking for the promised land—only to find discrimination, hatred, a world of little opportunity and less dignity. The dream deferred festered like a sore, waiting to explode. "There ain't no North any more," sighed an old Negro woman. "Everything now is South."[46]

46. Henry Lee Moon, "Danger in Detroit," *The Crisis*, LIII (January, 1946), 12-13, 28-29, and *Balance of Power: The Negro Vote* (Garden City: Doubleday & Co., Inc., 1948), p. 154; Louis Martin, "Detroit—Still Dynamite," *The Crisis*, LI (January, 1944), 8-10; Lester Velie, *Collier's* CXVIII (1946), 76; and John Dancy to Harold Kingsley, October 29, 1943, Detroit Urban League Papers. Riot appropriations are discussed by Charles S. Johnson in *First Annual Report of the Illinois Inter-Racial Commission* (Springfield: Commission on Human Relations, 1944), p. 37. The Negro woman is quoted in Lee and Humphrey, *Race Riot*, p. 141. Also see letter from Richard Wright to Senor Frasconi, *Twice A Year*, XII-XIII (1945), 259-60.

JANET L. LANGLOIS

The Belle Isle Bridge Incident
Legend Dialectic and Semiotic System in the 1943 Detroit Race Riots

Cities and Signs

Your gaze scans the streets as if they were written pages: the city says everything you must think, makes you repeat her discourse, and while you believe you are visiting Tamara you are only recording the names with which she defines herself and all her parts. [Calvino 1974:14]

ALTHOUGH TAMARA is one of those cities Italo Calvino encounters in the fabled East of Marco Polo's 14th century, and Detroit is its antithesis in almost every way, his proposition linking city, sign and discourse connects them. The question, shared by many anthropologists, folklorists, literary critics, semioticians and sociologists, of whether or not every culture or every era has characteristic communicative forms, has been pulled into a circumscribed urban space in the constricted time span of a visit. What is the city's discourse? How does it name itself?

The complexity of a city's texts makes it impossible to know that answer completely—one's gaze is only a glance, after all. Yet the attempt to read its streets is the essential first step for any traveler making his or her way through town. Initially, the city's representative sign systems appear heterogeneous. Pierre Guiraud has pointed out the spatial signification of urban demography. He says simply, "The division of cities into districts and streets forms another sign system. In many cultures, castes and professions are grouped in certain districts with a Potters' Row or Weavers' Lane, etc." (1971:85–86). Academic interest in city dwellers' cognitive maps possibly comes from just this recognition that people learn "about the meaning of locations, about what is expected to go on where and who is expected to be doing it," in what Lyn Lofland calls "locational socialization" (1973:69).

The connection between urban space and action in Lofland's definition points to other sign systems based on behavior. Peoples' movement in public spaces where all are strangers with diverse world views has special import in the city context. Being urban involves both competency and performance skills in getting through the city's multiple kinesic and proxemic systems. Urban interaction, whether in subway, shopping mall, central business district or ethnic neighborhood, can define the city as a pluralistic community or as one stratified into hierarchies (Karp et al. 1977:97–129, 165–208).

Verbal sign systems have multiple realities in the city as well. Graffiti, shop signs, and billboards (Guiraud 1971:85–86) combine with newspapers, magazines, and books produced for and consumed by different reading publics in making the city streets into palimpsests. Television, films, and video games extend streets into interstate highways (Eco 1976:13) while folk narrative fragments them into sidewalks, crossings, and front steps. Linda Dégh has written that rumor, legend, and personal experience narrative networks "do not seem to wither under the impact of urban life" but, on the contrary, "appear to be the hardiest of folk narrative forms, not only in adjusting easily to modern conditions but by generating new types based on the most up-to-date issues of contemporary life" (1972:77). These oral genres refract and diffuse the city's definition of itself.

Looking for connections between the streets is a traveler's second vital step in reading the city. Each person must develop for himself or herself what Umberto Eco has called a unified approach to significant phenomena (1976:3). What sign systems run parallel to each other; what others at right angles? What systems support each other and which conflict? Because urban folk narratives (like narratives in general) contain references to other urban systems, they are metasigns or second-order systems useful in tracing the city's total discourse. Their structure, transmission patterns, and social meanings have already recorded the city's names. Yet the study of rumor and legend has rarely coincided with that of urban signs. This study attempts that correlation.

A third and final step in learning street language emerges for a city traveler who focuses on these urban connections. The intersection of signs confirms Calvino's implication that names mediate the city's reality. Its presence is both expressed and suppressed by signification. Knowledge of what power struggles are secretly coded in street corners and of what the city *does not* say about itself ultimately makes one street-wise. The invisible city surfaces, however briefly.

Detroit: A Case History

The city, however, does not tell its past, but contains it like the lines of a hand, written in the corners of the streets . . . every segment marked in turn with scratches, indentations, scrolls. . . . [Calvino 1974:11]

Although the city has been defined by its tolerance for alternative realities (Karp et al. 1977:131–163), the relationships between diverse urban groups periodically explode, most clearly in interracial violence and rioting. Since Lerone Bennett Jr. saw the summer riots of 1943 as "a basic turning point in the Negro-white *dialogue*" (as quoted in Lee and Humphrey [1968:xxiii, emphasis added]), it seems appropriate to trace the rhetorical features of the riot of June 20–21 of that year that left 34 dead, hundreds wounded, and indelible scratches in Detroit's skin.

Expanding Linda Dégh's and Andrew Vázsonyi's concept of legend dialectics (1973, 1976) from the polemical positions of participants in specific performances vis-à-vis belief structures under debate to the ideologically opposed positions of entire urban groups allows one to see the dialectic encoded in the famous bridge rumors said to have triggered the riot action on the evening of June 20, 1943.[1] Black accounts tell of whites throwing a black baby and, often, a black woman and her baby, from the bridge connecting the city to Belle Isle, an island park in the Detroit River. White accounts reverse the situation, telling of a white baby, or a white woman raped and murdered, being thrown off the bridge by blacks (Knopf 1975:155–156; Lee and Humphrey 1968:20; NAACP 1943:30–31; McCormick 1970).[2]

Although neither of these equally matched but racially opposed versions has ever been verified, their narrative structure duplicates the black-white opposition contained in other sign systems making up the social reality of wartime Detroit. In 1943, Detroit was literally divided in half by Woodward Avenue running north from the Detroit River. The black community involved in the riot lived just east of the Avenue and the white community just west of it (Fig. 1). Both communities had increased in population due to the massive inmigration of southerners, 350,000 strong, responding to Detroit's war production needs. Residents in both areas faced similar problems: inadequate housing, substandard living conditions, adjustment stresses and relatively low economic status (Hartman 1975:5–7; NAACP 1943:1–29).

Each community was named and so becomes an illuminated manuscript on Detroit's semiotic landscape. The black ghetto, called "Paradise Valley," its southern tip "Black Bottom," centered in the business and entertainment district of Hastings Street. Many of the businesses were black-owned, although several Jewish merchants still had property there, a visible reminder of the street at the turn of the century when it had been the heart of a Jewish ghetto. Within its social clubs, blind pigs, and restaurants, many black celebrities got their start, including Lena Horne and Joe Louis. Robert Conot called Hastings Street "shabby, tawdry ... with a patina of mystery" (1974:379). One-time resident Betty De Ramus called it "part carnival sideshow, with hard-drinking dudes and loud street ladies, and part close community, with people who looked out for each other" (1980:77). In the war years, the Valley's boundaries pushed against the Polish community of Hamtramck in the north and against a mixed-ethnic neighborhood to the south. Wiped out by urban renewal and the completion of the Chrysler Freeway in 1960, it is now contained in one building, the 606 Horse Shoe Lounge (Moon 1974:13, 19).

The Valley's white counterpart, "Cass Corridor," had become the unofficial port of entry for Southern Appalachian migrants in 1943 Detroit. The migrants, mostly young men who were not yet married or older men who did not bring their families with them, lived in rooming houses or apartments up and down Third Avenue. Third was called "Tennessee Valley" or "Little Kentucky" throughout the 1940s and 1950s. Stigmatized by the label "hill-

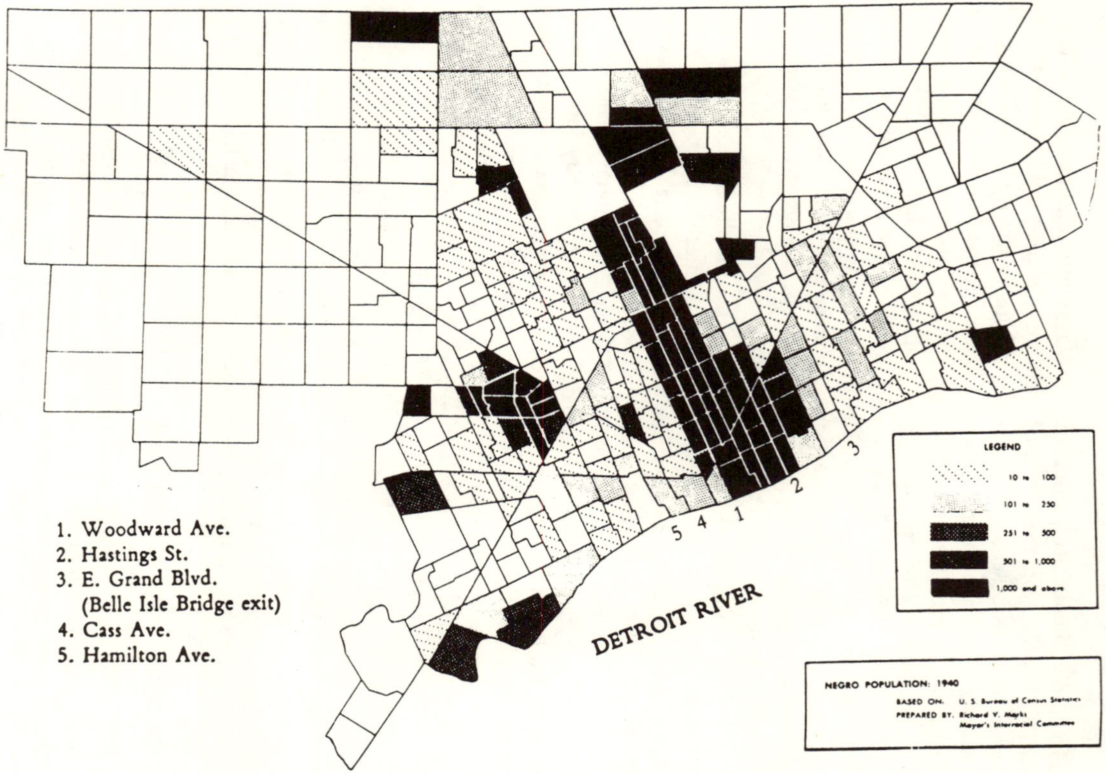

Figure 1. Demographic map of Detroit's black and white population in 1940. City of Detroit's Commission on Community Relations, *Maps of 1950 Detroit Population: Racial and Nationality Group Distribution.* Burton Historical Collection, Detroit Public Library.

1. Woodward Ave.
2. Hastings St.
3. E. Grand Blvd. (Belle Isle Bridge exit)
4. Cass Ave.
5. Hamilton Ave.

billies," the men formed a cohesive community. As an old-time Southern migrant told David Hartman, "That's where we were forced to live and now I can't see any reason for leavin'." When not at their jobs at factories spread throughout Detroit, Corridor residents turned to Hamilton Avenue, whose dance halls, pool rooms, cafes, and motion picture theaters matched up to those on Hastings Street. When the John Lodge Freeway cut through the area's commercial district in 1955, its viability as a working class community was destroyed. It began a steady decline into one of the deepest poverty areas in the city, a far cry from its upper-class status as a residential area for wealthy Detroiters at the end of the 19th century (Hartman 1975:1–15).

That the rumors pinpoint the Belle Isle Bridge as the place where blacks and whites met in reciprocal atrocity is also spatially appropriate. The bridge, an extension of Grand Boulevard at Jefferson Avenue east of Woodward, afforded one outlet for recreation to all the inner-city residents who were excluded from the parks in affluent suburbs. It was a location where the racial boundaries described above did not apply. On the Sunday evening when the riot began, a nearly equal mixture of people, estimated at 60,000 blacks and 40,000 whites, were picnicking on the island or starting on their way back to the city. Island and bridge were liminal spaces (Turner 1967:93–110) in Detroit's topography.

The riot action itself did begin on the bridge. Black/white confrontations throughout the city coalesced in the congested traffic coming off the island after a day of intermittent racial tension in the park. Young black men and sailors, who were mostly Southern Appalachian whites stationed at the Brodhead Naval Armory at the base of the bridge, began fighting. The violent action spread north, east, and west almost immediately, despite efforts by city police to contain the chaos on the liminal bridge. The movement of the rioting maintained the symmetry of the black/white dialectic, despite the memory of a bar owner in Paradise Valley that "police officers were not allowing the white people to go east of Woodward or the colored to go west of Woodward" in an attempt to stop the fighting (Horowitz 1970). White residents did go east of the line into Paradise Valley. Those who patronized the clubs on Hastings Street walked out in the early morning hours of Monday, June 21, unaware of the trouble. Others took their regular Monday morning or evening routes to and from work through the Valley. Still others entered past police barricades to fight. Black rioters stoned these pedestrians and motorists, sometimes fatally, and vandalized white-owned businesses.

Black residents also went west of the line. Black patrons coming out of the all-night theaters that lined Woodward Avenue on the edge of Cass Corridor were chased and beaten in the early morning hours. Black motorists, also on their way to and from work down the Avenue and not yet aware of the violence, had their cars overturned and ignited by groups of young white men who congregated on the street throughout the day. Several fatalities resulted. This violent double choreography was stopped only through the intervention of military police and federal forces early Tuesday morning, June 22.

The transmission of the bridge rumors was also a dual process in those few days in June. Dégh's and Vázsonyi's concept of legend conduit as "the sequence of individuals who qualify as legend receivers and transmitters" (1976:96–97) can be usefully applied to the double path the rumors etched in city streets. Equivalent but separate conduits of narrative were generated in the two communities east and west of Woodward. Contrary to T. A. Knopf's findings for the 1967 riots when the ghetto grapevine was opposed to the white suburban telegraph (1975:208), the opposed rumor networks in 1943 were both inner city. The localized spread of the alternate baby-throwing rumors in Paradise Valley and in Cass Corridor is supported by two pieces of negative evidence: (1) suburban oral histories of the riot make no references to them, and (2) contemporary newspaper reports of the riot gave them no coverage. Jay McCormick, a *Detroit News* reporter at the time, recalled, however, that "when they later sorted out the riot, they found that the same rumor had been spread in each community" (McCormick 1970).

At this point, social space and action are correlated with folk narrative in balancing racial rhetoric in the city. But what do these interlocking systems signify? What are they models of? Knopf's analysis of rumor in riot situations, congruent with Dégh's and Vázsonyi's general analysis of legend as the projection of folk opinions (1973:40), shows a major function to be the crystallization of the hostile beliefs held by each side: "The core of racial rumors is the animosity between blacks and whites. For white people, blacks are perceived as the cause of the trouble; for black people, whites are the cause" (Knopf 1975: 107–167, 206–212). Knopf notes that police brutality rumors are often spread in black communication networks and exaggeration of violence rumors in white, but that rumors about predictions of violence, conspiracy fears, and civilian brutality are common in both (1975:219). The bridge rumors, which Lee and Humphrey called "the myth so widely told and believed and so plausibly fitted into the crescendo of tension and violence," are certainly examples of this last category (1968:xvi). The shared narratives show that infanticide is a cultural code with overlapping meanings for blacks and whites in Detroit; one race's perception of the other's inhumanity becomes tangibly expressed. The rumors point to the semantic function of all the city's signs in textualizing Detroit's racial crisis (Turner 1974:37–42).

Yet the intersection of the lines in Detroit's past are complex and difficult to read. The invisible city reveals and hides itself in this layering of signs. The formal analogies that show the symmetry of the separate-but-equal status of the riot participants also conceal the city's disequilibrium. Knopf's analysis is useful once again in beginning to sort out the contextual features of the sign systems that ultimately lead to an awareness of asymmetry in the racial dialogue. She states that rumors with the same thematic content can be qualitatively different because each group circulating them has a different status within the social structure. She presents evidence, now all too well known, that inequities within the American social system, generally favoring white groups over black, have caused whites to fear the loss of status quo and blacks to demand justice (1975:149, 211). What Roger Abrahams has seen as essentially two different views of America, the first operating under the need for order (the equilibrium model) and the second for retribution (the disequilibrium model), underlies the formation of similar rumor networks and social action (1970:26-31). Following the lead of Knopf and Abrahams, then, it should be possible to show that the crisis in Detroit was actually two crises and that the infanticide rumor was actually two narratives from a semiotic perspective.

There is ample evidence that southern migrants were deeply frightened at the privileges they felt northern blacks were receiving (Conot 1974:378; Hartman 1975:5). J. Wallace Hushen, a *News* reporter at the time of the riots, remembered that a sailor who had fought on the Belle Isle Bridge told him that most of the southern sailors "thought that the northern Negroes were pretty uppity" (1970). It is possible, then, that the rumor circulating in Cass Corridor linked infanticide and rape to loss of control: "Look at what those blacks are doing. We have to keep them in their place. Equilibrium has been thrown off balance.

There is even more evidence that black residents of Detroit were deeply angered at the discriminatory practices they had to endure in the "Arsenal of Democracy" (Conot 1974:378-379; NAACP 1943:1-29). For example, 55 of the 185 wartime plants hired no blacks, and those that did hired only small percentages despite federal guidelines and the active work of local UAW and NAACP chapters. In early June, 13 days before the major riot, 25,000 white workers walked off the job at Packard Motors when several black workers attempted to upgrade their positions through the regular seniority channels. Julius Watson, one of two black skilled machinists in Ford's foundry in 1943, recalled that the pouring of iron, handling of heavy ladles, and working the molding machines were "black" jobs, traditionally the most difficult and lowest status positions in the factory system (Watson and Watson 1970). It is thus possible that the rumor circulating in Paradise Valley linked infanticide and murder to genocide: "Look what those whites are doing. They're trying to keep us in our place. We won't let them." Disequilibrium is confirmed.

Although there is no conclusive proof that these double linkages did create two distinct narratives in the riot dialectic, it is possible to know who won the argument. Only 43 of the 3,400 men on Detroit's police force were black in 1943. The unsuccessful police attempt to stop the riot, therefore, has generally been considered weighted against the black community. Of the 34 persons killed, 25 were black, and 17 of those were killed by police fire. Many more black rioters were arrested than white, although the case for equivalence of violent action has been presented above. The official riot report to the governor, coauthored by Detroit Police Commissioner John H. Witherspoon, charged black community members *only* for inciting the riot (Committee to Investigate the Detroit Race Riot 1943:1-13).

The asymmetry in the racial dialogue becomes most clear in an analysis of the part rumor was said to have played in the city's turmoil. Lee and Humphrey state that the baby-throwing rumors were "enough to turn the makings of a riot into a real one" (1968:xvi). Although Knopf argues that rumors cannot cause riots in and of themselves, she does agree that rumors can, and often do, intensify hostile attitudes that are, as Kenneth Burke notes, incipient actions (1975:160). This intensification function corresponds to Rosnow's and Fine's metaphor of rumor as the spark that ignites violence in stressful situations (1976:119) and to Knapp's analysis of the "wedge-driving" rumors that divide groups (1944:23–27).

The idea of rumor as a model for action has some validity in the Detroit context. The accounts of babies thrown off the bridge at Belle Isle presumably did have some rhetorical power in both the black and white communities because the rumor distribution and the riot action were remarkably synchronized, interweaving, and overlapping through the city's streets. It is possible that tellers and hearers acted because the stories were "real"; their narrative frames were erased in the moments of transmission (Stewart 1979:99–100; Katharine Young, personal communication 1981).

In retrospect, however, after the riot was over and when no babies, black or white, were found in the Detroit River, the accounts were found to be "false," for they stood in a paradoxical and metaphorical relation to the actual events (black and white men fighting) precipitating the massive rioting. Once the narrative frames were differentiated from the world, only the false rumor spread in the black community was officially remembered. The rumor spread in the white community was suppressed, and the rumor performance in the black was highlighted.

Jane Tompkin's poststructuralist warning about language and power is entirely applicable: "When discourse is responsible for reality and not merely a reflection of it, then whose discourse prevails makes all the difference" (1980: xxv). The official riot report is the discourse that prevailed. It was principally prepared by William E. Dowling, the Wayne County Prosecutor, and synthesized eyewitness accounts of the rumor event in Paradise Valley:

> The Forest Club is one of the larger recreational centers located in the Negro section of Detroit, commonly referred to as Paradise Valley. The club consists of a dance hall, a roller skating rink, and a bowling alley at the same address. Patrons, all Negroes, estimated at 700 in number, attended a dance there on Sunday evening, June 20. Shortly after midnight, Leo Tipton, an employee of the Forest Club Ballroom, assigned to the checkroom that night, appeared on the stage, and seizing the microphone in front of the orchestra leader, aroused the dancers with the following announcement: "This is Sergeant Fuller. There's a riot at Belle Isle. The whites have killed a colored lady and a baby. Thrown them over the bridge. Everybody get their hat and coat and come on. There is free transportation outside." Pandemonium broke loose! Some of the dancers dashed out of the building; others jumped out of the windows. . . . Tamble Whitworth, a special officer working at the ballroom, attempted to dissuade the people from leaving, but to no avail. The crowd milled about the intersection of E. Forest and Hastings Street. The transportation Leo Tipton had announced was available was not there to transport all of the mob. [Committee to Investigate the Detroit Race Riot 1943:10–11]

The report stated that "this occurrence excited passions and must be cited as the principal cause of the tragedy which followed," concluding that "more than 98% of the injuries" and "upwards of 95% of the property damage" would have been avoided if the fighting had stopped at the bridge and had not been fanned northward by Tipton's unfounded announcement. Footnotes recorded testimonies that Sergeant Fuller had been at home asleep at the time and that Leo Tipton, who already had a long police record, was arrested on July 30 on charges of inciting a riot for which he entered a plea of not guilty at his arraignment on August 5 (1943:10).

The NAACP's rebuttal to the Committee Report, prepared by Walter White and Thurgood Marshall, cited social inequities as the long-range causes of the riot but did not ignore the interplay of rumor and violent events as the short-term causes. The authors, however, reported the simultaneous circulation of both rumors in the Valley and Cass Corridor. They made it clear that the rumormonger discussed in the official report was only "an unidentified Negro at one of the Negro night spots" on Hastings Street and not necessarily Leo Tipton (NAACP 1943:30-31). This position is the one taken by Lee and Humphrey based on extensive interviewing of both black and white residents in Detroit immediately after the riot and by Knopf based on her work at the Lemburg Center for the Study of Violence at Brandeis University.

Despite these other voices, the Committee Report appears to be the model for most of the popular and oral histories of the 1943 riot. This situation should not be surprising, especially if one takes into account Alain Goldschläger's analysis of authoritarian discourse: "Power is based on silence, *not on dialogue*, and every authoritarian regime is based upon social and political structures that are univocal, meaning that they go from top to bottom, and do not allow movement in the opposite direction" (1982:12, emphasis added). Robert Shogan and Tom Craig use verbatim quotations, for example, in their book, *The Detroit Race Riot: A Study in Violence* (1964). The authors also use material from their 1963 inteview with Jesse Stewart, one of the few black officers on the force in 1943 and one of two suspended by the department for neglect of duty during the riot. Stewart told them that he had been off duty and was chatting with a friend in the checkroom at the Social Club while his wife visited nearby that Sunday evening, 20 years before. He had heard the incendiary announcement made by the bogus officer but was not able to locate him or to keep the dancers from erupting into the street (Shogan and Craig 1964:42-43).

Robert Conot, writing his influential *American Odyssey* ten years later, used both Lee and Humphrey's *Race Riot* and Shogan and Craig's work as sources. Nevertheless, he focused on the rumor performance in the black community in great detail and only briefly mentioned the rumors swirling through the white crowd on Woodward Avenue (Conot 1974:380-383). His account is similar to those quoted above, although the references to Leo Tipton and to free transportation are missing. Rumor event and its effect is channeled through the eyes of a young black, Donald Stallings, who may or may not be a fictional character.

In an unpublished 1970 interview, Louis Horowitz, who had a bar called Little Sam's in Paradise Valley that summer of 1943, recalled, "There's no doubt—no dispute about it. It was all started with rumor...." Mr. Horowitz briefly summarized the rumor content and transmission: "That there was a rumor that a white man took and threw a colored baby in the river at Belle Isle, and the rumor spread all the way to Forest and Hastings where Sonny Wilson had a bar." Mr. Horowitz continued: "And there was a crowd gathering at the corner there and there was two police officers that were walking a beat. Their names was Willie Williams and Jesse Stewart. The police department expected them to stop this so-called riot and they were suspended because the riot got out of hand." For Mr. Horowitz, "all the looting and shooting was taking place right in the colored neighborhood" and so it was not technically a riot between ethnic groups at all.

These accounts, metatexts of rumor performance and its effect, are themselves dynamic narratives. Detroit's past is not easily told. Its lines are smudged, ambiguous; they fragment. Events fall in and out of the interstices. Who told the rumor in Paradise Valley and where? Was it Leo Tipton? If so, did he impersonate Sergeant Fuller? If not, who did? Was the announcement made at the Forest Social Club or at Sonny Wilson's at the same intersection? Is it possible that the two bars were confused in memory, or that the same bar had two names, or that the same rumor was shared in all the bars along Hastings Street?

And what was Jesse Stewart's role in the riots? Was he off duty or on? In either case, his position, caught between the interests of his own black community and those of the police department, must have been untenable. Whatever his role in 1943, his narrative position as a mediator in two of the above histories signals a further power play of the city hierarchy. Not only was the white rumor erased from the city's past, but the white accounts of the black rumor performance use black informants to confirm black responsibility for "Bloody Week." This technique is clear in Louis Horowitz's response to the interviewer's open-ended question: "If'd you'd tell me about the 1943 riot?"

Actually, it happened on a Sunday night. I went to bed approximately say about, oh, close to midnight. I received a call from my manager. His name was James Davis at that time. He said that he'd received a call from the police department that there was rioting going on at Forest and Hastings. And I said, "What was it all about?" And he said that there was a rumor, and he used the term "rumor" (This is coming from a colored person), that a white man took and threw a baby into the river in Belle Isle. [Horowitz 1970]

This nesting of texts confirms Mr. Horowitz's status as an informed person, a feature of legend style here extended to oral history (Dégh and Vázsonyi 1976:102). It does so at the expense of black manager James Davis who, like Tamble Whitworth, Jesse Stewart and Donald Stallings, becomes a narrative pawn (Fig. 2).

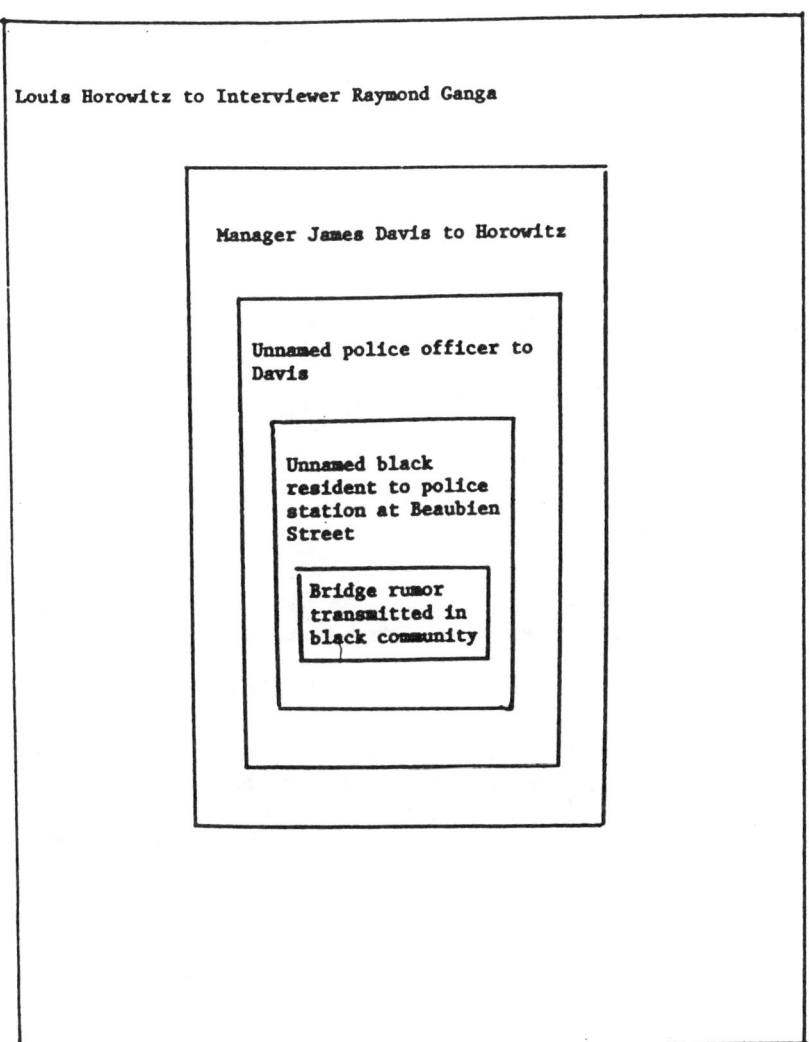

Figure 2. Nesting of texts in Louis Horowitz's oral history of the race riot.

Perhaps the final sign of the asymmetry discussed here is found in two of the oral histories created by interviews with black informants. Mrs. Everlee Watson, a Detroit resident since her 1935 move from Georgia, had been on Belle Isle with her family the evening the riot began and had later witnessed angry young blacks on Hastings Street. Mrs. Watson stressed that "it was really a race riot in 1943 . . . white and colored on the street rioting." Despite this conviction, her response to the interviewer's question about the cause of the riot, though more tentative, is similar to Mr. Horowitz's: "Well, I heard . . . but then you really never know. I heard someone said that this fellow came into the club where they had this dance, and said that a white man had just thrown a Negro woman and her baby into the Detroit River. Everybody filed out and it started" (Watson and Watson 1970).

Gordon and Lucille Hendrieth, born in Alabama, came to Detroit in the 1930s. Mr. Hendrieth, whose car had been overturned and ignited on Woodward Avenue, told the interviewer: "I heard it happened out to Belle Isle. Someone claimed that a child had been thrown into the water; I still say it was caused by the rough-ups in both groups." His wife continued: "A runner brought the word to the Forest Club, I remember having heard that. Predominantly young people were there. That's how it got out into the neighborhood" (Hendrieth and Hendrieth 1970). The suppression of racial balance and the oppression of memory seem complete when black residents know only this version of the riot's beginning. The dialogue has become a monologue. The city has not revealed all its past. As Goldschläger suggests, political rhetoric has created linguistic imperialism (1982:17).

Cities and Memories

The city is redundant: it repeats itself so that something will stick in the mind. . . . Memory is redundant: it repeats signs so that the city can begin to exist. [Calvino 1974:19]

The infanticide rumors that form the base for the discussion of Detroit's 1943 race riot set up reverberations. They carry overtones of the "castrated boy" legend complex that Barre Toelken has called "a startling kind of tableau that can express for a close group the most horrible aspects of interracial strife" and "a symbol of taking power away from someone" (1979:272). The racial asymmetry revealed in the previous sections edges up around these redundancies. What is it that the city is repeating? What power struggles, won or lost, are encoded in the semiotics of the city? What might be missing from our ethnographic record?

There are indications that the city of Detroit used social space, action and narrative as social signs in the riots of 1863 and 1967 in ways comparable to the 1943 situation. There are also indications that those recording the events did not see the hidden city, the suppressed discourse. In 1863, for example, recent Irish immigrants to Detroit were in much the same position as Southern Appalachian migrants almost a century later. They were confronted with discrimination in the housing and labor market while observing that northern blacks had their own homes and shops. The incident triggering the riot occurred after a failed attempt to lynch William Faulkner, a black man accused of raping two girls. On March 6, an Irish crowd turned to the black district, what would be the southern part of Paradise Valley, setting fire to businesses and homes, beating residents with clubs, and looking for the treasures rumored to be hidden there (Conot 1974:72–75). Conot cited the *Detroit Free Press*'s antiblack propaganda about baby-roasting and virgin-raping as instrumental in causing

"The Irish Riots," within the context of Civil War rhetoric about slavery.

Conot did not cite, however, the black community's response to white narrative and action. The baby-roasting charge was neutralized by the presentation of a similar charge against the Irish. A meeting was called at the A.M.E. church on Lafayette and Beaubien streets on March 11, 1863, five days after the riot ended, to draw up "An Expression by the Colored People of Detroit Concerning the Late Riot." One of the resolutions presented by the Chairman follows:

Resolved, that in the nature of this inhuman and unlawful mob, we find no equal . . . for the acts of violence and outrage committed on helpless females and infants, when endeavoring to make their escape from the burning flames and infuriated mob; especially in one instance, where a helpless babe was torn from the arms of its unprotected mother, and in her presence kicked and buffed until life was almost extinct. [Anonymous 1863:18]

This account, as well as a slightly different version first appearing in the *Detroit Free Press* on March 7 in which the woman and baby were driven back into the burning building by the crowd, was picked up by the abolitionist press. The pamphlet, *A Thrilling Narrative from the Lips of the Sufferers*, also gave the first-person testimony of Louisa Bonn, the wife of the black cooper whose shop was the first destroyed and the woman forced to retreat back into the flames with her child in her arms (Anonymous 1863:4-5).

The charge of virgin-raping was also neutralized by asserting that William Faulkner was not black but white. Testimonies in *A Thrilling Narrative* swore to this; a poem of sorts, composed by B. Clark, Sr., "a colored man," put it to verse:

Now be it remembered that Faulkner at right
Although call'd a nigger had always been white,
Had voted, and always declared in his shop
He never would sell colored people a drop. [Anonymous 1863:23]

In this case, the Irish monologue had become a dialogue through the defensive strategies of the black community. The offensive thrust of the white rioters had been counterbalanced, at least symbolically, with narrative.

The dialectic in the 1967 riots had quite a different configuration. Urban renewal and freeway construction in the late 1950s and early 1960s had caused many people to move from Cass Corridor and Paradise Valley. They had gone to the Twelfth Street area in Detroit's near northwest side where low-income housing was still available, following in the footsteps of Jewish residents of Paradise Valley who had taken the same path several decades before. By the mid 1960s, both Jewish and Southern Appalachian families had moved out to the northwest suburbs, leaving the area to blacks, although most of the businesses were still Jewish-owned. In a sense, the area was Paradise Valley transplanted, and Twelfth Street was Hastings Street with a difference (Conot 1974:435-440, 531).

The riot began here. The offensive was taken by black rioters this time, mostly young men who were caught in the inner-city trap of no skills in an increasingly technical world. A city police raid on an after-hours bar, where a party for two Vietnam veterans was in progress in the early morning hours of July 23, triggered them into action. Bottle and rock throwing at policemen assigned to cover the area escalated into city-wide confrontations with National Guardsmen. Looting and firing of Twelfth Street businesses also escalated into city-wide arson. The riot movement appeared to be an extension of H. Rap Brown's Detroit speech a month earlier: "Motown, if you don't come around, we are going to burn you down!" (Conot 1974:518–543).

The place of infanticide rumors within this tense situation is not clear. Stories of the child castrated by members of another race while his mother waited outside the public restroom had circulated for some years before the riot and for some years afterwards. In no way can they be seen as directly causal; they seem to form, instead, an interlocking network of narrative that contained the 1967 conflagration. In fact, the most often cited transmission of this story in Detroit occurred *after* the riot in the winter of 1967–68. Marilynn Rosenthal suggests that the narratives were symptomatic effects of the riot and not vice versa. She writes that the story had at least two versions in Detroit: "If the story is told in the white community, the boy is white and the teenagers are Negro. If it is being told by Negroes, then the mother and the boy are black and the teenagers white" (1971:36–37). At this point, the mutual transmission of the rumor, seen as a sign of Detroiters' mutual anxieties about further racial upheavals growing out of ethnic tensions, is similar to the 1943 situation (Rosenthal 1971:36–37; Rosnow and Fine 1976:3–4).

An analysis of Detroit's Rumor Control Center records from 1968 to 1974, however, shows that the black/white dialectic has once again been submerged. All the requests noted for rumor clarification came from white suburbanites.[3] They had either heard the story of the white child castrated or had read about it in a March 9 article in the *Windsor Star* (Windsor, Ontario, Canada) that, in attempting to debunk the rumor, had only spread it further (LaRonge 1979: 6–10). It is probable, given the deteriorated condition of black/police relations in the city, that no black resident hearing the story would check it out with the Control Center. The suburban telegraph as the most visible communication network appears to have cordoned off the inner city as effectively as the National Guardsmen did on July 27, 1967. The minority's voice was muffled once again through the nature of the city's power structure.

Since two folkloristic studies have concluded that this legend complex has always signaled the majority culture's fear of the minority (Ridley 1967: 153–156; Toelken 1979:176–179), it seems that every city has always hidden some of its past, muted some of its discourse. At the same time, the city gives just enough clues to keep one looking in the street corners for those revealing indentations. Detroit's 1943 Belle Isle Bridge incident offered unique possibilities for checking the equilibrium and disequilibrium of sign systems in the city due to the fullness of the record. The place of urban narrative was a central one in determining the use and abuse of power. It is the one instance that I know in which the ethnic dialogue was skewed by using the black version of the narrative about a victimized child against the black community as a conscious power play. In most cases, certainly those indicated briefly in the 1863 and 1967 city contexts, the black argument in the rumor exchange has simply not been noted in the literature, an unconscious and therefore more dangerous omission.

It is not commendable that atrocity stories are told by any group about another, or that any group has to live in segregated areas in the city, or that violence between groups must erupt as the final rhetoric. The full exchange, nevertheless, must be listened to and recorded. Folklorists are in a unique position to beat the city at its own game. We can hear Edwin Ardener's plea to see how social hierarchies can mute the very voices we most want to hear (1975a, 1975b). We must therefore record the city's total communication patterns. We owe that to the folk groups we have listened to for so long. Only then can the dialogue be fully played out, the violent conversation come to a close, and the city rest in its tolerances. Perhaps this peace can only be found in one of Calvino's invisible cities, but it is worth our ethnographic effort to find out.

Notes

An earlier version of this article was presented at the 1980 Meeting of the American Folklore Society. I would like to thank folklorists Michael J. Bell, Simon Bronner, Robert Winans, Katharine Young, and colleagues Leonard Tennehouse and Anca Vlasopolos for their comments. I would also like to thank the *Journal of American Folklore* reviewers for their useful criticism.

[1] The connection between these rumors and legends is supported by folk narrative studies that show the crystallization of rumor into legend or the reemergence of legend into rumor. See, especially, Mullen (1972:95–109), Rosnow and Fine (1976:11), and Toelken (1979:176–179). The relationship between these two genres, here treated as mutable forms, is explored more fully on pages 194–197 of the present article.

[2] Oral histories of the 1943 riot were created by students in Richard Reuss's 1970 seminar at Wayne State University and are now housed in the Folklore Archive there. Students were asked to develop their interviews around black, white, and suburban attitudes to the riot. I would like to thank Dr. Reuss, his students Raymond C. Ganga, Sister Joan Mumaw, IHM, and Kent E. Shafer, and the persons they interviewed for permission to use their material. Quotations from informants are cited in the references individually.

[3] Rosnow and Fine note the same situation for the Chicago Rumor Central (1976:122).

References Cited

Abrahams, Roger D.
  1970 Positively Black. Englewood Cliffs, NJ: Prentice-Hall.
Anonymous
  1863 A Thrilling Narrative from the Lips of the Sufferers of the Detroit Riot, March 6, 1863, with the Hair Bredth Escapes of Men, Women and Children, and Destruction of Colored Men's Property, not less than $15,000. Detroit: Published by the Author (Facsimile: Hattiesburg, Mississippi, Heartman's Historical Series, no. 72, 1945).

Ardener, Edwin
  1975a Belief and the Problem of Women. *In* Perceiving Women, ed. Shirley Ardener, pp. 1–17. New York: Wiley.
  1975b The "Problem" Revisited. *In* Perceiving Women, ed. Shirley Ardener, pp. 19–27.
Calvino, Italo
  1974 Invisible Cities. Translated by William Weaver. New York: Harcourt Brace Jovanovich. (Original: Le città invisibili, Torino, 1972.)
Committee to Investigate the Detroit Race Riot, 1943
  1943 Factual Report of the Detroit Race Riot of June 20–21st, 1943. Prepared by the Committee directed by Harry F. Kelly, Governor of the State of Michigan. Typescript copy housed in the Burton Historical Collection, Detroit Public Library.
Conot, Robert
  1974 American Odyssey. New York: William Morrow.
Dégh, Linda
  1972 Folk Narrative. *In* Folklore and Folklife, ed. Richard Dorson, pp. 53–54. Chicago: University of Chicago Press.
Dégh, Linda, and Andrew Vázsonyi
  1973 The Dialectics of the Legend. Vol. 1, No. 6. Bloomington, IN: Folklore Preprint Series.
  1976 Legend and Belief. *In* Folklore Genres, ed. Dan Ben-Amos, pp. 93–124. Austin: University of Texas Press.
De Ramus, Betty
  1980 Innocence and Vice on Hastings Street. *In* Blacks in Detroit: A Reprint of Articles from the Detroit Free Press, ed. Scott McGehee and Susan Watson, pp. 78–79. Detroit: Detroit Free Press.
Eco, Umberto
  1976 A Theory of Semiotics. Bloomington: Indiana University Press.
Goldschläger, Alain
  1982 Towards a Semiotics of Authoritarian Discourse. Poetics Today 3(1):11–20.
Guiraud, Pierre
  1971 Semiology. Translated by George Gross. London: Routledge & Kegan Paul. (Original: La Sémiologie, Paris, 1971.)
Hartman, David W.
  1975 The Development of Detroit's Cass Corridor: 1850–1975. Detroit: Wayne State University, Center for Urban Studies, Ethnic Studies Occasional Paper No. 3.
Hendrieth, Gordon, and Lucille Hendrieth
  1970 Interview conducted by Sister Joan Mumaw, IHM, on 14 March 1970. Mumaw Collection. The Race Riot of 1943: Negro Point of View. Folklore Archive, Wayne State University, Detroit, accession no. 1970(46).
Horowitz, Louis
  1970 Interview conducted by Raymond C. Ganga on 22 April 1970. Ganga Collection. 1943 Detroit Race Riot: Attitudes of the White-Man-on-the-Street. Folklore Archive, Wayne State University, Detroit, accession no. 1970(86).
Hushen, J. Wallace
  1970 Interview conducted by Raymond C. Ganga on 20 March 1970. Ganga Collection. 1943 Detroit Race Riot: Attitudes of the White-Man-on-the-Street. Folklore Archive, Wayne State University, Detroit, accession no. 1970(86).
Karp, David A., Gregory P. Stone, and William C. Yoels
  1977 Being Urban: A Social Psychological View of City Life. Lexington, MA: D.C. Heath and Co.
Knapp, R. H.
  1944 Psychology of Rumor. Public Opinion Quarterly 8:22–37.

Knopf, T. A.
  1975 Rumors, Race and Riots. New Brunswick, NJ: Transaction Books.
LaRonge, Philip
  1979 Legends Transmitted as Rumors Collected by the Rumor Control Center, Human Rights Department [Detroit, Michigan]. Folklore Archive, Wayne State University, accession no. 1979(87).
Lee, Alfred McClung, and Norman D. Humphrey
  1968 Race Riot (Detroit, 1943). With a New Introduction by Alfred Lee. New York: Octagon Books. (Originally published in 1943.)
Lofland, Lyn
  1973 A World of Strangers. New York: Basic Books.
McCormick, Jay
  1970 Interview conducted by Raymond C. Ganga on 27 March 1970. Ganga Collection. 1943 Detroit Race Riot: Attitudes of the White-Man-on-the-Street. Folklore Archive, Wayne State University, Detroit, accession no. 1970(86).
Moon, Elaine
  1974 (The Past Prologue) Paradise Valley. Detroit Discovery 1(5):13, 16–19.
Mullen, Patrick B.
  1972 Modern Legend and Rumor Theory. Journal of the Folklore Institute 9:95–109.
NAACP
  1943 What Caused the Detroit Riots? Written by Walter White and Thurgood Marshall. New York: NAACP.
Ridley, Florence
  1967 A Tale Told Too Often. Western Folklore 26:153–156.
Rosnow, Ralph L., and Gary Alan Fine
  1976 Rumor and Gossip: The Social Psychology of Hearsay. New York: Elsevier.
Rosenthal, Marilynn
  1971 Where Rumor Raged. Transaction 8(4):34–43.
Shogan, Robert, and Tom Craig
  1964 The Detroit Race Riot: A Study in Violence. Philadelphia: Chilton Books.
Stewart, Susan
  1979 Riddles and Proverbs of Textuality. Criticism 21(2):93–105.
Toelken, Barre
  1979 Dynamics of Folklore. Boston: Houghton Mifflin.
Tompkins, Jane P.
  1980 An Introduction to Reader Response Criticism. In Reader Response Criticism: From Formalism to Post-Structuralism, pp. ix–xxvi. Baltimore: Johns Hopkins University Press.
Turner, Victor
  1967 Forest of Symbols: Aspects of Ndembu Ritual. Ithaca: Cornell University Press.
  1974 Social Dramas and Ritual Metaphors. In Drama, Fields and Metaphors: Symbolic Action in Human Society, pp. 23–59. Ithaca: Cornell University Press.
Watson, Julius B., and Everlee Watson
  1970 Interview conducted by Sister Joan Mumaw, IHM, on 17 March 1970. Mumaw Collection. The Race Riot of 1943: Negro Point of View. Folklore Archive, Wayne State University, Detroit, accession no. 1970(46).

Wayne State University
Detroit, Michigan

THE HARLEM AND DETROIT RIOTS
OF 1943: A COMPARATIVE ANALYSIS

L. Alex Swan

INTRODUCTION

Traditional Definitions of Race Riots

Traditionally, race riots have been defined as a form of "group conflict in which members of race-conscious groups commit acts of violence indiscriminately against each other."[1] This is the definition upon which Gunnar Myrdal based his prediction, made in his classic study of the Black man in American society, An American Dilemma, that race riots were a disappearing phenomenon in the United States. Myrdal noted the large number of riots which had occurred in conjunction with the first World War--the most notorious of these was that of Chicago in 1919 during which fifteen whites and twenty-three Blacks were killed. The immediate cause of these riots was recognized as the unusually large migration of Blacks to the North and the "consequent displacement of some whites by Blacks in jobs and residences."[2] Myrdal concluded that since no such unusual migration marked the early years of World War II, "it does not seem likely that there will be further riots, of any significant degree of violence in the North."[3]

But between the time these hopeful words were written and their publication in 1944, America had suffered through a year of bitter racial strife, marked in particular by the Detroit riot of June 1943, and the Harlem outbreak in August of the same year. How could Myrdal have missed the signs, the ominous indications that riots, rather than a disappearing phenomenon were, in fact, the pattern for the future? And even more important, what was the nature of the 1943 riots? What can a study of two of them--

the riots of Harlem and Detroit--tell us about the state of American society during a crucial period of its history?

Signs: For and Against Riots

During the early years of World War II, it was easy to miss the signs of imminent racial crisis. In 1919, there had been riots in twenty-six American cities, but during the following two decades, few race riots had been recorded. Furthermore, there was increasing evidence that whites were more conscious than ever before of the demands of the American creed; there was a growing recognition that equality must have meaning in relation to the Black minority as well as the white majority. Finally, there were the obvious advances made by this Black minority--in education, in industry, in political power. In short, there were signs of a change in the pattern of Black-white relations that augured well for the future.

But in the opinion of most Blacks, the signs were indicative of only a superficial change: "Blacks saw progress but no real breakthrough; they saw cracks in the wall but no imminent emancipation from their second-class citizenship."[4] World War I had in truth marked not an end but a beginning, the beginning of Black racial consciousness. With his migration to the North, with his entry into American industry, the Black man was no longer an undifferentiated part of an ignored and isolated black mass.

To some degree, the Black man shared in the economic expansion of the twenties. The depression, however, proved the truth of the bitter adage with which the Black man memorialized his economic inequality: "Last hired, first fired." This was the policy of the day, and throughout the thirties "it became quite obvious that Blacks were suffering proportionately greater hardships than whites."[5] Although Blacks suffered discrimination in relief and work projects, the New Deal brought some relief, but almost as important, it brought to the Black leadership a new awareness of the possibilities of federal redress of racial grievances.

But the search for legal redress did not eliminate occasional outbursts of violence. On March 19, 1935, a riot erupted in Harlem. Thousands of Blacks stormed the business district causing more than two million dollars worth of property damage in what appeared to be a spontaneous, incoherent cry of protest. This riot was different from those that had attended the societal dislocations of World War I. Indeed by the traditional definition it hardly qualified as a riot: there was no engagement between warring racial groups but rather a frenzy of destruction by one minority group, an attempt to destroy the material and symbolic power which denoted their dependence and inferiority. The new Black spirit had found expression, and if the traditional meaning of riot did not seem to apply, it was the term that needed redefining in order to fit the actualities. Myrdal himself suspected that if riots were to mark future race relations they would follow the pattern of this Harlem riot of 1935.[6] Other commentators agreed.[7]

Old Versus New in Race Riots

In the 1943 riots of Detroit and New York are to be seen--virtually side by side--the old and the new in race riots. Detroit presents the traditional pattern of two race-motivated groups in violent opposition; New York, on the contrary, offers an example of destruction and looting by Blacks with virtually no contacts between whites and Blacks; in fact, opposition white groups never formed in New York, save for white police who attempted to enforce middle-class values with which the police themselves had identified. The causes of these two riots, as indeed of all race riots, are multiple rather than singular. Moreover, it is unlikely that any particular cause was present in one city and completely missing in the other. On the other hand, just as the nature of the two riots differs, so are there differences in the importance of specific irritants in each city. By ascertaining the general causes that underlie these 1943 riots and by noting the particular significance of individual grievances in Detroit and in Harlem, one can gain insight into the similarities and differences in the two situations. This insight can be deepened by comparing the two cities in terms of the behavior of rioters, of police and of government officials during the riot, and the sentiments expressed and action taken in the riot aftermath. Such comparisons should provide an understanding, first, of what is common to race riots--be they traditional or new--and, second, what combination of causes, behavior, and effects is peculiar to the new style: the style that, appearing first in Harlem in 1935, reasserting itself in the 1943 Harlem riot, had in the mid-1960's seared unforgettably the cities and the hopes of America.

Cause

The most basic and most general cause of the 1943 riots was the discrepancy between the promises of American democracy and the realities of Black life. This discrepancy did not, of course, first become apparent in that year, but during the year, it was spotlighted by the idealistic goals of World War II which were affirmed over and over again in an attempt to spur on the war effort. The idealism of the Four Freedoms--freedom of speech, freedom of religion, freedom from want, freedom from fear--was reiterated as an incentive to all Americans to share their blessings with others. But the Black man, alerted by his new race consciousness and by the aroused militancy of his leaders, felt that these vaunted blessings had never been his. Why should he fight to secure democracy and freedom for others when he himself had never known either? Such is the reasoning of the Detroit rioter who said: "I would rather die for democracy here than in Germany."[8] For the Black man, "freedom from want" and "freedom from fear" implied "freedom from unemployment, from barriers to jobs, and from inability to advance, and freedom from fear of discrimination, social humiliation, intolerance, and mob violence."[9] To gain these freedoms, he was willing to fight--at home as well as abroad. Black leaders did not hesitate to indict their country for continued injustice. One declared: "If the United States is going to assume a position of moral leadership in world affairs, it behooves her to clean her own house first."[10] A. Philip Randolph demanded: "There must be no dual standards of justice, no dual rights, privileges, duties or responsibilities of citizenship;" in short, "we want the full works of citizenship with no reservations. We will accept nothing less."[11]

In short, the idealistic banner under which World War II was fought furnished a rallying point for Blacks. Moreover, Blacks were aware of the awakening of large numbers of non-white peoples throughout the world. The Black American could identify, for example, with the people of India; both believed "that only as they push hard in this time of national need will their claims be heard."[12]

But the inevitable Black militancy, Black demands for full equality, Black identification with the emerging non-white peoples of other lands aroused fear and resistance among many whites. Friction between the two races was inevitable.

A major occasion for such friction was the racial situation in the armed forces. Here was the very essence of the American dilemma--segregated forces engaged in a war for freedom. Here also were the gradual changes which some whites found so threatening. Since the days of the American Revolution, the Army had maintained a strict policy of segregation of Black soldiers. World War II saw modifications of this policy but no basic changes, and the situation was even less promising in the Navy and Air Force.[13] "The paradox of the American people fighting racist tyranny abroad while the majority sanction the doctrine of white supremacy and racial discrimination at home has seared the souls

THE HARLEM AND DETROIT RIOTS OF 1943

of blackfolk" wrote one commentator.[14] And Walter White, president of the National Association for the Advancement of Colored People, declared: "No injustice embitters Blacks more than continued segregation and discrimination in the armed forces."[15]

Not only was the Black man relegated to all-black service units; he was further subjected to indignities and injustices at the hands of whites fearful of his new status as a soldier. In May, 1943, Judge William H. Hastie and Thurgood Marshall submitted a report on civilian violence against Black soldiers to the National Lawyers' Guild, which in turn formally placed it before the War and Justice Departments. The report called attention to an increase in the seriousness and frequency of acts of violence. The knowledge of killings was certainly present on the night of August 1, 1943, when Harlem crowds heard the rumor of the gunning down of a Black soldier by a white policeman.

The killings were known in Harlem and Detroit, but also known were the repeated irritations, the minor penalties imposed on a Black soldier because of what his color had come to mean.

Akin to the situation in the armed forces was the action taken by the American Red Cross which early in the war refused to accept blood from Negro donors. When this action was protested, the Red Cross, with the approval of Army and Navy officials, announced a new policy: Blacks could now contribute blood, but their blood would be segregated from that donated by whites. The sense of personal unworthiness and rejection that this policy imposed on many Blacks had an ironic footnote for those who knew that the scientist who perfected the technique of separating and preserving blood plasma was a professor of surgery at Howard University, the Black physician, Dr. Charles R. Drew.

If discrepancy between ideals and practices were the underlying cause of racial strife in 1943, and the situation in the armed forces and the Red Cross the most flagrant example of such discrepancy on a national scale, there was in every community a particular climate of unresolved tensions and accumulated grievances. The riot at Detroit was the product of one such climate.

PARTICULAR CLIMATE IN DETROIT

Employment

Detroit had its own peculiar history of race relations, of employment opportunities, of urban conditions, and it is only through a knowledge of this history that one can understand the nature of the Detroit riot as distinct from others of the same or of different pattern.

During the twenties Detroit had enjoyed an economic boom that sent the population soaring to 1.5 million, five times what it had been in 1900. Blacks comprised approximately ten percent of this total, although two decades earlier there had been only 5,000 Blacks in the entire city. The Depression years saw little change in these statistics, but with the initiation in 1940 of defense work in Detroit plants, a new surge began. It was estimated that half a million people moved into Detroit in the period 1940-43, and that in the fifteen months preceding the riots of June, 1943, this influx included as many as 50,000 Blacks.

This new wave of in-migration gave fresh stimulus to the racist organizations and individual hate-mongers that had long found in Detroit a license, even a welcome, for their propaganda. In addition to the Ku Klux Klan, which directed its appeal to the large number of transplanted Southerners, and the Christian Front of Father Charles E. Coughlin, who vented anti-Semitic tirades from his parish in suburban Royal Oak, there were Frank Norris--"the hell-shouting Negro-hating Texas preacher" whose tabernacle of intolerance was prospering[16]--and Gerald L.K. Smith, another inflammatory Protestant demagogue. In 1942 Life magazine predicted that "Detroit can either blow up Hitler or it can blow up the United States."[17] Local officials issued outraged denials of such charges, but Mayor Jeffries was later to admit that a riot was expected; it was clearly only a matter of time.[18]

The atmosphere of hate had long infected the employment situation in Detroit. The introduction of Black workers into firms where only whites had worked previously, or the upgrading of Blacks into jobs once exclusively the province of whites provoked alarm among many white workers throughout the country, but nowhere so much as in Detroit.

When the Packard Motor Car Company promoted two Black polishers to defense work in September, 1941, approximately 250 white workers staged a forty-minute sitdown strike; a similar work stoppage occurred a few months later at the Hudson plant.[19] The opposition of white workers was not ignored, but the Blacks had the support of the UAW-CIO and as a result the upgradings continued. So did the "hate-strikes". Whites, only too aware that Detroit tended to be a boom-or-depression town, feared the placement of Blacks in better positions as a threat to their own job security in the inevitable post-war readjustment. On May 27, 1943, twenty thousand Packard workers walked off the job to protest the upgrading of three Blacks in the aircraft division of the Packard Company.[20] For almost a week, war production was stopped. The bitterness of such encounters and that of the many that preceded it was still close to the surface when full scale rioting broke out a few weeks later.

Housing

In housing the situation in Detroit was equally explosive. Crowding and inadequate facilities had combined with a rapidly expanding population to force hundreds of families to settle in tents and shacks, families who had the money to pay for decent housing--if any had been available. Whites and Blacks were dependent upon the federal government for relief from this situation, but the federal government soon discovered that housing projects in the Detroit area inevitably became embroiled in the city's racial strife.

The Sojourner Truth project--named in honor of an ex-slave who had preached abolition and women's rights in various parts of the North during the nineteenth century--was completed in February, 1942. When the Black defense workers for whom it had been built tried to move in, they were opposed by white civilians protected by the police. The project adjoined a white residential area, and the local residents had brought pressure to bear on City Hall and on Congress to declare the housing units open to whites only. Federal officials had capitulated to the demand, but Detroit's mayor, Edward J. Jeffries, had forced them back to their original plan. Encouraged by the vacillation of the government and emboldened by sympathetic Detroit police, whites attacked and drove off the Black tenants. Black leaders charged that the violence had been instigated by the Ku Klux Klan. Although the charge was widely supported, no member of the Klan was ever brought to trial. Two months later the first Blacks moved into the Sojourner Truth project, under the protection of 1,750 city and state police.

A year later another housing project, this one a 3,000 unit development at Willow Lodge, was nearing completion. The National Housing Agency had ruled against bi-racial occupancy, but both Blacks and whites had appealed to the Detroit Housing Commission to open all units under its jurisdiction to any qualified tenant on a first-come basis. On April 29, 1943--seven weeks before the riot of June 20-21--Mayor Jeffries issued a statement, approved by eight of the nine City Councilmen, to the effect that the "racial characteristics" of Detroit neighborhoods must not be violated.[21] In short, Blacks were to be confined to such ghettoes as Paradise Valley.

Transportation and Recreational Facilities

Wartime had added other strains to the tension of urban life in Detroit. Transportation facilities were woefully inadequate, with many residents spending hours every day in bus or trolley queues. Nor did recreational facilities offer any relief. In 1943, Detroit had only two major parks; one of these was near the Black ghetto and was regularly fought over by white and Black teenage boys.

In short, all the classic ills--from sudden population expansion to employment strife to crowded housing to inadequate facilities for transportation and recreation--were present in Detroit. Furthermore, by June of 1943 the city had already established a pattern of reacting to these ills with violence. The Soujourner Truth riot and the Packard "hate-strike" were only the most notable incidents. Hardly a week passed in which a Black-white struggle did not demand police intervention.

CLIMATE IN HARLEM

By contrast the ills of Harlem were not quite so obvious, not so clearly on the surface. There was little overt antagonism between large numbers of whites and Blacks over jobs or housing. And yet Detroit and Harlem had much in common with each other and with the rest of the country. Blacks in both cities were experiencing the paradoxical combination of rising expectations and gnawing helplessness. Economically, socially, politically, the Black race was improving its position in American society, but the individual Black felt helpless to speed his own movement toward full and equal participation in the good things of American life. Even when he had the money, he found that he could not buy the standard of living that the white man enjoyed. He was hemmed in by prohibitions and discrimination.

After the Harlem riots of 1935, New York City showed some intention of displaying both leadership and tolerance. The full report of the committee appointed to investigate the 1935 riots was never released to the public, but there was evidence that some of its recommendations were being put into effect. City services in housing, health, education and recreation were expanded, and steps were taken to end discrimination in local civil service.

A major concern of the report was "the insecurity of the individual in Harlem against police aggression." This insecurity was said to be "one of the most potent causes of the existing hostility to authority." The report urged a "return by the police to the attitude that the first function of a police officer is to win the good will of those among whom he is stationed."[22] Whatever progress may have been effected in this direction, certainly no effort was made to implement the recommendation that a committee of from five to seven Harlem citizens of both race appointed to receive complaints of mistreatment by the police. Adam Clayton Powell, Jr., a Black member of the City Council, declared that police brutality complaints had been repeatedly ignored or whitewashed. He further asserted that the last few months had witnessed "a continual succession of unwarranted brutality perpetrated upon Black citizens in our city."[23] Two years earlier the City-Wide Citizens' Committee on Harlem had been organized, and by 1943, it could boast a good record of having secured employment for Blacks in department stores, insurance companies, and public utilities.[24] But the problems far outstripped the resources of one committee, no matter how well-intentioned. An editorial in the New York Times for May 29, 1943, noted the end of "Harlem Week"--but not of the "unfortunate conditions" that continued to plague that area: "segregation, high rents, low incomes, overcrowding, bad housing, a tuberculosis rate nearly four and a half times that of the city as a whole, a high street-accident rate, discrimination in employment, inadequate facilities for health education, lack of service opportunities for Black nurses and physicians."[25] There were calls for meetings and for investigations. There was even recognition of the fact that only a large-scale social reconstruction could really alter the situation. But the measures taken were never more than token--a few more playgrounds, an addition to the Black contingent of the police force, a promise of better schools after the war--and these were no longer enough.

Thus Harlem was seething, just as was Detroit. The half-million people who were crowded into the Harlem ghetto were in an ugly mood, and it was none the less dangerous because it did not involve the direct conflict with whites that marked the situation in Detroit. Physical clashes between the races in New York City might be confined to teenage gangs defending their "territory", but the individual Harlem Black was in no doubt as to the color of his enemy even if he did not fight him in the streets.

The enemy was the white man, often a Jew, who owned the tenements and the stores, and who forced the cost of living in Harlem "six percent higher than in all other comparable depressed areas."[26] The enemy was the white government that permitted segregation in its armed forces, that refused to pass the anti-poll tax bill, that made the FEPC another instance of mere tokenism, that failed to enforce in Harlem the ceiling prices set by the Office of Price Administration, that always offered too little too late. The grievances were both general and specific, abstract and concrete, but in no case were they really new; the enemy was "white power"; the mood was frustration. The combination was enough to provoke a race riot--new style.

SIMILARITIES AND DIFFERENCES IN EVENTS

Detroit

    As with the causes of these two riots, there were both similarities and differences between the events of Detroit and those of Harlem. In both cities the riots were ignited by the combination of a relatively minor incident and a succession of inflammatory rumors.

    The enkindling incident in Detroit was a fight between a Black man, Charles "Little Willie" Lyons, and a white man, Joseph B. Joseph, on the Belle Isle Bridge about ten o'clock on Sunday evening June 20, 1943. Belle Isle, a public island-park in the Detroit River, had been jammed that hot Sunday by about 100,000 persons, the majority of them Blacks. Since many whites resented the virtual Black monopoly of the park, and since some showed their resentment openly, racial incidents demanding police intervention had been numerous throughout the day. The one involving Lyons and Joseph burgeoned into a mass brawl, however, because of the frayed tempers of homeward-bound pedestrians and motorists caught in a traffic jam on the bridge. By the time police arrived "approximately 200 sailors were fighting with Blacks, and white men and Blacks were rushing into the fight," in the words of a police inspector.[27]

    Within an hour and a half fighting had spread to various parts of the city. Furthermore, a rumor had been started at a Black nightclub in Paradise Valley that whites had killed a Black woman and her baby on the Belle Isle Bridge. Whites returning from war plants also heard rumors--of the rape of a white woman by a Black man.

    During the early hours of Monday, large groups of Blacks began to loot and destroy white property in the Black ghetto. Looting and destruction of white property by Blacks had continued throughout the day. Whites who were caught in Black areas were beaten, stabbed and sometimes murdered. By noon white crowds had gathered on Woodward Avenue, and some of their number were hunting down and killing Blacks who ventured out from the ghetto. In the afternoon ten thousand whites mobbed the City Hall area, pulling Black victims from buses and trolleys.

The cost in blood and money set records that were not surpassed until the summers of the 1960's. Detroit could count thirty-four victims--nine white and twenty-five Black. Of the 675 injured, 219 were whites (including 75 policemen), and 156 Blacks. The loss in property--looted merchandise, gutted buildings, burned automobiles--was estimated at two million dollars.

The Aftermath

In the aftermath of the riot, Detroit made an effort to come to an understanding of its own behavior--but the attempt was never more than half-hearted. The city was so anxious to return to a "business as usual" policy that confrontation with the facts and with its own failures was made virtually impossible.

A special fact-finding committee appointed by Governor Kelly to investigate the riots included Detroit Police Commissioner Witherspoon and Wayne County Prosecutor William E. Dowling. By June 25, the committee issued its first report declaring that it had found "no evidence of subversive activities in connection with the riot."[28]

Other studies, investigations and reports were under way. Mayor Jeffries appointed a twelve-member inter-racial committee to study the race situation, but this committee quickly declined any responsibility for fixing the blame for the riots. Instead, the committee declared, it would confine itself to efforts to reduce race frictions. Obviously nothing very significant could be expected from an organization so anxious to evade the realities of the situation. In much the same way Police Commissioner Witherspoon and Mayor Jeffries issued reports designed to justify their own behavior during the time of crisis. In August the full report of the Governor's Fact-Finding Committee was made public. It proved to be a complete defense of official action and policy with all blame thrown on militant Black leaders, on the stridency of the Black press, and the actions of young Black hoodlums.

To balance such "white-washes" the National Association for the Advancement of Colored People undertook its own investigation. The Association's study was deeply critical of the Detroit Police Department, many of whose members, it was charged, were sympathetic with the white mob. One of the most memorable news pictures showed a Black held up by two policemen while a white man pummeled him in the face. There was also the grim statistic that out of twenty-five Blacks killed, seventeen died at the hands of the police, but not a single white died under such circumstances. And as _Life_ magazine reported: The police "used tear gas and (sometimes) night sticks on white mobs, tommy guns and pistols on Blacks."[29] The bitter cynicism to which such behavior was driving the Negro was evidenced in the columns of the Black press:

> What were the police doing when Negroes were being beaten in the Negro district? Arresting Negroes. What were the police doing when street cars were stopped by the mob and Negroes mobbed and beaten? They were arresting Negroes. What were the police doing when automobiles bearing Negroes were stopped, turned over and demolished and their occupants beaten? They were arresting Negroes. It is crystal clear that in no American community is the police power going to be used against the majority from which the mob comes to protect the minority from which the victims come. That much Negroes ought to face.[30]

The Detroit riot of 1943 gradually faded into history; soon it was only an unpleasant memory. But what had the city learned from its tragic experience? What steps were taken to guarantee that no such savagery should again tear at the very fabric of civilized life?

Detroit's failure was not unique. The federal government and the officials of other cities shuddered at what had happened but offered little in the way of prevention or cure. Weighed against the deep, entrenched prejudice that could ignite a Detroit riot, the radio dramatization by Columbia Broadcasting Station of the events at Detroit seemed well-intentioned but futile.[31] Yet this seemed the best the nation had to offer--good intentions--when what was needed was radical social reconstruction. Under the circumstances the Harlem riot of August 1 was to be expected.

Harlem

The enkindling incident that set Harlem ablaze with riot was the shooting of a Black military policeman, Robert J. Bandy, by a white policeman in the lobby of a Harlem hotel Sunday night, August 1. Bandy had come to New York from a New Jersey camp to spend Sunday with his mother and his fiancee. Bandy's mother, who lived in Middletown, Connecticut, had checked out of the Braddock Hotel around four Sunday afternoon. The three had returned to the hotel in the evening, after dinner and the movies, to pick up the mother's luggage. There they found an altercation between the room clerk and a Black woman over the refund of a dollar. Patrolman James Collins was called to the hotel desk when the woman, Margie Polite, was defined as obstreperous.

When Bandy saw the white officer pushing Miss Polite to the exit, he intervened, accusing the policeman of mistreating the woman because she was Black. A fight ensued. Either Collins threw his nightstick at Bandy and missed whereupon Bandy picked up the nightstick, or Bandy simply seized the nightstick and struck the officer across the cheekbone. At any rate, when Bandy failed to obey an order to give way, the policeman fired a shot, wounding Bandy in the left shoulder. The wound was not serious; the attitude of the police was negative.

An angry crowd quickly gathered, and in a few minutes the rumor spread that a Black soldier had been shot and killed by a white policeman. The rumor gained extra fillip from the emphasis on details such as "shot in the back," "before the eyes of his own mother," "in defense of a Black woman." Before long, thousands of Blacks were milling about in the streets.

The rumor had touched on one of the sorest points in the Black man's consciousness--the discrimination against Black men in the armed services. But this sore point lay close to many other grievances, and soon the crowd found an outlet for its aroused anger. The symbols of the white oppressor stood ready in the shining plate-glass windows of stores along 125th Street. Someone heaved a brick, glass shattered. Others picked up objects and flung them. The anger and hatred now turned outward in a burst of energetic destruction.

The large amount of looting was one reason for the later statement by the press and by both white and Black leaders that this was not a race riot. The other reason was the almost total absence of black-white clashes. There were only a few whites in the area at the time, and since the riot was almost completely quelled before daybreak, there was no opportunity for whites to gather. Furthermore, as already seen, the incentives to white mob action that existed in Detroit were not present to the same degree in New York City. Almost within minutes of the onset of riot conditions, Mayor La Guardia was on the scene. Accompanied by three leaders of the black community, he toured the district, appealing to the people to leave the streets and return to their homes. Occasionally he was jeered and booed--perhaps in response to his loudspeaker announcement that this was not a race riot--but in many cases his appeal was honored.

The leaders of Harlem were invited to a strategy meeting, and their suggestions acted upon. One of the most effective was to request the army to send Black as well as white MP's for removing of military personnel from the district. City police were instructed by Commissioner Valentine to use only as much force as was absolutely necessary, to remain impersonal in discharging their duties, and to disperse crowds as diplomatically as possible. Neither tear gas nor riot guns were used, and arrests were limited to those who appeared to be ringleaders.

Throughout the night the Mayor made radio broadcasts to the people, informing them of the situation and dispelling the false rumor that Bandy had been killed. Several Black leaders followed him on the air to appeal to the people to hasten the restoration of peace by returning to their homes.[32]

In spite of what was acknowledged on all sides to be the noble work of the Mayor and police,[33] the riot had proved to be most destructive. Five lay dead, and almost five hundred injured. Property damage was estimated to be in excess of five million dollars. Hundreds were under arrest.

The Aftermath

As in Detroit, the wake of riot brought forth various charges and counter-charges, studies and proposals, but very little constructive action. Perhaps the most curious reaction was that already referred to--the reiteration that this was not a race riot. If Mayor La Guardia did not start the trend, he was certainly one of the earliest to take up the cry. But there was virtual unanimity on this point.[34]

But even those who were most adamant in maintaining that Harlem had not experienced a race riot could not forego pointing to the social and economic conditions that provided the fuel for such an outbreak. Nor was it denied that these conditions were based primarily on racial discrimination. Apparently the term "race riot" was being restricted--rather arbitrarily and without strict attention to consistency--to clashes involving physical contact between the two races rather than to any riot with racial implications. One rather ludicrous result was an editorial in the New York Times which congratulated the city on having escaped a race riot: "We can be pretty sure that if race riots did not break out in Harlem and other parts of the city under the excitements and incitements of Sunday night's events they will not break out in this city."[35] But the editorial of the preceding day had listed enough grievances among the Black population to assure a race riot once the fuse was lit.[36]

The concern with terms and designations was one way of avoiding action. Another way was by making charges. The day after it had placed an advertisement in the New York Times praising the Mayor for his "prompt and well-tempered action,"[37] the City-Wide

THE HARLEM AND DETROIT RIOTS OF 1943

Citizen's Committee on Harlem attacked the La Guardia administration for failure to eliminate basic causes. The Mayor's attitude, it charged, "has been consistently that of minimizing the problem and of reducing appropriations for corrective services."[38]

Others joined in the accusation that the 1935 recommendations had been ignored and that the city as a whole had not done enough to prevent a riot. And certainly Mayor La Guardia had shown a certain insensitivity to Black feelings when he declared in one of his radio broadcasts on the night of rioting: "the people of West Harlem know that they have no cause to complain."[39]

Those who condoned the riots and those who condemned them were distinguished from each other not by awareness of racial injustices but by their frame of reference--those with a broad social-ethical orientation opposing violence condemned them. Those concerned with a specific subjective social injustice condoned them; their attitude as Kenneth Clark's study describes it was one of accepting "group violence as a means to the end of rectifying the specific injustice."[40] This study might well provide some understanding of the present rash of racial riots.

Clark's thesis is that in Harlem in 1943 the rioters were those who accepted violence as a legitimate social means of achieving a legitimate social end. Black acceptance of violence on this basis would seem to be more widespread today, than at any time in the past. Black spokesmen openly advocate violence, some charging that the white American has himself never chosen nonviolence as a strategy and that he shows no respect for those who do. If one accepts this argument, one might consider that the more ready acceptance of the Indian minority by the white majority can be traced in part to the image of the Indian as a "fighting brave" whereas the stock Black image is of a tractable or even cringing slave--an Uncle Tom. If the Negro seeks to establish a new image of himself as a non-pacifist activist, he cannot but find encouragement in the American heritage of violence and in the news coverage of Vietnam that makes war and violence as all-American as TV dinners.

Charges and studies could offer Harlem and the rest of New York City in 1943 at best only clarification of the issues. What was desperately needed was corrective action. The Citizens' Committee called for two immediate steps: the opening of new playgrounds, recreational facilities and summer schools in the Harlem area; and the enforcement of price ceilings set by OPA.[41]

Within a week an OPA office opened in Harlem with power to relieve the economic inequalities that admittedly existed.[42] The matter of playgrounds became quickly emeshed in city politics.

CONCLUSION

And so the riots had come; and they had gone--for a time. Whites would ask: "What does the Black man want?" And there would be answers: economic equality, an end to segregation in all areas of life, self-respect. The Black man had accepted white culture, its standards and values; now he wanted all that this culture offered the white man. And he would not accept postponement. Society was to learn that improvements could not keep pace with demands; if the one increased arithmetically, the other proliferated geometrically. Or in the terms of sociology: "when a group that has been discriminated against increases its group identification and opposes the discrimination more effectively, and when the majority group then reduces its discriminations, the conflict between the two groups increases for a while rather than decreases."[43]

It is this unhappy law that seems to explain the gradual displacement of old-style race rioting by new. The Detroit race riot was the product of intractable white opposition and ineptitude at all levels of city administration.[44] But in New York City officials were competent, even skillful, while most whites felt nothing much stronger than disinterest in Black affairs. In short, the new style of rioting betokens a certain advance in the Black's position. But this very advance makes the problem more difficult for solution.

The white feels the Black should be satisfied--"Look how far he's come." The Black finds that whereas race riots once aroused sympathy for his cause, now he is censured for "anarchy" and "lawlessness". In Detroit 1943 the Black man was clearly the victim of white intolerance and aggression; in Detroit 1967 this was not at all clear. In the first instance news photographs showed whites persecuting Blacks; in the second instance, the pictures were of Blacks setting fires, Blacks looting stores, Blacks sniping at firemen. And the cause is still essentially the same as ever-- the discrepancy between the American ideal and the actuality of Black life. The question in 1971 is the question not answered in 1943: Can this discrepancy be ended? Will it be?

Seemingly, it will take more than an appeal to the American conscience to solve the problems of racial conflict if Blacks and other oppressed people are to take their rightful places in the American life. Blacks have reversed their interaction perspective, and instead of interacting with whites on the basis of whites' concepts of their rights, they are interacting on the basis of their concept of their own rights. Consequently the 60's saw a new Black man; one who was in the process of changing his interaction perspective at another level. Formerly, Blacks interacted

THE HARLEM AND DETROIT RIOTS OF 1943

with whites, for the most part, on the basis of whites' distorted concept of them. Today, Blacks interact on the basis of their concept of themselves.

On a large scale, yet very subtle, white America seems determined to maintain the system of denial which Blacks and other oppressed people refuse to accept. Blacks shall continue to protest the system. In such an event racial crisis shall continue to be a part of the American scene.

NOTES

1. Maurice R. Davie, Negroes in American Society (New York: McGraw-Hill, 1949), p. 358.
2. Gunnar Myrdal, An American Dilemma: The Negro Problem and Modern Democracy (New York: Harper and Brothers, 1944), vol. I, p. 568.
3. Ibid.
4. Francis L. Broderick and August Meier (editors), Negro Protest Thought in the Twentieth Century (New York: Bobbs-Merrill, 1965), p. xxvii.
5. Carey McWilliams, Brothers Under the Skin (Boston: Little, Brown and Company, 1943), p. 293.
6. Myrdal, op. cit., p. 568.
7. Cf. Arnold M. Rose, The Negro's Morale: Group Identification and Protest (Minneapolis, Minn.: The University of Minnesota Press, 1949), p. 52.
8. Charles H. Wesley, "The Negro Has Always Wanted the Four Freedoms" in What the Negro Wants edited by Rayford W. Logan (Chapel Hill, North Carolina: University of North Carolina Press), p. 110.
9. Davie, op. cit., p. 328.
10. Rayford Whittingham Logan, The Negro and the Post-War World: A Primer (Washington, D.C.: The Minorities Publishers, 1945), p. 63.
11. A. Philip Randolph, "Keynote Address to the Policy Conference of the March on Washington Movement" in Negro Protest Thought in the Twentieth Century, pp. 202-203.
12. William Cecil Headrick, "Race Riots--Segregated Slums," Current History, September, 1943, p. 31.

13. Seymour Schoenfield, *The Negro in the Armed Forces: His Value and Status--Past, Present, and Potential* (Washington, D.C.: Associated Publishers, 1945), pp. 49-50.
14. Louis Martin, "Prelude to Disaster: Detroit," *Common Ground*, IV Autumn, 1943, p. 25.
15. Walter White et al., "A Declaration of Negro Voters" in *Negro Protest Thought in the Twentieth Century*, p. 242.
16. Thomas Sancton, "The Race Riots," *New Republic*, CIX July 5, 1943, p. 10.
17. "Detroit is Dynamite," *Life*, XIII, August 17, 1942, p. 15.
18. Earl Brown, "The Truth About the Detroit Riot," *Harper's Magazine*, CLXXXVII, November, 1943, pp. 488, 495.
19. Robert C. Weaver, *Negro Labor: A National Problem* (New York: Harcourt, Brace and Company, 1946), pp. 65-66.
20. "Race War in Detroit," *Life*, XV, July 5, 1943, p. 93.
21. Martin, *Common Ground*, IV, p. 22.
22. *New York Times*, August 6, 1943, p. 14.
23. *New York Times*, June 25, 1943, p. 8.
24. Russell B. Porter, *New York Times*, August 8, 1943, IV, p. 10.
25. *New York Times*, May 29, 1943, p. 12.
26. "Riots in Harlem," *New Republic*, CIX, August 9, 1943, p. 180.
27. As quoted by Alfred McClung Lee and Norman Daymond Humphrey, *Race Riot* (New York: The Dryden Press, 1943), p. 26.
28. *New York Times*, June 26, 1943, p. 28.
29. "Race War in Detroit," *Life*, XV, July 5, 1943, p. 93.
30. P.L. Prattis, *Pittsburgh Courier*, July 3, as printed in "The Negro Press on the Riots," *Common Ground*, IV, Autumn, 1943, p. 101.
31. Cf. William N. Robson, "Open Letter on Race Hatred: A Radio Document," *Theatre Arts*, XXVIII, September, 1944, pp. 535-552.
32. *New York Times*, August 2, 1943, p. 1.
33. Adam Clayton Powell, Jr., declared, "The police have acted most admirably. They have proven themselves as New York's finest." *New York Times*, August 3, 1943, p. 11.
34. C.B. Powell: "There is no element of race rioting in the situation." *New York Times*, August 3, 1943, p. 11. Walter White: "It cannot be too clearly emphasized that this was not a race riot in any sense of the term." *New York Times*, August 3, 1943, p. 11. Edward S. Lewis: "This outbreak was not a race riot in the usual sense of the term." *New York Times*, August 3, 1943, p. 11. *New Republic*: "Negro leaders denied that it was a race riot," p. 180. Walter Davenport: "Actually, it was not a race riot," Colliers, CXII, p. 11. The New York Newspaper Guild sent

a telegram to all members "urging Guild writers covering the recent Harlem riots to note that it was not a race riot." New York Times, October 16, 1943, p. 15.
    35. New York Times, August 4, 1943, p. 16.
    36. Cf. "Harlem's Tragedy," New York Times, August 3, 1943, p. 18.
    37. New York Times, August 3, 1943, p. 11.
    38. New York Times, August 5, 1943, p. 17.
    39. New York Times, August 2, 1943, p. 1.
    40. Kenneth B. Clark, "Group Violence: A Preliminary Study of the Attitudinal Pattern of Its Acceptance and Rejection: A Study of the 1943 Harlem Riot," The Journal of Social Psychology, XIX, 1944, pp. 319-337.
    41. New York Times, August 3, 1943, p. 11.
    42. New York Times, August 7, 1943, p. 13.
    43. Rose, The Negro's Morale, p. 142.
    44. The nearest comparable situation existed in Cleveland. Here as in 1943 Detroit there was a large proportion of whites with strong ethnic identification and an almost equally strong antipathy to Blacks. The Cleveland police force had made only token integration and was viewed by Blacks with the same cynicism and anger felt in Detroit in 1943. Cf. John Show, "Can Cleveland Escape Burning," Saturday Evening Post, July 29, 1967, pp. 38-49.

Blacks and the Los Angeles Municipal Transit System, 1941-1945

ALONZO N. SMITH

During the Second World War equal opportunity employment became a national issue. With the rapid expansion of production, and with a large portion of the workforce in uniform, severe labor shortages developed in several critical industries. When many employers continued to exclude qualified workers solely on the basis of race or religion, both the federal government as well as civil rights organizations took up the campaign for fair employment.

The overwhelming majority of complaints brought to the President's Committee on Fair Employment Practices involved discrimination on the basis of race, and of these most involved blacks.[1] Job discrimination in many vital defense industries such as aircraft and shipbuilding was investigated by the Committee. One industry considered vital to the war effort was municipal transit. A rigid system of segregation dominated the industry. The better-paying and more prestigious work — that of conductor and motorman on streetcars, and drivers on buses, was designated as "platform jobs," and reserved for whites. Afro American workers were confined to cleaning the vehicles, and to similar low-paying work which did not involve contact with the public. Prior to World War II, New York was the only major city where blacks had achieved gains in the public transportation system, and this had come only after vigorous protest.

During the war years, there were campaigns all across the country against discrimination in city transportation. In some instances these efforts bore fruit, while in others they were unsuccessful. Protests against exclusion in Springfield, Massachusetts brought promises from the Springfield Street Railway Company to hire blacks, but these promises were not fulfilled. In Pittsburgh, Pennsylvania the Pittsburgh Railways Company hired blacks to drive buses after the War Manpower Commission stopped referring applicants to the company. Gary Railways of Gary Indiana and the Kansas City Public Service Company of Kansas City, Missouri were both systems which held firm to exclusion, and in the latter city white workers threatened physical violence if blacks were hired.[2]

By far the most publicized instance of municipal transit discrimination was in Philadelphia. Here, the issue of equal opportunity employment became embroiled in a rivalry between an AFL and a CIO transit workers' union on the one hand, and efforts of management to prevent unionization on the other. When, under FEPC pressure, black workers were upgraded to platform jobs in August, 1944 a group of whites organized a strike which tied up the entire system. After the U.S. Army was called in, the strike was quickly broken, and blacks ran trolley cars and buses without further incident.[3]

The problem of discrimination in Los Angeles public transportation did not receive as much nationwide publicity as the Philadelphia case, and yet it was equally important. Added to the question of minority access to jobs were issues of housing discrimination and equal provision of municipal services.

The spatial distribution of employment, housing and transportation patterns has been recognized as an important aspect of low-income and minority life in

ALONZO N. SMITH is an Assistant Professor in the Black Studies Department, College of Arts and Sciences, University of Nebraska at Omaha, Omaha, Nebraska 68182

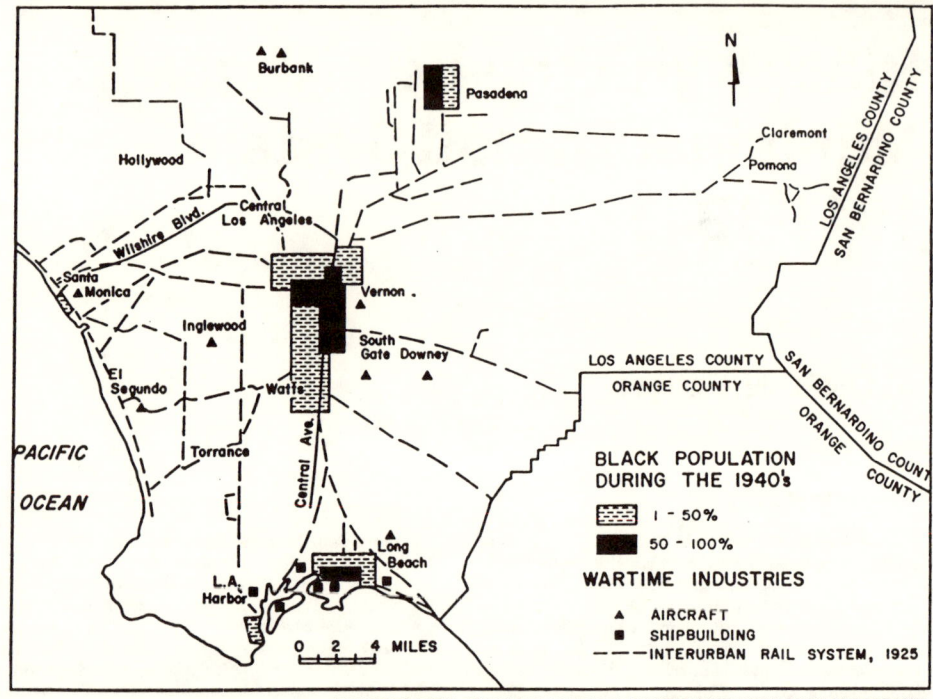

SCOTT ROBINSON, GEOGRAPHY-GEOLOGY DEPARTMENT, UNIVERSITY OF NEBRASKA

the city. Residential segregation and inadequate transportation have often been cited as major causative factors in black unemployment and poverty. It has been contended that suburbanization and the confinement of black people to certain sections of the city has increasingly separated them from the means to earn a livelihood. At the same time, this problem has been exacerbated by inadequate public transportation and a lack of access to private automobiles.

During the past fifteen years, a number of social scientists have addressed themselves to this question. Following the Watts Riot of 1965, the McCone Commission identified employment as the primary problem facing Afro American people in the Los Angeles area. It went on to note that inadequate and costly transportation was a major factor in creating disadvantaged employment consiridtions.

Following these conclusions, the Department of Housing and Urban Development sponsored several studies across the country. They were designed to test the hypothesis that improved transit service would help reduce high unemployment rates on low income and minority neighborhoods. But Falcocchio and Cantilli have concluded that "The results produced by these projects did not . . . present a clear picture of the role of transportation in the low-income labor market."[4]

However, in one study conducted by the Stanford Research Institute, it was found that transportation was a significant factor in hard-core unemployment, and that "Problems were most severe in the sprawling, automobile-oriented cities of the West . . ." The evidence from Detroit and Chicago compiled by John F. Kain strongly suggests that tight residential segregation has adverse effects on black employment levels, and that this condition has worsened with postwar suburbanization.[5].

Sam Bass Warner has also noted a relationship between spatial isolation and disadvantaged employment opportunities. He says that the private automobile and the freeway system have given Los Angeles area residents a high degree of spatial mobility and hence access to jobs. But to a large degree, these benefits of convenient transportation have been denied to low-income people, a group made up disproportionately of Blacks and Chicanos. With regard to the HUD project cited by Falcocchio and Cantilli, he feels that it was successful in Los Angeles, but was discontinued after the federal government failed to renew its funds. On the other hand, Alan Altschuler contends that it is not at all certain that urban sprawl has adversely affected the employment opportunities of the central city poor, and even if this question can be answered in the affirmative, he doubts whether any special programs will be effective.[6]

Thus, it can be seen from the foregoing survey of the literature in the field that there is a wide variety of opinion on the interrelationship of transportation, spatial isolation, and minority employment. All of the previously mentioned studies deal with phenomena in the present. There is, however, considerable evidence from urban history, and particularly from the Los Angeles metropolitan area, which can help to shed light on this question.

The Los Angeles Problem

While white wartime migration to California began around 1940, that of the blacks did not begin until about two years later.[7] The war industries of the state, as elsewhere, were very slow to open their doors to people of color, and aircraft company executives openly stated that, regardless of their training, blacks would simply not be hired. It required the setting up of the President's Committee of Fair Employment Practices, as well as an intense demand for labor following Pearl Harbor, before substantial numbers of Afro Americans got war industry jobs.[8] Between the FEPC and the critical demand for defense production labor, it was the latter which proved to be the most potent factor in breaking down the barriers to black employment.

Between 1940 and 1946 the black population in the City of Los Angeles increased from 63,774 to 133,082. The peak period of the in-migration of Afro Americans occurred during the summer of 1943, when they streamed into the area at the rate of about 1,000 a month.[9] However, housing facilities available to them hardly increased at all. The supply of housing was generally insufficient during the war, but blacks encountered more difficulties than the whites. When "Little Tokyo," an area in the central business district, was vacated by interned Japanese Americans, it was immediately jammed with blacks. But while several new residential areas in Los Angeles County opened up to whites, Afro Americans remained confined to a few areas.

Before they were outlawed by the Supreme Court in 1948, racial restrictive covenants were a common practice in Los Angeles, as elsewhere. Although most of the challenges to these contracts did not come until after 1945, there were several instances during the period in question when blacks who moved into "white" neighborhoods were subjected to harassment and vandalization of their property.[10]

Public housing projects were also a topic of controversy. In 1943, a project was begun in Venice, an ocean-front community near Santa Monica, and a proposal was made to open it on a nonsegregated basis. Several local residents wrote to the City Council to protest. Among the reasons they cited were that blacks already had a residential area of their own nearby, that they did not want more blacks coming into the area, and that white workers at the big Douglas Aircraft plant in Santa Monica did not want blacks living or working nearby. In 1945 the NAACP charged that the Federal Housing Authority had yielded to local pressure when an integrated project was proposed near the City of Compton.[11]

The Council of Social Agencies of Los Angeles, a private welfare organization, set up a Little Tokyo Committee. On August 19, 1943 several black community leaders brought a complaint to the Council, alleging that the Los Angeles County Housing Authority systematically segregated blacks. The Council also found that crowded conditions in the central city area were producing various social problems, including gambling and prostitution.[12]

In addition to employment discrimination and crowded housing, Los Angeles blacks also complained about unequal provision of municipal services. Wilshire Boulevard was the main commercial street in Los Angeles, and the black community had its counterpart in Central Avenue. When Wilshire was widened in 1940, blacks took the occasion to protest about the congestion and lack of traffic lights on Central. About this time there were also complaints of inadequate transportation service in black neighborhoods.[13]

The rapid growth in the black population after Pearl Harbor exacerbated these problems. Not only did crowding increase, but industrial and commercial land usage encroached increasingly on black residential areas. It was said that during the Second World War, the enforcement of zoning codes in black areas was "practically nonexistent." Prior to World War II, Los Angeles had an overwhelmingly middle-class black community, but it was during the 1930s and 1940s that the classic characteristics of what is commonly referred to as black "ghetto" life emerged.[14]

Added to deterioration within the black community was deterioration of public transportation in the Los Angeles metropolitan area. In the early 1900s the Los Angeles Railway and the Pacific Electric Railway played a crucial role in urban expansion. But by the mid-1920s the private automobile had clearly emerged as a competitor. By the late 1920s, many of the unprofitable lines were being removed from

27

service, and the Great Depression hastened this process.[15] When World War II came, the "Red Cars" of the Los Angeles Railway Company (LARY) were the major mass transit facility in the area. Most of the major routes were still in operation, including a line down Central Avenue to Watts.

Thus, the problem of discrimination in the Los Angeles transit industry touched several other major issues. Black residents in Los Angeles had the distinct impression that, despite the wartime prosperity, the quality of their lives was deteriorating in several tangible ways. Residential crowding was becoming acute. Provision of municipal services and transportation services seemed to be declining. And it was claimed that spatial isolation from the war plants hampered black access to the lucrative industrial jobs. Thus, the Los Angeles Railway Company became a major target for black activists during the war years.

In 1941 LARY made a collective bargaining agreement with Local 1277 of the Amalgamated Association of Street, Electric Railway and Motor Coach Employees, AFL.[16] This union, known as the Amalgamated, followed the general pattern of AFL craft unions in excluding Afro Americans from skilled jobs. By the time the war broke out, the union was admitting blacks, but preventing them from doing platform work.

Protests against this policy began to surface late in 1942. In October, 1942 the FEPC received its first complaint against LARY. On December 3 the *California Eagle*, one of the two major local black newspapers, ran an editorial on the problem. Noting that no publicly documented protest had yet been made to the FEPC, the newspaper expressed concern that there was some danger of a token agreement being concluded between certain black groups and the Company, whereby a few operators would be placed on the "U" and "J" lines, which went down Central Avenue. Condemning any deal of this sort, the *Eagle* insisted that the FEPC and the War Manpower Commission (WMC) were the most powerful weapons which the black community possessed against LARY.

The following week, in commenting on FHA quotas for segregated black housing in the area, the newspaper noted that Afro Americans were forced to jam the public transportation system in order to commute to work. It blamed the inadequate transportation services on the policy of job discrimination. The *Eagle* used harsh terms against LARY. In charging that inefficient transportation was causing many black workers to lose work hours in the war plants, it concluded that the Company's policy amounted to sabotage.

Finally, a mass protest meeting was held, and on December 18 a telegram of protest was sent to the FEPC by the Negro Victory Committee, a local wartime activist group. It was stated that no blacks were utilized as conductors or motormen, although there were 2,500 jobs in the system, of which 600 were unfilled. Three hundred busses and trolleys, with a maximum capacity of 30,000 persons, had thus been taken out of service.

The New Year's Day 1943 issue of the *Eagle* observed that gas rationing was taxing transportation facilities. Eight more "U" cars had been removed from the Central Avenue line. Charged the editor, "An ante bellum clique of company die-hards refuses to respect the law of the land . . . This is deliberate sabotage of the war effort." On January 15 a conference of FEPC, WMC, ODT (Office of Defense Transportation) officials, LARY and Amalgamated representatives, and black community leaders was held. According the FEPC officials, both labor and management took the position that the public was not ready for the upgrading of black workers. The Company did, however, agree to make an effort.

Finally, at the end of the month, LARY took steps to upgrade blacks. The *Eagle* ran a huge headline, "LARY HIRES NEGRO." Black workers, said the newspaper, were surprised at the Company's quick change in policy, and one refused to believe he had been promoted. As it turned out, his doubts were well-founded. Twice in February when blacks at LARY were promoted from car cleaner to apprentice mechanic, white workers staged wildcat strikes until they were returned to their menial positions.[17]

Joseph Prutsman, the business agent for the union, was one of the principal agitators against the upgrading. A foreman, Joe Spearing, also went around asking the men to protest "having to work with a bunch of niggers." Charges were made that blacks were "taking over the shop," and "stealing all the jobs." FEPC observers felt that this controversy did not necessarily mean that there was any basic white worker opposition to black upgrading. Rather, it was a reflection of internal union politics. One clique, led by Prutsman, was trying to oust the incumbent local president Edward Lenz, and was using the black employment issue against him.[18]

Both labor and management blamed the other, and refused to take any further steps toward relaxation of the discriminatory job policy, even when repeatedly requested to do so by FEPC officials. As black protest increased, racial tension also mounted. In March, 1943, a black passenger charged that a white conductor had pushed him off a streetcar, and then beat him with a wrench. White drivers and conductors complained of attacks from blacks on the Central Avenue line. One report to the Office of War Information quoted a local black as saying that LARY had "better put some Negroes on these cars or there won't be any running." The Negro Victory

Committee demanded a meeting of blacks, the government, labor and management, but FEPC officials declined.[19]

In September, 1943, the *Eagle* ran a full-page advertisement protesting housing discrimination:

> This situation, we believe, has a disastrous effect upon the production efficiency of these essential war workers, men and women who are forced to find cramped quarters in admittedly slum areas ... Today, thousands of workers are needlessly forced to travel as much as forty miles a day from their ghetto community to the job.

The letter was signed by several black attorneys and businessmen.

An *Eagle* editorial expressed similar views:

> War worker projects opened at Inglewood to accommodate workers at the North American plants to not permit Negroes ... The policy of race-exclusion throws a terrific burden upon transportation facilities, forcing upon minority group workers extended daily journeys to their far-off ghetto communities.[20]

Thus, in the minds of many Afro American leaders in wartime Los Angeles, there was a close relationship between residential segregation, commuting distances, and working conditions.

Viewing the situation in retrospect after 30 years, one black man recently expressed the same perspective to an oral history researcher. Those who worked in the San Pedro and Long Beach shipyards suffered especially hard. The Red Cars could only be used by those on the day shift, since there were no runs at night. Most of the Afro Americans who worked in the shipyards during the war labored between 12 A.M. and 8 A.M. A black employee could return to South Central Los Angeles on the 8:30 A.M. car from Long Beach. His problem was getting to work at 12 midnight. It seems that bus, taxi and jitney drivers did not want to drive in or out of South Central Los Angeles at night for fear of being physically harmed. In the words of the informant:

> I usually had some kind of job and didn't mind paying the Red Car fare; but I had real problems when I got a job at the Long Beach Naval Shipyard because it took the Red Car a long time to go from Watts to Long Beach and the damn thing broke down a lot. An when it didn't break down it would have to wait until the freight train passed. The Red Car always broke down and rarely got us to work on time. Man, let me tell you, it was a real hassle! It was a job getting a job, it was a job keeping a job, it was a job getting to the job ...[21]

By the beginning of 1944, only 493 out of 800 streetcars, and only 212 out of 256 buses were in operation. Many Los Angeles residents, black as well as white, were complaining about the deterioration in service. On February 28, the Los Angeles Central Labor Council, which represented the local AFL unions, called on LARY to abandon its discriminatory policy, and on March the Los Angeles Council of the CIO asked the government to deprive the company of its priority rating for manpower referrals. Accordingly, in March 24 the War Manpower Commission revoked the company's "essential" employer classification, after it had refused to employ 354 referred blacks. Likewise the Committee for Home Front Unity, appointed by Mayor Fletcher Bowron, called on LARY to end its jim crow employment.[22]

From April to August 1944, meetings were held by representatives of the federal government, management, labor, the Mayor's office, and the Chamber of Commerce. According to FEPC officials, the primary obstacle to a settlement was the attitude of LARY management. The officials of the Company claimed they were willing to upgrade black workers if they could be assured that the whites would not strike. Union leaders blamed a group of workers among the rank-and-file. Several workers ascribed the hostile attitude of their co-workers to black violence against streetcar operators, and to vociferous criticism by the local black press. City government officials felt that they could achieve a settlement without federal intervention. And the Chamber of Commerce was critical of the pressure-group tactics of black and interracial activist organizations.[23]

Finally on August 8, 1944 the FEPC held hearings in Los Angeles. Evidence indicated that LARY had refused to accept the responsibility for persuading white platform workers to accept blacks, attempting to pass it on the union. The Amalgamated had acted in the same fashion regarding the company. Over the objections of both management and labor, the FEPC issued a directive on August 9 to LARY to upgrade black workers. There was immediate compliance, and by the end of the month, fifteen black men were operating streetcars, and several black women were working as conductors, without any racial incidents. Doubtlessly, the federal government's firm action in the Philadelphia transit strike, previously alluded to, was a major factor in facilitating the smooth integration of black workers at LARY.[24]

On January 16, 1945, the name of the Los Angeles Railway Corporation was changed to Los Angeles Transit Lines. In June, the *Eagle* complained that the company had adopted a policy of not retaining Afro American mechanics. Black women car cleaners were also being terminated. But company spokesmen claimed that the layoffs were on the basis of seniority, and the blacks simply lacked seniority.[25]

Despite these problems, however, it appears that municipal transit was one occupation where blacks achieved solid gains in the Los Angeles area. Table I shows the increase in black workers at LARY in a nine-month period from 1944 to 1945. Although the total number of white operators decreased, that of the blacks increased.

Table I: Streetcar Operators at the Los Angeles Transit Company by Race, 1944-45.

	White	Black (%)	Total
Sept. 1944	2175	16(0)	2191
June 1945	2076	113(5)	2129

Source: Administrative Files, Region XII (reel 103), Field Records, FEPC files.

Looking at the municipal transit industry as a whole in the Los Angeles area, Afro-Americans appear to have scored important gains. Table II indicates the nonwhite percentage of the workforce in this industry. Although Mexican Americans outnumbered blacks, the Census reports at this time counted them among the Caucasian population, and so the overwhelming portion of those listed as "nonwhite" were actually black. While the total number of individually employed in the industry practically doubled from 1940 to 1950, that of the nonwhites increased almost sixfold, jumping from three to six percent of the total workforce.

Table II: Employment in the Street Railways and Bus Lines of Los Angeles by Race, 1940-1950.*

	Total	Nonwhites (%)	Blacks	Other
1940	4954	177 (3)	na	na
1950	9262	605 (6)	594	11

Source: U.S. Bureau of the Census, 1940, *Census of Population, Volume III: the Labor Force, Part 2: Alabama-Indiana*, p. 311, Table 19; Census, 1950, *Census of Population, Volume II: Characteristics of the Population, Part 5: California*, p. 5-416, Table 83

*The 1940 figures are for Los Angeles City, while the 1940 figures are for Los Angeles, Long Beach, and Orange County.

Summary and Conclusions

The problem of municipal transit discrimination was solved relatively well in Los Angeles when compared to Philadelphia, where the mobilization of the Army was required, or Gary and Kansas City, where no upgrading of blacks was achieved by 1945.

Several factors account for this. As we have seen, the federal government's firm action in Philadelphia had been taken just a few days prior to the issuance of the FEPC's directive in Los Angeles. The Mayor's office, as well as local black pressure-group activity, were also undoubtedly powerful factors.

Civil rights activists in the Los Angeles area were able to link their cause to pressing local problems. The drastic curtailment of transit service, coupled with gas rationing, focused public attention on an overcrowded, deteriorating public transit system. The moral cause of equal opportunity employment was strengthened by the critical need to use all available workers. Added to this was the fact that blacks were prevented by housing discrimination from living close to most of the war plants. Although further investigation into conditions in the other cities is necessary, it seems plausible that the long commuting distances in the Los Angeles metropolitan area made discrimination by the transit industry a particularly untenable policy.

In conclusion, the evidence presented by this study cannot provide definitive answers about the relationship between residential segregation, transportation facilities, and minority-group employment. What it does show quite clearly however, is that, at least in the minds of federal government officials as well as black civil rights activists, the three variables were indeed closely associated with each other. Thus, at least two decades before the "urban crisis" of the 1960s, the relationship between blacks and urban transit was a public policy issue.

The exclusion of Afro Americans from skilled jobs in municipal transit received considerable public attention during World War II. The Los Angeles experience suggests that further investigation of this problem can tell us much about civil rights during the black experience in the city. □

NOTES

1. Bruce I. Friend, *Guide to the Microfilm Record of Selected Documents of Records of the Committee on Fair Employment Practice in the Custody of the National Archives*, (np, October, 1970), p. 4.
2. Herbert Hill, *Black Labor and the American Legal System, Volume I, Race, Work, and the Law*, (Washington: Bureau of National Affairs, 1977), pp. 275, 309-311.
3. Hill, *Black Labor*, Chapter 11; Merle Reed, "The FEPC, the Black Worker, and the Southern Shipyards," *South Atlantic Quarterly*, 29:3 (April 1975).
4. *Violence in the City — An End or a Beginning?*, Governor's Commission on the Los Angeles Roots, Los Angeles, CA., 1968, cited in: John C. Falcocchio and Edmund J. Cantilli, *Transportation and the Disadvantaged*, (Lexington, MA: Lexington Books, 1974), pp. 6-7.
5. "Transportation and Poverty," *Stanford Research Institute Journal*, no. 24 (February 1969), pp. 4-9. John F. Kain, "Housing Segregation, Negro Employment, and Metropolitan Decentralization," *Quarterly Journal of Economics*, 82 (May 1968), pp. 195-197.
6. Sam Bass Warner, Jr., *The Urban Wilderness: A History of the American City*, (New York: Harper and Row, 1972), pp. 142-144. See also Robert M. Fogelson, *The Fragmented Metropolis, Los Angeles, 1850-1930*, (Cambridge: Harvard University Press, 1967), pp. 164-165. Alan Altschuler, *The Urban Transportation System, Politics and Policy Innovation*, (Cambridge: MIT Press, 1969), pp. 392-393.
7. Lawrence B. DeGraaf, "Negro Migration to Los Angeles, 1930 to 1950," (Ph.D. dissertation, History, UCLA, 1962), p. 273.
8. Alonzo N. Smith, "Black Employment in the Los Angeles Area, 1938-1948," (Ph.D. dissertation, History, UCLA, 1978), Chapters 3 and 4.
9. DeGraaf, "Negro Migration," pp. 155-158.
10. See the two major black newspapers, the *California Eagle* and the *Los Angeles Sentinel*, for descriptions of these incidents.
11. Walter Peterson to M. E. Diebold, 29 November 1943; M. E. Diebold to City Council, 20 October 1943; other letters, Fall 1943, City Records Center #12735, Council File 316009, Records of the City Council, Los Angeles City Archives, Los Angeles, CA. Thomas L. Griffith to Roy Wilkins, 14 March 1945, Box 329: Discrimination in Housing and Transportation, Branch files, Unprocessed Material, 1940-present, NAACP Records, Manuscript Division of the Library of Congress, Washington, D.C.
12. Council of Social Agencies of Los Angeles, Little Tokyo Committee, Minutes, October 8, 1943. Los Angeles Urban League Branch Files, 1943, Box 104, Urban League Papers, Library of Congress.
13. *California Eagle*, 30 March 1939, 28 September 1939, 14 March 1940.
14. Keith Collins, "Black Los Angeles: the Maturing of the Ghetto, 1940-1950," (Ph.D. dissertation, History, UC San Diego, 1975), pp. 115-120; Lawrence B. DeGraaf, "City of Black Angels, Emegence of the Los Angeles Ghetto, 1920-1940," *Pacific Historical Review*, 34 (August 1970), p. 328.
15. Fogelson, *Fragmented Metropolis*, pp. 92, 164-185.
16. Hill, *Black Labor*, p. 312.
17. Emanuel H. Bloch to Will Maslow, 31 December 1943, (microfilm reel #8), Records of the Legal Division, Headquarters Records, President's Committee on Fair Employment Practice, National Archives, Washington, D.C. (Available from University Microfilms); *California Eagle*, 3 & 11 December 1942, 1 & 28 January, 1943.
18. Lawrence Cramer to Guy Nunn, 10 February 1943, Guy Nunn to W. D. Mahon, 4 February 1943, Cramer to Nunn, 4 February 1943, (reel 103), Field Records, Region XII, FEPC Files.
19. *Eagle*, 17 March 1943 p. 1; "Report on Trip of Regional Director and Examiner Frank Pestana to Los Angeles on March 14-17," (reel 103), FEPC Files; Correspondence, Office of War Information Files, Race Tensions: California-Los Angeles, Box 27, Philleo Nash Papers, Harry S. Truman Library, Independence, MO. Maslow to Bloch, Ibid., Cramer to George H. Johnson, 3 March 1943, (reel 103), FEPC Files.
20. *Eagle*, 2 September 1943; 26 March 1943.
21. Collins, "Black Los Angeles," pp. 70-85.
22. Resolution of the Los Angeles Central Labor Council, 28 February 1944 (reel 103), FEPC Files; *Eagle*, 9 & 23 March 1944, Hill, *Black Labor*, pp. 313-314.
23. George W. Crockett to Malcolm Ross, 11 April 1944, Crockett to Ross, April 13 1944 (reel 103); Robert Brown to George M. Johnson (reel 1), Headquarters Records, "Statement on the LARY Case," by Maceo W. Hubbard, 29 June 1944, (reel 84), Headquarters Records, FEPC Files.
24. Hill, *Black Labor*, pp. 315-316.
25. *Eagle*, 7 June 1945.

The Black Worker and the Labor Movement in Cleveland, 1930–1945: Forging a New Relationship

Christopher G. Wye

One of the most dramatic changes in the black social structure during the thirties and early forties was the forging of a new relationship between black workers and the labor movement. Since the last decades of the nineteenth century, Cleveland blacks had been barred from union membership in most unions by a persistent color line in the American Federation of Labor. However, beginning with the rise of the more liberal Congress of Industrial Organizations in the middle thirties, black workers were increasingly included within the fold of the new industrial unions. At the same time competition from the CIO put pressure on the AFL to revise its racial policies, although it did so only haltingly and on a limited basis.

On the eve of the Depression, the black community had been largely on the periphery of the labor movement. To a significant degree this was the result of the dichotomy between the composition of the black labor force and the structural system of organization employed by the American Federation of Labor. Except for a few industrial unions—such as the United Mine Workers, the International Ladies Garment Workers, and the International Longshoremen's Association—the overwhelming majority of AFL affiliates were craft unions, whereas most blacks were unskilled and semi-skilled workers. Black participation in the labor movement was even further limited, however, by the discriminatory practices of many AFL unions. Although for a few years following its founding in 1881 the AFL had pursued a policy of nondiscrimination, a wide range of tactics was evolved in the 1890s to restrict black membership. Some unions denied black admission by means of a formal provision in their constitutions or rituals. Others excluded them by means of common agreement among their membership, higher initiation fees, more difficult examinations, special licenses, and inaccessible apprenticeship programs. Even where blacks were accepted into AFL unions, they were often discriminated against in matters concerning referrals for work and promotion or organized into Jim Crow auxiliaries which had little power to contract work agreements.[1]

This pattern of discrimination was clearly reflected in the practices of the AFL affiliates of the Cleveland Federation of Labor. In the construction industry, only the unions encompassing relatively unskilled occupations were open without restriction to blacks. Thus, both the Building Trades Laborers and Asphalt Pavers Unions traditionally maintained large black memberships and, on occasion, even elected blacks to positions of leadership.[2] In contrast, most of the unions in the highly skilled building trades restricted blacks in one way or another, some by barring them from membership and others by relegating them to a subordinate status. Despite a nondiscriminatory clause in each of their constitutions, the Plasterers, Bricklayers and Masons, and the

Cement Finishers admitted only a small number of blacks and then awarded them only the less lucrative, short-term contracts in the black community.[3] Blacks who sought access to the Carpenters and Joiners Union "just never seemed to pass the examination." The Parquet Floor Layers Union considered black membership undesirable because "most of our work is done in occupied dwellings and the people... object to having a Negro working therein." The Painters, Decorators and Paperhangers Union did not accept black members because it did "not desire the close association which would naturally be expected."[4]

Perhaps the most hostile of the building trades unions were the Plumbers and Steamfitters, the Structural Iron Workers and the Electrical Workers. These unions not only attempted to exclude blacks from membership through a combination of inaccessible apprenticeship programs, complicated and tedious licensing procedures, and prohibitive initiation fees, but they also sought to drive blacks out of their trades by destroying their work and harassing them with threats of physical violence.[5] The efforts of Charles E. West to gain admission to the Electrical Workers Union in 1928 are illustrative.

Since the customary apprenticeship channels were closed to him, West took a job at the Cleveland Electric Illuminating Company, where he managed to learn enough of the fundamentals to pass the municipal examination required for an electrician's license. His troubles really began, however, when he sought access to the Electrical Workers Union. When he applied for membership, he was quoted an initiation fee more than three times the normal rate; when he offered to pay it, his check was returned. In the next two years, West was continually harassed by carloads of men who would appear at his project site, inform him that he could not do electrical work without a union card, and then destroy his work by cutting the wires that he had installed. When West asked at the union office what they expected him to do when they refused to admit him to the union and at the same time refused to let him work unless he was a member, he was advised that "there must be some other work besides electrical work you can do." Although he struggled on for several more years, increasing union pressure on contractors not to "give that nigger any work" eventually forced West out of business.[6]

The situation in the manufacturing industries was similar to that in the construction industries, except that the skilled unions were even more solidly exclusionist. The industrially organized United Garment Workers, International Ladies Garment Workers, and Federal Laborers Unions, all of which had large number of unskilled workers, generally accepted black members.[7] In the skilled mechanical trades, however, blacks faced an unbroken line of opposition. Although around the turn of the century the Metal Polishers Union had taken in a few blacks, by the late twenties most of these had dropped away, and no new blacks were being accepted. The International Association of Machinists excluded blacks through a clause in its initiation ritual which made it applicable only to "sober white men."[8] Organized as fraternal lodges, the Molders, Pattern Makers, and Coremakers were tightly knit groups of friends and relatives who kept Negroes out by tacit consent. Commented one black about these lodges,

They were plant aristocrats. They held themselves aloof and few people knew where they met. You had to be a relative or close friend to get into their apprenticeship training programs and, of course, none of them had Negro friends or relatives.[9]

Black workers also encountered discrimination in the trade, transportation, and service industries, as well as in a wide variety of other occupations. Nearly all of the unions incident to retail and wholesale trade were hostile toward blacks. Skilled unions, like the Meat Cutters and Bakers Unions, excluded blacks from their apprenticeship programs, while semi-skilled unions, like the Gasoline Station Operators and the Retail Food Clerks unions, accepted blacks but refused to let them work outside the ghetto.[10] Similarly, in the transportation field, blacks were uniformly barred from the specialized Milk Drivers and Bakery, Tea, Coffee, and Yeast Drivers Unions, and only those independent movers who confined their operations to the black community were admitted to the more generalized Teamsters union.[11] Except for the Waiters, Waitresses, and Cooks unions, which excluded blacks entirely, and the Hotel and Restaurant Employees Union, which organized blacks into a separate local, much of the service industry was not well organized. Unions such as the Porters and Laundry Workers had a few black members, but these unions were quite small and relatively unimportant.[12] Blacks also faced varying degrees of union discrimination in a wide range of miscellaneous occupations. The National Federation of Postal Clerks, for example, generally accepted black members but opposed them for promotions, while the Teachers and Musicians unions admitted blacks only to separate auxiliaries.[13]

It was largely due to union influence that the trade schools conducted by the Cleveland Board of Education, particularly the Cleveland Trade School and East Technical High School, discouraged black applicants. The Cleveland Trade School, for example, was virtually an appendage of the several building and mechanical trades unions. According to the Board of Education's director of vocational and practical arts, "the entire objective of this school is cooperation with the various crafts and industries of Cleveland *through apprenticeship committees for the training of apprentices already employed in industry* [emphasis mine]." Therefore, despite the assurances of school administrators that "any boy may apply for admission," only those who were already employed and who were recommended by the appropriate apprenticeship committee had any chance of being accepted.[14]

The influence of union policies was also evident in a less direct way at East High School. Since it was not connected in any manner with the apprenticeship programs of the trade unions, East Tech was theoretically open to Negro students. In practice, however, the difficulty of placing black graduates, which was itself due in significant measure to union discrimination, caused the school's officials to discourage black applicants. "No boy will be refused admission," stated one counselor,

> but he enters with the full knowledge of what his chances are for success in any given vocation in so far as school officials are able to

inform him. Colored boys who have completed. . . technical trade courses have found difficulty in securing employment. . . .[15]

Faced as it was with this constant evidence of union discrimination, subordination, and exclusion, the black community developed a widespread antipathy toward the labor movement. Anti-union sentiment among black workers appeared to vary only in degree. Where union activity was weak or nonexistent, as in most categories of unskilled labor in the mass-production industries, black workers had little direct contact with labor organizations, and their hostility was more muted. There seemed to be only a rather general feeling that unions were "white men's organizations" and that "when Negroes got in they didn't do nothing for them."[16] Where union influence was stronger, as in many areas of semi-skilled and skilled work as well as in some government and service occupations, black workers experienced union discrimination more directly, and their reaction to it was more evident.

Blacks in these job categories not infrequently formed their own labor organizations to circumvent or oppose the discriminatory practices of white unions. For example, the Colored Waiters Club, a local branch of the National Alliance of Colored Waiters and Hotel Employees, was formed to protect the interests of black workers against the exclusionist policies of the white Cooks, Waiters and Waitresses Unions. Other black organizations such as the Messenger Bond Club, the National Alliance of Postal Employees, and the Fifth City Chauffeurs Association performed similar functions.[17]

Perhaps nothing better symbolized the cleavage between the black community and the labor movement at the outset of the Depression than the hotel strike of 1930–31. Faced with declining business and a pressing need to cut expenses, the Cleveland Hotel Owners Association announced that an open shop would prevail in all of the city's hotels when the current union contract expired on July 15, 1930. Almost immediately, the Cooks, Waiters, and Waitresses unions went out on strike, and within a week they were joined by the Operating Engineers, Firemen's, Musicians, and Deliverymen's Unions. In consequence, the hotel owners let it be known that they would hire black workers, whom the black community readily supplied. The Colored Waiters Club, for example, played a leading role in recruiting black strikebreakers, even going so far as to establish classes to train blacks in the skills needed for the hotel work. The Urban League did not officially endorse the use of blacks as strikebreakers in this instance, but it did refer black job-seekers to the Associated Industries, which was handling the employment problems of the hotels. Thereafter, the black strikebreakers were frequently beaten or threatened by members of the striking unions. The home of Ralph W. Rowland, the President of the Colored Waiters Club, was guarded twenty-four hours a day by the Cleveland police.[18]

Throughout the course of the strike, black leaders opposed all efforts to arbitrate a settlement with the union that did not assure black strikebreakers the right to remain in their new jobs at the hotels. Finally, a year and eight days after the strike began, the Hotel Owners Association announced that members of the striking unions would be "[re]hired as soon as the nonunion help can be weeded out" and black workers, their service done, began to filter back to the ghetto. The net effect of the strike was to reinforce the already deeply rooted antagonism between blacks and the unions.[19]

Nor was this mutual antagonism relieved during the AFL's expansion drive, which began in 1933, when the Congress passed the National Recovery Act containing Section 7A guaranteeing labor the right to organize and bargain collectively. Black workers encountered serious obstacles barring their participation in the movement. Although in some of the mass-production industries the AFL did make an effort to organize unskilled workers, very little effort was directed toward attracting black workers. At the same time, black workers frequently experienced considerable pressure from employers to join company unions, which were being fostered for the specific purpose of defeating the AFL's unionization drive. Faced with the half-hearted appeals of the AFL on the one hand, and the strong anti-union influence of business leaders on the other, black workers evidenced very little interest in the effort to organize unskilled workers. During the same years, the AFL's campaign to extend its coverage of semi-skilled and skilled workers aroused a great deal of hostility within the black community.

Although complete data are lacking concerning the role which blacks played in the AFL's attempt to organize unskilled workers in all of Cleveland's major industries, the experience of black steelworkers with the Amalgamated Association of Iron, Steel and Tin Workers Union probably exemplifies the general pattern. Before the advent of the NRA, the Amalgamated Association had been a small collection of closely knit fraternal benefit lodges whose members represented the skilled aristocracy among steel and ironworkers. Traditionally, it had been ill-disposed toward the notion of organizing unskilled workers, white or black. After the enactment of the NRA, however, the growing demand of the rank and file steelworkers for union organization, together with the increasing threat of competition from the emerging company unions, virtually forced the AA to make an attempt to bring unskilled workers into its fold.[20]

Yet the AA entered the field of industrial organization only with the greatest reluctance; its campaign among white workers was halfhearted from the first, and its efforts to enlist black workers were practically nonexistent. Although at the beginning of the AA's drive local AFL leaders declared that it was "anxious to organize Negro workers and . . . absolutely opposed to any discrimination against them,"[21] almost no attention was given to developing special tactics to overcoming the suspicion, distrust, and hostility that the long years of union prejudice had built up within the black community. Throughout its campaign the AA rarely sent speakers to churches and social welfare institutions, showed no interest in the more general problem of race relations in the city, failed to employ a single black organizer, and made no attempt either to include blacks in union social affairs or to elect blacks to office in the newly formed lodges. In fact, the AA seems to have been motivated almost entirely by expediency, for blacks were rarely solicited for membership unless they constituted a large enough portion of the labor force within a factory that failure to include them would have undermined the effort to secure union recognition.[22]

In complete contrast to the AA's irresolute attempt to enlist black members, the steel industry made a determined effort to bring blacks into its company unions. Immediately following the enactment of the NRA, the steel industry sought to parry the AA's expansion drive by instituting an Employees Representation Plan. Since blacks were often a substantial portion of the unskilled labor force at many steel companies, employers realized that the AA campaign could not be successful without black workers. Therefore, a carefully calculated strategy of intimidation and pressure was used to bring them within the ERP.[23]

Some black workers were threatened with the loss of their jobs if they did not join the ERP.[24] During the Depression years, when the unemployment rate among blacks was approximately 50 percent, this kind of threat carried a great deal of weight, especially among those who were approaching retirement age. Other blacks were persuaded to become members of the ERP because the employers made a definite attempt to assure them positions of leadership.

At the National Malleable Steel Company, for instance, three of the seven officials were black, and at the Midland Steel Company a black was elected president.[25] To insure that the ERP did not become a vehicle for interracial cooperation that might later evolve into a movement for an independent union, employers sometimes encouraged the development of separate social clubs for whites and blacks. Thus, at National Malleable, the Tribe Club was made up of white workers, while the Diamond C. Club was exclusively for blacks. The company supervised the activities of the black club through its president, who was at the same time an official of the ERP.[26]

Confronted with the vigorous efforts of employers to bring blacks within the ERP and the unconvincing solicitation of the AFL organizers, black workers were not well disposed toward the AA. Although some expressed an appreciation of the theoretical advantages of an outside labor organization, most seemed to feel that blacks would be better off with the ERP. "We know that labor organizations are best for the laborers if they are fair," explained one worker,

> but it is a matter of choosing between two evils—either the company union or the outside union. We colored have decided after studying that if the labor organization were to get a footing, the colored would lose out. There are a few jobs which the colored hold which they, the white union, would like to get. . . . There is more discrimination in the unions than in the company.[27]

Some black workers went even farther in their opposition to the Amalgamated Association. In several plants, blacks formed small anti-union groups whose members circulated among the other black workers, pointing out the problem which might ensue if the AA signed up the plant.[28]

If the AFL's campaign to organize industrial workers accomplished nothing toward bringing the black community and the labor movement closer together, its drive to unionize skilled and semi-skilled workers drove them even farther apart. Black workers in these occupations were rarely offered more than a subordinate or segregated status by the AFL during the early thirties, and when they refused to accept union status on this basis, they were not infrequently threatened with violence. After refusing a request by the Painters Union that they form a segregated auxiliary, several black painters were beaten, others were threatened, and still others had their work destroyed. Two black plasterers were assaulted with lead pipes after they declined to join the Plasterers Union because it would not permit blacks to work outside the ghetto. A black mechanic who refused to enroll in the Mechanics Union for similar reasons avoided a beating only because he carried a gun, which he used to fend off his assailants. And two black haulers who refused to accept a subordinate status in the Teamsters Union had their business offices burned out on several occasions.[29]

The most dramatic confrontation between white unionists and black workers during these years occurred when the Gasoline Station Operators Union attempted to organize Wright's Sohio Station, a business that was owned and operated by blacks. In 1934 almost every gas station in Cleveland was shut down when the Gasoline Station Operators Union staged a strike to secure union recognition. Wright's Sohio, however, was one of the few stations still open, because his workers, well aware that the union had never allowed blacks to work anyplace but within the black community, had refused to join the strike movement. Angry at the resistance of the black workers and feeling that it was necessary "to stop the supply of gasoline in this town" in order for their strike to be successful, the Gasoline Station Operators threatened to forcibly close Wright's Sohio. Wright countered by using his employees and other black bystanders to form a human barrier around the station. Tension mounted steadily as taunts and threats were exchanged between the black workers and the white strikers. Finally, the strikers attempted to crash through the line with a car. In the process, they knocked down two blacks, a fight erupted, a shot was fired, and a riot was only narrowly averted by the timely appearance of the police. This incident, and others like it, attracted a great deal of attention in the black press and served only to confirm the belief of many blacks that the AFL was a "white man's organization."[30]

Midway through the Depression decade, the combination of the increased protection given to the unions by the National Labor Relations Act and the newly established Committee on Industrial Organizations' campaign to unionize industrial workers ushered the country into a period of intense labor activity. Increasingly during these years the black community was drawn closer to the labor movement. From its inception, the CIO's industrial structure and racially egalitarian ideology impelled it to devote considerable attention to attracting black support. The black response to the new unions evolved through several stages. In the middle thirties, the most common reaction appeared to be a mixture of interest and skepticism; in the late thirties and early forties, large numbers of black workers were enrolled in the industrial unions, and the black community manifested a generally enthusiastic commitment to the CIO; then, in the later war years, blacks evidenced a somewhat more restrained endorsement as some CIO affiliates began to encounter sporadic resistance from whites toward the upgrading of black workers. As the industrial union movement gained momentum and as the expanding defense industries drew larger numbers of black workers into the labor market, some of the AFL unions were induced to reorganize themselves on an industrial basis and to liberalize their racial policies. These reform efforts, however, do not appear to have been extensive before the final years of the war.

The framework for the integration of negro workers into the CIO was provided by both the New Deal labor legislation and the character of the new industrial union movement. Enacted in 1935, the National Labor Relations Act went even farther than had Section 7A of the NRA in giving support to union activity. It not only reaffirmed the right of labor to organize and bargain collectively, it also outlawed company unions, protected workers against reprisals from anti-union employers, and created the National Labor Relations Board with the power to supervise and enforce elections to determine bargaining agents. These protections were of particular importance to black workers, who traditionally had been the segment of the labor force most vulnerable to intimidation from employers.

Also important in opening the door to the participation of blacks in the new unions were the structure and ideology of the CIO. Formed first within the AFL as the Committee on Industrial Organization in 1935, and later as the independent Congress of Industrial Organizations in 1938, the objective of the new organization was to unionize workers on an industrial basis. Since its very existence depended on its ability to secure the allegiance of a majority of unskilled workers, and since blacks constituted a substantial portion of the unskilled labor force, the CIO was virtually compelled to seek a large black enrollment. Yet it was not necessity alone that dictated the inclusion of blacks in the industrial unions. As one scholar has put it, to a certain degree the CIO was a "crusading movement" whose objective was to uplift the masses of neglected common workers. Its ideological underpinning, therefore, was a radical democratic impulse that involved an expressed commitment to racial egalitarianism.[31]

Probably the most important factor in attracting blacks to the CIO fold, however, was the multifaceted campaign that its leaders developed to overcome the anti-union bias of the black community. Following the establishment of the Cleveland Industrial Union Council in 1937, attempts were made to gain the support of key black leadership groups. CIO representatives presented their case to prominent black ministers and often made financial contributions to their churches. The Cleveland Council passed resolutions endorsing the Urban League's drive to secure a more equitable distribution of New Deal public housing within the ghetto as well as the NAACP's effort to garner public support for comprehensive anti-lynching legislation. Union leaders frequently appeared at political meetings in behalf of black Democratic politicians who sought election to the city council. The CIO also cooperated with the local arm of the newly formed National Negro Congress in its efforts to publicize the plight of the economically depressed black masses.[32]

However, the CIO's primary appeal, especially in its early years, was to black workers themselves. Mass meetings were held at which black and white speakers explained the importance to industrial unionism of interracial cooperation. Often these meetings were concluded with an attempt to gather interested blacks into smaller groups, which would then disperse to the homes of union workers for further discussion in a more social atmosphere. Leaflets and newspaper articles designed to appeal to the special sensibilities of the black working class were prepared. One such piece combined biblical phraseology with the vocabulary of racial persecution. "Ye are groping in the darkness," the writer declared, "so come let us reason together. The S.W.O.C. [Steel Workers Organizing Committee] has brought to your very doors the salvation of our race economically which is an opportunity to join in the fight for the liberation of steelworkers from the bondage and oppression of steel." A determined effort was made to assure the election of blacks to positions of leadership in the new unions. By late 1937, black union officials, some of whom had been elected in predominantly white unions, were not uncommon. Finally, union social affairs and conventions were scheduled at facilities known to have a nondiscriminatory policy so that blacks would be encouraged to attend.[33]

Of strategic importance in the CIO's effort to enlist the support of black workers was the use of black organizers. Although in the opening months of the Cleveland campaign these men were brought in from the United Mine Workers unions in West Virginia, as the drive got under way, a small corps of organizers was gradually recruited from the ranks of local union activists. With their intimate knowledge of the black subculture and their entree to many of its institutions, organizations, and facilities, these black organizers became the vanguard of the CIO attempt to penetrate the black community. They served as speakers at various churches, fraternal lodges, and social clubs; as leaders of informal discussion groups at taverns, poolrooms, and other centers of public congregation; as composers and distributors of racially oriented union literature; as representatives of the CIO in community-wide civic drives and protest movements; and as living symbols of the CIO's interracial character. Perhaps more than anything else it was the day-to-day activities of black organizers that established the credibility of the CIO's appeal to black workers.[34]

During the middle thirties, black workers evidenced considerable interest in the CIO drive, but there was no general consensus on the question of joining the movement. Although it is estimated that significant numbers of blacks joined the new unions in 1936 and 1937, few did so without some misgivings, and some would have nothing at all to do with the CIO.[35] At one extreme were a small number of blacks who actively supported the industrial unions. Generally younger men who were experiencing the inequities of the black employment situation for the first time and who were not yet reconciled to the inevitability of their plight, such individuals often formed the nucleus around which black organizers sought to build up a following within a particular plant. At the other extreme was a small group of blacks who scrupulously avoided any contact with the CIO. These men tended to be older workers with long years of service and better paying jobs who did not want to jeopardize their favored positions with their employers by getting involved in union activity. In between these two clusters lay the masses of black workers, who, as one observer put it, "waited at first to see which way the cat jumped." Although these workers were at once fearful of reprisals from employers, skeptical of the CIO's preachments regarding the "brotherhood of all workers," and apprehensive about the possibility of communist involvement in the new unions, they were also anxious not to pass up any opportunity for better pay and improved working conditions. In consequence, many eventually joined the CIO, but they were "hesitant about wearing their union buttons until the agreement was actually concluded" between union leaders and employers regarding union recognition.[36]

The divisions existing within the black community over the CIO issue during the midthirties were cast into sharp relief by the Republic Steel Strike of 1937.[37] Black workers could be found in about equal numbers on either side of the dispute. At the time the strike vote was taken, the S.W.O.C.—which was spearheading the CIO's organizational drive in the steel industry—had signed up approximately half of the company's black workers. Although most of these walked out with the white workers, some disregarded their union pledges and remained within the plant. Later, when Republic issued an appeal for black strikebreakers, some blacks responded to the call, but not enough to meet the company's needs, and others had to be imported from the South. In the only large-scale outbreak of violence between unionists and strikebreakers—an incident which began when the Republic Steel Company armed a gang of its workers with pick handles and sent them to attack a CIO soup kitchen—blacks were included on both sides. Summing up the reaction of black workers to the CIO–Republic Steel controversy, one contemporary later commented, "We didn't know which way to go. All we knew was we wanted good jobs and good pay. But how to get them—that was the question."[38]

Nevertheless, despite the apparent divisions among black workers over the question of endorsing the new industrial unions, the CIO's organizational effort seemed to be attracting increasing support within the black community during the middle thirties. In the same period, however, the AFL's expansion drive accomplished very little toward changing its discriminatory image among blacks. Although in 1936 the Cleveland Federation of Labor announced its intention to "organize our Negro brothers into bonafide trade unions," and though a special "Committee of 16" was created to implement this objective, the ensuing campaign was marked by contradictions. In the metal trades, the International Molders Union took in some Negroes, while the important International Association of Machinists continued to bar them from membership. Similarly, the Bartenders, Hotel Service Workers and Waiters Unions made vigorous efforts to recruit blacks, but only on the condition that they accept membership in separate auxiliaries. In one instance reported by the Urban League, union pressure forced the firing of forty-five black waiters at a large restaurant because they refused to accept a segregated union status. While the Amalgamated Meat Cutters and Butchers Union assisted the black press in its campaign against the sale of bad meat within the ghetto, it also refused to allow blacks to become union members and it strongly opposed the efforts of the Future Outlook League to get jobs for blacks at the large Woodland East 55th Street Market. The AFL's unionization efforts in 1936 and 1937 attracted very little comment from blacks, but it is probable that many would have agreed with an editorial that appeared in the *Call and Post* cautioning Negro workers to "beware of Greeks bearing gifts."[39]

In the late thirties and early forties, the relationship between blacks and both wings of the labor movement appeared to undergo certain changes. As industry tooled up for war production, and as black workers increasingly returned to the private sector of the economy, the CIO intensified its campaign within the black community. Innumerable resolutions were passed by union committees, conventions, and public meetings calling for such things as the passage of anti–poll tax and anti-lynching legislation, the prosecution of landlords and merchants who violated price ceilings established by the Office of Price Administration, discontinuance of discrimination in the armed services, termination of the segregation of black blood by the Red Cross, and abolition of the prejudicial treatment of blacks in a wide variety of local public and semipublic accommodations.[40]

Moreover, CIO representatives actively participated in drives initiated by black leaders to obtain more adequate health and recreational facilities, to secure the appointment of a black representative to the Cleveland Metropolitan Housing Authority and a black judge to the municipal court, to elect black Democrats to state and city offices and to create a citywide Fair Rent Committee. Probably the high point of the CIO's efforts to promote racial egalitarianism was reached in late 1943 when the Cleveland Industrial Union Council played a key role in persuading the city's mayor to form a Committee for Democratic Practices with the sweeping objective of abolishing "all forms of discrimination against Negroes."[41]

While the CIO increased its activities in support of communitywide racial movements, it also stepped up its efforts in behalf of black workers. Information gained from interview sources suggests that black union officials were elected to office in increasing numbers in these years. When black women encountered difficulties in securing employment in defense industries, individual CIO unions established special committees to carry on educational campaigns among white workers to promote their acceptance. White union leaders frequently made it a point to promote the improvement of working conditions for blacks, particularly in relation to safety conditions and job advancement in the city's steel foundries. At several plants CIO representatives were able to persuade employers to accept union contracts containing clauses that banned discrimination in both hiring and promotion.[42] Attempts were made to do away with segregated cafeteria, toilet, and lunchroom facilities.[43] When some local war industries sought to avoid employing blacks by importing white workers from the South, the CIO strongly supported the War Manpower Commission's effort to encourage the full utilization of local labor resources. The efforts of the new industrial unions in behalf of racial advancement were so extensive in these years that few activities for the improvement of conditions for either black workers in particular or the black community in general seemed complete without a CIO representative or resolution affirming "uncompromising opposition to all forms of discrimination."[44]

The persistent appeals of the new unions elicited a rather general pro-CIO sentiment among black workers during this period, although there were always some who continued to eschew all union activity. Often those workers who either had better-paying jobs or were approaching pension age refused even to join CIO affiliates that had already gained contractual recognition from employers. Others would not participate in union activity during the organizing period but readily enrolled after negotiations were completed.[45] Yet the available evidence indicates that there was a widespread inclination in favor of the new unions.

Although there are no reliable membership statistics, both black and white union officials agreed that at least a majority of black workers in Cleveland's mass production industries were enrolled in CIO unions by the early forties.[46] Indeed, some workers recall this period as marking the high point of amicable relations between blacks and whites in the industrial union movement. Perhaps reflecting a nostalgia born of old age, but also evidencing something of the idealism of the period, one former black union official who was interviewed for this study observed:

> We were brothers and sisters, whites and Negroes. . . We went on picnics together at Geauga park. . . white fellow came to my home for coffee after union meetings. . . There was an unselfish relationship between Negroes and whites.[47]

In the face of increasing competition from the burgeoning CIO unions during the late thirties and early forties, some AFL affiliates began to liberalize their policies toward blacks.[48] Yet the extent of this liberalization was both limited and uneven. To a considerable degree the impetus for reform originated with a small interracial group of local union leaders centered around Frank Evans, a black international representative of the United Auto Workers Union. A large, physically imposing man with a blunt and independent disposition, Evans became an influential figure in the clique of union leaders who sought to broaden the AFL's appeal to black workers.[49] It was largely through the influence of this group that the Cleveland Federation of Labor was persuaded to appoint additional black organizers, to take steps to assure the election of more black union officials, to pass resolutions condemning discrimination in war defense industries, and to form a special committee to root out prejudice within the local AFL. In the early forties, black leaders who felt that the AFL "still has much shirt cleaning to do in its relation with Negro workers" could agree that Frank Evans was entitled to "outstanding recognition as a labor leader."[50]

However, it does not appear that the combined influence of competition from the CIO and pressure from the reform group centering around Frank Evans achieved more than mixed results in these years. This was particularly true in regard to unions which were not in direct competition with the CIO.

The Amalgamated Meat Cutters and Butchers union enrolled blacks where they constituted a sizable portion of the labor force, as was the case at the Swift Packing Plant, but refused to let them work in the smaller retail meat shops. The Hotel Service Workers Union persisted in its efforts to organize blacks into segregated auxiliaries. And a whole range of skilled trade unions, particularly those in the construction industry, made no effort whatsoever to let down their racial bars. What little improvement there was came in unions that were more directly threatened with CIO competition. Both white and black workers agreed that the UAW affiliates for which Frank Evans himself was directly responsible were among the most liberal in the city. At several plants the Molders and Foundry Workers Union accepted significant numbers of black workers. And it was in this period that the International Association of Boilermakers reconstituted itself as an industrial organization and began to admit blacks for the first time, although the number who were enrolled was quite small and none was allowed to hold skilled positions before the later war years.[51]

Some of the difficulties confronting the AFL reform leaders in addition to the often limited nature of their achievements during the early war years are suggested in the history of the local International Association of Machinists. Like the International Association of Boilermakers, the IAM was induced by increasing competition from the CIO unions to cast off its craft structure and reorganize on an industrial basis, but the provision in its ritual limiting membership to "sober white men" continued to prevent black workers from gaining admission. Subsequently, in 1941 a small group of AFL officials—including the president of the Cleveland Federation of Labor, the president of the Machinists District 54 (the local supervisory body of the IAM), and Frank Evans—persuaded the union's Executive Council to adopt a resolution advocating the admittance of blacks into the IAM. Some months later, however, it became evident that the various locals were not following the policy laid down by the Executive Council, and the president of the CFL designated Frank Evans as a special mediator to promote the integration of blacks into the Machinists Union.[52]

Despite considerable effort, Evans was not able to gain membership for more than a handful of black workers. Typical placements included sixteen blacks at the Chase Brass company and fourteen at the Cleveland Tractor Company.[53] The general attitude of most IAM locals seemed to be that no blacks would be accepted in any position, skilled or unskilled, until the supply of white workers had been exhausted.[54] As late as 1943, the director of the local War Manpower Commission, who himself had sought in vain to get the Machinists Union to accept blacks, concluded that the discriminatory practices of the

IAM locals constituted the "major obstacle to the full utilization of manpower in Cleveland."[55]

Complicating the efforts of the reform faction in this period was a series of clashes between several AFL locals and the Future Outlook League. Although there was considerable variation in the circumstances surrounding each confrontation, the incident involving Local No. 52 of the Bakery, Tea, Coffee and Yeast Drivers Union indicates the general nature of the conflicts. In January 1940, the FOL initiated an attempt to open up jobs for blacks as drivers on trucks delivering baked goods within the ghetto by asking the drivers union if it would accept black members. When the union refused to permit this, the league began to present its case to bakery owners and was eventually able to place several black delivery men with the Kritzer Brothers Bakers.[56]

Thereafter, the union took extraordinary steps to force the firing of the black drivers. The business agent of Local No. 52 warned Eddie Kritzer that it was "foolishness" to hire blacks because "the union won't stand for it." Several days later Kritzer's father, who ran an independent bakery in another section of the city, was threatened with damage to his business if he did not persuade his son to "cooperate" with the union. When Kritzer gave no sign of compliance, the drivers union harassed local grocery stores with uncertain delivery schedules in an effort to pressure them into refusing to sell Kritzer products. In turn, the FOL countered by boycotting and picketing ghetto-based groceries that capitulated to the union's demands. By early February, the confrontation appeared to be a standoff, with perhaps a slight edge going to the league.[57]

The dispute, however, continued for another several months, during which time the FOL successfully withstood intensified union pressure. Embarrassed by the unexpectedly effective resistance of the FOL, the drivers union sought to extricate itself from the imbroglio by offering to accept black drivers for union membership on the condition that the league would agree to make no further attempt to employ blacks as delivery men. Although there was some pressure from conservative elements within the black community to accept these terms, the FOL, which had by this time gained the support of several other leadership groups, including the Baptist Ministers Conference, the Insurancemen's Congress, and the Colored Grocers Association, refused to agree to anything less than full and unrestricted union membership for black workers. Then Local No. 52, declaring that it would "not permit Negroes to . . . deliver bread to any grocery," persuaded the Typographical Union to forbid its members at the Cleveland Wax Paper Company to print the paper which the Kritzer Brothers used to wrap their bread. Later, when Eddie Kritzer succeeded in getting a nonunion company to print the needed wrappers, another AFL drivers union refused to allow its trucks to deliver the paper. In the end, Kritzer himself brought the wrappers to his bakery.[58]

By June 1940, the FOL appeared to have gained the upper hand, but the conflict ended with a bizarre turn of events. At the height of the struggle the Kritzer company sought to capitalize on the race consciousness which the league's fight with the union had developed within the black community by bringing out a new product called Brown Girl Bread. The FOL assisted in the marketing of the bread by mounting an intensive publicity campaign, which was so successful that within several months production of the new bread increased from three hundred to twelve hundred loaves a day, and additional black delivery men were hired. By the middle of June, however, six months after the confrontation began and just when it appeared that the FOL had established its claim to jobs for blacks as delivery men, the Kritzer Brothers Company "vanished in the night." A building that had housed a thriving bakery one day stood as nothing more than a gutted shell the next. Overnight the Kritzer Brothers, their delivery trucks, and all of their expensive baking equipment had simply disappeared. Although there was never any conclusive evidence to indicate why the Kritzers left town, it was widely rumored that the brothers had accepted a large sum of money from the Bakery, Tea, Coffee, and Yeast Drivers Union.[59]

This and other conflicts like it between AFL locals and the Future Outlook League attracted almost weekly front-page coverage in the black press and served to overshadow the limited, halting, and contradictory process of internal reform taking place within the Cleveland Federation of Labor. Realizing that this was the case, a small group of AFL reform leaders, including Frank Evans, called a conference with the FOL in August, 1940. The result of this meeting was a gentleman's agreement to the effect that certain unions would defer to the interests of the FOL provided that the League confined its activities to the community.[60] While that agreement was honored by those unions which participated in its formulation, others refused to follow its terms, and the conflicts between the AFL and the FOL continued. In succeeding months the League encountered stiff opposition, which sometimes erupted into street violence, from such unions as the Brewery Drivers, the Retail Food Clerks, the Milk Drivers, and the Ice Drivers.[61] Since by the early forties the FOL enjoyed widespread support from almost all levels of black society and was at the peak of its popularity, these incidents confirmed many blacks in the belief that the AFL's racial policies had not improved to any significant degree.

In the middle forties, when the city's industries were at the peak of war production, the relationship between the black community and each of the two major organizations entered a new period. Although the black community remained committed to the CIO, it was in these years that the first signs of stress became evident between black workers and the industrial unions. As the wartime labor shortage fostered greater occupational mobility and workers of both races were increasingly drawn into competition for better jobs, several CIO affiliates encountered resistance from whites toward the employment and upgrading of blacks. The most common manifestations of this antagonism were the unauthorized walkouts staged by white workers that contemporaries referred to as "hate strikes."

Of the approximately half dozen such incidents that occurred in Cleveland,[62] perhaps the most typical was the strike involving the Mine, Mill, and Smelter Workers Union at the Chase Brass and Copper Company in June, 1944. In the late thirties when the plant had been organized by the union, blacks were

180

accepted for membership on a basis of apparent equality. There were several black union officials, and there seemed to be no objection on the part of white workers toward the occasional promotion of qualified black workers. In the middle forties, however, when the company's need for skilled workers led it to upgrade blacks on a larger scale, a small number of white workers in the casting department left their jobs in protest. As in most instances of this kind, the union's leadership quickly responded by expelling the white strikers.[63] Yet, despite vigorous efforts by CIO officials to prevent such walkouts, they continued to occur with sporadic consistency and became a characteristic feature of race relations within the industrial union movement in this period.[64]

As a consequence of these and other difficulties experienced by black members of the CIO at the height of war production, the enthusiasm that the new union had engendered within the black community in the late thirties and early forties now became more restrained. Although still committed to the CIO, black workers took steps to protect their interests. The more realistic attitude toward the industrial unions was clearly manifested in the proliferation of intra-union racial organizations. In the late war and early post-war years, such organizations as the Negro Labor Council, Citizens Progressive League, Steelworkers Booster Club, and others were established to promote racial advancement within the CIO.[65] Although many of these clubs had some social functions, their primary objective was frequently to provide a forum for the exchange of information and experience regarding the inner workings of the CIO so that black workers could more effectively reap the benefits of union membership.

While the middle forties signaled the point at which the CIO began to experience its first serious difficulties in implementing its nondiscriminatory policy, they also marked the time when the AFL achieved its first really significant reforms. Unquestionably the most noteworthy of these occurred at the Warner and Swazey Company in March, 1943, when the International Association of Machinists began to accept black workers into full membership. The catalyst for the change in policy was provided when the Future Outlook League took the company to court in an effort to seek redress for its disregard of President Franklin Roosevelt's Executive Order 8802 prohibiting racial discrimination in industries under contract with the federal government.[66] During the course of the trial it became evident that the company's failure to employ more Negroes was due in large measure to resistance from the IAM. The attitude of union officials contrasted so sharply with the democratic ideology of the war effort that the IAM was widely criticized in the white press. Taking advantage of this public censure, representatives of the local War Manpower Commission, the AFL reform group that included the IAM's highest ranking district official, and black leaders brought considerable pressure to bear on the union. Yet only after a bitter internal struggle that involved the removal of the union's president did the IAM at Warner Swazey agree to unrestricted membership for blacks. Subsequently, IAM locals at other plants began to accept significant numbers of black workers, but the process of liberalization continued in such an uneven fashion that blacks continued to maintain a skeptical attitude toward the AFL.[67]

In conclusion, the melding of New Deal labor legislation and the rise of industrial unionism engendered a new relationship between the black worker and the labor movement and thus represented one of the most important developments in the black social structure that took place in the thirties and early forties. At the beginning of the Depression decade, the craft structure and discriminatory racial practices of the American Federation of Labor kept the largely unskilled black labor force on the fringes of the labor movement. This situation remained unchanged during the early thirties when the AFL expansion drive conducted under Section 7A of the National Recovery Act failed to attract black workers. However, beginning in the middle thirties and continuing at an increasing pace in the thirties and early forties, the emerging CIO brought large numbers of black workers into its industrial unions. In the same period competition from the CIO impelled some AFL craft unions to reconstitute themselves on an industrial basis as well as to liberalize their racial policies, although their efforts in this direction were limited and uneven.

A graph plotting the trend of black union relationships in the Depression and war years would reveal a steady, upward course. A similar graph plotted to reveal the trend of black business development would suggest quite a different picture.

Notes

1. For background on blacks and the American Federation of Labor see Sterling D. Spero and Abram L. Harris, *The Black Worker: the Negro and the Labor Movement* (New York: Columbia University Press, 1931), *passim*; Herbert R. Northrup, "Organized Labor and Negro Workers," *Journal of Political Economy*, LI (June 1963), 206–21; and Marc Karsen and Ronald Radosh, "The American Federation of Labor and the Negro Worker, 1894–1949," in *The Negro and the Labor Movement*, ed. by Julius Jacobson (New York: Doubleday, 1968), pp. 155–88.
2. The information on the Building Trades Laborers Union is from *Cleveland Press*, April 17, 1941, and May 30, 1942, while that for the Asphalt Pavers Union is from the *Cleveland Gazette*, January 5, 1935, and December 28, 1935.
3. For references to the constitutions of these unions see Spero and Harris, *Black Worker*, p. 69. The policies of these unions in Cleveland are mentioned in the *Cleveland Gazette*, December 6, 1930; interview, January 17 and 25, 1972; and *Cleveland Plain Dealer*, February 11, 1931.
4. The policy of the Carpenters and Joiners Union was mentioned in interview, September 15, 1971; the Parquet Floor Layers and Painters, Decorators, and Paperhangers Unions are covered in Ira De A. Reid, *Negro Membership in American Labor Unions* (New York: Department of Research of the National Urban League, 1929), pp. 40 and 45.

5. General statements regarding these unions are in Charles W. Chesnutt, "The Negro in Cleveland," *The Clevelander*, V (November 1930), 3. Information on the Plumbers and Steamfitters and the Structural Iron Workers Unions was discussed in interviews January 25 and September 15, 1971. The Electrical Workers Union is discussed in Thomas Wallace Fleming, "My Rise and Persecution" (unpublished typewritten manuscript, ca. 1930), p. 23, Western Reserve Historical Society; Herbert R. Northrup, *Organized Labor and the Negro* (New York: Harper and Brothers, 1944), p. 25; F. Ray Marshall, *The Negro and Organized Labor* (New York: John Wiley and Sons, 1965), p. 113; *Hearings Before the Subcommittee of the Committee on the Judiciary*, U.S. Twentieth Congress, First Session, s. 1482 (Washington, D.C.: Government Printing Office, 1928), pp. 603–14; and interview, January 25, 1972.
6. Interview, January 25, 1972; and *Hearings*, pp. 603–14.
7. The Garment Workers and International Ladies Garment Workers Unions are mentioned in *Cleveland Call and Post*, February 13 and July 23, 1936 and in Spero and Harris, *Black Worker*, pp. 337–47. Very little is known about the Federal Laborers Unions except that they were chartered directly by the American Federation of Labor, that they consisted of unskilled workers, and that they accepted some blacks. This information was obtained from interview, February 10, 1972.
8. The Metal Polishers Union is discussed in Reid, *Negro Membership*, p. 67; the International Association of Machinists is discussed in interviews, January 24 and February 10, 1972; Spero and Harris, *Black Worker*, pp. 88–89; and *Cleveland Call and Post*, October 5, 1940.
9. The attitude of the Molders, Patternmakers, and Coremakers Unions toward blacks was uncovered in interviews, January 18 and February 10, 1972. For a discussion of the effects of fraternal organization on union policies toward the Negro workers see Spero and Harris, *Black Worker*, pp. 66–67 and 287–88.
10. The Meatcutters Union is referred to in Charles Loeb, *The Future Is Yours: The History of the Future Outlook League, 1935–1946* (Cleveland: The Future Outlook League, Inc., 1947), pp. 65–69; the Gasoline Station Operators in *Cleveland Call and Post*, April 28, 1934; and the Retail Food Clerks in *The Voice*, March 30, 1940.
11. In regard to the transportation industry, it should be noted that most of the railroad brotherhoods excluded blacks, although these were independent unions not affiliated with the American Federation of Labor and were relatively unimportant in Cleveland, which was not a large railroad center. See Northrup, "Organized Labor," p. 129; and interview, January 17, 1972. In other parts of the transportation industry the major Drivers Unions are discussed in Loeb, *Future Is Yours*, pp. 66–67; and the Teamsters Union is discussed in interview, February 10, 1972; and *Cleveland Call and Post*, September 6, 1941.
12. In the service industry the Waiters, Waitresses, and Cooks Unions as well as the Hotel and Restaurant Employees Unions are referred to in Chesnutt, "Negro in Cleveland," p. 3; *Cleveland Gazette*, December 28, 1929; David

H. Pierce to Charles W. White, January 2, 1931, NAACP Branch Files, Library of Congress; William R. Connors to T. A. Hill, July 29, 1930, Urban League Branch Files, Library of Congress; *Hearings*, pp. 610–12; *Cleveland Call and Post*, January 3, 1942; interviews, January 24 and February 14, 1972. The Porters union is discussed in the *Cleveland Eagle*, November 15, 1935.

13. The Postal Clerks are referred to in *Cleveland Gazette*, March 30, 1929; the teachers union in *Cleveland Call and Post*, February 17, 1934; and the musicians union in Reid, *Negro Membership*, p. 94.
14. For general background on the Cleveland Trade School and blacks see Chesnutt, "Negro in Cleveland," p. 3; George A. Meyers to Cleveland Chamber of Commerce, 1926, George A. Meyers MSS, Ohio Historical Society; and Jane E. Hunter, *A Nickel and a Prayer* (Cleveland: Eli Kani Publishing Co., 1940), p. 153. The quotation is from Howard L. Briggs, directing supervisor of vocational education and is quoted in the *Cleveland Gazette*, December 6, 1930.
15. General background for blacks and East Technical High School may be found in Chesnutt, "Negro in Cleveland," p. 3–4; and interview, January 18, 1972. The quotation is from Briggs, *Cleveland Gazette*, January 18, 1972.
16. The quoted material is from interview, January 17, 1972. The general consensus expressed in this section emerged from various interview sources, the most important of which was interview, January 14, 1972.
17. The Colored Waiters Club was covered in interview, February 14, 1972; "Central Area Social Study" (unpublished report of the Research Committee of the Welfare Federation of Cleveland, 1944) pp. 130–31; the Messenger Bond Club in *Ibid.*, pp. 130–31; the Postal Employees in *Cleveland Call and Post*, February 27, 1936; and the Chauffeurs in *Cleveland Gazette*, April 26, 1930.
18. William M. Leiberson and John A. Fitch, "The Cleveland Hotel Controversy," *American Economic Review*, XXI (March 1931), 291–92; *Cleveland Press*, July 16, 1930; and "Hotel Help: Cleveland Lockout," *The Survey*, LXV (February 15, 1931), 531; W. R. Connors to T. A. Hill, July 29, 1930 and September 22, 1930, Urban League Branch Files, Library of Congress; "Minutes of the Board of Trustees of the Cleveland Urban League," July 31, 1930, Cleveland Urban League MSS, Western Reserve Historical Society; *Cleveland Press*, July 16, 1930; *Cleveland Plain Dealer*, July 16, 1930 and September 25, 1930; *Cleveland Gazette*, August 16, 1930, August 30, 1930; and interview, February 14, 1972.
19. In the forefront of the black opposition were the black councilmen who several times voted against creating an arbitration committee because there seemed to be little concern with the plight of the black strikebreakers within the City Council. See *Cleveland Plain Dealer*, September 16, 1930. The quotation is from *Cleveland Plain Dealer*, May 1, 1931.
20. Spero and Harris, *Black Worker*, pp. 249–57; Allan H. Spear, *Black Chicago: The Making of a Negro Ghetto, 1890–1920* (Chicago: University of Chicago Press, 1967), pp. 196–64; Horace R. Cayton and George S. Mitchell, *The*

Black Worker and the New Unions (Chapel Hill: The University of North Carolina Press, 1939), pp. 159–62; and *Cleveland Press*, August 15, 1933.
21. *Cleveland Gazette*, December 22, 1934.
22. Cayton and Mitchell, *New Unions*, pp. 159–81 and 162–75; *Cleveland Gazette*, December 22, 1934; interviews, January 18 and January 24, 1972.
23. Cayton and Mitchell, *New Unions*, pp. 104–10; and interview, January 18, 1972.
24. Interviews, January 17 and January 18, 1972.
25. The evidence is conflicting as to whether there were three or four black representatives at National Malleable. Data from interview, January 18, 1972, indicate there were three, while Cayton and Mitchell, *New Unions*, p. 110 suggests there were four. The exact number of black representatives, however, is less important than the fact that there were any black officials at all. Midland Steel was referred to in interview, January 17, 1972.
26. Some information on the Diamond C Club is contained in the interviews cited by Cayton and Mitchell, *New Unions*, pp. 387–88. The data on the Tribe Club and the general interpretation given to both clubs were suggested in interview, January 18, 1972.
27. Cayton and Mitchell, *New Unions*, pp. 405–406.
28. *Ibid.*; and interview, January 18, 1972.
29. *Cleveland Call and Post*, August 4, September 15, and December 1, 1934; *Cleveland Eagle*, November 29, 1935; and interview, February 10, 1972.
30. *Cleveland Plain Dealer*, April 18, 1934; "Strikes and the Public," *Business Week*, May 12, 1934, pp. 11–12; *Cleveland Call and Post*, April 28, 1934; and interview, January 31, 1972.
31. The quotation is from St. Clair Drake and Horace R. Cayton, *Black Metropolis: A Study of Negro Life in a Northern City*, 2 vols.; (New York: Harcourt, Brace, 1945), I, 313. The democratic and racially egalitarian elan which characterized the early CIO organizational drive was confirmed in interviews, January 18 and interview, January 19, 1972.
32. These facts of the CIO campaign in the black community were gleaned from William Ganson Rose, *Cleveland: The Making of a City* (Cleveland: The World Publishing Company, 1950), p. 939; interviews, January 24 and March 6, 1972; *Cleveland Call and Post*, January 21, 1937; *Cleveland Union Leader*, December 9 and December 16, 1937; and *Cleveland Gazette*, June 12, 1937.
33. See *Cleveland Call and Post*, May 13, May 13, September 30, and October 7, 1937; and September 1, 1938; and *Cleveland Gazette*, November 20, 1937; *Cleveland Eagle*, September 4, 1936; and interviews, January 18 and March 6, 1972.
34. The first CIO black organizer in Cleveland, John Hart, is well remembered by local blacks. Hart had been with the United Mine Workers Union in West Virginia before coming to Cleveland. See interviews, January 2, January 24, 1972 and January 26, 1972; *Cleveland Call and Post*, May 13, 1937, September 30 and October 17, 1937; *Cleveland Eagle*, September 4, 1936.

35. Unfortunately, there are no data regarding black membership in the CIO unions. According to one estimate the Cleveland CIO had 65,000 members in 1937. Assuming blacks constituted about 10 percent of this figure, there could have been as many as 6,500 blacks in the CIO. Since the total black labor force numbered about 35,000 workers at this time, this figure represents about 17 percent of all black workers. However, in view of the fact that there was still considerable skepticism regarding the CIO in the black community in this period, this proportion seems quite high. See Rose, *Cleveland*, p. 939.
36. The data on which this interpretation was based were put together from interviews, July 18, 1971; January 19, 24, 26, and 29; and February 1, 1972. The quotations in this paragraph are from Rosemare Bearden, "The Negro in 'Little Steel'," *Opportunity*, XV (December 1937), p. 363.
37. It should be noted that the conclusions presented in this paragraph refer only to the Cleveland theater of the Republic Steel strike. In the nearby towns of Warren and Niles the interaction between the CIO and the black community was much different. See Bearden, "Negroes in 'Little Steel'," pp. 362–65; and Cayton and Mitchell, *New Unions*, pp. 193-98.
38. This account was put together from interviews, January 18, 19, 21, 24, 29, and 31, 1972, and the depositions of two black strikebreakers, Cooper Wilson and Richard McCand, in the Marvin C. Harrison MSS, Western Reserve Historical Society. The white press covered the strike in detail, but made almost no mention of blacks. The black press virtually ignored the strike, even to the extent of not reporting the role of black workers.
39. The quotation is from *Proceedings of the Ohio State Federation of Labor, 1936*, p. 77. The business agent of the Molders Union estimated that about fifty blacks were admitted to the local. *Cleveland Eagle*, April 17, 1938. The International Association of Machinists did not admit blacks to membership in Cleveland until early 1943. See *Cleveland Call and Post*, April 17, 1938. The Bartenders Union was discussed in *Ibid.*, October 8 and October 15, 1936; the Hotel Service Workers and Waiters unions in interview, February 14, 1972, and in "Report of the Executive Secretary of the Cleveland Urban League," May 1937, Cleveland Urban League MSS, Western Reserve Historical Society; the Meatcutters and Butchers in *Cleveland Call and Post*, October 15, 1936 and Loeb, *Future Is Yours*, pp. 54–55. The final quotation is from *Cleveland Call and Post*, July 23, 1936.
40. *Proceedings of the Ohio CIO Conference*, 1939, p. 58 and 1941, pp. 68–69. *Cleveland Union Leader*, September 12 and 20, 1941, January 8 and 29, 1943; and *Cleveland Call and Post*, January 24, 1942, and September 20, 1941.
41. *Cleveland Union Leader*, October 3, 1941, August 13, 1943, April 18, 1944; and *Cleveland Call and Post*, April 4, 1940, July 25, 1942.
42. The election of black union officials as discussed in interviews, January 18, 24, and 29, and February 1, 1972. The remaining references in the paragraph are to *Cleveland Call and Post*, September 13, 1941; and E.G. Young to R.A. Strong, January 6, 1941, Files of William Muldoon, War Manpower Commission, National Archives.

43. "Annual Report of the Urban League of Cleveland," 1941, Cleveland Urban League MSS, Western Reserve Historical Society.
44. *Cleveland Union Leader*, January 8, November 26, and December 17, 1943. The quotation is from *Proceedings of the Ohio CIO Conference*, 1941, pp. 68–69.
45. Interviews, January 26 and March 6, 1972.
46. *Ibid.*, and interviews, January 18, 19, and 24, February 10, and March 3, 1972.
47. Interview, February 10, 1972.
48. Explicit references to the effect of the CIO unionization drive on liberalization within the AFL are rare. Several are reported in R.A. Strong to William Muldoon, February 7, 1941 and Elliott G. Young to William Muldoon, October 3, 1941, files of the War Manpower Commission, National Archives; and William T. McKnight to Will Maslow, December 17, 1943, records of the Fair Employment Practices Commission.
49. Although generally critical of the AFL, the black press gave Frank Evans a great deal of publicity. See, for example, *Cleveland Call and Post*, May 9, 1942, and December 12, 1942; and *Cleveland Gazette*, March 25, 1939. The glimpses of Evans's activities revealed in the press accounts were pulled together in interview, January 18, 19, 24, and March 3, 1972.
50. *Cleveland Call and Post*, January 25, 1941; March 28, 1941; September 20, 1941; and January 31, 1942.
51. Compare, for example, *Cleveland Call and Post*, September 20, 1941 with Loeb, *Future Is Yours*, pp. 54–55 on the Meatcutters'; the Hotel Service Workers are discussed in *Cleveland Call and Post*, January 31, 1942. Skilled trade unions such as the Plumbers and Steamfitters, Electrical Workers, and Structural Iron Workers did not admit blacks until after the war. See interview, January 25, 1972. The views of white workers were obtained from interview, January 19, 1972, and those of black workers from interview, January 18, 1972. The Molders and Foundry Workers Union is referenced in *Cleveland Call and Post* (July 29, 1942), and the Boilermakers are discussed in Robert C. Weaver, "Negro Labor Since 1929," *Journal of Negro History*, XXXV (January, 1950), 30–31.
52. *Ibid.*, interviews, January 26, June 24, 1972; and *Cleveland Call and Post*, November 22, 1941.
53. *Cleveland Call and Post*, November 27, 1941; and *Cleveland Press*, January 5, 1943.
54. Interview, January 24, 1972; and Confidential Labor Market Report, October 16 to November 30, 1942, Bureau of Employment Security, files of the United States Employment Service, National Archives.
55. *Cleveland Press*, July 5, 1943.
56. *Cleveland Call and Post*, January 18, 1940; February 22, 1940; and Loeb, *Future Is Yours*, pp. 66–67.
57. Loeb, *Ibid.*; *Cleveland Call and Post*, January 25, 1940; and *The Voice*, January 16, 1972.

58. *Ibid.*, February 10, 1940; *Cleveland Gazette*, February 3, 1940; *Cleveland Call and Post*, February 8 and 29, 1940; Loeb, *Future Is Yours*, pp. 67–88; and interview, January 10, 1972.
59. Loeb, *Future Is Yours*, pp. 68–69; and *The Voice*, March 2, 1940, and June 13, 1940.
60. *Cleveland Call and Post*, August 17 and 24, 1940; interviews, January 16, 21, and 24, 1972.
61. The opposition of the Brewery Drivers is noted in *Cleveland Call and Post*, July 12, 1941; that of the Retail Food Clerks in *The Voice*, March 30, 1940; that of the Milk Drivers in Loeb, *Future Is Yours*, pp. 47–50; and that of the Ice Drivers in *Cleveland Call and Post*, August 17, 1940.
62. Several representative "hate strikes" are referred to in Northrup, *Organized Labor*, pp. 207–208; "Equality Campaign: Political Pressure Exerted in Cleveland for Local Drive to Further Employment of Negroes in the City's War Industries," *Business Week*, May 9, 1942, pp. 70–72; and *Cleveland Call and Post*, February 28, 1942, April 3, 1943, and April 10, 1943.
63. *Cleveland Call and Post*, June 3, 1944 and July 1, 1944; and interview, January 26, 1972.
64. E.L. Zeeman to William T. McKnight, June 1, 1945, War Manpower Commission, National Archives; and E. L. Keenan to William T. McKnight, April 30, 1945, Records of the Fair Employment Practices Commission.
65. The Negro Labor Council is mentioned in an unidentified news clipping dated 1943 in the NAACP Branch Files, Library of Congress; the Citizens Progressive League in *Cleveland Call and Post*, November 27, 1943, and interview, January 25, 1972, the Steelworkers Club in interview, January 26, 1972.
66. The FOL's suit against the Warner Swazey Company is discussed in Chapter IV.
67. Untitled memorandum, March 31, 1943; Daniel R. Donovan to William T. McKnight, December 6, 1943, William T. McKnight to Will Maslow, May 22, 1944, and William T. McKnight to Will Maslow, October 26, 1944, Records of the Fair Employment Practices Commission; *Cleveland Call and Post*, September 19, 1942, September 26, 1942, March 20, 1943, and April 3, 1943; *Cleveland Press*, January 5, 1943; and interview, January 24, 1972.

Table 17
The Status of Blacks in Unions Affiliated with the Cleveland Federation
of Labor by Industry in the Early Thirties

Black Members	No Black Members	Separate Black Union
Construction		
Hod Carriers	X	
Brotherhood of Carpenters and Joiners	X	
Plumbers and Steamfitters Union	X	
Sheet Metal Workers Union	X	
International Brotherhood of Electrical Workers	X	
Structural Iron Workers Union	X	
Plasterers Union	X	
International Brotherhood of Painters, Paperhangers, and Decorators	X	
Parquet Floor Layers Union	X	
Asphalt Pavers Union		
Building Trades Laborers Union	X	
Cement Finishers Union	X	
Bricklayers and Masons	X	
Manufacturing		
Metal Polishers Union	X	
Pattern Makers Union	X	
Molders Union	X	
International Association of Machinists	X	
Paint and Varnish Makers Union	X	
Amalgamated Association of Iron and Steel Workers	X	
United Rubber Workers Union	X	
International Ladies Garment Workers Union	X	
Coopers International Union	X	
Stationary Engineers Union	X	
Professional		
American Federation of Musicians	X	
American Federation of Teachers	X	

Note:
This summary of the status of blacks in the Cleveland Federation of Labor's affiliated unions is based on a wide variety of sources ranging from newspaper, manuscript, and other published sources to personal interview. Since documentation of the policy of each union would have taken up a great deal of space in the text, it has been left to an Appendix. See Appendix F.

Table 17 (continued)
The Status of Blacks in Unions Affiliated with the Cleveland Federation of Labor by Industry in the Early Thirties

Black Members	No Black Members	Separate Black Union
Government		
National Federation of Postal Clerks	X	
Transportation		
Teamsters Union	X	
Waiters and Beverage Dispensers Union	X	
Milk Drivers Union	X	
Bakery, Tea, Coffee, and Yeast Drivers Union	X	
Ice and Coal Drivers Union	X	
Amalgamated Association of Motormen and Conductors	X	
Streetcarmen's Union	X	
Brewery Drivers Union	X	
Trade		
Retail Food Clerks Union	X	
Meat Cutters Union	X	
Bakers Union	X	
Juke Box Operators Union	X	
Gasoline Station Operators Union	X	
International Maritime Union	X	
Service		
Waiters Union	X	
Waitresses Union	X	
Cooks Union	X	
Hotel and Restaurant Custodians Union	X	
Window Washers Union	X	
Greasers Union	X	
Porters Union	X	
Mechanics Union	X	
Laundry Workers Union	X	
Bartenders Union	X	
Cleaning and Dye Workers Union	X	

Public School Integration in Missouri, 1954-64

MONROE BILLINGTON

Professor of History, University of Toledo

On May 17, 1954, the United States Supreme Court issued its historic decision declaring state-supported segregated schools unconstitutional.[1] In the decade following that decision a few Deep South states successfully resisted the Court's implementing order of 1955 requiring state schools to admit pupils on a racially nondiscriminatory basis "with all deliberate speed,"[2] but several Southern and border states initiated the process of desegregation. Integrating large numbers of Negroes and whites soon after the Court's rulings, the border state of Missouri received much praise for its progress.[3] However, desegregation slowed down each succeeding year and essentially came to a halt by 1958. Indeed, some resegregation of schools occurred, especially in the urban areas, and in 1964 less than one-half of Missouri's Negro pupils were actually attending schools with whites.[4] The following paragraphs elaborate the limited progress and some of the problems of public school integration in Missouri from 1954 to 1964.

Missouri's population in 1954 contained approximately seven and one-half per cent Negroes.[5] Despite this relatively small percentage, Jim Crow practices were common in the state. Because of customs or laws, Negroes generally did not share equally in places of public accommodations and recreational facilities. Segregated residential areas were the rule rather than the exception, and Negroes and whites were statutorily prohibited from marrying.[6]

These traditions had been established in the latter part of the nineteenth century after the Civil War and the abolition of slavery, and Missouri's constitutions and laws for separate schools were in accord with them. The state's constitution of 1865 read, "Separate schools may be established for children of African descent,"[7] and shortly thereafter, the General Assembly "authorized and required" the townships' boards of education to provide separate

---

[1] Brown v. Board of Education of Topeka, 347 United States Reports 483-96 (1954).

[2] *Ibid.*, 349 United States Reports 301 (1955).

[3] A popular weekly news magazine in 1955 rated Missouri well ahead of other border and Southern states on the progress of school desegregation, and NAACP officials Roy Wilkins and Thurgood Marshall commended Missouri for "outlawing" school segregation. "Report Card Progress of the States Toward School Desegregation," *Time*, LXVI (September 19, 1955), 25; St. Louis *Post-Dispatch*, October 25; December 17, 1956.

[4] *Southern School News*, June 1964.

[5] In 1950 Missouri counted 297,088 Negroes in its total population of 3,954,653 for a percentage of 7.53. U. S. Bureau of the Census. *U. S. Census of Population:* 1950. Vol. II, *Characteristics of the Population.* Part 25, *Missouri* (Washington, 1952), 47.

[6] On the other hand, public transportation was legally nonsegregated, voting was unrestricted, and sports events, parks, auditoriums, libraries, and civil service jobs were generally open to all races. "Report to the United States Commission on Civil Rights on Desegregation of Schools in Missouri by the Missouri Advisory Committee" (mimeographed, July 1959), pp. 2, 99-102; *Report of the United States Commission on Civil Rights*, 1959, (Washington, n. d.), p. 207; *Revised Statutes of the State of Missouri*, 1949, Sec. 451.020; *ibid.*, 1957 Supplement.

[7] Missouri Constitution (1865), art. IX, sec. 2.

252

schools for colored children.[8] The mandatory language of the laws became a part of the constitution of 1875, and subsequent statutes contained words in keeping with that document.[9] A new constitution adopted in 1945 retained the provision requiring separate schools for white and colored children, and Missouri was being governed under this document in 1954. This constitution contained an important phrase permitting the state legislature to abolish the separate school system. The key sentence read, "Separate schools shall be provided for white and colored children, except in cases otherwise provided by law."[10] In view of this qualifying phrase, proponents of integrated schools had tried to legislate the separate school system out of existence in 1951 and 1953, but their attempts had been unsuccessful.[11] Missouri, therefore, was included among those seventeen states plus the District of Columbia which had compulsorily segregated schools in 1954.

Because the Supreme Court's ruling in May 1954 did not conform to Missouri's constitution and laws, the state's Commissioner of Education requested Attorney General John M. Dalton to clarify the situation. Dalton issued a formal opinion on July 1 declaring that the separate schools provisions of the state constitution and statutes were "superceded [sic] by the decision of the Supreme Court of the United States and are, therefore, unenforceable. . . . "[12] In spite of Missouri's Southern traditions, the Supreme Court's decision and Dalton's opinion on it raised few overt objections. The state Board of Education quickly adopted a resolution to implement the Supreme Court's ruling to the full extent of its authority under the Missouri constitution, and Governor Phil M. Donnelly stated publicly that Missouri would not resist the decision.[13]

Why were Missourians so amenable to school desegregation? Basic in the answer to this question was the work after World War II of many religious, civic, educational, and social groups, as well as a number of instances where desegregation in other areas had been successful, all of which help set the tone for smooth integration of the public schools. Many of the efforts for closer cooperation between the races prior to 1954 were made in St. Louis. Indeed, the St. Louis story was a dramatic one in view of the city's manifold southern traditions. Numerous agencies marshalled unpleasant facts about human relations in the city, helping to change significantly existing attitudes and conditions. The various organizations supporting desegregation in general and school integration in particular included the press, the League of Women Voters, the YMCA, the YWCA, the NAACP, the Urban League, the Metropolitan Church Federation of St. Louis, the National Conference of Christians and Jews, the Mayor's Commission on Human Relations, and several citywide parent and patron organizations

---

[8] *General Statutes of the State of Missouri:* 1866, chap. 46, sec. 20.
[9] Missouri Constitution (1875), art. XI, sec. 3; *Revised Statutes of the State of Missouri,* 1879, sec. 7052; *ibid.,* 1889, sec. 8002; *Ibid.,* 1909, sec. 10793.
[10] Missouri Constitution (1945), art. IX, sec. 1(a).
[11] St. Louis *Post-Dispatch,* April 12, May 2, 1959, March 5, 1953.

[12] *Race Relations Law Reporter,* I (February 1956), 282; see also St. Louis *Post-Dispatch,* July 1, 1954.
[13] *Race Relations Law Reporter,* I (February 1956), 277; St. Louis *Post-Dispatch,* May 19, 1954.

and alliances.[14]

Many events in St. Louis reinforced the foundation for voluntary compliance with the Supreme Court's ruling. These cracks in the color wall included increasing desegregation of leading hotels in the city, desegregation of the major league baseball park (1944), initiation of desegregation policies by Saint Louis University (a Roman Catholic institution) and nonsectarian Washington University (1944 and 1947, respectively), desegregation of the school system of the Roman Catholic Church (1947), desegregation of municipal swimming pools and other recreational facilities, including children's playgrounds (1950), desegregation of the city's largest legitimate theatre (1951), considerable progress in equalization of employment opportunity, illustrated by the hiring of Negro streetcar and bus operators (1953), and the formation of an Intergroup Education Association of public school teachers and principals to improve the teaching of human relations in the schools.[15] Integration of St. Louis' public schools was the next logical — if not easy — step.

Inasmuch as the major newspapers of St. Louis had statewide circulations, publicity concerning desegregation in the state's largest metropolis undoubtedly softened resistance throughout the state, making it easier for many school boards to initiate integration in their communities. Thus, when Missouri's Attorney General stated that school boards were free to desegregate their schools, a number of districts immediately made plans for mixed schools, and numerous small and medium-sized towns in every section of the state desegregated part or all of their schools when the 1954-55 term began in September. Negroes resided in 75 of Missouri's 114 counties, and the process of desegregation was reportedly underway in 52 of them.[16] With few Negro pupils, towns such as St. Joseph, Mexico, Neosho, Clarksville, Macon, Madison, and Fulton desegregated with no serious problems or opposition. Uneventful change-overs were evident when most of the schools witnessed Negroes and whites participating without incident in sports, social events, and other extracurricular activities.[17]

The total school population in Missouri in 1954 was 710,000 of which 63,100 were Negroes. Of these, 55,500 Negro pupils resided in the city and county of St. Louis, Kansas City, and six rural counties in Missouri's southeastern corner, leaving only 7,600 Negro pupils spread thinly over the remainder of the state.[18] Since nearly 90 per cent of the Negro pupils were concentrated in two metropolitan centers and a half dozen rural counties, attention must be directed to these areas for an understanding of what happened respecting public school integration in Missouri.

Supervising a public school system embracing nearly 99,000 children of which 32,800 were Negroes, the St. Louis Board

---

[14] *Ibid.*, May 18, June 4, 7, 1954; St. Louis Public Schools, Instruction Department, "The St. Louis Story: The Integration of a Public School System" (mimeographed, February 1955), pp. 11-12.
[15] Bonita H. Valien, *The St. Louis Story: A Study of Desegregation* (New York, 1956), pp. 8, 10-12; *Civil Rights U.S.A. Public Schools [in] Cities in the North and West 1962* (Washington, n. d.), pp. 255-57.

[16] *Kansas City Star*, October 14, 1954.
[17] *Southern School News*, September 3, October 1, November 4, December 1, 1954; St. Louis *Post-Dispatch*, June 14, July 12, 13, August 8, 13, 24, 28, 31, September 5, 9, 1954, June 23, 1955.
[18] *Southern School News*, September 3, 1954.

of Education announced on June 22, 1954, that racial segregation would be brought to an end in the city of St. Louis by means of a three-stage plan. Unanimously adopted by the Board, this program provided for consolidating Stowe Teachers and Junior College (for Negroes) with Harris Teachers and Junior College (for whites) in September 1954. At the same time special schools and classes for the handicapped were to be desegregated. The second step, to be taken at the beginning of the second semester in January 1955, provided for desegregation of the adult education program and all of the city's public high schools except the technical schools. The final phase, desegregation of the elementary and technical high schools, was to be inaugurated in September 1955. The plan stipulated that new boundary lines were to be fixed to provide the best use of all school facilities without regard to race. Students were to be required to attend schools according to the new boundaries, but under certain conditions transfers would be granted. The board's justification for making the transition over a twelve-month period stemmed from the considerable work related to the drawing of new school district lines, assignment of pupils, teachers, and other personnel, and transferring books and auxiliary materials. By integrating in steps, school administrators could concentrate on particular schools — thus doing a better supervisory job.[19]

Because of a delay in the construction of the new O'Fallon Technical High School, the board postponed until September 1956 the implementing of desegregation at the city's technical schools. Except for this change, the plan was carried out on schedule with no major problems or objections. The easy integration of the student bodies and faculties of the teachers and junior colleges foreshadowed equally simple transitions when the other phases were taken. The burning of two crosses, occasional altercations between white and Negro students, and some mutterings of discontent among white parents indicated minimal opposition and only served to illustrate how well St. Louisans were accepting the new conditions.[20] Thus, over a two-year period St. Louis, with slightly more than one-half of Missouri's total Negro pupil population, had accomplished a major feat on the desegregation front.

With 21 suburban school districts, St. Louis County in 1954 had almost as large a school population as the city of St. Louis. But while one-third of the school children in the city were Negro, less than five per cent (3,500) of the pupils in the county's schools were colored. Furthermore, the Negro children were concentrated in a few population centers, and when county school districts desegregated between 1954 and 1957, little actual integration occurred. Under such circumstances, St. Louis County had minimal opposition and considerably fewer administrative problems than did the city of St. Louis.

Kansas City, with 10,400 (16%) Negroes in a pupil population of 65,000, followed a stage-by-stage transition to an integrated school system not unlike the city of St. Louis. Having voted to con-

---

[19] St. Louis Public Schools, "St. Louis Story," pp. 8-9. See also St. Louis *Post-Dispatch*, June 23, 1954. For a detailed account of the execution of the plan, see St. Louis Public Schools, Instruction Department, "Desegregation of the St. Louis Public Schools" (mimeographed, September 1956), pp. 22-63.

[20] St. Louis *Post-Dispatch*, October 4, November 10, 1954, March 2, 5, August 28, 1955, October 4, 1956.

duct mixed classes during the 1954 summer session in two high schools and the Junior College of Kansas City, the Board of Education announced in July that Negro students at Lincoln Junior College would be transferred to the formerly white junior college in September, and that at the same time two vocational high schools would be integrated. Plans were laid for the other high schools and elementary schools to be integrated in 1955. Again, the reason for the delay was to gain time for solving administrative problems.[21] The plans were put into effect as scheduled, and Kansas City received its share of commendation for school integration. The editor of a widely-circulated Negro weekly newspaper in the city wrote that not a "ripple of difficulty" occurred in any of the schools with mixed student bodies.[22]

The half dozen rural counties in the southeastern corner of Missouri are referred to collectively as the Bootheel. Bordering Arkansas, Kentucky, or Tennessee, these Mississippi River delta counties are economically dependent upon cotton and, except for the two large urban centers, have a higher percentage of Negroes than other areas in the state. With Southern customs and traditions well ingrained, resistance to school integration was strongest in these counties where 8,800 Negro pupils lived, but some changes did occur during the decade under consideration. Four schools in the area desegregated in 1954 with no untoward incidents, and a few additional schools followed in 1955. Two counties — Pemiscot and New Madrid — had the dubious distinction of being the state's only counties having taken no steps toward desegregation by June 1956, and several schools in the Bootheel counties had made only token efforts to integrate. In 1956 seven high schools in Missouri had not desegregated and 8,000 elementary pupils were still required to attend separate schools. Six of the high schools and half of the elementary pupils were in the Bootheel counties.[23] But it was generally believed that the Bootheel would soon be integrated, and little publicity was given to the lack of change in that area after 1956. Most observers preferred to look at other parts of the state where additional schools were dropping the color bars.

Economy of operation was a major consideration in the minds of school board members all over the state as school integration was put into effect. Many districts with a few Negroes had been paying dearly to maintain separate schools, and they welcomed the Supreme Court's ruling because a considerable saving resulted when the schools were combined.

Approximately one-half of the school districts in Missouri dismissed one or more Negro teachers upon desegregating their schools. The greatest mortality was in the rural or semi-rural areas where each district often hired only one or two Negro teachers. Desegregation resulted in the loss of positions for some 125 to 150 Negro teachers in the state.[24] In some instances, Negro teachers were able to find positions in nearby segregated schools, while others migrated from the state. Many

---

[21] *Kansas City Call*, May 28, 1954; *Southern School News*, September 3, 1954; "Missouri Advisory Committee Report, 1959," p. 45.
[22] *Kansas City Call*, September 23, 1955.

[23] *Southern School News*, June 1956.
[24] "Missouri Advisory Committee Report, 1959," pp. 112, 118-19; Southern Education Reporting Service, *A Statistical Summary, State By State, of School Segregation-Desegregation in the Southern and Border Area from 1954 to the Present* (13th rev., Nashville, 1963-64), p. 331.

moved to Missouri's larger school systems and because of rising school populations in Kansas City and St. Louis, much of the state's gross loss of Negro teachers as a result of initial desegregation was soon overcome.[25]

St. Louis' school board integrated teachers as well as pupils in 1954-1955, guaranteeing tenure rights and promising to make future appointments from a single examination-rated list without regard to race or color. If a school's enrollment decreased because of redrawn boundary lines, surplus teachers were transferred to schools where they were needed. No Negro teacher in St. Louis lost his job because of integration.[26] Kansas City was slower than St. Louis in initiating teacher integration and continued to lag behind throughout the decade, although the western city integrated a few teachers early and mixed faculties increased each year.[27] But neither St. Louis nor Kansas City was free from criticism. Schools in the two cities which enrolled a disproportionate number of either white or Negro pupils usually had faculties of the majority race. Biracial faculties often existed only in schools with mixed populations, and racial distributions of teachers closely paralleled racial concentrations of pupils.[28] Seldom did white teachers work under Negro principals, but St. Louis school authorities insisted that they did not assign teachers on the basis of race, and they refused to reassign teachers with race in mind.[29]

Having desegregated more school districts in 1954 than any other state, Missouri was publicized each year as being progressively more desegregated (75% in 1954, 85% in 1955, 88% in 1956, 90% in 1957, 95% in 1958.)[30] But progress in Missouri was not as great as it seemed. The published per cents referred to school-age Negroes enrolled in the state's public schools who were in "integrated situations,"

---

[25] *Southern School News*, July 1958. When the town of Moberly desegregated its schools in 1955, eleven Negro teachers were dismissed. Convinced that their contracts were not renewed solely because of their race, eight of the teachers went to court to regain their jobs. They contended that the Moberly school board violated their rights under the due process and equal protection clauses of the Fourteenth Amendment when it refused to rehire them. The petitioners lost when the district court ruled that the school board had acted honestly in awarding teachers' contracts in 1955. This decision was upheld in the Eighth Circuit Court of Appeals, and by refusing to review the case, the United States Supreme Court tacitly agreed. Kansas City *Call*, May 6, 1955, February 17, 1956, March 6, December 4, 1959; *Southern School News*, September 1956, November, December 1959.
[26] Valien, *St. Louis Story*, p. 15.
[27] *Southern School News*, February 1959; Kansas City *Star*, July 28, 1963; Kansas City *Times*, August 30, 1963. For complaints about Kansas City's limited progress, see Kansas City *Call*, July 8, 1955, June 14, 1957, July 13, 1962.

[28] *The 50 States Report Submitted to the Commission on Civil Rights by the State Advisory Committees, 1961* (Washington, n. d.), p. 354; "Missouri Advisory Committee, 1959", pp. 123-24; *Southern School News*, February 1959, February 1960.
[29] St. Louis *Post-Dispatch*, April 26, 1963; *Southern School News*, July 1963. Having received many informal complaints about discrimination against Negro teachers, the Missouri Commission on Human Rights in 1964 conducted a survey to determine whether the state's fair employment practices law was being followed in the schools.
[30] *One Hundred Fifth Report of the Public Schools of the State of Missouri, School Year Ending June 30, 1954* (Jefferson City, n. d.), p. 23; *One Hundred Sixth Report of the Public Schools of the State of Missouri, School Year Ending June 30, 1955* (Jefferson City n. d.) p. 24; *Southern School News*, October 1955, September 1956, June 1957, June, September 1958; Southern Education Reporting Service, *Status of School Segregation-Desegregation in the South and Border States* (Nashville, 1958), p. 17; "Missouri Advisory Committee Report, 1959", pp. 46-49, 62; *Report of the United States Commission on Civil Rights*, 1959, pp. 205, 207-208.

i.e., in districts where segregation of the races had been officially abolished with colored students attending classes with whites or *theoretically* entitled to do so. Many Negroes in "integrated situations" were not, in actuality, integrated but little publicity was given to this fact. In 1959 the Missouri Advisory Committee to the United States Commission on Civil Rights reported that the "vast majority" of Negro pupils were still attending segregated schools. In a long report based on considerable research, the Committee pointed out that Missouri school integration had reached its peak in 1954 and thereafter the process had slowed down. The Committee concluded that "perhaps there has crept in a certain amount of complacency, as a result of the favorable comments which Missouri's attitude toward desegregation has elicited outside the State."[31] When the Committee reported again two years later it found virtually no change.[32]

The primary reason many Negro pupils attended segregated schools stemmed from residential housing patterns. The problems were especially acute in St. Louis. Because of economic opportunities, large numbers of Negroes from the South poured into the city during and following World War II, the trend continuing after 1954. With the Supreme Court's decision many whites who preferred uniracial schools joined an already significant number of their neighbors who were rushing to the suburbs in St. Louis County. These population shifts resulted in the resegregation of some schools as Negroes formed a belt through the central part of the city from the Mississippi River to the western city limits.[33] Schools which had been all-white before 1954 found that their student bodies gradually became all-Negro or nearly so. This was especially apparent in the West End area. From 1950 to 1960 the West End shifted from 98 per cent white to 64 per cent Negro. As a result, Soldan High School, serving the West End and contiguous neighborhoods, was 74 per cent white in February 1955, but 90 per cent Negro in 1964. A number of elementary schools such as Arlington, Columbia, and Scullin underwent comparable changes during the same period.[34]

The subject of pupil transfers was related to the resegregation problem. Negro parents believed that the Board of Education's transfer policies were partially responsible for the racial imbalance in the schools. They charged that "wholesale" special transfers of white students from Soldan High to Southwest High were granted when the schools were desegregated. Despite Superintendent Phillip J. Hickey's vigorous denials that the transfer policy was discriminatory and although a 1962 impartial report to the U. S. Commission on Civil Rights concluded that the Negroes' claims were unfounded, the charges reflected Negro misgivings of the board's policies.[35]

---

[31] Missouri Advisory Committee Report, 1959," pp. 40, 80, 81; *The National Conference and the Reports of the State Advisory Committees to the U. S. Commission on Civil Rights,* 1959 (Washington, 1960), p. 218; St. Louis *Post-Dispatch,* June 7, 1959.

[32] *The 50 States Report,* pp. 354-55; *Southern School News,* October 1961.

[33] American Civil Liberties Union, *Work Ahead in Hope; 39th Annual Report July 1, 1958 to June 30, 1959* (New York, [1960]), p. 73. Population movements primarily accounted for the fact that while Negro children constituted 33 per cent of the total number of pupils in St. Louis in 1954, a decade later they comprised 57 per cent. St. Louis *Post-Dispatch,* February 12, 18, 1964.

[34] *Civil Rights U.S.A.,* p. 268; see also St. Louis *Argus,* December 7, 1962; St. Louis *Post-Dispatch,* December 2, 5, 1962.

[35] *Civil Rights U.S.A.,* pp. 278-81; *Southern School News,* June 1963.

A more explosive issue arose over the board's attempt to solve overcrowding in certain schools by transporting pupils to less crowded schools in the city. In 1960 Negroes constituted most of the 1,000-plus pupils being transported from over-populated schools, and when civil rights leaders charged that these children were not being taken to the nearest uncrowded school if that school were all-white, the board readily admitted the charge. The board believed in "neighborhood schools" and contended that school authorities were not obligated to change deliberately the character of a neighborhood or its school.[36]

In the fall term of 1961-62, St. Louis school officials provided bussing facilities for some 3,200 elementary school children from overcrowded school districts to available classroom space in other parts of the city. Over 90 per cent of the transported children were Negro, and many of them were sent to all-white schools, but they went as classroom units. Moreover, the transported pupils used the school grounds and cafeteria facilities at times other than when the regular pupils used them. While 106 rooms of children were transported every day from sending to receiving schools and back in 1961-62, the following year saw the bussing program swell to 4,800 pupils in 136 rooms. The board held that classrooms as separate units could be administered more easily and that lunchroom and recreational facilities were less strained if transported and resident children had different eating and recess periods. These explanations did not satisfy the Negro community, and criticism of school officials and their policies increased.[37]

When Negroes hinted that a court test might come over the bussing of children, Superintendent Hickey appointed a special committee to investigate the transporting system. In the spring of 1962 this three-member committee headed by James A. Scott suggested a series of measures to insure that transported children not be segregated from other children at the host schools. Two of the committee's twelve recommendations dealt with the organization of school days at receiving schools, urging greater efforts to bring resident and transported pupils together in all aspects of school life — with emphasis on integration of classrooms, playgrounds, lunchrooms, schoolwide projects, picnics, and parents' activities.[38] By the time the committee issued its report in June 1962, one of its suggestions was already in effect: transported pupils were having their noon, recess, and lunch periods at the same time as local pupils. If shortage of facilities and space required dividing the children into groups, the divisions were not being made on whether the children were transported. But when school officials in June 1963 indicated that they intended to continue to segregate transported pupils in the classrooms at the receiving schools, Negro parents objected and organized a Committee for Parents of Transported Pupils. On one occasion these parents stood in the streets in the West End area to prevent a dozen busses from operating.[39]

In the meantime, other Negro groups

---

[36] St. Louis *Post-Dispatch*, February 18, 1960; *Southern School News*, March 1960. In metropolitan areas a neighborhood school is one which limits enrollment, or most of it, to pupils who live either within walking distance or no farther than a short bus ride away.

[37] St. Louis *Argus*, July 14, 28, August 4, 1961.

[38] St. Louis *Post-Dispatch*, June 13, 1962; *Southern School News*, July 1962; *Civil Rights U.S.A.*, pp. 271-73.

[39] St. Louis *Post-Dispatch*, June 6, 7, 9, 12, 1963.

protested not only the bus program but also such matters as transfer policies and resegregation. After weeks of charges and countercharges involving these and other concerns, Negroes in March 1963 requested the establishment of a special fact-finding committee to probe the broad range of Negro problems in the public schools.[40] In the following month Board of Education President Daniel L. Schlafly appointed a twelve-person Citizens Advisory Committee to discover whether St. Louis public schools had engaged in policies, procedures, or practices causing resegregation and to evaluate numerous other criticisms leveled at the board and school administrators.[41] Led by the Rev. Trafford P. Maher, head of the Department of Education, Saint Louis University, this biracial committee issued its final report in June, recommending sweeping changes to promote maximum desegregation in the St. Louis public schools. Among other recommendations, the committee suggested that some district boundaries be redrawn to promote desegregation and that Negro pupils transported by bus be "fully integrated" in all classrooms and extraclassroom activities of the receiving schools. Although supporting the neighborhood school concept, the committee recommended that an open enrollment principle be instituted, permitting some students to transfer to available classrooms regardless of their residence.

Adopted unanimously by the committee members, the report expressed the belief that the school board and administrative officials had acted in good faith in the past. However, with regard to future policy, it urged lines of action which Negro and civil rights leaders had proposed and which the school system had resisted. Recognizing that implementing problems would be difficult, the committee felt that "creative procedures" were needed. The committee acknowledged that the school system was being blamed, in part at least, for problems the schools had not created and could not solve. But it suggested that the board work so that "integration of the facilities and activities of the public schools may continue the progress thus far made in an orderly fashion and in a climate of good will."[42]

In a report to the school board in July, Superintendent Hickey recommended that a modified open enrollment policy be established, that buses be rescheduled so that all children could have the same lunch period, and that partial but not total classroom integration be inaugurated in several of the host schools. But while Hickey made these and other concessions, he rejected a Maher committee suggestion that school boundaries be redrawn to achieve more mixed schools. As a result, representatives of eleven Negro and civil rights organizations immediately termed Hickey's report unacceptable. These groups picketed the Board of Education's subsequent meeting held to act on Hickey's recommendations, but the board accepted Hickey's plan and updated its pledge to achieve desegregation. In a new policy statement the board asked the help of "the entire community in eliminating practices which prevent maximum integration through the denial of equal opportunities in housing, employment and other benefits of human dignity and worth."[43]

Negroes did not respond to this plea

---

[40] *Ibid.*, March 6, 17, 18, 1963.
[41] *Southern School News*, April 1963.
[42] St. Louis *Post-Dispatch*, June 21, 1963; *Southern School News*, July 1963.
[43] *Ibid.*, August 1963.

in the way the board hoped. Opposed to the bussing program and continued segregated classes, the St. Louis branch of the NAACP announced that it planned to encourage a boycott of segregated public schools in September 1963. The Board of Education filed a suit in the U. S. District Court at St. Louis in August asking for a judgment upholding the legality of the board's bus transporting program and seeking an injunction prohibiting interference with the bussing of the pupils. Two weeks later the NAACP instituted a suit accusing the board and school administrators of violating the Constitution by operating a segregated school system and asking that school officials be restrained from segregating transported Negro pupils. The NAACP deferred the "pupils-stay-at-home" campaign pending more extensive evaluation of desegregation proposals by the Board of Education, but Negro leaders made it clear that direct measures and pressure tactics would be applied if board action on desegregation was not forthcoming.[44]

Because of the controversial bus transportation program and with a growing classroom shortage, the St. Louis school board in January 1964 approved construction of 34 temporary classroom buildings (called "transportables") in the city's crowded West End section. But the transportables were opposed by an organization of Parents for Integrated Education which demanded that Negro pupils lacking space be bussed to schools in other neighborhoods and integrated into classrooms there. The organization strongly opposed the construction of the supplementary buildings, saying that this would only intensify the Negro "ghetto" in the West End.[45]

Replacing Philip J. Hickey who retired in August 1964, Superintendent of Instruction William Kottmeyer supported the transportables and hoped to keep the bus transporting to short runs by "block transportation instead of by rooms." Kottmeyer was criticized by some Negro and civil rights leaders because of *de facto* segregation in the schools, but he had the support of the majority of the Board of Education, including the Negro members.[46]

When Kansas City desegregated, it continued a liberal transfer policy allowing students to move from crowded schools to those with vacancies.[47] As increased requests for transfers were made, especially those taking white students away from high schools with heavy Negro enrollments, the Kansas City *Call* feared that the liberal transfer policy might be carried too far, spoiling an otherwise good record of the Kansas City school board.[48] But the Negro community in Kansas City generally accepted school conditions until the summer of 1963. The relative calm was abruptly disturbed when several Negro groups criticized the board's operation of its schools. Joining the nationwide protest of Negro inequities and sponsored by the Congress of Racial Equality (CORE), over 200 persons calling for "total integration" marched on the Board of Education building. With Kansas City's Negro pupil population rising from 16 per cent in 1954 to 34 per cent of the total in 1964, the

---

[44] *Ibid.*, July, September, October 1963; St. Louis *Post-Dispatch*, August 13, 20, 1963.
[45] *Southern School News*, February, April 1964.

[46] In 1964 the St. Louis school board had three Negro members, one of which was the Rev. John J. Hicks who had been elected to the board in 1959, the first Negro to serve on a school board in Missouri. Hicks was unanimously elected President of the Board in October 1963.
[47] *Southern School News*, April 1956. Also, Kansas City *Times*, June 4, 1963. Transfers were allowed for academic and "other legitimate reasons."
[48] September 14, 1956.

CORE-led group sought a policy statement from the board looking toward greater desegregation in the redrawing of school district boundaries, in the selection of new school sites, in granting transfers, and in faculty assignments. It also asked for the appointment of a biracial committee to help plan along these lines.[49]

Sensitive to Negro demands, the Board of Education announced in August 1963 a general policy which favored maximum racial desegregation "without destroying the fundamental principle of the school as a major service unit to the neighborhood of which it is a part." CORE leaders expressed approval of the new policy, and the board and Superintendent of Schools James A. Hazlett made a point of continuing discussions with representatives of the NAACP and in general trying to cooperate with the Negroes' requests. But tension in the community and schools continued because of *de facto* segregation, and sporadic gang fighting along racial lines near some schools was attributed in large part to the lack of integration.[50]

In 1964 the school boards of Missouri's two urban centers were committed to neighborhood schools (for both theoretical and practical reasons), and these stands were pitted against Negro demands for the end of *de facto* segregation. Under these circumstances, what of the future? Resolution of this conflict — not peculiar to the cities of Missouri — will undoubtedly ultimately come from the United States Supreme Court.[51] Meanwhile, many schools in Missouri will retain a large degree of racial imbalance.

Missouri's problems and partial success in integrating its schools during the first decade following the Supreme Court's decision were not unlike those of other border states having segregated schools in 1954.[52] This being true, this case study of one state emphasizes that after ten years school integration was far from complete in the border and Southern states.

---

[49] Kansas City *Times*, June 27, July 3, August 19, 1963; *Southern School News*, August, December 1963, May 17, 1964.
[50] *Ibid.*, September 1963; Kansas City *Times*, September 17, 1963; "A Report of the Missouri Advisory Committee to the United States Commission on Civil Rights" (mimeographed, June 1963), pp. 16-18, 21.

[51] Assuming good faith and the absence of a policy of segregation, may a board overlook segregation in its schools caused by neighborhood racial concentrations? After reviewing a number of legal cases, one researcher has concluded that school boards cannot constitutionally ignore *de facto* segregation and that they must act reasonably to prevent it or to minimize it if it is unavoidable. Robert Allen Sedler, "School Segregation in the North and West: Legal Aspects," *Saint Louis University Law Journal*, VII (Spring 1963), 228-75.
[52] E.g., see this author's, "Public School Integration in Oklahoma, 1954-1963," *Historian*, XXVI (August 1964), 521-37.

Race Relations in an Urbanized South

Lewis Killian and Charles Grigg

Often overlooked in discussions of race relations in the South is the fact that in 1960, 48.2 percent of all Negroes living in urban places in the United States resided in the South.[1] This represents the largest number of Negro urban dwellers found in any of the four regions. Of 13,563,000 Negroes in the United States living in places of 2,500 population or more, 6,536,000 (48.2 percent) live in the South. This compares with 2,846,000 (21.0 percent) in the Northeast, 3,215,000 (23.7 percent) in the North Central region and only 966,000 (7.1 percent) in the West.

Reflecting the agrarian history of the South is the fact that, as of 1960, 41.5 percent of the Negro population in the South was classified as rural and 58.5 percent as urban, as compared with 3.2 percent rural in the Northeast and 96.8 percent urban. Table 1 gives a more detailed breakdown by regions. The point that stands out is that while the South has the highest proportion of Negroes classified as rural, it is still the region with the largest number of Negroes living in both rural and urban areas. A similar observation can be made if the distribution of Negro population residing in SMSA's is examined.[2] In 1960, 11,917,000 Negroes were classified as living in SMSA's in the U.S.; 42.6 percent or 5,089,000 were located in the South; 23.6 percent or 2,826,000 were in the Northeast; 25.8 percent or 3,081,000 resided in the North Central states; and 8.0 percent or 951,000 were located in the West.

Marches, such as the ones at Selma, and voter registration projects spotlighted the struggle of Negroes for political equality during 1964 and 1965. This drive was concentrated primarily in the rural areas of the South. These tactics have been supplemented, but not replaced,

---

[1] South, Northeast, North Central and West represent the four regions defined by the U.S. Census.

[2] SMSA—Standard Metropolitan Statistical Area. An area used by the United States Bureau of the Census for reporting population data and described as "one or more contiguous nonagricultural counties containing at least one city of 50,000 or more and having a generally metropolitan character based on the counties' social and economic integration with the central city. (William Peterson: *Population*. New York, the MacMillan Co., 1961, p. 186.)

20

TABLE 1*

Distribution of Negro Population by Urban and Rural Residences by Region, 1960 (in thousand)

	U.S.		South		North East		North Central		West	
	No.	%	No.	%	No.	%	No.	%	No.	%
Total	18,455	100.0	11,166	100.0	2,940	100.0	3,335	100.0	1,014	100.0
Rural farm	1,498	8.1	1,467	13.2	5	.2	24	.7	2	.2
Rural nonfarm	3,394	18.4	3,163	28.3	89	3.0	96	2.9	46	4.5
Urban places	13,024	70.6	6,224	55.7	2,773	94.3	3,125	93.7	902	89.0
Other urban	539	2.9	312	2.8	73	2.5	90	2.7	64	6.3

* Derived from Tapes of 1 in 1,000 sample U.S. Census, 1960.

by the activities of federal registrars in counties where resistance to enfranchisement remains adamant. But this is only one facet of the struggle of the Negro to enter the mainstream of American life. Already the emphasis is shifting to the goal of economic equality. Picket lines and boycotts aimed at private employers are likely to join demonstrations against local governments as the principal techniques of direct action is this effort. The main thrust of this phase of the civil rights movement will be in the urban areas.

As indicated above, the South has 42.6 percent of all Negroes living in SMSA's. An overall measure of the relative deprivation of the urban Negro is found in the distribution of the S.E.S. (Socio-Economic Status) index used by the Bureau of the Census. In 1960, 77.7 percent of the Negroes living in the central cities of all SMSA's had an S.E.S lower than 50. The index ranges from 0 to 100. The South is faced with the immediate and critical problem of socio-economic inequality to an

TABLE 2*
PROPORTION OF NEGRO POPULATION IN STANDARD METROPOLITAN STATISTICAL AREAS WITH S.E.S. (SOCIO-ECONOMIC STATUS) LESS THAN 50 BY REGION, 1960

S.M.S.A.	U.S.	South	North East	North Central	West
Central City	77.7	86.3	73.4	72.7	65.7
Other	82.9	88.9	73.0	85.5	67.8

* Derived from Tapes of 1 in 1,000 sample U.S. Census, 1960.

even greater extent than are other regions. In fact, Table 2 indicates that 86.3 percent of some 5,089,000 Negroes in the South have an economic basis for dissatisfaction as compared with 73.4 percent of some 2,826,000 Negroes living in the Northeast. Income levels within the central cities of SMSA's also reflect this basic source of Negro inequality. In the South 83.1 percent of the families living in the central city of an SMSA report an annual income of less than $3,000. In the Northeast, 70.5 percent report incomes of less than $3,000; in the North Central region, 69.8 percent; and in the West, 69.9 percent.[3]

Yet the hottest spot of the long, hot summer of 1965 proved to be Los Angeles, not a southern city. There, the reactions of economically deprived Negroes burst the limits of carefully designed strategy and there was a riot, not a demonstration. The possible significance for the South of this spontaneous outburst of undisciplined aggression was reflected in the warning of Charles Evers, Field Director of the NAACP, to the white leaders of Natchez, Mississippi, a few days after the Watts riots. In the midst of non-violent demonstrations aimed at

---

[3] Derived from Tapes of 1 in 1,000 sample U.S. Census, 1960.

securing equal employment opportunities and desegregation of public facilities, Evers warned that Natchez might experience the kind of violence that Los Angeles had seen unless the stalemate in negotiations were broken. While Evers pleaded with his followers to remain nonviolent, he used the specter of the Los Angeles riot as a warning to white leaders.[4] In the past it has been southern white officials who have used the threat of violence beyond their control as a warning to Negroes not to press their demands too rapidly. Now the tables are turned.

In March of 1965 the focal point of the Negro revolt was Selma, Alabama, and the surrounding rural counties, as Birmingham had been the focal point in the spring of 1963. Each had, in its turn, been chosen by the strategists of the civil rights movement as a key strongpoint in the whole defense system of southern race relations.

But ironically Selma and its hinterland are more typical of the past than of the future. It is not to the Selmas but to the Birminghams and the Huntsvilles, and even to the ghettoes of New York, Detroit, Chicago and Los Angeles, that we must look to discern the pattern and problems of race relations in an urbanized South. The tide of Negro migration is flowing steadily toward the cities. With this movement there is coming a replication of the northern pattern of concentration of Negroes in the central cities. And as for years the current of Negro protest flowed from the North to the South, so today it flows from the cities of the South to the hinterlands. From southern cities there is coming the dynamic Negro leadership which is reaching into rural counties and arousing Negro citizens from apathy and fear. Even after freedom to vote and to assemble peacefully are attained in the small communities, it will still be to the cities and the expanding communities that Negroes must turn for jobs.

The consequences of urbanization for the South and its Negro population have long been anticipated by some sociologists. In 1946 Rudolph Heberle wrote:

> The sociological implications of this change are well-known; while the worker gains in freedom he loses the landlord's protection and care, and his economic insecurity increases as he is exposed to the vicissitudes of the labor market. A relationship of community based on a shared interest in the output, on reciprocal service and protection and on steady, often intimate, contacts gives way to loose, intermittent, contractual relations based solely on the cash nexus (1946, p. 1).

More recently, Vivian Henderson has voiced the same theme in saying that the Negro in the South is moving into an "economized culture" (1961).

---

[4] "Protest March Canceled," Los Angeles Times, Sept. 3, 1965. P. 9, Part I.

Thus the most obvious implication for Negroes of the urbanization of the South is that they escape the heavy, albeit sometimes benign, hand of white paternalism. In the areas of Negro concentration in the central city they escape not only the hand but the eye of the white man. It becomes far easier for the individual Negro to achieve anonymity. As the pressure of the 1964 Civil Rights Act destroys the form of segregation in public places he may experience the "equality of anonymity" so long characteristic of the northern city.[5] As the initial shock of his presence in public gatherings and places of public accommodation wears off the Negro may find that he is once more "the invisible man."

This freedom and anonymity may extend not only to the individual Negro but also to the Negro organization. This first became evident when Negro churches changed from *other-worldly* refuges to which Negroes retreated from an oppressive white world. In Montgomery, Birmingham, Tallahassee, Atlanta, in cities all over the South, they became command posts where militant Negro leaders planned strategy, garnered spiritual and financial resources, exhorted their followers and formed them into the shock troops of the Negro Protest. This change is dramatically symbolized by the practice of some police forces of sending spies into meetings at Negro churches to find out "what the Negroes are up to!"

It is in the cities, too, particularly the larger ones, that the NAACP, the Urban League, and the newer protest organizations are able to base their chapters and their professional staff. It is not just that there is more scrupulous regard for their legal right to exist in the urban milieu than is found in many small towns. It is also that a large proportion of the white population is only vaguely aware, if knowledgeable at all, of their existence. They are part of the Negro world of which the average white citizen knows less and less as his community grows larger. The authors have personally witnessed the astonishment and dismay of some southern white people when they were told that Black Muslim Temples actually existed in their own cities, not just in Harlem, Detroit and Chicago.

Finally, there is the hope of many Negro migrants that the urban center offers more tangible sorts of freedom, freedom from unemployment or agricultural serfdom, freedom to vote, freedom to purchase the wider variety of goods and services which the city offers. But an important turning point of the Negro Revolution was the full, traumatic realization of Negroes that this hope has not been fulfilled "on the other side of Jordan"—in northern cities.

Such freedom and anonymity as the city does offer will, for many

---

[5] The phrase, "The equality of anonymity" was used by Drake and Cayton in *Black Metropolis* (New York: Harcourt and Brace, 1945).

Negroes, be accompanied by alienation and anomia. Henderson has pointed out that one of the most important effects of urbanization and the "economized culture" will be the lifting of Negro aspirations (1961). But not all Negroes will find that the city offers them the means to match their aspirations. Thus the discrepancy between aspirations and means to attain them postulated by Robert Merton as one of the conditions productive of anomia will exist (1949).

In one of the very few studies of the relationship between urban residence, education, occupation and anomia among Negroes, Killian and Grigg found evidence of this (1962). Comparing samples of Negroes in a small southern town and a large southern city, they found that the small town was an anomic milieu for Negroes regardless of class. In the city, however, Negroes characterized by relatively high occupational status had lower scores on the Srole Anomie Scale than did small town Negroes or blue-collar urban Negroes. The Negro who lived in the city but was of low occupational status scored high in anomia as frequently as did the low-occupation rural Negro. Among whites, regardless of class, there was greater frequency of high anomia scores in the urban environment. Of all categories, it was only the Negro with high social position (as measured by education, occupation and class self-placement) who displayed less anomia in the urban setting than in the rural.

There is the implication here that the urban South is indeed the "city of hope" for the Negro who has the type of job which enables him to take advantage of the opportunities it offers. But for the Negro who is unable to enter the "Black Bourgeoisie," it may be the "city of despair." That the consequences of alienation and despair might be the same in a southern city as in a northern "Black Belt" was discovered by the city of Jacksonville, Florida, in 1960. After three days of violence by whites against Negro non-violent demonstrators who were protesting segregated restaurants, groups of Negroes armed with sticks and rocks began indiscriminate attacks on white people entering the Negro slum areas. Suddenly the city awoke to the fact that conditions assumed to be confined to northern cities also existed in Jacksonville.

> The Negro youth gangs, which had been in existence for some time and include more than 3000 youngsters, had become unified and were taking up the role of "protector" of the general Negro community. Previously they had fought among themselves, and confined their activities to the Negro housing areas. Now they were prepared to match blow for blow with the general white community (Florida Council, 1960, p. 2).

The incident which triggered this reaction was a racial conflict which, although it was in the central business district, was close enough to the Negro slums to be highly visible to the inhabitants. Just as four years later alleged acts of police brutality in Rochester,

Philadelphia and New York precipitated widespread aggression in the ghettoes, this incident was the occasion for an uprising of previously non-involved Negroes. There is evidence that a condition of readiness for such action had been created by conditions in the Negro slums from which the youth gangs erupted. A middle-class Negro youth, president of the Youth Council of the NAACP, observed of these gangs:

> A lot of these Negro juvenile gangs live in housing ghettoes. The housing conditions of gang members here are the worst I have ever seen of any of the many cities which I have visited. . . . Their actions in large degree stem from lack of recreational facilities, bad housing, broken homes, etc. . . . I've heard some gang members say, "There is no place to go; there is nothing to do" (Florida Council, 1960, p. 3).

Surveying the continued underemployment of Negroes in the modern South and the lack of adequate vocational and technical training for Negroes in southern cities, Henderson predicts:

> Without extraordinary economic expansion and rapid improvement in the distribution of income, without swift changes in southern race relations, it is apparent that in the next decade the bulk of southern poverty will complete its shift from the country to the city.
> Negro poverty will take its place in the urban slums of the South as a substitute for the traditional rural poverty—which, at least, was relatively self-sufficient (1964, p. 17).

It has been suggested above that the freedom of the city creates a milieu in which Negro organizations, especially protest groups, may flourish in a manner not permitted in the small town. It may also be postulated that, for the individual, "the more extensive political participation, and the greater freedom to participate in protest organizations may soften somewhat the impact of minority status." (Killian and Grigg, 1962).

But in spite of the dramatic impact that protest organizations have had in many southern cities, evidence is not available to show that any large proportion of urban Negroes are actively and continuously involved in any sort of organization. The assumption, dating back at least to de Tocqueville, that Americans of all sorts are "joiners" has been seriously challenged insofar as white Americans are concerned. But Myrdal's assertion that Negroes are even greater "joiners" than are whites, at least of "expressive" associations such as churches and lodges, has not been subjected to the same sort of critical scrutiny (1944, p. 952). Simons, studying a sample of Negroes in Jacksonville, in 1962, found evidence to the contrary (1964). The Chapin social participation scale was administered to a sample of 500 adult Negroes. It was found that only 15.6 percent were actively affiliated and 29.6

percent were nominally affiliated with one or more voluntary association. Only 2 percent were found to be members of "political" or "protest" organizations.

Nor is it evident that urbanization of itself contributes to greater political participation by Negroes, with or without organization, Matthews and Prothro, in a study of social and economic factors and Negro voter registration in the South, found that when other factors are controlled neither urbanization nor industrialization is significantly associated with Negro registration. They state:

> There is no meaningful difference in the rate of Negro registration between metropolitan and non-metropolitan counties when Negro concentration is controlled. Thus, neither "urbanism" nor "metropolitanism," as crudely defined by the census categories, appears to be independently related to high Negro voter registration."
>
> ... Urbanization and industrialization may provide necessary conditions for high levels of Negro political participation but, by themselves, they are not sufficient to insure them (1963, p. 36).

Whatever the reactions of Negroes to urbanization may be, it must not be forgotten that the lives of southern white people are also being affected by this trend. The intimacy across the lines of color-caste which paternalism permitted is destroyed for them as well as for Negroes, to be replaced by impersonality, anonymity and sometimes by generalized hostility. That desegregation brings whites and Negroes into new, apparently equal-status relationships does not mean that integration is achieved. Better, franker communication and greater mutual respect may for a long time be confined to very small numbers of whites and Negroes who work at breaking down the psychological barriers. Larger numbers of both races are likely to find themselves more isolated than ever before, seeing each other only as white or black faces in the urban crowd.

Urbanization will also have psychological consequences for southern whites. Charles Lerche, a political scientist, suggests that one consequence has already been a southern political protest which has even changed the historic position of southern congressmen on foreign policy. He argues:

> Southern protest, whatever its immediate referents in any particular place, grows ultimately from the almost inchoate resentments of the back-country farmer or small-towner (who may or may not have already moved to the city) in revolt against a changing society that denies him his old place but fails to provide a new and satisfying one. (1964, p. 257).

Thus it should not be forgotten that many of the very changes which have engendered the Negro Protest have, along with the Negro Revolt itself, produced a counter-movement among southern whites.

The fact that Negroes, with the aid of federal intervention, have coerced external changes in the pattern of race relations does not preclude the creation of a new spirit of hostility, along with a pattern of conflict long familiar to northern cities.

Nevertheless, small and embattled as the group of activists in the Negro Protest organizations may be, they have opened many doors to Negroes, particularly in southern cities, and will open many more. But the persistent question remains, "How many Negroes will be able to go through these doors, and how soon?" As formal barriers are lowered, the low socio-economic status of large numbers of Negro southerners will loom larger as a pervasive deterrent to entry into the mainstream. The consequences of this barrier are illustrated in the Cape Kennedy area of Florida, the most rapidly urbanizing area in the nation. Here the full impact of the new national morality in race relations is felt, for the entire economy of the area is directly or indirectly "federalized." The largest employers are government agencies or government contractors; the schools receive large sums of federal money; private businessmen, public officials and real estate brokers are intensely aware of the dependence of the area upon federal funds. The schools are desegregated, places of public accommodation are as open as any in the South, Negroes are free to register and vote without interference and the largest employers are seeking Negro workers with a missionary zeal. But their search has come to be concentrated in areas far from the Cape, for the indigenous, southern Negro population cannot supply workers qualified for the job vacancies in the industries of the space age. Research on Negro high school graduates throughout the state of Florida reveals that most of the small minority who reach achievement levels high enough for admission to the better universities are lured away from the South to colleges in other regions.[6] Thus the employers in the space industries are confronted with the task of luring Negro scientists, engineers and skilled craftsmen to come to the South to work. It seems, however, that it is easier to get Negroes from other regions to come to the South to demonstrate than to become part of the regional society. Many who consider jobs in the Cape area find that much of the change is superficial. As is true in the North, the federal executive order of 1962 has not drastically changed housing patterns. While white schools are desegregated, Negro schools serving the housing ghettoes remain all-Negro. While Negroes may vote freely, they are still outnumbered by white voters and their influence is manifested subtly and slowly.

Even though the South is in a period of transition, the hand of the past still rests heavily upon it, and it is from this past that Negroes

---

[6] This finding reported to the authors by A. A. Abrahams of the Florida A. and M. University, on the basis of unpublished research.

have been fleeing to the North for generations. The shape of the South that is emerging in the transition is not yet clear. It may be that in some distant future the Negro will find in a new, integrated South a freedom which he has not yet found in the cities of the North and West. In the present stage of the transition, however, he is more likely to find the impersonality, the subtle patterns of exclusion and the separation of whites and Negroes in hostile worlds which have caused him to become disillusioned about the North.

REFERENCES

FLORIDA COUNCIL ON HUMAN RELATIONS. *Special Report*, "The Jacksonville Riot," September, 1960. 4241 S. W. 109 Court, Miami, Florida.

HEBERLE, R. "A Sociological Interpretation of Social Change in the South," *Social Forces*, 1946, 25, 9-15.

HENDERSON, V. "Economic Dimensions in Race Relations," in J. Masouka and P. Valien (Eds.), *Race Relations: Problems and Theory*. Chapel Hill: University of North Carolina Press, 1961.

HENDERSON, V. *The Economic Status of Negroes: In the Nation and in the South*. Atlanta: Southern Regional Council, 1964.

KILLIAN, L., AND GRIGG, C. "Urbanism, Race, and Anomia," *American Journal of Sociology*, 1962, 67, 661-665.

LERCHE, C. *The Uncertain South*. Chicago: Quadrangle Books, 1964.

MATTHEWS, D., AND PROTHRO, J. "Social and Economic Factors and Negro Voter Registration in the South," *American Political Science Review*, 1963, 57, 24-44.

MERTON, R. *Social Theory and Social Problems*. Glencoe, Illinois: Free Press, 1949.

MYRDAL, G. *An American Dilemma*. New York: Harper, 1944.

SIMONS, W. "An Analysis of Negro Formal Social Participation Patterns in a Segregated Southern Community," unpublished Master's thesis, Department of Sociology, The Florida State University, 1964.

GOOD-BYE TO JIM CROW: THE DESEGREGATION OF SOUTHERN HOSPITALS, 1945–70*

E. H. Beardsley

In the popular mind the struggle for racial integration in the American South after the Second World War is identified almost exclusively with education, voting rights, and places of public accommodation such as hotels and restaurants. Yet concurrent with those very visible and highly charged campaigns, another and quieter fight was going on, out of sight of newspaper reporters and television cameras, a fight that was to be as important to blacks as the more dramatic struggles for schools, ballots, and beds. This was the fight aimed at discrimination in hospital care, a contest that affected the health and well being of all Southern blacks. Yet it was a contest that involved very few of them. Unlike more celebrated civil rights battles, the fight to desegregate white hospitals, while aided by legislative action and court decision, took place primarily in the pages of medical journals, at professional meetings, and in firm but fairly friendly talks between black and white physicians and hospital administrators.

When long-standing racial barriers in the South finally began to fall, progress was in no small part due to white physicians themselves. Although largely sharing the racist assumptions of other whites, as medical professionals they had also felt the counter-pull of a set of ideals having no relation to color. Moreover, most had had years of frequent and generally sympathetic contact with black patients and black physicians. Thus, as they began, in the 1950s, to grasp more fully the fiction of "separate but equal" in their domain, these white doctors were able to set aside traditional racial practices in favor of a new order that was medically and ethically sounder than the old.

But if white doctors deserved credit, along with the federal government, by far the major impetus behind hospital desegregation was the persistence and energy of black physicians, who sought to create a climate of opinion in which change was not only possible but irresistible. Although many black

---

*A shorter version of this paper was presented at the fifty-eighth annual meeting of the American Association for the History of Medicine in Durham and Chapel Hill, North Carolina, 17 May 1985. The material in it forms part of a chapter of a forthcoming book on the health history of Southern blacks and mill workers, to be published by the University of Tennessee Press.

doctors played important parts, the most influential figures were two black physicians from Washington, D.C., Howard University's Paul Cornely and W. Montague Cobb, two men who found activism as much to their taste as academe.

In contrast to the effort to integrate medical societies and schools, which was going on simultaneously and which also commanded attention from Cornely and Cobb, the struggle against all-white and segregated hospitals was vastly more difficult, complex, and protracted. For one thing, professional associations and schools were essentially under the control of medical elites, while hospitals had to serve and be sensitive to the feelings of a mass clientele. One obvious barrier to hospital desegregation was economic. Many hospital administrators might personally have favored abandonment of second-rate segregated wards and of policies that excluded blacks altogether. But they balked at taking any initiatives ahead of popular opinion for fear of losing their white patients. And in the South, until well into the 1960s, that opinion dictated that hospital care would be delivered on a segregated basis. A sizeable number of blacks, in fact, were still accommodated in all-black institutions, which in Paul Cornely's view remained "only high grade convalescent homes...."[1]

In the North the situation was not much better. Predominantly white institutions claimed to be integrated, but actual practice was usually more restrictive than open. Commonly, hospitals either limited the number of blacks in wards, or put them in private rooms—or double-occupancy rooms, provided another black was already there.[2]

Hospital opportunities for black physicians and interns whether in the North or the South, remained sharply limited. A growing number of black doctors did enjoy admission privileges at segregated hospitals in both regions, but only in connection with their paying patients. For the would-be black intern, the South offered no prospects. Shut out of positions at accredited white institutions, his or her only options were an unaccredited black hospital or departure from the South. The outflow of youthful talent, so apparent before World War II, continued in the post-war decades and affected the profession left behind. In 1951, a Charleston black physician, Carr McFall, could only count three black doctors in South Carolina under fifty, a result of the fact that "there was no place in the state where a Negro physician could get their [sic] intern training."[3]

With the passage by Congress of the 1946 Hospital Survey and Construction Law, prospects for Southern black patients and doctors had bright-

---

[1] Paul Cornely, "Race relations in community health organization," *Amer. J. Pub. Health*, 1946, *36*: 990.
[2] Paul Cornely, "Trend in racial integration in hospitals in the U.S.," *J. Nat. Med. Assoc.*, 1957, *49*: 10.
[3] Advisory Council Minutes, 14 Nov. 1951, box 16460, South Carolina Board of Health Executive Committee Papers, State Archives, Columbia, South Carolina; see also W. Montague Cobb, "Hospital desegregation must end," *J. Nat. Med. Assoc.*, 1953, *45*: 284–85.

ened considerably. Popularly known as the Hill-Burton Act, the new law authorized an initial, five-year federal appropriation of $75,000,000, to be used by the states—on a matching basis—to create a system of hospitals and public health centers that would enable all Americans to receive health care at modern institutions. Although the Hill-Burton Act allowed the continuance of segregation, it also asserted that blacks should be provided with services and facilities of equal quality to those of whites, whether the setting was an all-black hospital or, as was more likely, a segregated ward in a white institution. Thus, in new federally-sponsored hospitals, black patients, if they were still segregated, at least had the benefit of modern facilities and enjoyed roughly equal treatment.[4] In 1950 when a new hospital opened in Greenville, South Carolina, as a result of the Hill-Burton Act, black surgical and maternity patients were accommodated for the first time in a county facility. Equality, though, was still some distance away. Comparing blacks' facilities with those of whites at that time, a hospital administrator in Greenville, Robert Toomey, admitted that while they were "now better" than before, they were "still separate" and "scarcely equal...."[5]

Yet as time passed, acceptance of a black presence became more and more routine at hospitals opened after the Hill-Burton Act, and the quality of service was less distinguishable by race. Savannah, Georgia, got its first federal hospital in 1957, and two black doctors sat on its planning board. According to one, Henry Collier, by then white physicians accepted the idea of cooperating with blacks because of long interracial contact at the city's two black hospitals.[6] Raleigh, North Carolina, got its Hill-Burton hospital, Wake Memorial, even later, in 1961, and the next year the dean of the Tuskegee Institute in Alabama, Bennie D. Mayberry, had occasion to inspect it while his wife was receiving treatment. He later wrote to the administrator of Wake Memorial, William Andrews, that it was an unexpected pleasure "to visit your institution. In the Admission Room, I found the personnel most courteous and prompt to act." While his wife was convalescing, Mayberry saw several other departments in the black wing and found them all "clean [and] orderly...."[7]

White patrons, to be sure, were not always as eager to welcome black patients, even in segregated wings. Wake Memorial nearly collapsed financially in its first year because white patients were unwilling to go to what

---

[4] "A decade of Hill-Burton (editorial)," *Amer. J. Pub. Health*, 1957, 47: 1446–47; also "The hospital survey and construction program (editorial)," *ibid.*, 1949, 39: 1468–69; on the law's tolerance of segregation, see W. Montague Cobb, "Progress and portents for the Negro in medicine," *Crisis*, 1948, 55: 117. Hill-Burton funding continued into the 1970s.
[5] Interview by the author with Robert Toomey, 19 Nov. 1979; also "Self-Study Report," Southern Regional Council Community Survey (Greenville), n.d. but c. 1952, box 5, SRC Papers, Robert W. Woodruff Library, Atlanta University, Atlanta, Georgia.
[6] Interview by the author with Henry Collier, 20 May 1982.
[7] Bennie D. Mayberry to William F. Andrews, 29 Oct. 1962, Memorial Hospital of Wake County, North Carolina, file 92C, Duke Endowment Papers, Duke Endowment administrative offices, Charlotte, North Carolina.

was popularly derided as a "colored" hospital. As Andrews, the administrator, admitted to the Duke Endowment, "the continued low census at Memorial Hospital has ... forced us into some rather drastic measures."[8] Eventually overcrowding at Raleigh's other hospitals—Rex and Mary Elizabeth, neither of which admitted blacks—plus a resurgence of common sense deflated the boycott. A white patient reported that she had received "excellent food and service" at Wake. Moreover, she "did not see a Negro patient." Her conclusion, shared by a growing number of whites, was that "having both races in the same hospital produced no problem."[9]

Black doctors benefited almost as substantially from the Hill-Burton Act as black patients, for new hospitals and hospital additions gave many their first access to modern equipment and technology, as well as increased contact with specialists and exposure to advanced clinics and seminars.[10] What especially impressed many black doctors was their ease of entry to these hospitals. Certainly, the law helped considerably. But there was also a willingness on the part of many to do the right thing. White physicians and hospital administrators (in federally funded facilities at least) sometimes welcomed black physicians so openly that the latter were startled. For Greenville's hospital, Toomey said, the awarding of full privileges to black physicians (to serve *black* patients) in 1953 came out of a "sense of correctness and dignity. There was no other reason for it.... People within the hospital just felt that the continuation of [professional] segregation was wrong...."[11]

Although Toomey's explanation played down the influence of the law, blacks remembered the same cordiality. About the time that Greenville was according equality, in another part of South Carolina a black internist, Ranzy Weston, was seeking to join the Aiken County hospital staff. He was fully prepared to be rebuffed "because of the way things had been...." When the administrator told him that all he had to do was "make an application," Weston was flabbergasted. It must have shown on his face because the administrator, "a Yankee," went on to tell him that "this hospital belongs to the county of Aiken, and we get Hill-Burton funds...." Weston was a taxpayer, and if qualified, he had a "right to get on the staff."[12] Likewise, when Mayberry of the Tuskegee Institute visited Wake Memorial the thing that he found most surprising was "the extent of integration of hospital personnel." And the question raised in his mind was, "if it could be done here, why not other places in the South?"[13]

[8] Andrews to Marshall Pickens, Duke Endowment executive, 29 Dec. 1961, Memorial Hospital of Wake County, file 92C, Duke Endowment Papers.
[9] Mrs. R. W. Strickland, letter to the editor, *Raleigh News and Observer*, 14 July 1961.
[10] Interview by the author with Augusta, Georgia, black physician Ranzy Weston, 20 May 1982.
[11] Toomey, interview, 19 Nov. 1979.
[12] Weston, interview, 20 May 1982.
[13] Mayberry to Andrews, 29 Oct. 1962.

One answer was that many Southern institutions *were* doing what Wake was. In an earlier study Paul Cornely found that 25 percent of Southern general hospitals had blacks on the active staff, 25 percent extended them admission privileges, and 12 percent accepted black interns. Further, in every category, hospital staff integration in the South was substantially equal to that in the North.[14]

Yet Mayberry's question had merit: if 50 percent of Southern hospitals had opened their doors to practicing black physicians by the late 1950s, an equal number still shut them out. In the admission of black patients, discrimination was even more evident. Despite the Hill-Burton Act, the situation for patients remained into the 1950s close to what it had been in the period before World War II. In 1956, 90 percent of Southern hospitals were white-run, and of those, about one-third did not admit any black patients.[15]

Among the two-thirds who did admit blacks, over half had not received any Hill-Burton funds, and they were thus under no compulsion to accord equal treatment to the black patients they did admit. In the late 1950s at Columbia General Hospital, in South Carolina (not yet a Hill-Burton facility), there was no X-ray equipment in the "colored wing," and black patients needing this procedure had to be carried across a wide, open court to the main building. In the seven hospitals associated with the Medical College of Virginia, not only were no black physicians allowed to practice in them as late as 1957, but black patients were quartered in "sub-standard buildings, with sub-standard equipment, [and] greatly overcrowded."[16] Hence, despite the Hill-Burton Act, in the late 1950s at least 60 percent of the South's public and private hospitals either did not admit black patients or accorded them inferior care.

One group of hospitals in the South, though, had accepted patient integration by the late 1950s. These were the South's veterans' hospitals, which in 1950 had opened their wards to black patients under the pressure of a directive from the chief medical administrator of the Veterans' Administration. Nine hospitals in the Carolinas and Georgia had been affected by the new policy. Joan Kirshner, at the time a new staff member in one of them in Atlanta, remembered that the order stated simply that henceforth new admissions were to be assigned to wards without regard to race. She also recalled that there was considerable apprehension about the problems that would arise. But those worries proved to be needless. Integration proceeded without difficulty. The same unexpectedly smooth transition occurred at

---

[14] Cornely, "Trend in racial integration in hospitals," p. 9.
[15] Paul Cornely, "Segregation and discrimination in medical care in the U.S.," *Amer. J. Pub. Health*, 1956, 46: 1079.
[16] "Imhotep conference proceedings," *J. Nat. Med. Assoc.*, 1957, 49: 212–13, 351–42; also interview by the author with Modjeska Simkins, 14 Dec. 1979. Simkins, a black civil rights leader in South Carolina, has been involved with health matters since 1930, when she took a post as head of Negro work for the state's anti-tuberculosis association.

the veterans' hospital in Columbia: the former chief surgeon, Richard Ferguson, recollected that there was "a little griping," but that "no one left the hospital because of it."[17]

But the relatively few Veterans' Administration hospitals offered no place for care of the average black patient. For a growing number of black physicians, solutions (for doctor and patients, alike) were also not going to be found in more separate-but-equal Hill-Burton hospitals, nor even in new all-black structures. Opportunity and equity lay in the complete overturning of hospital segregation, and in the early 1950s a movement began within the National Medical Association (NMA, the major black professional group) aimed at that goal. The initial leaders were Cobb and Cornely, but by the late 1950s they had help from a number of black doctors in the deep South. Inspired by the civil rights fervor of ministers and students, they began making their stand for justice, too.

Yet, for about a decade, the hospital desegregation fight did not lead to any results for black doctor or patient. The white medical establishment ignored the appeals of the Cobb-Cornely group. As for black physicians, until the later 1950s, most were unwilling to support the cause actively, while a sizeable number firmly, if silently, opposed desegregation. For that group, according to Cobb, desegregation was a threat because it would destroy the fiefdoms they had built up in third-rate black hospitals. It would also throw them into competition with younger, abler blacks (not to mention whites), putting their very careers in jeopardy.[18] Yet, in spite of this, the few activist black physicians did have an impact. When hospital integration finally came, it was the earlier efforts of the Cobb-Cornely group which had prepared the way.

In challenging the segregation of Southern hospitals, Cobb, as editor of the *Journal of the National Medical Association*, saw that his first task was to heighten black doctors' awareness, to make them an instrument for change. His approach was both to assail and inspire. As he wrote in one editorial, what were needed were "pioneer spirits," who rather than yield to the allure of "fundamentally insulting placebos" would "tighten their belts and continue the struggle for principle."[19]

Cobb gave *Journal* readers as many examples as he could of the fight for principle. Even where there was little occasion for celebration, Cobb found elements of victory. When the Memphis NAACP branch reversed an earlier decision and rejected a plan for a new, all-black hospital, Cobb ap-

---

[17] Interview by the author with Joan Kirshner, 20 Sept. 1985. Kirshner said that Gen. Omar Bradley, the Veterans' Affairs Administrator until 1948, was the catalyst for the directive. Determined to make needed changes in the VA system, he believed that if blacks were good enough to fight for their country they were also deserving of equal medical care. The only hospital exempt from the order was Tuskegee's all-black hospital. In an interview by the author with Richard Ferguson, 12 Aug. 1985, Ferguson recalled that the VA dispatched human relations specialists to local hospitals to prepare staff for the upcoming integration.

[18] *Journal of Negro Education*, Special Health Issue, 1949, *18:* 342.

[19] W. Montague Cobb, "The crushing irony of deluxe 'Jim Crow' (editorial)," *J. Nat. Med. Assoc.,* 1952, *44:* 387.

plauded. He likewise congratulated blacks in Columbia, South Carolina, and St. Petersburg, Florida, when they helped defeat local bond referendums calling for improvement of black hospitals. As he had done in the fight against segregated societies and schools, Cobb tried to link the energies of the NAACP to hospital desegregation. By 1953 the NAACP was urging state chapters to form local physician health committees to survey and report on the extent of hospital segregation. Touting the NAACP as the action arm of the NMA, in 1954 Cobb urged every doctor to contribute $100 to the NAACP's anti-segregation fund, a substantial part of which would be directed at hospitals. By the time of its 1954 meeting in Washington, the NMA was able to give $2,000 to the civil rights group. Its legal counsel Thurgood Marshall came to receive the money and stayed to make the major address.[20]

By the mid-1950s a number of Southern blacks were also beginning to take action against hospital segregation. Aroused not just by Cobb's editorials but also by the landmark 1954 school desegregation decision, in 1956 three Wilmington, North Carolina, doctors brought suit against that city's large Walker Hospital to force the admission of black doctors. Though they lost their case (they would win it in a second suit in 1964), the effort was significant. For the first time, Southern black physicians had challenged the status quo in the courts. After Wilmington, legal action was no longer unthinkable or unethical. One of the plaintiffs, Hubert Eaton, underscored the new possibilities: "if you don't know what to do, go to court; that is the only way we know of in Wilmington, North Carolina."[21]

Not many were yet ready to follow that advice. But a new militancy was gaining ground, even if its object was only the desegregation of hospital staffs. A black doctor in Richmond, Virginia, Daniel Webster Davis, had been trying for several years to get the Medical College of Virginia to open its associated hospitals to black physicians. By 1957 he was tired of begging: "I shall recommend that our next battleground be the federal courts."[22] In Gastonia, North Carolina, that same year, George R. Watts began challenging the system as soon as he arrived in town. As a black physician he could not practice at the town's two white hospitals. So his first visit was to the larger one, Gaston Memorial Hospital, where he introduced himself to a shocked white superintendent and asked for a tour of the building. On being given access to the emergency room—apparently to forestall his asking for more —Watts soon found that even that privilege was a facade, for the hospital refused his first emergency patient. Watts thereupon rebuked the superin-

---

[20] "Memphis NAACP branch rescinds endorsement of Negro hospital," *J. Nat. Med. Assoc*, 1952, 44: 314; on Columbia, see "Negro voters defeat hospital bond issue," *ibid*, 1953, 45: 438; on St. Petersburg see *ibid*, 1960, 52: 216. The involvement of the NAACP is shown in W. Montague Cobb, "The national health program of the NAACP," *ibid*, 1953, 45: 337; "Support the Fighting Fund for Freedom," *ibid*, 1954, 46: 192–93, 274; also Thurgood Marshall to Cobb, 7 Sept. 1954, in *ibid*, 1954, 46: 439, 441.
[21] "Proceedings Imhotep national conference on hospital integration," *J. Nat. Med. Assoc*, 1957, 49: 199.
[22] *Ibid*, p. 198.

tendent for unprofessional behavior and made a formal application for full staff membership. By 1957 he, too, was ready to go to federal court if the hospital turned him down.[23]

Inevitably, the interest in staff desegregation led to a desire to bring about patient mixing as well. As the Wilmington plaintiff Hubert Eaton had noted, "we don't want a partially integrated hospital where everything will be integrated except patients; we want [a] completely 100 per cent integrated hospital or no hospital at all."[24] But opening white wards to black patients would never occur as a result of black initiative alone. The backing of the federal government was needed, and to bring that about sizeable support from white professionals was essential. In this effort Cobb continued to play a leading part, but he also got substantial help from his colleague at Howard, Paul Cornely.

The primary target of Cornely's effort was the American Public Health Association (APHA), a group largely in sympathy with black professional goals. Cornely was a member of the APHA's committee on medical care, and in 1954 he helped to draft a resolution repudiating discrimination and segregation in its delivery. The next year, with Cornely playing a lead role, the APHA adopted this resolution as the will of the Association. In 1956 he returned to the APHA convention to urge members to assume responsibility for putting the Association position into action. "Every public health worker, whether in the North or South, ought not to accept the patterns of his community as sacrosanct." Where they impeded the health of any group, the health professional should seek to change them. The destructive effect of segregation and discrimination, Cornely insisted, was no longer in doubt: they "are environmental factors and are just as damaging to health as water pollution, unpasteurized milk, or smog."[25]

In the same address he drew the attention of Association delegates to a recent Illinois statute which denied tax-exempt status to any private hospital refusing admission on account of race. That ban should be widened, Cornely thought, and he urged his APHA colleagues to join him in recommending the addition of non-discriminatory clauses to all federal and state health laws, denying public money to any hospital or health center maintaining separate facilities for blacks. If legislatures were unwilling to do that, Cornely warned, "it may be necessary to pursue this matter through the ... courts until it reaches the Supreme Court" as was done in education.[26]

In the late 1950s, however, such an amendment had no chance of passing Congress. That body had only just reached the stage of enacting the weakest sort of voting rights law. Not until 1962, in fact, was New York

---

[23] *Ibid.*, p. 213.
[24] *Ibid.*, pp. 199, 200.
[25] Cornely, "Segregation and discrimination in medical care in the U.S.," p. 1081.
[26] *Ibid.;* see also "Rann holds Imhotep planning meetings," *J. Nat. Med. Assoc.,* 1961, *53:* 616; and "New weapons against hospital discrimination," *ibid,* 1955, *47:* 342.

Senator Jacob Javits, long a foe of segregation, willing to introduce a restriction on Hill-Burton funds in a Senate committee.[27]

The mainstream medical and hospital associations, however, were not under such constraints and in carrying the hospital desegregation fight to them, Cobb, Cornely, and allies launched their most venturesome political campaign, the Imhotep Conferences of 1957 to 1963. Largely the brainchild of Cobb, but strongly supported by Cornely, these national meetings sought to assemble white and black physicians and hospital administrators for face-to-face discussions on hospital segregation. The Imhotep (from the Greek for "he cometh in peace") conferences reflected the hope that integration could be achieved voluntarily, without divisive court and legislative battles, which Cobb saw as a "waste of time, energy, emotional tension, and money."[28] Even if friendly persuasion did not move the white establishment, blacks would at least have a forum for presenting their grievances, plus the moral certitude that it was whites, not they, who had turned their backs on rational, peaceful solutions.

It was quickly clear that a forum was all Imhotep would provide. Not a single white medical or hospital association—not even Catholic or Protestant hospital associations—sent delegates to the initial 1957 sessions. The American Medical Association sent only an observer. But the standoffishness of the federal government was the greatest disappointment. The Department of Health, Education, and Welfare (HEW), which also sent only an observer, would not even let the group use its auditorium in Washington, a place regularly used for NMA meetings (not even Howard University, in fact, would give the group a meeting place). As a consequence of white lack of interest, the first 175-delegate meeting was almost a solid phalanx of black faces. In all, thirty-two organizations from twenty-one states participated. Although no one came from Georgia, eleven physician delegates travelled from North Carolina and one from South Carolina.[29]

Without any whites to address, Cobb, Cornely and the other conveners of the conference were in the position of having to preach to the converted. Cobb presided over the first session (as he would at all others) and used the occasion to lambast the Hill-Burton Act and call for its revision. Cornely, too, urged action but cautioned that hospital desegregation would not come easily, for many private hospitals would rather close down than accept black staff and patients on all wards. But the session was not a total loss. Black delegates felt a sense of mission and common purpose which they had not had before. The Richmond physician, Daniel Webster Davis, expressed the sense of the meeting when he said that "we have gotten great benefit and

---

[27] "Javits bill to end hospital discrimination under Hill-Burton Act," *J. Nat. Med. Assoc.*, 1962, *54*: 120–23.
[28] "Rann holds Imhotep planning meeting," *J. Nat. Med. Assoc.*, 1961, *53*: 645.
[29] "An appraisal of the Imhotep conference," *J. Nat. Med. Assoc.*, 1957, *49*: 181; see also "Imhotep conference proceedings," *ibid*, 1958, *50*: 225; for a photo of conferees, *ibid*, 1957, *49*: 187; and for state delegations, "Summary of conference," *ibid*, 1957, *49*: 193–94.

inspiration ... and I do hope that we will go on from year to year with these meetings until ... we shall receive complete emancipation."[30]

The meetings did continue, but so did the white boycott of them. At the next two conferences the shrinking number of delegates had to content themselves with petitioning Congress to amend the Hill-Burton Act and with requesting HEW to block all federal monies going to segregated facilities. Between the 1959 and 1960 conferences Cobb sought to promote local hospital desegregation by getting the NAACP more involved. At his urging the NAACP asked its state conferences to initiate a broad attack on medical discrimination, including encouragement of physician activism and meetings with white hospital authorities. If nothing else, the sessions might make whites more sensitive to such offensive habits as labelling beds and linens with the word "Negro," and addressing black patients by their first names.[31]

But those approaches had no visible impact, and the fourth Imhotep conference (1960) shrank to thirty registrants. North Carolina's delegation dropped to five, and South Carolina (like Georgia) sent no one. In desperation, conference leaders sought to shift entirely to the grass roots, by creating local action committees which would press for desegregation at the community level.[32] That did not work either, and in 1963 Imhotep held its final session, in Atlanta. After calling on churches to "eliminate unChristian attitudes" in their hospitals, Cobb, Cornely, and other backers ended the seven-year effort with a rather hopeless appeal for a mass letter-writing campaign by black citizens.[33]

All involved were disappointed, but the principals did not think that their venture had been futile. Cornely felt that it had heightened awareness of deficiencies in hospital care for blacks and perhaps also "helped to push the concept of equity in health services."[34] Cobb saw its influence working in another direction, on the thinking and, eventually, the policies of national Democratic administrations—notably on the passage of the 1964 Civil Rights Act. Beginning with the election of John F. Kennedy, Cobb made a practice of funneling the findings of Imhotep conferences to the White House. There was little response to Imhotep alerts until 1962, when the administration began to press for Medicare. At initial hearings on that proposal, and subsequently, the Imhotep group in the NMA gave strong backing to the administration bill. They were, in fact, the only physician group to

---

[30] Davis is quoted in "Proceedings Imhotep national conference," p. 198; for Cobb's remarks, see "An appraisal of the Imhotep conference," p. 181; Cornely's views are in "Imhotep conference proceedings," *J. Nat. Med. Assoc.*, 1957, *49*: 233.

[31] "Second Imhotep conference on hospital integration," *J. Nat. Med. Assoc.*, 1958, *50*: 381, 383; see also "NAACP resolutions on health, 1959," *ibid.*, 1959, *51*: 399, 401.

[32] "Fourth Imhotep national conference," *J. Nat. Med. Assoc.*, 1960, *52*: 283–86; see also "Call for nationwide formation of local Imhotep committees," *ibid.*, 1961, *53*: 83. The recollection of black and white physicians and hospital administrators was that the NAACP played little or no role in hospital integration in the late 1950s and 1960s (interviews by the author with Robert Toomey, 19 Nov. 1979; I. D. Newman, 17 Dec. 1979; and Marshall Pickens, 15 Dec. 1982).

[33] Paul Cornely and Emory Rann, "The Imhotep conference—why a conference?" *Crisis*, 1963, *70*: 275.

[34] Interview by the author with Paul Cornely, 14 May 1979.

support it, and as Cobb interpreted events, the NMA thereby won both the gratitude of the White House and, as a sort of *quid pro quo,* its close attention to Imhotep recommendations concerning hospital desegregation.[35]

Assessing the actual impact of the Imhotep conferences on the 1964 Civil Rights Act is difficult. The law, which banned segregation in places of public accommodation and withheld federal funds from any state or local agency still practicing it, affected many institutions and activities besides hospitals. Moreover, the most immediate stimulus for its passage came from Martin Luther King's 1963 Birmingham campaign, which shared the goals of the later law.[36]

The most likely effect of the Imhotep conferences was to provide an added dimension to the picture of social discrimination, to which the administration of Lyndon B. Johnson was increasingly responsive. Apparently Johnson was eager to push ahead rapidly with hospital desegregation. Shortly after the 1964 act's passage he directed the Surgeon General and the Justice Department to meet with hospital administrators and leaders of the NMA and AMA to make clear the requirements of the new law. Cobb attended the meeting and recalled that federal officials adopted the tone that everyone should "be good boys and girls and settle down and get this plan initiated." The 1964 Civil Rights Act was, after all, the law of the land, and "we might as well abide by it."[37]

And abide by it they did. Between 1964 and 1970 the large majority of Southern hospitals accepted desegregation of patients and physician staffs without the application of federal sanctions. Compared to the history of school desegregation, the story of hospital integration provided a chapter in Southern race relations of which the region could be proud. Hospitals were in fact the first vital social institution, apart from the armed forces, to implement full scale integration—putting them ahead of schools, colleges, neighborhoods, and of course, churches. And they did it on the whole with surprising speed and unexpected good will.

That was largely because in hospitals the primary consideration was quality of care, not the color of patients on the floor. Of course professionalism could not assert itself until hospital administrators had the assurance that racial tolerance would not cost them patients. As the Savannah black doctor Henry Collier noted, hospital managers might have favored patient desegregation before 1964, but "everybody was afraid to do it." White patients "just didn't want to lay in bed next to the 'nigger,' " and administrators were understandably unwilling to put them there.[38]

Therein lay the chief value of the 1964 act. By putting nearly all hospi-

---

[35] Interview by the author with W. Montague Cobb, 22 May 1979.
[36] Paul H. Douglas, *In the Fullness of Time: The Memoirs of Paul H. Douglas* (New York: Harcourt, Brace, Jovanovich, 1971), p. 298.
[37] Cobb, interview, 22 May 1979.
[38] Collier, interview, 20 May 1982.

tals under the same requirements, previously inconceivable changes could now be made. When Greenville General in South Carolina announced in the mid-1960s that it was fully desegregating its wards, the hospital simply referred to the Civil Rights Act as the reason. As its administrator Robert Toomey saw the situation, the law gave hospitals the opportunity "to finish off the entire process of desegregation."[39]

But civil rights legislation was not the only factor in bringing about desegregation. The federal courts also played a key role. While the federal bench did not rule often on the issue of hospital desegregation, it did speak early and effectively. The most important case by far was a 1963 judgment of the Fourth United States Circuit Court of Appeals, which began to have an impact just as Congress passed the 1964 law. The case was *Simkins v. Moses H. Cone Memorial Hospital* (Greensboro, North Carolina), and according to former United States attorney Terrill Glenn of Columbia, South Carolina, it was the "granddaddy of hospital desegregation suits," for it did what black medical reformers had been unable to do for fifteen years: eliminate segregation from hospitals funded by the Hill-Burton Act.[40]

The origins of *Simkins v. Cone* went back to 1962 when a group of black doctors, dentists, and patients in Greensboro, North Carolina, brought suit in federal district court to force the desegregation of the city's two private, all-white hospitals, Moses H. Cone and Wesley Long. Cone and Long hospitals had recently received Hill-Burton grants, even though both remained closed to black physicians and patients. In fact, the two institutions had admitted their discriminatory intent. Yet North Carolina's hospital regulatory body had approved the requests on the grounds that a simultaneous award to Greensboro's all-black L. Richardson Memorial Hospital satisfied the federal requirement of equal provision for blacks.[41]

The plaintiffs disagreed. Charging that Richardson Memorial was inferior to the two white hospitals in staff, equipment, and facilities, they protested that their exclusion from Cone and Long hospitals was a denial of constitutional rights under the due process and equal protection clauses of the Fifth and Fourteenth Amendments. In December, District Judge Edwin N. Stanley ruled against the plaintiffs. Though agreeing that there was discrimination, Stanley found that he was unable to give the blacks relief because, as private facilities, the hospitals were not bound by the Fifth and Fourteenth Amendments.

Four months later the black plaintiffs took the ruling to the Fourth United States Circuit Court of Appeals. There, the presiding judge, Abraham Sobeloff, and two of his four colleagues, Albert V. Bryan and J. Spencer Bell, were not deterred by the barrier of privatism. Their decision was that pri-

---

[39] Toomey, interview, 19 Nov. 1979.
[40] Interview by the author with Terrill Glenn, 26 Jan. 1983.
[41] The account that follows of the *Simkins v. Cone* case is taken from the *Federal Reporter*, 2nd series, (St. Paul, Minnesota: West Publishing Co., 1964), *323*: 959–77.

vate hospitals which received money as a result of the Hill-Burton Act were sufficiently involved with the state "to bring them within the Fifth and Fourteenth prohibitions against racial discrimination."[42]

As for denial of equal protection, there was no doubt about that: the exclusion of blacks from more modern white hospitals had helped impose "severe consequences" on black doctors and the black populace, for the latter had an infant death rate twice that of North Carolina whites and a maternal death rate five times greater. Looking for a solution going beyond the plaintiffs' petition, the judges struck at the statute which had underwritten the discrimination. In November 1963 they declared that that portion of the Hill-Burton Act "tolerating 'separate-but-equal' facilities for separate population groups" was unconstitutional and therefore null and void.[43]

In expunging racism from the Hill-Burton Act, *Simkins v. Cone* revealed the broad influence that the 1954 school desegregation ruling had had on the Southern federal judiciary. In his majority opinion Sobeloff conceded that the two North Carolina hospitals had taken federal money "without warning that they would thereby subject themselves to restrictions on their racial policies." In fact they were now being told to do what the government promised they would not have to do. "But in this regard the defendants, owners of publicly assisted facilities, can stand no better than the collective body of Southern voters who approved school bond issues before the *Brown* decision...."[44] Every white Southerner had to be prepared to sacrifice for the larger good of justice. As for what that sacrifice would entail, *Simkins v. Cone* was unequivocal. All hospitals which had accepted Hill-Burton money in the past (or would in the future) were duty bound to admit black doctors and patients on an equal footing without delay.

The new will of the Southern federal judiciary got prompt illustration in South Carolina. In 1962, a year before *Simkins v. Cone,* a black woman had been forcibly removed from an all-white waiting room of the Orangeburg Regional Hospital, a new facility built with Hill-Burton funds. Gloria Ratchley promptly sued the hospital to force its desegregation. The United States District Judge, George Bell Timmerman, however, had ruled for the defendants, accepting the hospital's argument that segregation was necessary for its smooth operation, as well as for the physical and mental health of patients.[45] Two years later (after *Simkins v. Cone*), the Fourth Circuit Court of Appeals vacated Timmerman's decision and ordered a re-trial at the district level. This time the new judge, Robert Hemphill, decided that integrated facilities were a right and that (white) patient health would not be jeopardized by them. In January 1965 he gave the hospital sixty days to desegregate fully or have the court do the job.[46]

[42] *Ibid.,* p. 961; see also pp. 967, 969.
[43] *Ibid.,* p. 959; see also p. 969.
[44] *Ibid.,* p. 970.
[45] "Orangeburg regional hospital ordered integrated," *Orangeburg Democrat,* 19 Jan. 1965.
[46] *Ibid.;* Timmerman had resigned by the time of the re-trial.

White opinion was outraged. A month after the order, the *Charleston News and Courier*, the major paper in the region and a bastion of segregation, castigated Hemphill for "forcing racial integration down the throats of patients...." It was a prescription, said the paper, that ran counter to all laws of "spiritual and physical healing."[47] Considering the intensity of the opposition, Judge Hemphill remained remarkably faithful to the mandate of *Simkins v. Cone*. The desegregation plan that he approved provided black plaintiffs (and patients) nearly all of that for which they had asked. His two concessions were loopholes for whites rather than restrictions against blacks.[48]

Thus by 1965 the federal courts and the 1964 Civil Rights Act were working in tandem to pull Southern hospitals toward integration. The *Simkins v. Cone* decision imposed the new ethic on hospitals which had enjoyed Hill-Burton funding in the past. The public accommodations statute reined in those recalcitrant hospitals which hoped for future federal assistance, whether from the Hill-Burton Act (which continued until 1975) or any of a multitude of other medical programs and agencies, such as the National Institutes of Health, the National Science Foundation, the Kerr-Mills Law, and HEW.

Yet, in practice, it was more the prospect of federal enforcement than its actuality which led Southern hospitals to abandon segregation. And in fact, it was neither federal agencies nor the courts which applied most of the pressure for change. That came, rather, from private associations and community groups which either threatened hospitals with punishment if they did not alter policy or promised reward and advantage if they did.

The chief threateners were civil rights groups. Early in 1965, just as HEW and other agencies were beginning to implement the 1964 law, the NAACP announced that it was requesting an HEW investigation of twelve Southern hospitals, all allegedly guilty of gross discrimination but still receiving federal aid. One, in the North Carolina Piedmont region, was found to be maintaining separate wards, dining areas, and operating rooms. Another denied blacks the right even to visit white patients.[49] In the meantime, local NAACP groups threatened to take hospitals to court. Following Hemphill's ruling in the Orangeburg case, the head of the South Carolina NAACP, I. Dequincy Newman, warned that he would soon initiate suits against other state hospitals if they did not voluntarily integrate all areas.[50]

---

[47] "Bad medicine," *Charleston News and Courier*, 21 Feb. 1965.
[48] "Orangeburg hospital's plan to desegregate approved," *Charleston News and Courier*, 21 Apr. 1965; when Columbia's Richland Memorial Hospital opened on a totally integrated basis in 1972 there was a large flight of white patients, causing financial instability (interview by the author with Diane Berry, 8 Feb. 1983). White abandonment of Southern public hospitals has continued, posing the problem of gathering sufficient revenues from paying patients to offset the load of no-pay and part-pay patients, many of whom are black and whose government insurance covers only a part of the costs (interview by the author with Blease Graham, 31 Mar. 1983); see also Charlotte LeGrand, letter to the editor, *The State*, 3 Apr. 1983.
[49] "NAACP seeks probe over hospital discrimination," *Orangeburg Democrat*, 15 Jan. 1965.
[50] *Ibid.*

Not all civil rights groups were so quick to look to federal authority. Some, like the Richland County, South Carolina, Citizens Committee, under the leadership of Columbia's Modjeska Simkins (no relation to plaintiff Simkins), a long-time civil rights and medical activist, tried first to work to gain voluntary compliance. In the summer of 1965, Columbia General Hospital, a recent beneficiary of Hill-Burton funds, still maintained a segregated black wing, separate washrooms, and an all-white nursing dormitory. Having just revealed the abuses of black patients at the state mental institution, Simkins and the committee approached hospital officials and urged them to take steps to end segregation. Only when that approach failed did they request an "on-site" visit from HEW officials in Atlanta. In the end (about 1967), Columbia General was integrated without a court order or a withdrawal of federal money.[51]

But desegregation came not only from the pushing of civil rights activists. It was also a result of *pulling* by mainline white groups, which had their own reasons for wanting to desegregate public institutions. In Columbia, South Carolina, at about the time of the 1964 act, the mayor and insurance executive, Lester Bates, formed a Community Relations Council, composed of prominent black and white citizens, to work for peaceful, gradual integration of public facilities. In part the Council reflected the city's willingness to bow to the inevitable. But it was also evidence of new thinking among the South's urban white elites. To them segregation still had emotional appeal, but more important was a stable social climate, deemed essential to business. As one Columbia physician recalled, the feeling was that "federal legislation was in the wings, and ... desegregation would go over better if citizens were led to do it gradually and voluntarily rather than have it forced down their throats."[52] And so two physician members of the mayor's council called on the Columbia hospital superintendent James M. Daniel and sought his cooperation, arguing the wisdom of changing before change was forced. Simkins was applying her pressure at about that time, and the push plus the pull was the combination which led hospital trustees to start dismantling more than a century of segregation.[53]

Nor was Columbia exceptional in witnessing that sort of pressure and response. In Greenville, South Carolina, a similar blue ribbon committee emerged in 1964. It promptly began to press for the desegregation of such institutions as restaurants, stores, and hospitals. Agitation from civil rights groups was not a factor there, according to Robert Toomey, who was part of the citizen effort. Not only was the NAACP presence non-existent, but "the black leadership was working with us, and we were delighted."[54]

---

[51] Simkins, interview, 14 Dec. 1979; "Columbia hospital is investigated by HEW officials," *The State*, 29 July 1965; for the mental hospital inquiry, see "Dr. Hall reveals deaths in Negro mental hospital," *Orangeburg Democrat*, 7 Feb. 1965.
[52] Interview by the author with Dr. Frank Owens, 2 Feb. 1978; on the pace of the Columbia Hospital integration, see Graham, interview, 31 Mar. 1983.
[53] Owens, interview, 2 Feb. 1978.
[54] Toomey, interview, 19 Nov. 1979.

The same sort of apparatus was at work in Charlotte, North Carolina, although there black medical and civil rights activists also played a role. Though spurred by the 1964 law, the Charlotte Race Relations Commission owed its creation to the Greensboro sit-ins of 1960. The Duke Endowment's Marshall Pickens was Commission vice-chairman, and he and his colleagues had learned a lesson from Greensboro: "not to let the situation get out of control but to control it and do what you're supposed to do." Well before 1964, then, Charlotte leaders were calling on restaurateurs and retailers to urge that "things should simply be opened up to avoid somebody coming in here insisting on having a seat."[55] After the Civil Rights Act, the commission shifted its attention to hospitals and schools. "Hospital people would come talk to us," Pickens recorded, "and we told them to put the black doctors on the staff and put the black patient in the hospital." In Charlotte, Pickens noted proudly, integration was achieved without rioting in the streets, without even any conflicts. That was so because the leadership said, "we're going to do it, and let's just move it along.... [Don't] raise questions about it, just do it."[56]

The only cost of volunteerism was in the length of time for the transition. As the Columbia physician and one-time mayor Frank Owens noted, there was "no overnight change."[57] Indeed, once hospitals showed signs of shifting away from segregation, HEW largely let them set their own pace. Such an attitude encouraged hospital stability and eventual community acceptance of change, but it also gave room for foot-dragging and outright flouting of the law. Columbia General Hospital did not integrate its obstetric wards until 1969, and it acted then largely because declining births made having two wards redundant. Before putting white women in once all-black quarters, however, the black section was remodelled and refurbished. On opening it, the superintendent announced that the unit now stood ready to give patients the "best care possible...."[58] According to the NAACP, such evasion of the 1964 Civil Rights Act was all too common, and the federal government did nothing to stop it. For years after the Act's passage, HEW continued to fund hospitals that "excluded Negro doctors and limited desegregation under so-called 'patient choice' policies."[59]

There was also the problem of hospitals that lay beyond the reach of the law or the courts. These were institutions which had never taken Hill-Burton money before 1964 and afterwards chose to forgo federal funding rather than disavow segregation. Most were small, inconsequential institutions with little to offer patients of either race, but a few were large, modern

[55] Interview by the author with Marshall Pickens, 15 Dec. 1982.
[56] Ibid.
[57] Owens, interview, 2 Feb. 1978.
[58] "Columbia hospital plans to consolidate obstetrics," *Columbia Record*, 13 June 1969; as late as 1969 the NAACP complained strongly that HEW was certifying hospitals which continued to discriminate against both black patients and physicians. See "NAACP health resolutions," *J. Nat. Med. Assoc.*, 1969, *61*: 357.
[59] "NAACP health resolutions," p. 357.

hospitals with sufficient financial resources (often provided by Southern Protestant churches) to resist racial equity. Of course many caved in with the passage of Medicare (1965), whose funds—and patients—were denied to segregated hospitals. Raleigh's Rex Hospital in North Carolina was one such institution integrated by Medicare. After being refused funds early in 1966, Rex promptly accepted its first black maternity patient and shortly afterwards assured the Raleigh black community that it "intends to comply with the Civil Rights Act so it can accept Medicare patients."[60] Over the next three months the hospital undertook further desegregation measures, and in 1967 a federal court judged the hospital sufficiently in compliance with the law to receive Medicare funding.[61]

A few hospitals held out longer by rejecting Medicare patients, but their course became increasingly difficult. For all their toleration of gradual desegregation, the courts showed little patience for overt discrimination, and by the end of the 1960s they were laying all manner of unforeseen snares in the way of those institutions which practiced it. The fate of Charleston's "new Roper" hospital (built in the 1940s) showed just how difficult being exclusively white had become. This privately-owned institution got into trouble because of its own cafeteria.

"New Roper," so named to distinguish it from "old Roper," which had closed in 1959, had never accepted black patients. When the issue of compliance had first arisen in 1964, Roper's chief of staff recommended that the hospital open its 330 beds to blacks so that it could qualify for federal funds. But the Medical Society of South Carolina, which owned the hospital, refused on the ground that federal aid would only mean federal interference with its operation.[62]

If it had been permissible ten years before, such exclusion of blacks now could not be tolerated in the Democratic-controlled Justice Department. In August 1968 the Attorney General, Nicholas deB. Katzenbach, brought suit against the doctors who owned the hospital to force them not only to integrate hospital facilities but to abandon discriminatory employment and promotion policies. The Justice Department's case centered on the hospital's cafeteria and snack bar. Because they served visitors from other states, they and the hospital which housed them fell under the provisions of the Interstate Commerce clause and were thus places of public accommodation subject to the 1964 Civil Rights Act.

In March 1969 the United States District Judge, Robert Martin, accepted that reasoning, and ordered an end to segregation and discrimination as they affected both patients and employees at Roper. But Martin went further

---

[60] "Rex doctors don't change by-laws," *Raleigh Times*, 12 July 1966.
[61] "Rex hospital sued after Negro's death," *Raleigh News and Observer*, 1 Aug. 1970.
[62] "Hospital integration is sought," *Charleston Evening Post*, 30 July 1968; the story of the integration of "New Roper" is taken from *United States v. Medical Society of South Carolina*, in *Federal Supplement*, 1969, 298: 145.

and closed all loopholes that might be used to defeat the spirit of the decision. The hospital could not ask a white whether he was willing to share a room with a black. Nor could a white patient be moved from a room occupied by a black, unless a doctor attested to a compelling medical reason. Further, for the next two years, Roper's director had to give evidence that the hospital was not discriminating against employees or patients. By the end of the decade the kind of judicial tolerance shown earlier by Hemphill, the South Carolina judge, was no longer possible.[63]

Seen in broader perspective, the denial of funding and court orders in the Rex and "new Roper" cases were the exceptions, not the rule. They were mostly characteristic of that group of hospitals with no black patients, even on segregated floors. Outside compulsion to integrate was the exception because the majority of hospitals, as they saw changes coming, moved forward voluntarily to accept them. Rarely had white hospital administrators and physicians—and the same could be said of most black doctors—agitated for change, or even invited it. But when it no longer appeared avoidable (and pressure from civic and civil rights groups prompted that conclusion), they accepted it willingly and with apparent good grace.[64]

The bowing of Savannah, Georgia, to the inevitable might serve as an illustration of this. As soon as it became apparent that Washington was serious about the 1964 Civil Rights Act, the city's white hospitals wrote to all black doctors, inviting them to apply for staff privileges. According to one physician, Henry Collier, hospitals were even willing to lower some standards to allow black doctors to perform minor surgery. By the 1970s, however, standards were being raised again, as more black physicians began to obtain the needed board certification.[65]

Ranzy Weston of Augusta, Georgia, was another black doctor whose experience spanned both eras, and his account suggests the gains that desegregation brought to all black doctors, even those working in modern Hill-Burton facilities. Weston had had privileges in the county hospitals in Aiken, South Carolina, and neighboring Augusta, Georgia, since his arrival in the area in 1953. But he and his patients were isolated in somewhat second-rate black wards. Occasionally, he crossed the color line to treat a white patient, but he recalled with rueful humor that "they didn't want me to treat white women.... No matter how old they were they didn't want me to treat white women."[66]

---

[63] The Roper Hospital case proved influential, not only in pushing segregated private hospitals to integrate but also in adding strength both to the 1964 law and to the federal courts' ability to implement it. See, for example, *Gray v. Greyhound Lines, East* in *Federal Reporter*, 2nd series, 1976, 545: 176; and *United States v. Medical Society of South Carolina* in *American Law Reports, Federal*, 1972, 11: 734. The publication of the Roper case in *American Law Reports* was one sign of the importance which lawyers and judges assigned to it.

[64] Collier, interview, 20 May 1982. Ranzy Weston, interview, 20 May 1982, noted that black doctors were not pushing very strongly for desegregation.

[65] Collier, interview, 20 May 1982. Weston, interview, 20 May 1982, reported the same sort of sudden reversal.

[66] Weston, interview, 20 May 1982.

With integration, things changed markedly. As Weston recalled, if a black doctor had the qualifications, he had equal access to the best facilities available and was admitted fully into the company of specialists whose help he had never totally enjoyed before. If a specialist, usually white, did not want to help, that no longer counted. He *had* to assist. That was the new ethic.

Most black patients, especially those in non-Hill-Burton hospitals, also moved up from second-class status. They, too, could now routinely gain access to a bevy of specialists generally unavailable to them before. Moreover, black cases came under the review of the entire hospital staff. This was an important new development, for it insured that the black patient's well-being was not subject any longer to control by just one or two doctors of perhaps average-to-limited competence, as was often true in all-black and segregated hospitals. Black patient welfare was now guarded by the practice of case survey and review, long a tradition in white hospitals but extended to most black patients only with integration.[67]

The only losers were the South's all-Negro hospitals. They had never taken sturdy root. They had been overlooked, even weakened, by the Hill-Burton Act. With the 1964 law their end was at hand, for as Marshall Pickens of the Duke Endowment put it, once integration came, "blacks preferred to patronize the local white hospital."[68] Not all black hospitals disappeared, certainly. The strongest institutions, such as L. Richardson Memorial in Greensboro and Flint-Goodrich in New Orleans continued on a strong course. But by the mid-1970s the great proportion had been absorbed into white hospital systems, collapsed entirely, or been converted to out-patient clinics.[69]

The fate of Columbia's Waverly-Good Samaritan Hospital illustrates the general trend. The product of a 1939 merger between two sub-standard black hospitals, Waverly-Good Samaritan began to enjoy new credibility after World War II, owing to successful private fund-raising and the garnering in 1950 of a substantial Hill-Burton award (both the result of efforts led by Modjeska Simkins). But the approval in 1967 of a new county hospital by Columbia area voters was the beginning of the end for the black institution. The large, modern, fully integrated Richland County Memorial Hospital opened in 1972. Waverly closed the next year. By mid-decade, the small

---

[67] *Ibid.;* Pickens, interview, 15 Dec. 1982.
[68] Pickens, interview, 15 Dec. 1982.
[69] Anne Bishop (Duke Endowment), in a letter to the author, 28 Feb. 1983, reported that in 1964 the Endowment was aiding fifteen black hospitals in the Carolinas; but that by 1976 only one of them (L. Richardson Memorial in Greensboro) was still operating; also see "Hospital survives alone," *Greenville (North Carolina) Daily News*, 29 Aug. 1982. Not all change was loss: Lincoln Hospital (Durham) survives in spirit, today, as a modern $5,000,000 health center, thanks largely to the efforts of a long-time Lincoln surgeon, Charles Watts (interview by the author with Charles Watts, 17 May 1984).

black hospital sat abandoned and for sale, a home only for occasional derelicts.[70]

Otherwise, hospital integration in the South signalled a gain for everyone. And one reason why it proceeded as smoothly as it did was because white Southern physicians and hospital administrators, in contrast to school superintendents, for example, had no real stake in maintaining segregation. White patients might have been as touchy on the subject as white school patrons, but public opinion did not intrude into the hospital as it did into the classroom. Staff physicians and administrators were more in control of their publics than their counterparts in secondary education. The main thing holding back hospital administrators was assurance that the public could not escape to some still segregated hospital across town. Once that was provided—by force of federal law and judicial decision and by pressure from white and black community leaders—the pace of change was rapid and certain. To Henry Collier, the Savannah black doctor, the really amazing thing was how swiftly and completely the whole segregationist edifice collapsed. White doctors, said Collier, "acted like it was never any different, like segregation had never existed."[71]

---

[70] The history of Waverly-Good Samaritan is based on Simkins, interview, 14 Dec. 1977. On the new Richland County Hospital, see "Richland hospital bond issue voted," *The State*, 30 Aug. 1967, and "Richland Memorial is born," *Columbia Record*, 4 Mar. 1972. Waverly remains a derelict, unused structure, still for sale.
[71] Collier, interview, 20 May 1982.

RONALD H. BAYOR

Urban Renewal, Public Housing and the Racial Shaping of Atlanta

A number of American cities experienced urban renewal in the 1950s and 1960s. Historians and others who have chronicled the urban changes of those decades have cited economic redevelopment as the motivating factor in the rebuilding of the downtown and the relocation of the black population from that area. For example, Carl Abbott in his analysis of Sunbelt cities noted that "the rebuilding of downtown districts was intended to secure two related economic goals." The first was to make the city more appealing as a center of investment and business activity as opposed to competing cities; the second was to enhance the downtown area in light of suburban development which might attract business away from the central city. Clarence Stone in his study of Atlanta's renewal also indicates the primacy of economic factors as the motivation for rebuilding the city's downtown and uprooting the black population.[1]

While economic motivations were certainly evident in the revitalization of Atlanta's downtown, renewal's other components—the large-scale relocation of a poor black population and the building and placement of public housing—when looked at historically reveal the culmination of a long-term effort to guide and segregate the black population and were not simply incidental by-products of the economic redevelopment process. Race as a motivating element and the racial consequences of the decisions made during urban renewal have only recently received attention by historians, such as Arnold Hirsch and Christopher Silver in their books on Chicago and Richmond, respectively.[2] In Atlanta, too, renewal did not occur in a historical vacuum. Actually the renewal decades of the 1950s and 1960s fit in with a long-standing use of public power in order to shift and confine the black community to certain parts of the city. Seen historically, it was part of a decades-old segregation pattern: urban renewal, as critics in the 1950s were inclined to say, was actually "Negro removal." Postwar redevelopment simply added to the segregative process that was already evident. The difference by the 1950s and 1960s was that blacks now had some political power, a result of the end of the white primary in 1946 and a subsequent increase in black registration. Therefore housing needs for blacks had to be met by white politicians in order to secure the black vote. There was, however, that same pattern to manipulate black residential mobility and open only certain sections of the city for black housing. Therefore the racial factor by the 1960s included both racism based on segregating the black population and racially based decisions to acknowledge and appease black discontent during a decade of increasing black political power.

The clearance of low-income housing from neighborhoods adjacent to the Central Business District (CBD), the building of a stadium and civic center, and the relocation and public housing problems all illustrate the racial functions of redevelopment and connect postwar renewal to previous efforts to control black residential patterns. Urban renewal in Atlanta sought to redevelop the downtown for commercial purposes but also, given the historical record, to sort out and further segregate the black population. As a result of the 1950s and 1960s renewal process, by 1967–68, 95 percent of those displaced were black and 83 percent of Atlanta's newly built public housing units were located on the city's west side (northwest and southwest) with the rest in the southeast.[3] No public housing was ever built in the affluent white northeast part of the city.

The historical background for the postwar residential manipulation begins in 1913, when a segregation ordinance was passed.[4] White public officials in Atlanta tried to control legally the areas in which the black population could live. The 1913 segregation ordinance and a number of others which were passed in subsequent years until the 1930s curtailed black movement into white areas through a number of tactics. For example, the 1913 law established "Colored and White blocks." A 1929 law denied the right of an individual to move into a building on a street in which "the majority of the residences . . . are occupied by those with whom said person is forbidden to intermarry." A 1931 law made it illegal for "a member of one race to move into a house previously occupied by a member of the other race, if the dwelling was within fifteen blocks of a public school" of the other race. Although the U.S. Supreme Court in 1917 declared segregation ordinances unconstitutional, Atlanta's city officials made repeated attempts to pass ordinances that would maneuver around the Court's ruling. These laws plus a comprehensive zoning plan in

1922, which included racial zoning, determined on which streets and in which parts of the city blacks could live. Blacks were therefore confined to central Atlanta near the CBD, to parts of the west side, and adjacent to industry. The north side was determined to be a white area. A white area would be rezoned as black only if the rezoning fit in with the general plan to regulate black residential growth. Also, racial buffers were widely employed. The zoning law therefore set the limits of black residential mobility. Even after the racial aspects of the zoning law were declared unconstitutional in 1924, city officials thought of these sections as the only ones suitable for black residential use. The urban renewal, relocation, and public housing site selection of the 1950s and 1960s used the basic racial framework of the 1922 law, with some variations, in order to provide racial buffers with which to protect the CBD and push more of the black population westward. The goal throughout the twentieth century was to direct and segregate the movement of the city's black population.

Before 1945 two plans had also been developed to build highways that would serve as racial barriers and buffers thereby holding the black community to predetermined areas. The first attempt in 1917 envisaged a parkway that would limit the ghetto's expansion on the east side of the city and maintain the area closer to the business district for whites. The second plan in 1941 involved a highway on the west side to control black expansion in that section.[5] Neither road was built, but together with the racial zoning and ordinances they served as the direct predecessors of the highway, urban renewal, and public housing plans of the 1950s and 1960s.

Another action that served as a predecessor to city policy in the 1950s was Fulton County's slum clearance of 1947, which removed all black housing in its Bagley Park section of the county and built a park for whites on the property. No plans were made for housing the displaced blacks; they were simply evicted and forced to move into Atlanta's already overcrowded black neighborhoods.[6]

The black community was not always easily confined, for prior to 1945 they had established growing neighborhoods in the areas east, south, and west of the central business district. Particularly since the 1920s there had been a movement into the west side and an effort to expand beyond the section in this area designated for blacks by racial zoning.[7] As a result of black movement into white west-side neighborhoods, various factors were used to control that expansion.

It was during the postwar decades that highways became a factor in the buffers and barriers created to try to confine blacks to certain parts of mainly west-side Atlanta. Although the development of highways, access roads, and public housing served legitimate purposes of easing traffic flow, enhancing commercial activity and supplying needed housing, when possible this development had clear racial functions as well, which were carryovers from earlier attempts to control spatially the black community. A case in point was the laying out of Interstate 20 (I-20) west on the west side, which in certain areas was used to form a racial wall between black neighborhoods to the north and white ones to the south. Whites in various sections of the area the expressway was to go through were told by city officials that the road would serve as a racial boundary. Not only the highway itself but access roads were planned and used in a number of neighborhoods in the same way. For example, the white residents of the Center Hill and Grove Park communities on Atlanta's west side were assured that a proposed access road "will be a boundary which will protect them as Negro citizens move farther out."[8]

It is certain that a racial factor was not the only consideration in planning these highways; yet it appears that it was a significant factor. When I-20 west was first planned in 1946, it was to carve its way through a west-side section north of where it was eventually placed. The initial location of the highway was based on an analysis of traffic conditions and property values. When the road was in the final planning stages, rather than holding to the 1946 plan, it was laid out along the black (on north) and white (on south) boundary in sections of the west side. However, when the road was finally completed in the mid-1960s, it no longer served any racial purpose. Black migration had been so rapid that by the time of completion the highway boundary had been crossed. Nonetheless, the highway's intended role as a racial barrier is evident in the final plans.[9]

Thus the highway development taking place in Atlanta beginning in the 1950s not only had the intended effect of displacing blacks in the downtown area but also of regulating and confining their residential mobility in the areas into which they were being pushed. The fact that the roads were more successful as displacement than confining instruments is due to the class level of the black population affected. Displacement had its main impact on poor inner-city blacks, who had few resources to fight urban renewal and were forced to move. Confinement was directed at all blacks, including many on the west side with substantial economic and political resources with which to resist and thwart the process. At no time were blacks totally at the mercy of white planners and city officials. The initial movement into the west side before 1945 and the usually successful attempts afterward to leap over racial barriers and buffers in order to expand their residential area indicate that black leaders were not powerless. Through a well-planned but quiet effort engineered by the Atlanta

238

Urban League beginning in the late 1940s to buy land beyond the racial barriers, and through such black institutions as the Atlanta Life Assurance Company, the Citizen's Trust Bank, and the Mutual Federal Savings and Loan Association, which provided mortgages, the black community, particularly the middle class, was able to jump over various obstacles to their mobility, including highways.[10]

Also, in the 1950s black leaders in such groups as the Empire Real Estate Board and in the biracial city-affiliated West Side Mutual Development Committee sought to work out racial land arrangements and quiet racial transition of neighborhoods rather than face the white violence and opposition to black mobility that was all too evident during this period. As a result, black leaders were part of the compromises that resulted in using access roads or unpaved streets as racial boundaries. And city officials as well viewed these agreements and tactics as a way to avoid violence, and also to maintain segregation and divert blacks away from white areas.[11] However, while white leaders saw these decisions as final statements on the black housing issue, blacks viewed it as temporary. Eventually, by the 1960s, white resistance to black expansion on the west side broke down, with the last effort being Mayor Ivan Allen's building of a short-lived concrete and wooden barricade on Peyton Road in 1962—a north-south street on the west side along which blacks were moving into a white neighborhood.[12] Yet the black community's inability to prevent the destruction of large parts of their eastern and southern neighborhoods for commercial and civic redevelopment, the subsequent relocation of many of the displaced to the west side, and the use of highways and roads as racial dividing lines also indicate that final decisions served the white business elite and fit in with a long history of residential control.

The first phase of urban renewal in the 1950s consisted of tearing down the slums for commercial rebuilding; in the second stage in the 1960s, slum clearance was used for the needs of the city—a stadium, civic center, expressway; the third phase in the 1970s finally centered on the rehabilitation of the slums. In all stages, including the last, more housing was destroyed than was built or repaired, even though the federal government had ordered by 1968 "that a city could no longer destroy more housing than it created."[13] The large-scale elimination of housing, the city's policy until 1962 to maintain segregated public housing, and the policy until the mid-1960s not to use renewal land for public housing resulted in major displacement of the black population near the central business district and a shortage of housing. Initially, in the early period of urban renewal in the 1950s, the Atlanta Housing Authority was convinced, over black objections, that two new outlying housing projects, in addition to empty units in both existing public and private housing, would be enough to handle the displaced black population.[14] They totally miscalculated the problem, or perhaps never gave it serious analysis in the first place.

It was clear in the very beginning stages of the postwar renewal planning that there would be a continuation of earlier segregative efforts. The all-white Metropolitan Planning Commission in 1952 laid out its design for future planning in its "Up Ahead" report. This plan called for relocating housing for blacks "in designated areas on the periphery of the city" and for the destruction and relocating of the black business enclave on Auburn Avenue. Business spokesmen in the black community complained that not only were blacks not consulted about "Up Ahead," but the design would leave blacks "out of the expansion of the downtown business area." Furthermore, black leaders such as John H. Calhoun also saw the plan as an attempt to weaken black political power by dispersing the black voters to the outskirts of the city. Calhoun urged that black residents be allowed to return to cleared areas, which would then be protected from further blight by zoning and green belts. As Calhoun noted, "it is indeed unfortunate that we were forced to live in central areas, but since we are here, is it democratic to attempt replacement with other citizens?" While decentralization of the population was important, it should not be accomplished "at the expense of the well-being of one-fourth of the population." Although complaints from the black community drew support from Mayor William Hartsfield and resulted in the rejection (although temporarily) of plans to demolish or weaken the black hold on Auburn Avenue, renewal, relocation, and public housing development followed the intent of the 1952 plan (and its unconstitutional predecessors), which was to control black residential mobility and maintain the segregation of the black population.[15]

Initial efforts to relocate the downtown black population in surrounding neighborhoods met with strong opposition, as seen in the dispute over the Egleston Hospital site in 1959–60. Because of the need of black housing and the increasing political presence of blacks in the city by the late 1950s, white political leaders had to address the issue of a black housing shortage. There was also a need, felt by many white leaders, to shore up moderate black support through housing concessions during a time of sit-ins and protests. The black leadership was opposed to the displacement and renewal policy that moved blacks out of the downtown area and wanted instead public housing to be built in or near the CBD renewal areas. After much discussion with white and black leaders, Mayor Hartsfield agreed in 1960 to support the building of a small 350-unit black public housing project in the area east of the CBD, where Egleston Hospital, now abandoned, was located. A second site was chosen in a far-off section and met little opposition. The Egleston site selection, however, caused strains in Atlanta's race relations and raised the issue of where to reclocate displaced blacks. The main opposition came from nearby white Georgia Baptist Hospital, white churches in the area, and white neighborhood residents. The concern was that the public housing would result in further and quickened racial transition in this section of the city. Thereby both whites who supported rezoning Egleston for public housing and those who did not had as their aim the control of black residential mobility. Hartsfield commented that if the Egleston rezoning were not approved it could result in "uncontrolled infiltration [of blacks] all over the city and very largely to the detriment of the people who are fighting this site."[16] The support of the white business and political leadership was based on the desire to manipulate black migration and, at the same time, maintain their contacts with the black leadership.

When the Board of Aldermen voted against the rezoning in 1960, due to neighborhood pressure, the first director of the Department of Urban Renewal, Malcolm Jones, commented to Hartsfield that "I am convinced that the pressure on East Atlanta has been aggravated by the failure of the city to permit housing for Negroes on the Egleston site. This is, of course, exactly what we have been predicting would happen if adequate living space for Negroes is not provided in an orderly manner." He suggested that land be offered to blacks "even though some White people may be hurt, but where the least amount of damage be done to existing White Communities." Also agreeing with the idea that black residential mobility must be carefully guided was Thomas Parham, the Metropolitan Planning Commission's Housing Relocation Coordinator, who warned Hartsfield that if outlying land was not offered to blacks, white neighborhoods would face transition and the central city would become solidly black, with the "political, social, and economic consequences of which you are well aware."[17] As a result, city officials and the business elite did not abandon their efforts to direct black relocation, but simply turned to the easier solution of putting black displacees from CBD renewal into the confines of the black neighborhoods, mainly on the west side but also to a lesser extent to the south of the CBD. The continuing goal was to try to hold them to certain locations in those sections with minimal infiltration into white neighborhoods, or in the cases of the black neighborhoods still on the fringe of the CBD, to develop racial buffers. When black migration did push into white sections and racial transition was taking place, the neighborhood then became suitable for rezoning for low-income projects.[18]

While discussions went on regarding rehousing displaced blacks, highway development and renewal in the CBD area continued unabated. The east/west and north/south expressways (I–20 and I–75/85, respectively) were completed by the mid- to late 1960s and resulted in the displacement of many low-income blacks in or near the CBD. While blacks had little or no input into the early planning decisions affecting highway placement, black leaders were able to sway some opinion later on. The highways did tear through black neighborhoods and displace many people—which the black leadership could not stop. However, black leaders were influential in getting the north/south expressway moved a few blocks east when it threatened to cut through the black-owned Atlanta Life Assurance Company on Auburn Avenue and virtually destroy that street—a major close-in retail section for Atlanta's blacks. However, black influence was limited in regard to the highways since Auburn Avenue was still affected in that the highway did cut it, although in a less damaging place. Nonetheless, this retail area, clearly hurt by being cut off from many of those who patronized its stores, never recovered.[19] The destruction of black neighborhoods and the negative impact on Auburn Avenue was in line with historic city policy, as noted in the earlier reference to the 1952 "Up Ahead" plan.

Replacing the destroyed black housing, besides the expressways, was the stadium on the south and the civic center on the east. The initial plan for what became the stadium site was to build a white public housing project there. Mayor Ivan Allen, Hartsfield's successor in 1962, thought the white project would serve as a racial buffer between the CBD and black communities to the south. However, black leaders protested against the plan, since black housing was so desperately needed in the city, and urged the development of a black housing project. Allen, caught between the white business elite who did not want a black project on renewal land on the edge of the CBD, and the black leadership, who had helped elect him, opted for a stadium (the building of which he had supported anyway) and asked for a feasibility study that would show that the stadium had to be built on that renewal property. On the basis of the racial tug-of-war that went on constantly in Atlanta, black housing demands were not met at a time of extreme housing shortages for black families. Instead, the stadium was put in place as a racial buffer on cleared land that had removed many blacks from near the CBD.[20] There was never any difficulty rehousing displaced whites.

For the civic center, also an Allen suggestion and also serving as a racial buffer, a dispute emerged in 1963 between white and black leaders regarding the extent of black displacement and the need for a relocation plan before work began on the center. The area where the center was to be built was the Buttermilk Bottom section on the east of the downtown business district. Only the intervention of the federal government (the Urban Renewal Administration) brought an increasing concern from city and business leaders for the rehousing problem in regard to both the civic center and stadium areas. After years of neglecting public housing in favor of slum clearance and nonresidential renewal as indicated in the Housing Act of 1954, the federal government in 1963 stated that support for continued renewal in Atlanta would be granted only if applications were accompanied by consideration of and an appeal for more public housing. As a result of federal and black pressure, the city agreed to only a partial redevelopment of the Buttermilk Bottom section, thereby limiting also the number of displacees; and the earlier agreement, which called for no public housing in renewal areas, was terminated. Allen was still under considerable pressure to provide housing.[21]

The previous Egleston controversy and its aftermath, the expressway, stadium, and civic center issues, and the relocation problems in general were part of Atlanta's long-term attempt to control black residential patterns. In a statement before the Advisory Committee of the U.S. Civil Rights Commission meeting in Atlanta in 1967, the NAACP warned of the danger that the " 'relocation program' may be used to rebuild the ghettos as *ghettos.*" The organization also noted that "the pattern was established and continued through the past 25 years or more—where all available housing for Negroes—publicly aided or not—has been done either in the ghetto or adjacent to it." According to interviews in 1967 with those in the black community who were knowledgeable about housing patterns in the city, the "interviewees repeatedly cited Expressway route location and urban renewal project location selections as being dictated by a desire to create and maintain segregated patterns of residences in the city in the past." Public housing, it was stated, "has been and is being used to force segregated housing patterns," particularly through the use of segregated housing application offices. In this way whites and blacks could be pushed in certain directions. Some interviewees further claimed that housing code enforcement "was deliberately not carried out in some areas in order to speed deterioration so that Negro families could be removed through urban renewal."[22]

As a result, the NAACP became so disturbed by the attempt to control black spatial mobility and solidify and perpetuate the ghetto that they asked Robert Weaver, Secretary of HUD, in 1967 "to withhold all funds to public housing and Urban Renewal Programs until all discriminatory practices are eliminated and a balanced dispersion of public housing units are accomplished."[23] As Robert Flanagan, executive secretary of the Atlanta branch of the NAACP, noted in 1967 in regard to plans of placing another public housing project on the west side, any more rezoning for public housing in western black neighborhoods "would lend confirmation to the obvious attempt by the power structure to systematically relocate Atlanta's Negro citizens to the southwest and northwest sections of the city."[24] And Amos Holmes of the Atlanta NAACP, as part of a report to the U.S. Commission on Civil Rights in 1968, commented that "we must insist that the Federal and State governments have a responsibility to insure that local housing authorities and urban renewal agencies stop using public funds to entrench and extend segregation." By 1967, 88 percent of the land approved for high-density zoning was in the western and southern parts of Atlanta.[25]

Although land on the west side was cheaper—and this reason was often cited by Atlanta officials as the rationale for putting public housing there—the economic factor in Atlanta's racial patterns has only limited application, since public housing placement fit in with the general efforts to segregate the black population in certain parts of the city. During the Civil Rights Commission hearings in Atlanta in 1967, Kenneth Wexler of the Commission's Research Division stated that "segregated housing patterns in Atlanta have increased since 1940, although the economic justification for them has diminished." By 1960 more than two-thirds of the residential segregation could not be explained by differences in economic status between the races.[26]

The appeals to HUD to halt the further construction of segregated public housing presented a dilemma for the black community. In a situation very similar to the Dorothy Gautreaux suit in federal court in Chicago in 1966, in which the judge's ruling to place public housing in white areas resulted in a long-term halt in its construction, blacks in Atlanta also faced the question of whether to acquiesce to needed public housing no matter where it was put or to insist on a program to disperse this housing into white areas.[27] Furthermore, there were other benefits to be derived from accepting the racial design for Atlanta. The white business elite from the early stages of renewal had held out enticements to the black community to win their approval. These included promises to rehabilitate some black neighborhoods, to support the construction of low-cost private housing for displacees with incomes above the maximum for public housing (called 221 housing), and to provide the black colleges on the west side with land for expansion. And black real estate firms could and did benefit from the business created by renewal.[28]

Regardless of the consequences, Atlanta's black leaders, as those in Chicago, pursued their effort to force a change in the city's housing policy. The concentration of low-income black housing primarily on the west side finally led the federal government in 1967 to accede to black demands and stipulate that no more federal housing was to be placed in racially identifiable areas unless some effort has been made previously to build housing in other areas. They wanted the dispersal of public housing with particular attention to fringe neighborhoods, where the housing would attract both white and black tenants:[29] The black leadership and residents of black neighborhoods were concerned that the west-side areas could no longer sustain more population; the schools were already overcrowded and city services strained.[30] The black community therefore made an effort to force city officials to scatter or disperse the public housing and move it particularly into the northeast—the elite white enclave. The black leaders' demands were supported by interracial groups in the city, such as the Council on Human Relations of Greater Atlanta, and by some neighborhood organizations on the west side, such as the West End Businessmen's Association. There was also a simultaneous movement supported by some of the same groups to secure open housing and fair housing laws in order to ensure a dispersal of the black population.[31] The mayor therefore was faced with either adhering to the new federal guidelines and also giving in to primarily black pressure or losing all further renewal money or federal support for much-needed low-income housing. As expected, the regional administrator of HUD refused to approve further northwest sites for public housing that the mayor had suggested.[32] Mayor Allen looked for a solution to the problem.

The Housing Resources Committee (set up by the mayor in 1966 to study housing needs and accelerate construction of low-income housing) proposed in 1968 as a way out of the impasse a "package deal" for the rezoning of a number of sites at once and the dispersal of low-income housing in all parts of the city.[33] The mayor was faced with a split in the white political-business leadership. The Chamber of Commerce supported the plan, but the Board of Aldermen or Atlanta Housing Authority did not. However, while the Chamber favored the general plan it never acknowledged support for specific sites where the housing was to go, and the business and political leadership never fought strongly for the "package" plan. Eventually business support waned because of fear over the future of their own and other white neighborhoods, as well as concern that building more public housing would just bring more blacks into the city. Mayor Allen rejected the "package" plan and opted instead for a plan by which the city would consider only individual sites rather than a number of sites at any given time.[34] However, the only future low-income housing developed was either in outlying areas or in sections earlier determined as areas for black expansion. All efforts to put public housing in the northeast failed. On one occasion in 1972 a north-side site that a federal-court-appointed housing committee recommended for public housing was quickly rezoned by the Board of Aldermen for commercial development, even though the board had turned down two earlier requests to do so. The neighborhood civic association which had opposed commercial zoning for this property previously now supported this rezoning.[35]

The regional office of HUD eventually relented on its ruling regarding the development of future public housing in racially identifiable areas. Surrounding counties also remained opposed to public housing, so low-income housing that was built went into areas that were already black or were expected to be black soon.[36] The housing difficulties remained, further concentrating blacks in their designated ghetto areas.

It was not only black housing projects that were used for racial purposes; white projects also were part of the segregation design. In general, low-income projects were placed in areas in which either one or the other race predominated. As a result, according to a report by the Greater Atlanta Council on Human Relations in 1959, "racial segregation is much more complete in new housing developments than in established neighborhoods. Public housing developments have extended and strengthened patterns of segregation in some localities."[37] This was evident from the early stages of public housing.

Techwood, the first federal housing project in the United States, was built in an area in which the majority of inhabitants were white (72.4 percent in 1930), but in which a number of blacks also lived (27.6 percent). The project was intended for use only by whites, and none of the 224 black families on the Techwood site was living in the project after its opening. As part of the effort to remove blacks from the Techwood area, the Atlanta delegation to Col. H. B. Hackett, general manager, Public Works Emergency Housing Corporation, recommended that the boundaries of the project be amended "in order to remove all of the colored population from the area." It was clear what the intentions of the Atlanta representatives were in regard to controlling what residential sections were available to blacks. Techwood's building and opening in 1936 therefore displaced many blacks in that neighborhood and led to a more segregated area than before (only 15.8 percent of the neighborhood population remained black by 1938), but with the expectation that the remaining blacks would soon be forced out by business and further white occupancy.[38]

In another situation, occurring during the urban renewal period in 1957, the white-only Joel Chandler Harris Homes was strategically placed on the border of a black-white fringe area—blacks to the north and whites to the south. Before the Harris project was built, the white section was beginning to see an influx of blacks. The building of the project, along with a cyclone fence on its northern boundary and the city's refusal to pave one hundred yards of road connecting the black and white areas, served as a barrier to protect the white West End neighborhood from black incursion. At least until 1965, long-standing vacancies at white Harris Homes were not filled with those on the long waiting lists of black prospective tenants in an effort to maintain the racial buffer of the Harris project.[39]

The 1960s residential manipulation was made easier as a result of earlier segregation practices, further connecting renewal and relocation to its historical past. One of the problems with developing public housing sites was the earlier racially oriented zoning in Atlanta, which provided too little land for multifamily structures and too much for commercial or industrial building. A report by the Housing Resources Committee noted that the amount of land zoned industrial was excessive, especially in relation to the problem of finding land for low-income housing.[40] It was clear, as Mayor Allen and others acknowledged, that an artificial shortage of land for blacks had occurred because the city used zoning to develop racial buffers between black and white areas. "The result was," as Allen stated, "Atlanta city maps were dotted with scores of these unused plots of land. And this at a time when we needed all the good land we could find for housing."[41] The problem was recognized as early as 1959 by Malcolm Jones, the director of the urban renewal department, who commented that finding land for black housing was a major problem and "unless solved quickly this will greatly hamper the progress of the Urban Renewal program throughout the city." He called for a reanalysis of the zoning ordinances in order to meet the need for black housing.[42]

Nonetheless, there was little attempt to rezone or use land in areas of Atlanta where city officials had determined black housing would not be built. This was true of multifamily low-income housing and also 221 housing. Race again appeared to be the prime motivation as indicated by a number of situations. "It is clear most of the additional vacant acreage within the city which is zoned for residential use is," stated a report on housing prepared for Atlanta's business leaders in 1961, " 'politically unavailable for Negro use.' " The report continued that there was an "artificial scarcity of land available for black housing in a community in which there are no natural barriers to geographic expansion and in which the white community has effective possession of considerable residential acreage which is vacant or very thinly occupied."[43] As the Atlanta Bureau of

Planning noted in 1965, "it should be remembered that there would be more than enough land for construction of Negro housing—as well as all that needed for whites—if it were not for the restrictions inherent in our community customs." Land that was politically suitable for blacks followed the racial land patterns of earlier decades. Applications for rezoning for high density secured the approval of the Board of Aldermen during the 1965–67 period mainly in black areas. As one analyst of Atlanta's zoning concluded, "It is inescapable that zoning within the City of Atlanta is utilized to preserve the status quo and to segregate the white and nonwhite populations."[44]

Also as a federal judge stated in 1971 in regard to a controversy concerning the placement of two apartment projects in an area just to the north of the city limits in Fulton County, "This court is constrained to find that the only objections the county authorities have to Boatrock and Red Oak [the two projects] is that the apartments would be occupied by low-income black tenants." The Fulton County Commissioners had refused to issue building permits until ordered to by the judge. Other tactics used to limit low-income black expansion were to zone for large lot sizes and square-footage floor space and also low density, which would make the zoned area too expensive for moderate and low-income housing.[45]

Ironically, Atlanta was becoming more segregated in terms of housing and neighborhoods at the very time that lunch counters, public accommodations, and schools were being integrated. Also, black voting power was increasing in the city and their strength was acknowledged by white politicians who sought their votes. Since the the 1950s Atlanta had seen itself, in the phrase coined by Mayor Hartsfield, as the "city too busy to hate." The contrast between image and reality and between a city that was the headquarters of a number of national civil rights organizations but which became more and more residentially segregated is not difficult to explain. As blacks increased their pressure on city officials to achieve desegregation in schools and public facilities, issues that were very much in the newspapers of the nation, Atlanta's white leaders acquiesced, although reluctantly and slowly, rather than ruin the city's image and damage economic growth. The lessons of Little Rock and Birmingham were clear to Atlanta's white elite.[46] However, Atlanta's housing was not a front-page issue; it rarely attracted the attention of the nation's newspapers in the same way as did lunch-counter desegregation. As a result, the conscious attempt to resegregate and control black spatial mobility could be achieved more quietly, and with black demands for dispersed public housing more easily ignored.

Efforts to confine blacks already on the west side and to use roads as buffers and barriers received national attention on only one occasion. The building of the Peyton Road barricade in 1962 and the controversy that ensued found its way into the national press. Coming at a time when the Berlin Wall was being built, the newspapers dubbed the Atlanta structure the "Atlanta Wall." It hurt the city's image, embarrassed Mayor Allen, and therefore was quickly demolished. The attention focused on the "Wall" also led to a change in city policy. The Southern Regional Council accurately reported that "the city's planning and zoning policies once were bent toward the maintenance of racial boundaries and the confinement of the Negro population through the use of barriers and buffers. Since the Peyton Road conflict was resolved, there has been a substantial easing of such applications of public policy." Also, the city's realtors eschewed any further use of physical barriers to hold the segregation line.[47]

Only with the election of Maynard Jackson in 1973, the city's first black mayor, and a change in federal government policies through the Housing and Community Development Act of 1974, which led to a greater interest in "upgrading existing communities," did priorities shift in regard to housing and renewal for blacks. The goals for central Atlanta (an area larger than the CBD) now was to increase housing for the middle and upper class but "without relying on displacement of low and moderate income households." Any renewal that results in displacement should entail "no net reduction in city-wide stock accessible to the type of households displaced." For those who did not wish to move elsewhere, housing in the site area should be provided.[48]

However, the damage had already been done. By 1959 the black community, which was 35.7 percent of Atlanta's population, was confined to 16.4 percent of the land, and by 1965 blacks, now 43.5 percent of the city's population, were on only 22 percent of the land, although, as noted, there was much vacant land, incorrectly zoned commercial or industrial, in the city. The segregation index in Atlanta increased from 87.4 in 1940 to 91.5 in 1950 to 93.6 in 1960 (the third highest in the nation) as attempts were made to confine the black community through renewal displacement, public housing, and highway-road barriers. Between 1950 and 1970, census tracts that were mainly inhabited by blacks (90 percent or more) increased from 13 to 21 to 37.[49] The policy of placing public housing mainly in one section of the city led to the already noted statistic of 83 percent of the housing being built on the west side by 1967 in areas where the schools were already overcrowded and the other city services strained. Black areas became severely overcrowded by the 1960s: overcrowding in black households "was four times more frequent . . . than among white households," with 40 percent of black-occupied rental units characterized as overcrowded.[50]

Also, those black projects placed in outlying areas, such as Perry Homes on the northwest (built in 1955), were not near any public transportation or jobs and thus for years were isolated, with residents restricted in their employment opportunities. According to a report on Atlanta's housing completed in 1966–67, "Many Negroes have found it necessary to live in areas which are inconvenient to their place of employment. This has resulted in both higher transportation costs for low-income Negro families and in some cases has prevented Negroes from taking jobs of their choice." The report recommended that in the future more attention be paid to the location of jobs before selecting public housing sites. The failure to locate public housing particularly in the northeast resulted in removing blacks from proximity to jobs in that section. According to the Council on Human Relations of Greater Atlanta in 1966, the refusal to disperse public housing had increased the problems of those living in public housing elsewhere in the city to get to the jobs on the white north side. The divergence of jobs from job-seekers was just one of the consequences of Atlanta's control of black spatial patterns.[51] The removal of black housing from some sections near the central business district and the expansion of the CBD also created an area largely devoid of neighborhoods and street life, an area that is deserted after the commuters return to the suburbs. Had urban renewal been used to build decent housing for the poor in the CBD area rather than engage in massive destruction of housing, large-scale relocation, and racial buffers, Atlanta's downtown might today be a more vibrant district.

Furthermore, the predominately black south side of metro Atlanta, as opposed to the largely white north side, has experienced relatively little development into the 1980s. Northern regions have become overdeveloped and choked with traffic, while the south has been neglected, even having difficulty attracting retail investments.[52] The economic development of the Atlanta metro area has been warped by the racial residential manipulations of earlier years, creating in essence separate cities, separate metro areas, which was not conducive to balanced economic growth.

On the west side the policy of using highways and access roads as buffers and barriers and at times terminating roads between black and white areas led to later problems regarding traffic flow, linkages between various parts of the city, and city expansion in certain directions. Samuel Adams, former director of research for the Southern Regional Council, noted in 1967 that there were few streets on the west side that offered easy travel between the black northern neighborhoods and the white southern ones.

He concluded that this situation was caused by the attempts to impede movement between the two racial areas. The eventual outcome is noted in the 1980 Atlanta Comprehensive Plan, which stated that the west sides' traffice congestion was due to "limited street network" and "lack of adequate north-south arterial capacity."[53]

Atlanta, with its deserted downtown at night, concentrated public housing, uneven economic development, distance between jobs and housing for the low-income, segregated city neighborhoods, segregated schools based on those neighborhoods (Atlanta city schools are presently "among the top eleven most racially segregated systems in the country"),[54] and traffic problems, stands today as the product of decisions based on long-term racial considerations that culminated in the relocation and public housing policies of the renewal decades.

Georgia Tech

Notes

The research for this article was supported by grants from the American Association for State and Local History—NEH, and the American Historical Association (Beveridge grant).

1. Carl Abbott, *The New Urban America: Growth and Politics in Sunbelt Cities* (Chapel Hill, 1981), 144–46; Clarence N. Stone, *Economic Growth and Neighborhood Discontent: System Bias in the Urban Renewal Program in Atlanta* (Chapel Hill, 1976).

2. Arnold R. Hirsch, *Making the Second Ghetto: Race and Housing in Chicago, 1940–1960* (Cambridge, 1983); Christopher Silver, *Twentieth-Century Richmond: Planning, Politics and Race* (Knoxville, TN, 1984).

3. "Toward Equal Opportunity in Housing in Atlanta, Georgia—A Report of the Georgia State Advisory Committee to the United States Commission on Civil Rights," May 1968, 7, Southern Regional Council papers (hereafter cited as SRC), The Atlanta University Center Woodruff Library, Special Collections; Atlanta branch, NAACP, presentation before the Advisory Committee of the United States Civil Rights Commission, 8 April 1967, SRC.

4. The segregation ordinances and racial zoning plans and their effect on Atlanta are covered in: Barbara J. Flint, "Zoning and Residental Segregation: A Social and Physical History, 1910–1940" (Ph.D. dissertation, University of Chicago, 1977), 135, 207, 212, 239–40, 276, 303, 309, 313, 317, 320, 325–26, 334–36, 341–43, 357; Gilbert T. Stephenson, "The Segregation of the White and Negro Races in Cities," *South Atlantic Quarterly* 13 (January 1914), 1–4, 7–10; John Dittmer, *Black Georgia in the Progressive Era, 1900–1920* (Urbana, 1977), 13–15; Roger L. Rice, "Residential Segregation by Law, 1910–1917," *Journal of Southern History* 34 (May 1968), 181, 193–94; E. Bernard West, "Black Atlanta—Struggle for Development, 1915–1925" (M.A. thesis, Atlanta University, 1976), 34–36, Appendix; "The Atlanta Zoning Plan," *Survey* 48 (22 April 1922), 114–15; Howard L. Preston, *Automobile Age Atlanta: The Making of a Southern Metropolis, 1900–1935* (Athens, GA, 1979), 96; John Hammond Moore, "Jim Crow in Georgia," *South Atlantic Quarterly* 66 (1967). 558; Blaine A. Brownell, "The Commercial-Civic Elite

and City Planning in Atlanta, Memphis, and New Orleans in the 1920s," *Journal of Southern History* 41 (August 1975), 357,. 359, 362, 364; *Atlanta Journal*, 11 April 1922; Atlanta General Council Minutes, 20 May 1929, 525; 16 March 1931, 518.

5. Preston, *Automobile Age Atlanta*, 98, 101–3.

6. *Atlanta Daily World*, 22 October 1948; Statement of Atlanta Urban League presented to Joint Congressional Committee on Housing in Atlanta, 29 October 1947, in SRC.

7. Preston, *Automobile Age Atlanta*, 106–7; Robert A. Thompson, Hylan Lewis, and David McEntire, "Atlanta and Birmingham: A Comparative Study in Negro Housing," in *Studies in Housing and Minority Groups*, Nathan Glazer and David McEntire, eds. (Berkeley, 1960), 19–20; Timothy J. Crimmins, "Bungalow Suburbs: East and West," *Atlanta Historical Journal* 26 (Summer/Fall 1982), 88–89.

8. William B. Hartsfield to Clarke Donaldson, 20 March 1954, Atlanta Bureau of Planning papers (hereafter cited as ABP), Atlanta Historical Society. Robert C. Stuart to W. O. Duvall, 19 March 1954, ABP; "Report on the Adamsville Transition Area," 26 August 1960, ABP; Timothy J. Crimmins, "West End: Metamorphosis from Suburban Town to Intown Neighborhood," *Atlanta Historical Journal* 26 (Summer/Fall 1982), 46–47. For more on the racial uses of highways and roads, see Ronald H. Bayor, "Roads to Racial Segregation: Atlanta in the Twentieth Century," *Journal of Urban History* 15 (November 1988), 3–21.

9. H. W. Lochner and Company, and DeLeuw, Cather, and Company, *Highway and Transportation Plan for Atlanta, Georgia*, Prepared for the State Highway Department of Georgia and the Public Roads Administration, Federal Works Agency (Chicago, January 1946); Leon Eplan, a city planner and Commissioner of the Department of Budget and Planning from 1974 to 1978, stated that "even the interstate highway system was, as in the case of I–20 West, used to form a racial wall." John H. Calhoun noted that I–20 West was developed as a racial buffer, and L. D. Milton commented that it was supposed to be the racial dividing line, but it did not hold up. Leon Eplan, "Background Paper," for Metropolitan Atlanta Conference on Equality of Opportunity in Housing, 29 May 1968, SRC; Interview with John H. Calhoun, 7 August 1985; Interview with L. D. Milton, 18 September 1985. Calhoun was active in the founding of the Atlanta Negro Voters League and All-Citizens Registration Committee in the 1940s. He was also a real estate broker and a member of the Empire Real Estate Board, a coalition of black real estate firms; co-chair of the Georgia Voters League; executive director of the Atlanta branch, NAACP, in the 1960s; a city councilman in the 1970s; and a member of the Atlanta Regional Commission. Milton was president of the black-owned Citizen's Trust Bank in Atlanta from 1930 to 1971 and was involved in developing some west-side communities for blacks.

10. Interview with Robert A. Thompson, 17 July 1985; telephone interview, 15 August 1986; interview with Milton; Thompson, Lewis, and McEntire, "Atlanta and Birmingham," 29, 31, 34; *Atlanta Journal-Constitution*, 11 October 1959. Thompson was housing secretary and associate director of the Atlanta Urban League from 1942 to the 1960s, secretary of the Atlanta Housing Council, and assistant to the Regional Administrator of HUD for equal opportunity in the late 1960s. He was personally involved in most housing and expansion issues in Atlanta during this period.

11. Interview with Thompson; Interview with Milton; Stephens Mitchell to Robert C. Stuart, 18 February 1954, ABP; Westside Mutual Development Committee and Advisory Panel to Collier Heights resident, 5 March 1954; ABP; *Atlanta Journal*, 9 December 1952.

12. *Atlanta Journal*, 17, 19, 20, 1962; Ivan Allen, Jr., with Paul Hemphill, *Mayor: Notes on the Sixties* (New York, 1971), 71–72; Interview with Ivan Allen, Jr., 29 July 1985.

13. "Atlanta's Fight Against Substandard Housing—Is It Working?" *Research Atlanta Report*, October 1972, 47, 53, 73.

14. Stone, *Economic Growth*, 62–63, 97; *Atlanta Journal-Constitution*, 18 May 1958; *The Renewer* (Newsletter of the Citizens' Committee for Urban Renewal), August 1963. As of

1968, Atlanta still had separate white and black public-housing application offices and thereby discouraged integration of the public housing. Therefore, the official desegregation of public housing in 1962 had little immediate effect on decreasing housing segregation in public units. See "Toward Equal Opportunity," 8, 11, 30, 40.

15. Presentation of J. H. Calhoun, representing Atlanta branch, NAACP before Metropolitan Planning Commission Hearings, 30 May 1952, NAACP papers, group II, series C, branch files, 1940–55, Box 38, Library of Congress; L. D. Reddick to W. E. B. DuBois, 6 October 1952, W. E. B. DuBois papers, reel 68 (microfilm edition); remarks of L. D. Reddick at the public hearings, Metropolitan Planning Commission, 26 May 1952, DuBois papers, reel 68; remarks of John Wesley Dobbs at the public hearings, Metropolitan Planning Commission, 3 June 1952, DuBois papers, reel 68.

16. Stone, *Economic Growth*, 68–71; *Atlanta Constitution*, 21 February 1960; *Atlanta Daily World*, 15 May 1960, 19 July 1961, 8 and 10 August 1961; Interview with Cecil Alexander, 17 December 1984. (Alexander was chairman of the Housing Resources Committee from 1966 to 1969, the Citizens Advisory Committee on Urban Renewal in the 1960s, and the Long-Range Planning Committee of the Chamber of Commerce in the 1970s.)

17. Malcolm D. Jones to Hartsfield, 6 May 1960, ABP; Thomas M. Parham to Mayor William B. Hartsfield, 11 May 1960, ABP.

18. Claudia M. Turner, "Changing Residential Patterns in Southwest Atlanta from 1960–1970" (M.A. thesis, Atlanta University, 1970), 37–38. In 1961 a one-time exception to the policy of not building public housing on renewal land came after the devastating Egleston rejection, when land had to be found quickly for those displacees who were to be put into the Egleston site housing. A project for elderly blacks (Antoine Graves Homes) was built in the Butler Street renewal area near Grady Homes, adjacent to the CBD on the south, and an addition was made to the Perry Homes project in the northwest. This action was taken because of the dire need for housing and the opposition of white neighborhoods to locating any black projects in their areas. See Stone, *Economic Growth*, 75–76; *Atlanta Daily World*, 23 June 1961; *Atlanta Constitution*, 14 and 22 June 1961.

19. Floyd Hunter, *Community Power Succession* (Chapel Hill, 1980), 6, 26; interview with Calhoun; interview with Thompson, 17 July 1985. *Atlanta Daily World*, 4 June 1958.

20. Interview with Leon Eplan, 15 October 1985; interview with Robert B. Flanagan, 3 December 1985. (Eplan, a city planner, did the feasibility study on the stadium. Flanagan was executive secretary of the Atlanta branch, NAACP, in 1967–68 and later president of the Georgia NAACP.)

21. Stone, *Economic Growth*, 94–98, 100–101, 108, 110, 113, 177–78.

22. Atlanta branch, NAACP, presentation before the Advisory Committee of the United States Civil Rights Commission, 8 April 1967, SRC; Final Report, City of Atlanta, Georgia, "Equal Opportunity in Housing," Atlanta Community Improvement Program, 1966–67, Box 1, City of Atlanta, Reports, Atlanta Historical Society.

23. Atlanta branch, NAACP, presentation before the Advisory Committee of the U.S. Civil Rights Commission, 8 April 1967, SRC.

24. Flanagan to John M. Flanigen (chairman, zoning committee), 3 November 1967, Cecil Alexander files (privately held). Also, interview with Clarence Coleman, 24 April 1986. (Coleman was the Southern Regional Director of the National Urban League from the mid-1960s to 1972 and prior to that was deputy executive director of the Atlanta Urban League.) *Atlanta Daily World*, 25 March 1962.

25. "Toward Equal Opportunity," 8. Samuel Ira Spector, "Municipal and County Zoning in a Changing Urban Environment," Research paper 53, June 1970, Bureau of Business and Economic Research, Georgia State University, 7.

26. *Atlanta Constitution*, 8 April 1967; "Toward Equal Opportunity in Housing in Atlanta, Georgia—A Report to the Georgia State Advisory Committee to the United States Commission on Civil Rights," First Draft, 13 October 1967, 26, SRC.

27. Hirsch, *Making the Second Ghetto*, 265–66, 268.

28. Stone, *Economic Growth*, 63–65, 68, 85–87, 142–43.
29. Housing Resources Committee, Minutes, 31 May 1967, in Cecil Alexander files; "Toward Equal Opportunity," May 1968, 48; *Atlanta Constitution*, 8 April 1967; *Atlanta Journal-Constitution*, 27 August 1967.
30. *Atlanta Constitution*, 5 and 15 August 1967; Stone, *Economic Growth*, 144–45; *Atlanta Journal-Constitution*, 27 August 1967.
31. *Weekly Star*, 14 September 1967, 16 November 1967; Housing Resources Committee, Minutes, 2 August 1968, in Cecil Alexander files; *Atlanta Constitution*, 21 April 1967; Council on Human Relations of Greater Atlanta to members of Board of Atlanta Housing Authority, 20 September 1966, in SRC; Atlanta branch, NAACP, "Citywide Housing Conference," 11 February 1967, in Sam Williams collection, Community Relations Commission Papers, The Atlanta University Center Woodruff Library, Special Collections; Spector, "Municipal and County Zoning," 7.
32. Edward H. Baxter (Regional Administrator of HUD) to Ivan Allen, Jr., 5 May 1967, SRC.
33. *Atlanta Constitution*, 13 December 1968; Spector, "Municipal and County Zoning," 544; Stone, *Economic Growth*, 146–48.
34. Resolution of Atlanta Chamber of Commerce, 10 April 1968, in Cecil Alexander files; Stone, *Economic Growth*, 146–50; Housing Resources Committee Minutes, 12 December 1968, in Cecil Alexander files; *Atlanta Constitution*, 1 December 1967.
35. *Atlanta Journal*, 19 April 1972; *Atlanta Constitution*, 20 April 1972.
36. Stone, *Economic Growth*, 143, 146–47; Malcolm D. Jones (Housing Coordinator) to Frank Carter, 16 August 1968, Cecil Alexander files.
37. Greater Atlanta Council on Human Relations, "Report," 19 March 1959, SRC.
38. "Techwood Neighorhood," Report 1: Social Base Map Survey of Atlanta, Georgia, WPA of Georgia, 1939, 7–8; H. A. Gray (Director of Housing, PWA) to K. S. McAllister (Housing Manager, Federal Emergency Administration of Public Works, Housing Division), 19 January 1937; and McAllister to Gray, 22 January 1937, National Archives, RG 196, Records of the Public Housing Administration, Box 32, folder H1101–4; Leopold Hass and D. L. Stokes to Col. H. B. Hackett (General Manager, Public Works Emergency Housing Corporation), 21 March 1934, National Archives, RG 196, Federal Program Project files, Box 23, folder H–1101; "Memorandum and Report on Techwood and University Housing Projects, Atlanta, Georgia, January 9, 1934," by N. Max Dunning, Assistant Director of Planning, National Archives, RG 196, Federal Program Project files, Box 23, folder H–1100.
39. Thompson, Lewis, and McEntire, "Atlanta and Birmingham," 21, 27–32; Greater Atlanta Council on Human Relations, "Report," 19 March 1959, SRC; Francis X. Servaites (Acting Commissioner, PHA) to A. R. Hanson (Director, Atlanta Regional Office, PHA), 22 October 1965, National Archives, RG 196, Commissioner of Public Housing Correspondence, Box 7, folder, Atlanta Regional Office, Atlanta, 1965.
40. Housing Resources Committee memo, "Report on Vacant Land in Atlanta," 9 August 1967, SRC.
41. Atlanta branch, NAACP, "Citywide Housing Conference," 11 February 1967 in Sam Williams collection; Atlanta Chamber of Commerce, Board of Directors, 13 September 1967, in Grace Hamilton papers, The Atlanta University Center Woodruff Library, Special Collections; Allen, *Mayor: Notes on the Sixties*, 71.
42. Malcolm D. Jones to Mayor and Board of Aldermen, "Year-End Review of Urban Renewal," 1959, Department of Urban Renewal, Atlanta: (Mimeo) in Charles Palmer papers, Emory University, Special Collections.
43. Hamilton Douglas, Jr., "Housing the Million," report prepared for a group of Atlanta business leaders, 10 January 1961, SRC.
44. Atlanta Bureau of Planning, "The Story of Negro Housing in Atlanta," 1965. ABP; Spector, "Municipal and County Zoning," 5–6; *Atlanta Journal-Constitution*, 18 May 1958.

45. Spector, "Municipal and County Zoning," 5, 54; *Atlanta Constitution*, 8 September 1971.

46. Ronald H. Bayor, "A City Too Busy to Hate: Atlanta's Business Community and Civil Rights," in *Business and Its Environment*, Harold Sharlin, ed. (Westport, CT, 1983).

47. Southern Regional Council, *Proposed Immediate Steps on the Immediate Problem: Housing Discrimination and Low-Cost Housing Shortages*, n.d., SRC; Samuel L. Adams, "Blueprint for Segregation: A Survey of Atlanta Housing," *New South* 22 (Spring 1967), 77.

48. Abbott, *New Urban America*, 151; "Back to the City: Housing Options for Central Atlanta," Full Technical Report, Central Area Housing Strategy Study, June 1974 (Study Director, Richard C. D. Fleming of Central Atlanta Progress; Project Coordinator, Frank Keller of Atlanta Department of Planning).

49. "Housing and Negroes in Atlanta, Georgia," Hearings testimony before U.S. Commission on Civil Rights held in Atlanta, 10 April, 1959, SRC report, 24 June 1959; Samuel Adams, "Blueprint for Segregation," 74; Virginia H. Hein, "The Image of 'A City Too Busy to Hate': Atlanta in the 1960's," *Phylon* 33 (Fall 1972), 219; James W. Harris, "This Is Our Home: It is Not for Sale" (Princeton Senior's Thesis, 1971), 35.

50. Final Report, City of Atlanta, Georgia, "Equal Opportunity in Housing," Appendix I-1; "Toward Equal Opportunity," May 1968, 4; "The Growth and Extent of Segregation in Housing in the City of Atlanta," n.d., in Clarence Bacote papers, The Atlanta University Center Woodruff Library, Special Collections.

51. "Toward Equal Opportunity," May 1968, 10; C. R. Yates to Fulton County Grand Jury, 15 April 1960, in Whitney Young papers, Columbia University; Final Report, City of Atlanta, Georgia, "Equal Opportunity in Housing," 19; Council on Human Relations of Greater Atlanta to members of the Board of Atlanta Housing Authority, 20 September 1966, National Archives, RG 196, Commissioner of Public Housing Correspondence, Box 7, folder, Housing Assistance Regional Directors, Atlanta, 1966.

52. *Atlanta Constitution*, 27 December 1987; Preston, *Automobile Age Atlanta*, 157-58.

53. Adams, "Blueprint for Segregation," 78. Atlanta, Department of Budget and Planning, *1980 City of Atlanta Comprehensive Development Plan*, vol. 1, August 1979, 48, 54.

54. *Atlanta Constitution*, 22 July 1987.

Breaking Racial Barriers to Public Accommodations in Indiana, 1935 to 1963

*Emma Lou Thornbrough**

I went into a restaurant today and asked for a sandwich. The waitress told me she could not serve me. Had this place been a top hat and tail's place I would not have gone in. But it's in the midst of the steel district and only the workers go there. I am working in the same block as the restaurant, and I felt like it was all right for me to go in. I was clean.

Thus wrote an East Chicago woman to Walter White, secretary of the National Association for the Advancement of Colored People (NAACP), in 1943, a year when the United States was engaged in a desperate war against Nazi Germany, a fascist, racist power. "Mr. White," the writer continued, "we have any number of places in Indiana Harbor, E. Chicago and Hammond. Some even display signs in there [sic] windows 'white only.'" She asked White for guidance as to action that might be taken in the face of widespread discrimination, adding: "We need some action out here. I don't want riots or anything like that. But I do want justice for all, and I don't believe in any isms but Americanisms. I want my sixteen year old son to know the true meaning of Americanism by seeing it practiced toward men regardless of color."[1]

Other letters about racial discrimination and segregation in Indiana came regularly to the national office of the NAACP. Blacks complained of exclusion from eating places. They were rarely allowed to sit down at lunch counters or tables, although some establishments permitted them to buy food to carry off the premises. Eating places frequently displayed signs which read, "We cater only

---

* Emma Lou Thornbrough is professor emeritus of history, Butler University, Indianapolis. She is currently writing a history of school segregation and desegregation in Indianapolis. The staff of the *Indiana Magazine of History* wishes to thank Wilma Dulin, program archivist at the Indiana Historical Society, for her tremendous help in finding the illustrations for this article.

[1] Mayole Nelson to Walter White, May 11, 1943, National Association for the Advancement of Colored People Papers (Library of Congress, Washington, D.C.); cited hereafter as NAACP Papers.

to whites." The few blacks who had the money to travel could not stay at hotels. There were reports that blacks in Indianapolis were sometimes relegated to the back seats of public buses. In some cities railroad stations displayed signs designating waiting rooms "For Colored." Numerous complaints about the denial of access to public parks and recreational facilities were sent by Hoosier blacks to the national NAACP office. In Indianapolis a separate park (Douglass Park) and golf course were developed "for colored people." When blacks sought to use facilities in other parks, authorities made it clear that they were not welcome and refused to issue permits for such events as picnics.[2]

In Gary there were numerous racial incidents over the use of public parks. Park police drove black children away from public playgrounds. In 1937 state troopers were used to drive blacks away from public beaches. Another continuing grievance was the denial of use of hospital facilities. Blacks were admitted to Jim Crow wards in the Indianapolis City Hospital and a few other hospitals in the state but were completely barred from most. An 1879 law permitted, but did not mandate, authorities to maintain segregated school systems. Following the increase in black population that began with the "Great Migration" during World War I, segregation in schools as well as other areas of society tightened during the 1920s. In Indianapolis, Gary, Evansville, and some other cities and in smaller communities in the southern part of the state, school systems were segregated. There were many complaints over the dilapidated and inferior school facilities and the unequal educational opportunities for blacks in these schools. As high school athletics became a subject of major interest and school pride, the rule that barred teams from black schools from participation in tourneys with teams from white schools became an added grievance.[3] In 1933 Freeman Ransom, a lawyer and one of the most highly respected members of the Indianapolis black community, wrote to the national office of the NAACP that: "The Negro suffers every type and kind of discrimination in this state that he suffers anywhere, even jim-crow theaters and moving picture houses. In fact our pictures in the mile square—that is downtown—refuse absolutely to admit Negroes."[4]

---

[2] Robert Bailey, a civil rights lawyer, wrote about a case of assault and battery that arose out of the refusal of a restaurant to allow a black customer to sit on a stool while waiting for a hamburger to be cooked for him to carry out. Robert Bailey to White, September 16, 1929, NAACP Papers. See, also, Robert Bailey to William Pickens, January 28, 1937, *ibid.*; Milton Kaplan to National Legal Committee, January 16, 1940, *ibid.*; and Indianapolis *Recorder*, July 24, 1926.

[3] For some examples see L. Campbell to Robert Bagnall, August 4, 1930, NAACP Papers; Resolution of Gary NAACP to Gary City Council, August 12, 1932, *ibid.*; Kathryn Bailey to White, August 23, 1937, *ibid.*; Thurgood Marshall to Kathryn Bailey, August 26, 1937; and Emma Lou Thornbrough, "Segregation in Indiana during the Klan Era of the 1920's," *Mississippi Valley Historical Review*, XLVII (March, 1961), 594-618, *passim.*

[4] Freeman Ransom to Pickens, March 10, 1933, NAACP Papers.

From the foregoing it is apparent that in spite of its northern location Indiana was indeed a segregated society. Segregation in public education was authorized by state law, but other forms of segregation and discrimination persisted and increased in spite of a state civil rights law that was enacted in 1885 and never repealed or amended. The law declared that all persons were "entitled to the full and equal enjoyments of the accommodations, advantages, facilities and privileges of inns, restaurants, eating-houses, barber shops, public conveyances on land and water, theaters, and all other places of public accommodations and amusement, subject only to the conditions and limitations established by law and applicable alike to all citizens." Violation of the law was a misdemeanor punishable by a fine of one hundred dollars or imprisonment for thirty days or both or by payment of a forfeit of one hundred dollars to the injured party.[5]

From the time of its enactment the law was generally a dead letter, so widely ignored that most citizens were probably unaware of its existence. Because enforcement was almost entirely a discretionary matter on the part of the county prosecutor and because nearly all prosecutors hesitated or refused outright to act, it was almost impossible to get the law before the courts to establish a precedent-making rule. On the rare occasions when a case was tried the law was given the narrowest possible interpretations. In 1920 the Indiana Appellate Court ruled that an ice cream parlor was not an "eating place" within the meaning of the 1885 law. In 1941 the state Supreme Court ruled that requiring "colored persons" to occupy a separate section of a theater was not a violation of the law and that the injured party did not have the right under common law to sue for damages in excess of the amount provided for in the law. Most blacks lacked the money and the will to prosecute seemingly hopeless cases. In the unlikely event that a successful suit appeared probable the defendants usually preferred to settle out of court rather than risk the publicity of a trial which might have the effect of opening their establishment to unwanted black patrons.[6]

For blacks the only answer appeared to be a stronger civil rights law with machinery for enforcement. This necessitated action by the state legislature. Blacks were politically weak, but in spite of the other legal and extralegal disabilities which they suffered, they could exercise the right to vote without restrictions. From the time they first acquired the franchise through the adop-

---

[5] Indiana, *Laws* (1885), 76.

[6] *Chocos et al. v. Burden*, 74 Indiana Appellate Reports 242 (1920); *Bailey v. Washington Theater Co.*, 218 Indiana Reports 513 (1940); Emma Lou Thornbrough, *The Negro in Indiana before 1900: A Study of a Minority* (Indiana Historical Collections, Vol. XXXVII; Indianapolis, 1957), 260-66.

tion of the Fifteenth Amendment after the Civil War, Indiana blacks, like most members of their race in the nineteenth century, were nearly all loyal to the Republican party. In a period when political power was almost evenly balanced between the Republicans and Democrats in Indiana, Republican politicians sought their votes and awarded a few with minor political appointments. After 1896, when the Republicans entered upon a long period of dominant status and the "lily white" movement in the party spread northward, black voters and issues of concern to them were ignored. In the 1920s the close identification of the Republican party with the Ku Klux Klan in Indiana caused many blacks to defect from the GOP and vote the Democratic ticket for the first time.[7] The Great Depression and the relief programs of the New Deal brought a permanent exodus of the rank and file of black voters from the Republicans to the Democrats. After 1930 both parties began for the first time to seek black votes actively and to nominate a few black candidates.

From 1896 until 1932 not a single black candidate had been nominated for the state legislature, but in 1932 both parties named black candidates. Two black candidates, both Democrats, were elected to the lower house, the first Democratic members of their race to serve in the Indiana General Assembly. In every campaign during the 1930s blacks from Indianapolis and other large cities were nominated for the House of Representatives and municipal offices. After 1936 a majority of white voters in the state returned to their traditional support of the Republican party, giving it control of the state legislature in most of the sessions of the following years. Although an overwhelming majority of black voters continued to support the Democratic party, some black leaders remained loyal to the Republican party. In the hope of dividing the black vote the Republican organization in Indianapolis customarily designated one black candidate for the legislature.[8]

The number of blacks elected was miniscule—never more than one or two at any session in the House and none in the state Senate until 1941 when Republican Robert Lee Brokenburr was elected—but certain individuals succeeded in raising issues which were of special concern to the black community. The most notable black member in the 1930s was Henry J. Richardson, Jr. Elected in 1932 and reelected in 1934, he was a man who was to play a long and important part in the struggle for civil rights and racial justice. In his first session, in a House with a large Democratic majority in which organized labor had strong representation, Richardson spon-

---

[7] William Giffin, "The Political Realignment of Black Voters in Indianapolis, 1924," *Indiana Magazine of History*, LXXIX (June, 1983), 133-66.

[8] Emma Lou Thornbrough, *Since Emancipation: A Short History of Indiana Negroes, 1863-1963* ([Indianapolis, 1963]), 30-31, 33-36.

HENRY J. RICHARDSON, JR.

Courtesy Henry J. Richardson, Jr., Collection, Indiana Historical Society, Indianapolis.

sored a measure that required every contract made by a state or municipal corporation for construction or repair of a public building or public works contain an agreement that there would be no racial discrimination in hiring. This measure passed, but another bill that he proposed that was designed to strengthen the 1885 civil rights law died in committee.[9]

At the next session, after his reelection in 1934, Richardson with six other legislators cosponsored a bill "to prohibit discrimination and intimidation on account of race or color." At a public hearing before a packed gallery Richardson challenged his colleagues to follow the example of other northern states and "put teeth" into the 1885 law, declaring that denial of rights ostensibly protected by law was "unconstitutional, un-Christian and anti-social." Few members of the House were willing to voice open opposition to the measure, but according to the black press, they were under pressure from a lobby representing theaters, hotels, and restaurants to kill the bill. Democrats from Indianapolis and the Calumet area continued to support Richardson, but other Democrats

---

[9] Indiana, *Laws* (1933), 122-28; Indiana, *House Journal* (1933), 588, 711. Richardson, a native of Alabama, was sent north for his education. He graduated from Shortridge High School before Indianapolis high schools were segregated and later received degrees from the University of Illinois and the Indiana University School of Law.

joined with Republicans in trying to defeat the measure through the use of delaying tactics. A somewhat weakened version was not brought before the House for a vote until the end of the session on March 4 when any action by the Senate would have been impossible even if the bill had passed the House. A motion to postpone action on the bill indefinitely by a Democratic member was lost, but fifteen Democrats refused to vote on the motion by walking out of the House. In a roll call vote 43 members voted for the bill, 45 voted against it. A motion to call in the absent members was defeated.[10] The attitude of the white politicians and the tactics used to defeat Richardson's bill anticipated the course that would be followed to kill public accommodation bills in future legislative sessions.

In a speech following the defeat of his bill Richardson declared that the record of both political parties in Indiana was "one of shameless exploitation of the colored vote and a brazen insult to colored voters." He also offered a stinging rebuke to members of the black community who had been reluctant to support his efforts. " 'Negroes have made invaluable contributions to America,' " he proclaimed. " 'Why in God's name should they cringe, fawn, and beg some one, possibly a foreign born, for the things considered inalienable to All American citizens?' "[11]

The distaste and alarm which Richardson's demands and aggressive tactics aroused in old-line Democrats was made clear in 1936 when he declared himself a candidate for reelection to the General Assembly. He entered the May primary but was not endorsed by the Democratic organization and was not nominated. The only black Democrat slated by the Marion County (Indianapolis) organization was Marshall Talley, a Baptist minister who had not sought the nomination. In the Democratic landslide of 1936 Talley was the only black in the entire state elected to the legislature. During the single term he served he sponsored no controversial bills and remained inconspicuous.[12] After Richardson's abortive attempt in 1935 no bill to strengthen the public accommodations law was introduced in the General Assembly until after World War II.

The war years intensified the awareness of blacks of discrimination and disabilities, but economic revival stimulated by the demands of war brought hopes of jobs and new opportunities of winning rights hitherto denied. Many blacks noted the inconsistencies between the nation's professed war aims and the realities of the experience of black Americans in the military and on the home front. One publication complained: "To lament and condemn the

---

[10] Indiana, *House Journal* (1935), 154, 187, 228, 262, 716-17, 784-85; Indianapolis *Recorder*, February 2, 9, 1935.

[11] Indianapolis *Recorder*, March 23, 1935.

[12] Indianapolis *Recorder*, April 11, May 9, November 7, 1936.

discriminatory and segregated policies of Hitler or Tojo to the point of sending American boys to destroy their system, while at the same time allowing some of their practices to be levied against American citizens is a paradox beyond our comprehension.... We must excise this paradox which gives a system hypocracy and not democracy."[13] As young black men began to be called for selective service the Indianapolis *Recorder* protested, "These young men, whose parents and grandparents and great-grandparents helped build this great nation, will be segregated, put into a program of militarization not anxious to have them nor ready even for their coming."[14]

On the home front the most insistent demands of blacks were for equal job opportunities in the burgeoning war industries and for access to training programs for jobs in industry. A detailed treatment of the struggle for a fair employment program is beyond the scope of this paper, but a brief summary will be attempted since employment practices and access to public accommodations were often related.

Unemployment among blacks declined as Indiana factories received war contracts. There was some upgrading of the kinds of jobs held by blacks and some opening of training programs for jobs in industry. These came about in part due to a voluntary program for the employment of blacks in industry instigated by the Indiana State Chamber of Commerce and the Indiana Defense Council and President Franklin D. Roosevelt's executive order establishing a Fair Employment Practices Commission and prohibiting discrimination in companies with war contracts. Probably the most important reason for hiring blacks was simply the shortage of white workers as the labor demands of war industries grew while more and more men were being called into military service. This situation allowed employment of some blacks in factories formerly closed to them, and enabled other blacks to take other nonfactory jobs as whites went into the service or found better jobs in war industries.[15]

In their efforts to find employment in war industries blacks found valuable allies in the state chapter of the Congress of Industrial Organizations (CIO) and its member unions, which were ex-

---

[13] *Federation News*, May 10, 1943, quoted in Dallas Daniels, "History of the Federation of Associated Clubs, 1939-1949" (A.M. thesis, Department of History, Butler University, Indianapolis, 1975), 48.

[14] Indianapolis *Recorder*, January 25, 1941. The editorial added that naturalized citizens were able to enter any branch of military service without difficulty and to serve without discrimination. Many other comments can be found in the *Recorder* and in the NAACP Papers contrasting the treatment of naturalized aliens and native-born blacks.

[15] For a good account of the employment and treatment of blacks in Indiana war industries, see Max Parvin Cavnes, *The Hoosier Community at War* (Bloomington, Ind., 1961).

Dedication Ceremonies of the Senate Avenue YMCA, Indianapolis, 1913.

From Left: George Knox, Freeman B. Ransom, Madame C. J. Walker, Booker T. Washington, Unidentified, Joseph Ward, Unidentified, Thomas E. Taylor.

Courtesy Madam C. J. Walker Collection, Indiana Historical Society, Indianapolis.

SENATE AVENUE YMCA MEMBERSHIP DRIVE, 1936.

Courtesy Bass Photo Company, Indianapolis.

panding during the war. From its founding the national CIO, which was organized on the principle of incorporating all workers in a given industry into the same union, had opposed racial discrimination in determining its membership, but local unions were not always cooperative with national and state efforts. Entrance of blacks into factories and unions also brought questions of social relationships. Eating together as well as working together raised the possibility of "social equality," which working-class whites had long resisted. In some unions blacks were excluded from all but the nominal privileges of membership. They were told by white members that they were not welcome at social events and were barred from activities at union halls.[16]

While black workers encountered discrimination in seeking employment and membership in labor unions, the treatment of black servicemen on leave who came into towns seeking lodging and recreation emphasized the realities of Indiana society in contrast with professed war aims. In Indianapolis, in spite of their reluctance to accept segregation, members of the black community, recognizing that local whites would not tolerate blacks at the United Services Organization center, organized volunteer efforts to provide facilities for black soldiers. The Service Men's Activities Organization, which later received some government funding, established headquarters at the Senate Avenue Young Men's Christian Association (the YMCA for blacks) and arranged for lodging and recreational centers and social activities.[17]

When black soldiers ventured into private "white" restaurants, they were usually refused service. Occasionally there were protests. In one instance five black girls quit their jobs as waitresses in a chili parlor in Indianapolis when the manager refused service to black soldiers. They left in spite of his offer to try to make it possible for the soldiers to eat in the rear of the establishment. In Evansville a waitress told three black soldiers entering a restaurant that they would not be served there. While they were protesting, a plainclothes policeman entered and told them it was the rule of the restaurant that blacks were not served there but that they could get food at the back of the place. On hearing this twenty white soldiers who were in the restaurant walked out.[18]

Developments during the war years and protests such as the ones described above (usually isolated and spontaneous) paved the way for a vigorous campaign against all forms of racial discrimination in the postwar years. Black veterans demanded fulfillment of the ideals they had fought for, while blacks at home sought to

---

[16] Indianapolis *Recorder*, June 17, September 23, 30, October 21, 1944; Cavnes, *Hoosier Community at War*, 124.
[17] Cavnes, *Hoosier Community at War*, 149-50.
[18] Indianapolis *Recorder*, May 8, 1943, May 27, 1944.

strengthen the gains they had made during the war. The improved overall economic status of blacks and a growing black middle class made blacks more assertive of their rights. It was a period of rising expectations. Among whites also there was a new awareness of racial injustice and its incompatibility with American ideals.[19]

Discrimination in public accommodations was but one of the practices to be eliminated. Other objectives were fair employment legislation, abolition of segregated schools, and access to decent housing on a nondiscriminatory basis. A weak, though much publicized, fair employment act was passed by the state legislature in 1945, and a law abolishing segregation in public education was enacted in 1949. However, it was not until 1963 that legislation creating a Civil Rights Commission with enforcement powers in employment and public accommodations was enacted, and it was 1965 before a housing law was passed.

Meanwhile other, nonlegislative methods of ending discrimination and winning access to places of public accommodation were undertaken. A small group of civil rights activists from the Indianapolis branch of the NAACP spearheaded the campaign and planned strategies. They were joined by a loose coalition of members, black and white, of NAACP branches, other black social and fraternal organizations, members of CIO unions, and a variety of church-related groups.

The NAACP had a long but uneven history in Indiana with periods of vitality followed by periods of decline. During the 1920s, a period when segregationist measures were being strengthened, a vigorous NAACP had successfully challenged an Indianapolis residential zoning ordinance and had fought, albeit unsuccessfully, increased segregation in the public schools. In the depression years of the 1930s membership had dwindled, and efforts at fighting discrimination had lagged. The failure of the civil rights bill sponsored by Henry J. Richardson, Jr., in 1935 was attributed in part to the absence of a strong local NAACP.[20]

During the war years membership in the Indianapolis chapter of the NAACP had begun to grow substantially, while elsewhere in the state new branches were organized or old ones revived. Some of the new members were drawn from the white community. White members served on the board of the Indianapolis branch. A branch of about seventy members organized in Fort Wayne in 1946 was "about half and half as to color" and included members of several religious denominations. The first president was a white Unitarian minister. In 1947 a state conference of branches was formed.[21]

---

[19] Thornbrough, *Since Emancipation*, 38-42.

[20] Emma Lou Thornbrough, unpublished manuscript history of the NAACP in Indiana in the 1920s (in the possession of the author); Pickens to Olivia Taylor, April 17, 1935, NAACP Papers.

[21] Indianapolis *Recorder*, January 20, 1945; typewritten account of first Fort Wayne branch meeting, January 9, 1946, NAACP Papers.

The preeminent figure among civil rights activists in the state was Willard Ransom, the son of Freeman Ransom. The elder Ransom, a lawyer, executive director of the Madame Walker Co., and influential community leader, had become prominent in Democratic circles in the New Deal years. The son, after graduating with honors from Talladega College, had attended Harvard Law School, the only black member of a class of more than three hundred. During World War II he rose to the position of captain in the department of the judge advocate general. Most of his time in the military was spent in Alabama, where he was outraged by the discriminatory racial practices in the army and engaged in protests against the treatment of black officers and enlisted men. He returned to Indianapolis determined to continue the fight for racial equality in his home community. In addition to drafting civil rights legislation and planning strategies, he was an activist. Because of his activism, and especially because he supported Henry Wallace and the Progressive party in 1948 and 1950, he was vilified by some as a dangerous radical. Certain NAACP members regarded his leadership as a dangerous liability. But in spite of efforts to oust him he was elected state president five times in the years when the NAACP enjoyed its greatest influence and success in Indiana.[22]

The Indianapolis branch of the NAACP played a particularly important role in the fight for civil rights in Indiana because of its location in a city that was both the state capital and the city with the largest black community in the state. Although most black voters, and probably most NAACP members, were Democrats, leadership of the Indianapolis branch was bipartisan. The president, William T. Ray, a Republican, was the son-in-law of Robert Lee Brokenburr, the first black state senator and the most prestigious of black Republicans. Jessie Jacobs, another Republican, who had sought nomination to the state legislature, was an especially dynamic and indefatigable member of the board. Henry J. Richardson, Jr., continued to furnish legal advice, while other Democrats were leaders in civil rights activities.[23]

Many members of the Indianapolis branch were also members of the Federation of Associated Clubs (FAC), a local organization with objectives similar to the NAACP that was founded at a time when the latter organization was languishing. The moving spirit in the FAC and its longtime president was Starling James, a pub-

---

[22] Lynville G. Miles to Indianapolis State Conference of the NAACP, October 18, 1948, NAACP Papers; Edna B. Morris to Willard Ransom, October 3, 1949, *ibid.*; Gil [Aron S. Gilmaster] to White, June 26, 1952, *ibid*; Vera Brechtel to Gloster Current, October 7, 1952, *ibid.*

[23] Indianapolis *Recorder*, November 1, December 6, 1947; Speech of Gloster Current at Senate Avenue YMCA, December 3, 1948, NAACP Papers.

Robert Brokenburr with fellow Indiana legislators. James Hunter on Brokenburr's right; Jesse L. Dickinson with pipe.

Courtesy Indianapolis *Recorder* Collection, Indiana Historical Society, Indianapolis.

lic school teacher. James was not a radical. A middle-class black whose favorite recreation was playing bridge, he felt an obligation to oppose racial discrimination while at the same time trying to educate the black community in middle-class values and standards of conduct.[24] In 1937 James and friends in nine small social clubs banded together to found the Federation of Associated Clubs. Within ten years there were about 125 affiliates. The FAC monthly newspaper reported the social events of the member clubs but also published editorials by James and Richardson. All clubs in Indianapolis were urged to affiliate with the FAC and join in "fighting for the economic, civil, and social liberties of our people." Because the total membership of the affiliates numbered in the thousands and the

---

[24] Daniels, "History of the Federation of Associated Clubs," 16, *passim*. There was no local chapter of the National Urban League in Indianapolis in this period, but in some cities, notably Gary, the National Urban League played an important part in developing programs against discrimination. Indianapolis *Recorder*, June 23, 1945; Ronald D. Cohen, "The Dilemma of School Integration in the North: Gary, Indiana, 1945-1960," *Indiana Magazine of History*, LXXXII (June, 1986), 161-84.

NAACP had only a fraction of that number, the FAC was an effective instrument in promoting NAACP programs.[25]

The Indiana CIO also played an important part in the campaign to break down racial barriers under the dynamic and idealistic leadership of Walter Frisbie, its president in the postwar years. "We must show him [the black worker] by our good faith and our good works that his interests, our interests and our country's interests are one and the same," said a CIO report. At the state level a vigorous antidiscrimination committee worked for these objectives while also trying to organize antidiscrimination committees in all of the CIO's locals.[26]

The CIO and its member unions and the NAACP often worked together at the state and local levels. There was a considerable overlapping of membership. In Muncie the president of the NAACP also served as chairman of the antidiscrimination committee of the United Automobile Workers. The CIO and the NAACP also cooperated in politics. Two of the most influential black members of the state legislature in the 1940s and 1950s, James Hunter of East Chicago and Jesse Dickinson of South Bend, were identified with CIO unions.[27]

In the absence of a law enforced by government authorities, a nonviolent direct action campaign to bring about compliance with the 1885 civil rights law was begun by private groups. There were meetings with the managements of establishments that barred blacks and with government officials in efforts to negotiate with them to persuade them to observe the law. These were followed by nonviolent attempts, usually by racially mixed groups, to secure service in the establishments. If they were refused service, an appeal to law enforcement officials for help might follow. The nonviolent direct action campaign in Indianapolis appears to have been largely indigenous, although the leaders were no doubt aware of similar efforts in other cities. During the 1930s chapters of the Congress for Racial Equality (CORE) had carried out negotiations and sit-ins to gain access to restaurants in several northern cities. CORE, an offshoot of the Fellowship for Reconciliation, was strongly

---

[25] *Federation News*, July, 1941, quoted in Daniels, "History of the Federation of Associated Clubs," 18. Affiliates of the FAC included a wide range of types of organizations: bridge clubs, music clubs, men's clubs, women's clubs, labor organizations, and an American Legion post.

[26] *Yearbook of the Indiana State Industrial Union Council CIO* (1943), 83; "Anti-Discrimination Committee Report in Synopsis of Sixth Annual Convention of Indiana State Industrial Council, 1943," mimeograph, pp. 23-25, Indiana Division (Indiana State Library, Indianapolis).

[27] H. Hubert Cameron to White, October 25, 1943, NAACP Papers; Indianapolis *Recorder*, April 19, 1947, August 26, 1950, July 13, 1957. Hunter and Dickinson were Democrats. The only black legislator from Evansville was Charles Decker, a Republican elected in the GOP landslide of 1946. Decker was an organizer for the CIO.

religious and pacifistic, characteristics not evident in the Indianapolis movement. A more probable influence on the Indianapolis campaign was the use of sit-ins and demonstrations by NAACP Youth Groups in border cities—Washington, D.C., St. Louis, and Baltimore—to desegregate theaters and eating places.[28] A significant difference between the Indianapolis movement and those in the border cities was that its efforts were directed at securing compliance with a state law, whereas in the other cities there was no such legal basis. The nonviolent direct action campaigns in the other cities were often accompanied by picketing and demonstrations to gain public attention. In Indianapolis there was almost no newspaper publicity except in the black press. Perhaps out of deference to white businesses which might be embarrassed by reports of efforts of blacks to gain service, the nonviolent direct action campaign was ignored by the "white" press.

The most obvious targets of the movement were restaurants, lunch counters, and hotels. Motives for ending discriminatory treatment in these establishments were partly ideological but also practical. No doubt the most important reason for securing service at eating places (the right to sit down at a table or a counter and receive service) was simply that educated middle-class blacks were fed up with being subjected to indignities and humiliation and being treated as second-class citizens. In the postwar years more of them had sufficient money to patronize the better "white" establishments. Prevailing segregation was also embarrassing to whites who could not invite black friends and associates to "white" establishments. The United Council of Church Women, for instance, was reported to have canceled plans for a national board meeting in Indianapolis because the city's hotels refused to accommodate the black members of this racially mixed group.[29]

Discrimination was particularly burdensome to travelers. In urging the enactment of a stronger civil rights bill, black representative Jesse Dickinson told his fellow lawmakers: "There are hardly any drive-ins, especially south of U.S. Highway 40, where I can stop and get a sandwich. There are more motels where I'd be denied admission than where I could get accommodations." During the war Chester Allen, who traveled over the state as the governor's representative to persuade industries to hire black workers, after making a speech in one city, often had to travel many miles

---

[28] August Meier and Elliott Rudwick, *Along the Color Line: Explorations in the Black Experience* (Urbana, Ill., 1976), 351-52.

[29] Indianapolis *Recorder*, February 15, 1947; Indianapolis *Star*, February 7, 1947. In 1956, after some progress had been made toward acceptance of black guests, the Sheraton Lincoln Hotel admitted that it did not rent private dining rooms to Negro groups and that this exclusion rule was the hotel "policy" in spite of the 1885 law. Indianapolis *Recorder*, April 13, 1957.

before finding a place where he could get a night's lodging. In 1946 two black disabled veterans who came to Indianapolis to attend an American Legion convention were refused rooms at an Indianapolis hotel even though they had made reservations in advance. When Walter White, the national secretary of the NAACP, was making plans to come to Indianapolis in 1948 to give a lecture, the president of the local branch of that organization wrote to suggest that he might "try" the Claypool, a leading hotel, but added, "You can get reservations at the Ferguson Hotel . . . a modern, up-to-date hotel owned by Negroes." When Jackie Robinson, the famed baseball player, came to Indianapolis to campaign on behalf of Richard M. Nixon during the 1960 presidential campaign, he was refused accommodations at a motel.[30]

The first concerted attack on discrimination in hotels and restaurants was made by the CIO. In 1942 when two member unions were forced to move their convention from Indianapolis because the Claypool Hotel refused to house black delegates, the state CIO had protested publicly over the "vicious Jim Crow policies" of the hotel. In 1946 plans were carefully drawn for an attack on Jim-Crowism at the time of the state convention in Indianapolis, recognizing, as the antidiscrimination committee put it, that this city "with the largest percentage of Negro population of any city in the mid-west also has the reputation of being one of the worst offenders against equal rights." At a meeting attended by trade union leaders, representatives of Negro organizations, veterans' groups, and civil rights attorneys, a strategy to break down discrimination in restaurants was planned. CIO representatives first met with city and county law enforcement officials to ask assurances of legal redress if service was refused. The police "flatly refused" to promise to make arrests. The prosecutor grudgingly agreed to issue arrest affidavits. After the meeting CIO representatives informed the Chamber of Commerce of their plans. At the convention volunteers were invited to form racially mixed groups to seek service at six of the best downtown restaurants. "The restaurants chosen," reported the antidiscrimination committee, "were not little one-arm joints or greasy spoons. They included some of the fanciest in Indianapolis; in fact, one in which a group was served was so fancy that a couple of the delegates had to borrow money to pay their checks." In all cases the racially mixed groups were served "with no restrictions" by the restaurants. "In the biggest demonstration against

---

[30] Indianapolis *Recorder*, February 16, 1957, October 26, 1946, November 5, 1960; Cavnes, *Hoosier Community at War*, 18; William T. Ray to Gloster Current, February 7, 1948, NAACP Papers. The two veterans, represented by Henry J. Richardson as their counsel, filed suit against the Antlers Hotel.

jim-crow in the history of Indianapolis," the committee exulted, "we proved to everyone's satisfaction that jim-crow can be beaten."[31]

As CIO members recognized, claims that this was a definitive, lasting victory were premature: Jim Crow was by no means dead in Indianapolis. In 1947 the antidiscrimination committee reported that the "restaurant issue" in Indianapolis was still a key concern before the committee. An incident a few weeks later furnished strong evidence of the unwillingness of Indianapolis officials to enforce the law. The chief of police refused to issue a permit for a dance for a racially mixed CIO group, declaring that it was his "personal policy" that there would be no mixed dancing. The mayor, who backed the decision, was reported to have said that his term of office was almost over and he did not want a race riot to mar his administration. Although a judge issued a temporary injunction barring the police chief from refusing to grant the permit for the dance at a downtown hotel, the latter avoided complying with the order. When no permit had been issued one hour before the dance, it was moved to the union hall.[32]

An important reason that the CIO-sponsored invasion of Indianapolis restaurants did not produce lasting results was that it was a one-day affair staged by convention delegates most of whom were not Indianapolis residents. The kind of follow-up that the CIO leaders recognized as necessary did not occur. Early in 1947 an Indianapolis group under NAACP leadership began a more persistent "eating crusade" that proved to be more effective and to produce more lasting results. A Civil Rights Committee drawn from social and fraternal organizations in the black community, white church groups, and labor groups was led by Wilson Head, a member of the staff of Flanner House, a social settlement center for blacks operated under a racially mixed board of directors.[33]

Early in the campaign, Head, Willard Ransom, Jessie Jacobs of the NAACP, and Charles Preston, a white reporter from the Indianapolis *Recorder*, met with the secretary of the Indiana Restaurant Association to seek a commitment that local restaurants would obey the law. They met with little success, receiving only a promise that copies of the law would be sent to restaurants. The "eating

---

[31] *Yearbook of the Indiana State Industrial Union Council CIO* (1942), 50; "Anti-Discrimination Committee Report in Synposis of Proceedings, Eighth Annual Convention, Indiana Industrial Council, Indianapolis, July 1946," mimeograph, Indiana Division (Indiana State Library).

[32] Indiana CIO Anti-Discrimination Committee, "Fighting Discrimination," April 8, 1947, mimeographed report, Indiana Division (Indiana State Library); Indianapolis *Recorder*, May 24, 31, 1947. The dance was a closed affair for union members and their guests. No tickets were sold.

[33] Head, a native of Alabama, received his B.S. degree from Tuskegee and his Master's degree from the Atlanta School of Social Work. He had worked with the Friends Service Committee before coming to Indianapolis. Ray to Current, [1947], NAACP Papers.

crusade" invaded all kinds of establishments, ranging from lunch counters at variety chain stores like G.C. Murphy, Co., and Woolworth's to expensive restaurants. Participants carried copies of the civil rights law and sometimes displayed them to the managers of the restaurants they entered. They received a mixed reception. Sometimes they were served without hesitation; more often they encountered obstacles. Some restaurants and lunch counters suddenly closed in order to avoid serving their unwanted patrons. In other places they were forced to wait for long periods and subjected to discourtesies, but they were finally served. In the two leading downtown department stores they were accepted in the downstairs lunchrooms but were not welcome in the upstairs restaurants. When patrons who were identifiably black appeared in one of these upstairs establishments, they were escorted to a "special table" which "happened" to be behind a screen. In other places the crusaders were sometimes served but were offered seats behind screens or in partitioned areas. The management of one chain of drugstores promised that in the future they would comply with the law, but in practice they continued to refuse service until threatened with a lawsuit.[34]

The reluctance of "white" establishments to comply with the law and accept black patrons stemmed in part from simple race prejudice and stereotyped images of the consequences of interracial social mixing. However, a more important reason, though it was seldom stated explicitly, was the perceived threat to business—the fear that black patronage would drive away that of whites. One evidence of the apprehension aroused in the white establishment by the "eating crusade" was the abrupt dismissal of Wilson Head from his position at Flanner House. The excuse used to justify his dismissal is not clear. One reason appeared to be that Flanner House stationery had been used by the Committee for Civil Rights, though without Head's knowledge. Whatever the excuse, he was dismissed without an open hearing on the causes. A letter written by William T. Ray, president of the Indianapolis branch of the NAACP, with the support of Willard Ransom, the president of the Indiana NAACP, to Robert L. Brokenburr, chairman of the board of trustees of Flanner House, declared that Head had been one of the most active leaders in Indianapolis against "second class citizenship" and suggested that his leadership in the drive against discrimination in eating places might "quite conceivably have roused the ire of interested parties." Ray said he sought assurances that Head was not to be "victimized for his civil rights activities." Nevertheless, in spite of protests from the NAACP and the Asso-

---

[34] Indianapolis *Recorder*, January 11, February 15, March 15, April 19, 1947, January 1, 1949; Daniels, "History of the Federation of Associated Clubs," 52.

ciation of Social Workers, Head was not reinstated. In the black community it was believed that an official of the largest Indianapolis department store, who served on the Flanner House board, was responsible for ousting him.[35]

After his dismissal the Indianapolis branch of the NAACP hired Head as executive secretary for a short time but soon discovered that it did not have funds to continue to pay him. After he left to take employment in Chicago only a dwindling group of activists remained to keep up the fight against discriminatory treatment, but the fight continued. Foremost among the fighters was Jessie Jacobs, who temporarily took over the position of executive secretary without pay. In a letter to Gloster Current at the national office of the NAACP, she deplored the unwillingness of most members of the NAACP, black and white, to participate actively. "Truly," she wrote, "about six people are actually carrying the load, with another six helping at times." But, she added: "If I don't break under this load I believe I can make NAACP mean something here. The dozen of us have sure raised enough H--- in the city. People believe we are 10,000 strong in numbers and cash. (Smile)."[36]

Some attempts were made to file suits against businesses that flouted the law. Public officials, however, were reluctant to prosecute, and there appeared to be no way under the existing law to compel them to act. In 1947 the Marion County prosecutor was quoted as saying to a reporter, "I'm for the enforcement of all laws, but this is a delicate question." He also cited the 1920 Appellate Court decision that ice cream parlors did not fall within the scope of the 1885 law. Under pressure he finally said he would prosecute, but he added that he hoped there would not be a "deluge" of cases. When cases involving refusal of service at drugstore lunch counters were filed, another prosecutor said that the law prohibiting discrimination in public places did not apply to drugstores; an interpretation without any recognizable precedent and one with which the state attorney general disagreed. Finally, in 1950 a restaurant employee who refused service to a black high school teacher was found guilty in municipal court and fined ten dollars and costs. But the judge criticized the man who had brought the suit for having waved a mimeographed copy of the civil rights law in the face of the defendant, saying "the problem could not be worked out by such methods."[37]

---

[35] Indianapolis *Recorder*, January 3, April 10, 1948; clipping from the Shreveport, Louisiana, *Sun*, January 10, 1948, NAACP Papers.

[36] Jessie Jacobs to Current, October 28, 1948, NAACP Papers.

[37] Indianapolis *Recorder*, March 29, April 12, 1947; July 15, 22, September 23, 30, October 7, 15, 1950; Indianapolis *News*, September 25, 1950. This was believed to be the first time a criminal penalty was imposed in Indianapolis under the 1885 law. In 1957 Patrick Chavis, a black deputy prosecutor, began more vigorous efforts to prosecute suits under this law. Indianapolis *Recorder*, March 30, 1957.

Such progress as was made—and there was progress—was the result of pressure from private groups. In 1950 Willard Ransom reported to the national headquarters of the NAACP that:

> direct action to open restaurants etc [was] succeeding in forcing compliance with the Indiana Civil Rights Law in many restaurants, hotels and theaters. Methods—test groups, persuasion, affidavits, suits. The Indianapolis hotels recently opened their doors to Negro members of the National Bar Association, Veterans of Foreign Wars, CIO, etc. While much discrimination in these accommodations still exists the Association program is steadily winning on all fronts.[38]

Efforts to break down barriers to public accommodations were carried on in some of the smaller cities in the state as well as in Indianapolis. For example, in 1942, before organized efforts had begun in the state capital, the South Bend branch of the NAACP succeeded in launching the prosecution of a manager of a Hook's drugstore for refusing service to two black women at the lunch counter. The branch appealed to the national office for support to secure a conviction after the case was delayed, warning that if it was lost, "the practice of discrimination against colored people in public places will be increased with impunity." In Fort Wayne, even before a branch of the NAACP was formally organized, a suit was begun against a restaurant which had refused to serve a racially mixed group. After a branch was organized, its secretary wrote, "We do want to wake this very reactionary city to its often unrealized discrimination." In Bloomington protests from Indiana University students ended refusal of service to blacks in most eating places. However, over the state as a whole progress was spotty and sporadic. In 1948 it was reported that the leading hotel in Elkhart had begun to accept blacks as overnight guests and to serve them in its dining room, but as late as 1961 most restaurants in that city refused to serve black patrons, requiring them to buy food and carry it off the premises for consumption.[39]

Terre Haute was one of the most segregated communities in the state and one in which, according to NAACP leaders, blacks were reluctant to protest publicly. "These people want relief from discrimination and prejudice," said the president of the local branch, "but do not want to be involved in the process of getting it." In Terre Haute in 1952, she continued, "We may eat at two of the Ten Cent Stores; the bus and Union Station; the YWCA Snack Bar and the cafeteria at the Ind. State Teachers College." Hotels refused accommodations to blacks, but a committee from the NAACP was

---

[38] Willard Ransom to Current, April 17, 1950, NAACP Papers.

[39] NAACP bulletin release, South Bend branch, March 6, 1942, NAACP Papers; Joyce Humphrey to Director of Branches, undated, *ibid.*; Indianapolis *Recorder*, January 24, 1948, January 21, 1961.

working to remedy the situation. Only one theater in the city allowed blacks unrestricted choice of seats.[40]

In some communities discrimination went unchallenged. At a regional conference of state NAACP branches in 1949, an attorney from the national headquarters emphasized the need for action to enforce civil rights statutes. A branch had a duty "to see that there is not segregation and discrimination in theaters, restaurants, and other public accommodations." Yet branches in Ohio and Indiana and other states in the Middle West were found to do little or nothing to break down Jim Crow, with the result "that the civil rights law is never enforced and Negroes cannot eat in restaurants, live in hotels, or buy first class tickets in local theaters."[41]

Efforts against discrimination in places of recreation and amusement were carried on as well as campaigns for access to restaurants and hotels. In some places blacks were simply refused admission to motion picture theaters; more often they were seated in segregated sections. In Indianapolis, with its large black community, there were a number of black-owned or black-operated theaters that showed the same films as the downtown "white" theaters that refused to sell tickets to blacks. The presence of large numbers of black soldiers during World War II and the lack of any kind of recreational facilities for them led to changes. The leaders of the Federation of Associated Clubs succeeded, without publicity, in opening many theaters to black patrons through negotiations with the managers of the theaters. In black neighborhoods black-owned theaters continued to operate successfully. In white neighborhoods most theaters continued to bar blacks, but this situation rarely caused friction. An exception was the Esquire Theater, the only one in the city which showed foreign films. When Wilson Head, with the assistance of Willard Ransom, began a suit after he was denied admission, the Jewish Community Relations Council intervened to persuade the theater owner, a member of the Jewish community, to change his policy. The case was settled out of court, but the negotiations and the outcome established a precedent for admission to other neighborhood theaters.[42]

---

[40] Daisy E. Hand to Jack Greenburg, July 31, 1952, NAACP Papers. In 1957 members of a United Auto Workers delegation were refused service by the proprietor of a cafeteria in Terre Haute. The man said he knew the law but did not intend to obey it and called the police. When told by the police that he must serve the unwanted customers, he complied but then closed the cafeteria. Indianapolis *Recorder*, June 1, 1957.

[41] Lucille Black, acting director of branches, to Paul E. Day, Kokomo branch, May 11, 1949, NAACP Papers.

[42] Indianapolis *Recorder*, July 7, 1945 (Victory Progress Edition), July 7, 1948; Report of Wilson Head, acting executive secretary, Indianapolis Branch NAACP, June 11, 1948, NAACP Papers; Indianapolis Branch Secretary's Report, June 11 to July 9, 1948, *ibid.*

In smaller cities blacks were often seated in segregated areas of theaters, a practice which the Indiana Supreme Court had held was not a violation of the civil rights law. These arrangements brought few protests. On the other hand, in both large and small cities discriminatory practices concerning use of public parks and other recreational areas were a frequent source of dissatisfaction and complaint. In Indianapolis, for instance, there were *de facto* arrangements under which certain parks and one golf course were "for colored" and other public recreational areas were for whites. In 1945 representatives of the local NAACP met with city officials to seek changes in these segregated practices, but their efforts met with no immediate success. In 1947 the same Civil Rights Committee which launched the "eating crusade" appealed to local groups to use all city parks and recreational facilities and not accept segregated arrangements.[43]

Access to parks and golf courses in Indianapolis raised no serious problems, but city authorities were sometimes less than cooperative. In 1946 two black girls were excluded because of their race from participation in the Ice-O-Rama, an ice skating show sponsored by the city recreational department. When a delegation from the NAACP went to the mayor in protest, he told them that it was too late to do anything since the Ice-O-Rama had already taken place. He was reported to have added that, "agitation of Negro groups in certain cases in the past has [had] a corrupting influence on racial attitudes in the community and serve[d] in many instances to foster racial prejudices."[44]

A long-standing source of irritation for blacks in Indianapolis was Riverside Park, a privately owned amusement park open to white patrons only. For several years the management opened the park to blacks once a year on Negro Day, an occasion used for fund raising by black charitable organizations. As blacks became increasingly sensitive to discrimination during the war, resentment against Negro Day and all it symbolized mounted, and the Federation of Associated Clubs and the NAACP began a campaign to discourage blacks from attending it. "It is hard," said the FAC newsletter, "for well thinking, liberal whites, to understand a race of people" who would support campaigns to end segregation in drugstore lunch counters, theaters, and parks and then "turn right around and spend money to be insulted and to promote racial separation." In 1945 a boycott of Negro Day reduced attendance to about fifty persons, most of them children. "Riverside Park's 'jim-crow season' was dealt what may be a mortal blow," exulted the Indianapolis *Recorder*.[45]

---

[43] Indianapolis *Recorder*, June 23, 1945, June 28, 1947.

[44] Indianapolis *Recorder*, June 23, 1945, February 23, 1946, June 28, 1947.

[45] Daniels, "History of the Federation of Associated Clubs," 35; Indianapolis *Recorder*, quoted in *ibid.*, 49; Lowell Trice to Ella J. Baker, September 15, 1945, NAACP Papers.

The boycott of Negro Day did not cause the Riverside management to change its policy of barring blacks on other days. Signs saying "White Patronage Only Solicited" were not removed. A fifteen-year campaign by blacks and sympathetic whites resulted in reducing the size of the signs but not in eliminating them. The manager insisted that he was not breaking the law by posting signs that said "solicit," and that his use of the signs was merely an exercise of his constitutional right of free speech. Since the signs were not a clear-cut violation of the civil rights law, the Marion County prosecutor would not act.[46]

In the years following the war moves for nondiscriminatory access to parks were made all over the state. When the CIO sought to hold camp schools in the state parks, it was refused access. The governor insisted that the decision was not racially motivated and that it was state policy to limit use of the parks to groups interested in nature study and conservation. But in many places restrictions began to ease. In Evansville, for example, a Mayor's Commission on Civil Rights created in 1948 reported that segregation in public playgrounds had ended, ovens for picnics in public parks were now being assigned on a nondiscriminatory basis, and segregated washrooms in the parks were being eliminated. In Gary use of public beaches was a continuing source of friction. Although black use of the public facilities was not prohibited, there was a strong feeling against their presence, and use of the beaches by blacks was likely to precipitate racial incidents.[47]

Whites were more sensitive to attempts by blacks to use public swimming pools than to their presence at public beaches. After they had gained access to most other public recreational facilities in the 1950s, blacks began to demand use of the pools. Their demands were sometimes answered by the offer of the use of the pools on certain days or hours, arrangements which were unacceptable to black leaders.[48] The most notable controversy occurred in Marion, where armed attendants barred blacks from using a pool in a public park. At the instigation of the recently formed local branch of the NAACP, a suit was filed in federal court against the mayor, members of the city council, the president of the park board, and the park superintendent, charging them with violating the United States Civil Code and the Fourteenth Amendment to the United States Constitution (violation of the Indiana law was not cited). After the suit was filed, the president of the park board resigned, and the city offered part-time use of the pool to blacks. This com-

---

[46] Indianapolis *Recorder*, July 21, August 4, November 10, 1962.

[47] Indianapolis *Recorder*, July 13, 1946, January 1, 1948; Edna Morris to Current, October, 1949, NAACP Papers.

[48] When Noblesville authorities made such an offer, it was rejected, and the park board faced the possibility of a lawsuit. Indianapolis *Recorder*, August 8, 1953.

promise was rejected. After this rejection the city council admitted there was no question of the legal rights of blacks to use the pool but also expressed the fear that opening it to them would lead to racial disturbances. Nevertheless, the council agreed to open the pool rather than face a federal suit. Thereafter, blacks used the pool without incident, although some whites boycotted it. Other Indiana cities also ended segregated use of public pools in 1956. In Muncie and some other communities the integration of public pools was followed by the formation of private pool clubs open only to whites.[49]

In 1952 Willard Ransom wrote to Jack Greenburg of the NAACP Legal Defense and Educational Fund that there was no doubt that the Indiana civil rights law was being violated in most communities in Indiana but that progress in enforcement was being made. He continued:

I am convinced that with the weaknesses as are present in our Indiana Civil Rights Law—the most effective way to break discrimination in public places in Indiana is through a mass, direct action campaign, utilizing educational techniques and legal action at the same time. This technique ended restaurant discrimination in Bloomington, Indiana and greatly eased theater and restaurant discrimination in East Chicago, Indianapolis and other areas.

This technique requires an NAACP leadership that is militant and unafraid.[50]

Although the methods Ransom described produced results, they were usually localized and sometimes temporary. A stronger civil rights law was clearly needed to bring about general, statewide compliance, a fact which led to increasing emphasis on political action beginning in the 1949 session of the General Assembly. Enactment that year of a school law abolishing segregation in public education was a significant victory, but effective fair employment legislation and a strong public accommodations law eluded the civil rights forces for many years.

The 1948 state Democratic platform declared that the denial of the rights of minorities, "most overtly asserted in the fields of employment, education and in the full use of the public conveniences," was a direct contravention of the rights of these citizens. The platform pledged "to work unceasingly to end all discrimination on account of race, color, creed, or national origin or sex," and to try to rewrite the 1885 civil rights law at the next session of the legislature. A bill to strengthen the existing law by increasing penalties and, more importantly, by granting injured parties the right to seek injunctions against businesses that failed to comply with

---

[49] Willard Ransom represented the plaintiffs with the assistance of Patrick Chavis and Charles Wills, members of the NAACP legal redress committee. Indianapolis *Recorder*, September 5, 1953, July 7, 1956; Indianapolis *News*, June 30, July 25, 1956.

[50] Willard Ransom to Greenburg, July 28, 1952.

Willard Ransom with Senator Glen Hearst Taylor of Idaho, South Bend, May, 1948. Both Ransom and Taylor were active in the Progressive party.

Courtesy Indianapolis *Recorder* Collection, Indiana Historical Society, Indianapolis.

Federation of Associated Clubs Legislative Dinner, 1959.

From Left: Birch Bayh, James Hunter, Unidentified, Robert Brokenburr, Henry J. Richardson, Jr., Jesse L. Dickinson, Unidentified, Unidentified, Mercer Mance, Matthew Welsh, Unidentified, Starling James.

Courtesy Indianapolis *Recorder* Collection, Indiana Historical Society, Indianapolis.

the law was introduced into the Democratically controlled House of Representatives, read a first time, referred to committee, and never heard of again.[51]

Despite this setback NAACP strategists remained optimistic. Although the bill was killed in committee, Ransom said, "The NAACP had its fight, prepared the way for a fight in 1951, publicized the issue, and laid the basis for opening many places of public accommodation by direct action." However, the anticipated fight in the 1951 session, in which Republicans had majorities in both houses, did not occur. NAACP lawyers drew up a bill, but the three black members of the legislature were unable to find a white member who was willing to act as cosponsor; therefore, it was not even introduced.[52]

Civil rights played little part in the outcome of the 1952 state elections, which were swept by the Republicans. Of the Republican platform that year the Indianapolis *Recorder* said, "If the Hoosier GOP has any ideas about the equality of citizenship, and implementation of civil rights ... pronouncements as to such will have to come later, if at all." Nevertheless, a bill to strengthen the public accommodations law introduced by William D. Mackey, a black Republican representative from Indianapolis, showed signs of vitality, passing the House of Representatives by a vote of 74 to 11 on February 26. In the Senate it was referred to the Committee on Labor, which took no action on the bill before the end of the session. Another effort was made in 1955 when a white Republican member joined Jesse Dickinson as cosponsor of a strengthened public accommodations bill. Referred this time to the social security committee, it was not heard of again.[53]

By 1956 civil rights as a national issue had begun to attract some attention. In Indiana both political parties sought to use the issue to their advantage. Republicans tried to appeal to black voters by campaigning against white Southern Democrats. Although Republican Homer Capehart had refused to vote for the cloture resolution that would have stopped a southern filibuster against a civil rights bill in the United States Senate, he nevertheless denounced Southern Democrats as responsible for the lack of progress in federal civil rights legislation. At the state level Harold Handley, the Republican candidate for governor in 1956, reminded voters that he had been a member of the 1949 legislature that had passed the

---

[51] Indianapolis *Recorder*, June 19, 1948; Indiana, *House Journal* (1949), 380; Willard Ransom to Current, April 14, 1950, NAACP Papers.

[52] Willard Ransom to Current, April 14, 1950, NAACP Papers; Indianapolis *Recorder*, January 20, February 3, 1951.

[53] Indianapolis *Recorder*, June 14, June 28, 1952, January 17, April 25, 1953, January 1, 1955; Indiana, *House Journal* (1953), 91, 675, 728, 831; *ibid.* (1955), 329; Indiana, *Senate Journal* (1953), 714.

bill abolishing segregated schools, while his Democratic opponent pointed out that the Republican candidate had not been recorded as voting for or against the school bill. In speeches and interviews during the campaign, Handley, who was elected, appeared to take a strong stand in behalf of civil rights. Prospects for legislation appeared better in the 1957 legislative session, in which Republicans controlled both houses, than in previous sessions. A public accommodations bill introduced by Jesse Dickinson was reported favorably and passed the House by the wide margin of 60 to 8. Introduced into the Senate on March 5, it was reported favorably the following day, but a motion to permit action on it on March 11, at the end of the session, by suspending a rule that prohibited a bill from being called up for third reading after the fifty-ninth day of the session was lost by a vote of 23 to 15.[54]

In 1958 the Democrats won a majority of the seats in the Indiana House of Representatives; it was the first time in a decade that the Democrats had won control of either chamber of the legislature. Among the Democratic House members were a number of strong civil rights supporters, including the future United States Senator, Birch Bayh, who was elected speaker of the house. Another new impetus to action on civil rights was the organization of the Indiana Human Rights Legislative Association, a broad coalition of groups supporting civil rights legislation. Jessie Jacobs, an experienced lobbyist and the state legislative chairman of the NAACP, played an important part in coordinating lobbying efforts.[55]

In addition to supportive legislators and more effective lobbying, the chances of new civil rights legislation was enhanced by a new strategy intended to prevent a repetition of the experience in past sessions of legislation being killed at the close of the session by introducing similar public accommodations bills in both houses. In the Senate, Jesse Dickinson, now a member of the upper chamber, and Robert Brokenburr sponsored a bill for a much stronger law than that enacted in 1885. If it had been enacted, the bill would have outlawed indirect methods, including advertisements, of denying access to equal accommodations and would have made it pos-

---

[54] Indianapolis *Recorder*, October 13, 1946; Indiana, *House Journal* (1957), 353, 724, 795, 896-97; Indiana, *Senate Journal* (1957), 836, 838, 850, 956-57. All of the negative votes in the House were cast by Republicans. Since only 68 votes were cast out of a total House membership of 100, it is obvious that some members avoided commiting themselves by failing to vote. The list of members voting for and against the Senate motion to suspend was not printed.

[55] The Indiana Human Rights Legislative Association coalition included the NAACP, United Automobile Workers, National Council of Negro Women, Jewish Human Relations Council, Council on Human Rights, American Federation of Teachers, Women's Council of Federated Clubs, and representatives of several church groups. Indianapolis *Recorder*, January 17, 1959.

sible for actions under the law to be brought in the name of the state by the attorney general, thereby bypassing the local prosecutor. The bill passed the Senate by a vote of 37 to 0, but it was not until March 6 that it was received in the House, where it died in committee. A similar measure passed the House of Representatives by a vote of 66 to 12 but was not acted upon by the Senate. The bills were not sent to a conference committee and died without further action. The new strategy and the lobbying done in support of it had failed.[56]

During a decade of persistent effort civil rights advocates had encountered only frustration and failure. Efforts to enact a fair employment bill "with teeth" had followed a course similar to public accommodations legislation. A member of the NAACP with some experience in lobbying described the legislative process on civil rights as a "shell game."

> There will be plenty of credit to pass around, but no civil rights laws. . . .
> The bill is referred to committee and the committee sits on it for three weeks. Finally the committee decides to report it out. 'That makes them champions of civil rights.
> But it's too late to get the bill passed— which has been the idea of the committee members all along. Or maybe the House makes a superhuman effort and passes the bill. All the . . . [members] who vote for it are thus recorded as champions of civil rights.
> The Senate of course has no time left to act on the measure. The Senators claim that they too are champions of civil rights but never had a chance.[57]

The civil rights issue, and in particular the campaign for a strong public accommodations law, seemed to have little appeal for either white or black voters. Black leaders were constantly chiding black voters for their apathy and failure to retaliate against white politicians who ignored them and their needs. Only a tiny fraction of the black community belonged to the NAACP, and only rarely was there any kind of mass action against discriminatory treatment. Although the attitudes of whites were changing and there was a growing awareness of the injustice of racial discrimination, few white citizens were actively engaged in civil rights causes. Among white lawmakers only a few were genuinely committed to the cause. In contrast to the campaign for a fair employment law, which was widely denounced in editorials in the press and vigorously opposed with much publicity by the Indiana Chamber of Commerce, there was little overt lobbying against public accommodations legislation. However, while lawmakers did not want to be recorded as voting against measures which bore words like

---

[56] Indiana, *Senate Journal* (1959), 56, 514, 594-96; Indiana, *House Journal* (1959), 66, 814, 829, 982. In the House seven Republicans and five Democrats voted against the measure.

[57] Indianapolis *Recorder*, February 12, 1949.

"equal" or "fair" in their titles, they also feared that if they strongly supported civil rights legislation they might alienate white voters. Politicians resolved their dilemma by avoiding both direct confrontation with civil rights issues and overt opposition to civil rights legislation on the one hand, while on the other hand they used the legislative tactics of delay and inaction to defeat all civil rights bills.

The Republican party was clearly politically dominant in the years between 1949 and 1959. It controlled both houses of the legislature except when the Democrats had a majority in the House of Representatives in 1949 and 1959. Republican efforts to woo black voters back to their traditional allegiance to the GOP were usually halfhearted and futile. In every election a large majority of black votes went to Democrats, and this fact allowed the Democratic party to take the black vote for granted. The Democrats included civil rights planks in their platforms, but when the legislature met, they gave priority to other issues. In his weekly column in the Indianapolis *Recorder*, Andrew Ramsey, one of the most tireless fighters for civil rights among Indiana blacks, observed that politics for blacks was a "one way street." Party workers depended on black "ward heelers" to deliver the black vote and rewarded them with minor political jobs, but once the election was over, the black constituency as a whole was ignored until the next political campaign.[58]

The fact that the black population and black voters were concentrated in a few areas undoubtedly influenced political attitudes and contributed to indifference or opposition to minority rights. By 1960 over 85 percent of the black population was found in only seven highly industrialized counties. Census figures also showed that in about one third of the counties in the state there were no blacks or only two or three. Some rural communities had a reputation of hostility toward blacks, and so-called "sundown laws" in these towns prevented blacks from settling in them or even staying temporarily. Moreover, there had been no legislative reapportionment in Indiana since 1921; hence, rural areas and small towns were overrepresented in the General Assembly, while urban areas and their growing black populations were underrepresented.[59]

During the 1960s developments within Indiana and the tide of events nationally gave increased vitality to the movement for civil rights legislation. During the 1960 elections, however, civil rights

---

[58] Indianapolis *Recorder*, April 25, 1959.
[59] Thornbrough, *Since Emancipation*, 19-20. In 1960 blacks made up about 6 percent of the total population of Indiana. Almost 80 perecent of Hoosier blacks lived in six cities: Indianapolis, whose population was 20 percent black; Gary, 38 percent black; East Chicago, 23 percent black; South Bend, 9 percent black; Fort Wayne, 8 percent black; and Evansville, 6 percent black. *Ibid.*

issues received relatively little attention, although there were some encouraging signs. The Democratic state platform, for instance, pledged the party "to continue fighting for civil rights of all people, until such rights are assured in the fields of employment, education, and public conveniences." In more ambiguous language the Republicans called for "improvements" in the fair employment practices law and endorsed the right of any citizen to "exercise all of his talents and rights, anywhere, at any time."[60] Also, both gubernatorial candidates, Democrat Matthew E. Welsh and Republican Crawford F. Parker, promised to make a strong stand for civil rights if elected. At a rally at the Walker Theater in Indianapolis before a largely black audience, Welsh made the strongest commitment to civil rights yet made by a candidate for governor. He called for an effective fair employment law, decent housing without discrimination, educational programs to enable blacks to enter all fields of employment, and declared:

No one should ever be denied service in any public hotel or public restaurant on the basis of race. When present laws, properly enforced, aren't enough, we'll fight for new ones as a step toward fair play and decency.

All these issues must be faced squarely. We must stop this terrible waste of human ability. Your Indiana government must set the moral tone with bold, imaginative action—under the leadership of a Governor who is indignant enough about present conditions to do something about them.[61]

After the election NAACP lawyers and their allies began drafting bills and planning strategies for persuading and exerting pressure on lawmakers. The most significant development was the formation of the Indiana Conference on Civil Rights Legislation, a coalition of groups representing a wide spectrum of concerns. Some of the groups were primarily interested in a fair employment law, but all of them supported public accommodations legislation. At an organizational meeting Rufus C. Kuykendall, a black Republican lawyer who had served on the staff of the United States Civil Rights Commission, was elected state chairman; Irving Levine, executive director of the Jewish Community Relations Council, executive secretary; and John Preston Ward, a brilliant young black lawyer, legal counsel. At this same meeting, which was attended by a few members of the legislature, Governor-elect Welsh said he would ask the General Assembly for a strong fair employment practices law and legislation to end discrimination in housing, hotels, and restaurants. A resolution was also adopted at this meeting that

---

[60] *Civil Rights Indiana, 1960* (n.p., 1960), 14.
[61] Matthew E. Welsh, *View from the State House: Recollections and Reflections, 1961-1965* (*Indiana Historical Collections*, Vol. LIV; Indianapolis, 1981), 62-63.

called for the creation of a Commission on Human Rights to administer antidiscrimination laws.[62]

For the first time a governor included a plea for civil rights legislation in his inaugural address. "My administration," said Welsh, "will make a determined effort to secure for all our citizens the rights and the privileges now arbitrarily denied to many. For if we fail to achieve this, we fail not only our own high principles, but we fail our nation in its struggle against both those here and abroad, who would strip from man all his rights as an individual and make of him only a tool of the state." He asked for legislation that would create a Civil Rights Commission, guarantee freedom from discrimination in private facilities and accommodations, and empower the state to initiate proceedings when local authorities failed to act.[63]

In the Senate, where Democrats were in a majority, a public accommodations bill was introduced under bipartisan sponsorship. It was a strong measure that stiffened penalties, gave the right to file civil suits, and contained a section modeled after a Connecticut law on discrimination in housing, including public housing, publicly assisted housing, and developments of five or more units. A second bill principally dealing with fair employment provided for a Civil Rights Commission. After surviving efforts to weaken it by amendments, the public accommodations bill passed the Senate by a vote of 40 to 8 on February 14, early enough to give the lower chamber ample time to consider it. In the House the measure was drastically altered. The enforcement provisions were deleted and the language on housing amended to include only facilities owned by city, town, or state.[64]

As the legislature deliberated on these bills, public demonstrations reinforced the behind-the-scenes lobbying efforts that were taking place. While the Senate considered the bills before it, for instance, outside the statehouse several ministers offered prayers,

---

[62] Indianapolis *Times*, December 18, 1960. Ward, at that time executive secretary of the Indiana Civil Liberties Union, was later one of the attorneys in the Indianapolis schools desegregation case in the federal courts. Rufus Kuykendall, a graduate of Indiana University and the Indiana University School of Law and a longtime worker in the NAACP, was on the staff of the United States Civil Rights Commission from 1959 to 1960, during the Eisenhower administration. Indianapolis *News*, August 6, 1964. John Preston Ward, a graduate of Indiana University, with a law degree from New York University, practiced law in Indianapolis and served as counsel to the Indiana Civil Liberties Union. Indianapolis *Recorder*, January 26, 1963. In the 1970s he was one of the lawyers for the black plaintiffs in the Indianapolis schools desegregation case in the Federal District Court. Irving Levine was a professional social worker who lived in Indianapolis only a short time. His position in the Indiana Conference on Human Rights is evidence of the interest of the Jewish community in civil rights legislation.

[63] Indiana, *House Journal* (1961), 51; Indianapolis *Recorder*, January 14, 1961.

[64] Indianapolis *Recorder*, January 14, 1961; Indiana, *Senate Journal* (1961), 118, 246, 350, 411, 455.

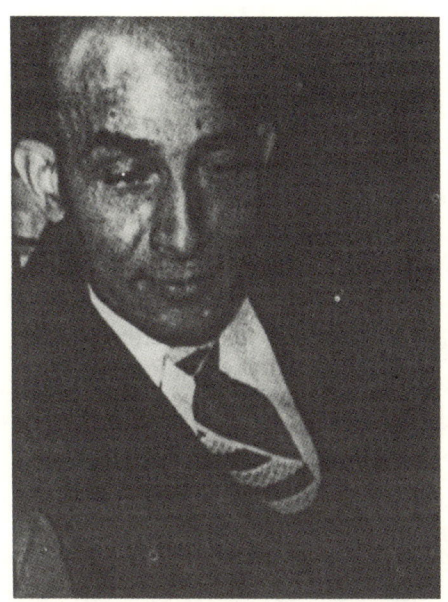

JAMES HUNTER, EAST CHICAGO

ANDREW W. RAMSEY, COLUMNIST
FOR THE INDIANAPOLIS *RECORDER*

Courtesy Indianapolis *Recorder* Collection, Indiana Historical Society, Indianapolis.

and a crowd sang "America." It was a peaceful show of support. The Reverend Ford Gibson admonished the crowd not to make any noisy demonstrations. "We just want them (the legislators) to know we're here," said the state NAACP president. Also, an audience of about one thousand attended a public hearing sponsored by the Indiana Conference on Civil Rights Legislation, and another crowd of six or seven hundred NAACP supporters from all over the state staged a march. And after the House amendments were made a rally was sponsored by the NAACP at a Methodist church. At this rally a standing-room-only crowd cheered the Reverend Ralph Abernathy of the Southern Christian Leadership Conference when he declared: "walls of segregation are popping and cracking all around us. We are going to bury it in our generation. We want our freedom now, not next month, next year or next century."[65]

Before a final vote was taken, strenuous efforts were made to kill the proposed amendments. A long list of speakers urged adoption of the Senate version at a public hearing. But the pleas, protests, and efforts of Democratic members in the House were futile. A minority report by Birch Bayh and James Hunter that sought to restore the language of the Senate bill was rejected by a vote of 62 to 30. The vote was almost entirely along party lines: twenty-nine Democrats and one Republican voted in favor of the minority report. The weakened bill then passed the House by a margin of 82 to 9. Some Democrats in the Senate were so bitter at what they considered the emasculation of the bill by the House that they wanted to scuttle it, but Welsh urged its adoption as the best possible bill under the circumstances. The House version was then approved by the Senate by a vote of 36 to 11. In addition to providing for criminal action and penalties, the public accommodations measure (an amendment to the 1885 law) in its final form enabled injured parties to bring civil suits, a provision which made it possible for individuals to initiate legal actions if the county prosecutor was reluctant to do so.[66]

A second measure adopted at the 1961 session created the Indiana Civil Rights Commission. The law creating the Civil Rights Commission said that its function was "to discourage any person from engaging in discriminatory practices by informal methods of persuasion and conciliation, to induce compliance with this act." In

---

[65] Indianapolis *Times*, February 3, 1961; Indianapolis *News*, February 10, 1961; Indianapolis *Star*, February 25, 27, 1961. Part of the crowd at the hearing was there to oppose the fair employment bill, which the Indiana State Chamber of Commerce strongly opposed.

[66] Indiana, *House Journal* (1961), 451, 525, 705-706, 817-19; Indiana, *Senate Journal* (1961), 915; Indiana, *Laws* (1961), 585; Indianapolis *Recorder*, March 3, 1961. Of the nine votes against the bill in the House, seven were by Republicans and two were by Democrats. In the Senate both of the original sponsors, Brokenburr and Dickinson, voted against the final weakened version.

addition to dealing with employment practices, the commission was authorized to receive written complaints of violations of the public accommodations law or "other discriminatory practices based upon race, creed, color, national origin or ancestry" and to investigate them. The commission might also conduct investigations "in the absence of complaints whenever it deems it in the public interest" and transmit recommendations to the legislature for aid in removing such discrimination. However, when it began operations in August, 1961, no research had been done on the extent of discrimination in public accommodations in Indiana. Information of this sort was necessary if the commission was to carry out its functions. In particular, it wanted information about the effect of compliance with the law on business operations and white patronage.[67]

Groups which had worked so tirelessly for a strong, enforceable public accommodations law "with teeth" were disappointed and skeptical about the watered down version finally enacted. However, the 1961 law and the bill creating the Indiana Civil Rights Commission proved to be much more than meaningless gestures: they paved the way for a stronger civil rights law adopted at the next session of the General Assembly.

The personality and performance of Harold Hatcher, the man whom Welsh appointed as the first director of the Civil Rights Commission, did much to convince the public as well as the lawmakers that civil rights legislation served a legitimate and worthwhile purpose. Hatcher, a Quaker with long experience in civil rights as director of field service for the American Friends Society and as director of the Association for Merit Employment, a private fair employment program, interpreted his responsibilities under the law broadly to include receiving complaints and investigating all kinds of discriminatory practices, not merely those in employment. He also saw his role as an educational one—to inform the public about the need for civil rights legislation and the function of such legislation.[68]

---

[67] Indiana, *Laws* (1961), 500-505; Welsh, *View from the State House*, 192; Indiana Civil Rights Commission, *Civil Rights Bulletin*, I (July, 1963), 8. The commission created in 1961 was officially called the Fair Employment Practices Commission (FEPC). Since, however, the FEPC was commonly called the Civil Rights Commission in the press and elsewhere and the commission itself used this name in its bulletin, the name Civil Rights Commission is used in this article. Jesse Dickinson, longtime advocate of civil rights legislation as a member of the General Assembly, was appointed by Welsh to the Civil Rights Commission.

[68] Welsh, *View from the State House*, 192 n. 6; Indianapolis *Recorder*, June 3, 1961. Harold Hatcher, a native of Kentucky, graduated from Indiana University and held a divinity degree from the University of Chicago. In Indianapolis he headed a Jobs Opportunity Program sponsored by the American Friends Service Committee, headed the Association for Merit Employment, and served on the Mayor's Commission on Human Rights before becoming director of the Civil Rights Commission. Indianapolis *Recorder*, June 3, 1961.

During its first two years the commission received numerous complaints, nearly all of which were resolved voluntarily. In fact, in about one half of the cases no evidence of discrimination was found. Out of about two hundred cases of alleged discrimination during the first year only one progressed to the calling of a public hearing. The operator of a skating rink in Bloomington was charged with refusing admission to a racially mixed group of Indiana University students. Because the proprietor chose not to attend the hearing and the commission lacked the power of subpoena or the power to issue cease and desist orders, there was no way short of prosecution in court to force him to comply with the law. Apparently, he simply ignored the finding of the commission. This case illustrated so well the inadequacy of the 1961 law that it helped create support for a stronger law.[69]

At a Governor's Conference on Civil Rights attended by more than three hundred people in September, 1962, Welsh promised to work for stronger laws when a new legislature met after that fall's elections. However, civil rights was not a major issue in the 1962 political campaign, and the governor's party lost control of the Senate, thereby giving the Republican party control of both houses of the legislature. Nevertheless, a new civil rights bill was introduced in the Senate early in the next session with the backing of the Indiana Civil Rights Commission. The bill contained enforcement provisions but fell short of the expectations of some black leaders because it did not cover discrimination in housing. After some amendments that strengthened the enforcement provisions were made, the bill passed the Senate by a vote of 45 to 2 early in the session and was sent to the House. In the House it appeared that the bill was bogged down, and some intense personal lobbying efforts were initiated. The Indiana Conference on Civil Rights, the same coalition which had worked for a strong law in 1961, was again active. During the closing days of the session, by a vote of 80 to 7, the House passed the Senate bill with some slight amendments, which the Senate later concurred in.[70]

Declaring that "equal educational and employment opportunities and equal access to and use of public accommodations are . . . to be civil rights," the 1963 law said it was the public policy of the state to provide equal opportunities for the enjoyment of these rights. The Civil Rights Commission was to induce compliance with laws forbidding discriminatory practices "by informal methods of

---

[69] Indianapolis *News*, September 9, 1963.

[70] Indianapolis *Star*, September 23, 1962; Indianapolis *Recorder*, November 3, 1962, January 12, February 23, March 2, 1963; Indiana, *Senate Journal* (1963), 69, 101, 127, 137, 681; Indiana, *House Journal* (1963), 745-46. Brokenburr, a Republican, and Marshall Kizer, a white Democrat, were the cosponsors of the bill in the Senate. The two Senate votes against the bill were by Republicans.

persuasion and conciliation" if possible. It was also empowered, upon receiving written complaints, to make preliminary investigations into charges, to hold public hearings, subpoena witnesses, take testimony under oath, and examine books and papers for matters relating to the investigation. Refusal to obey a subpoena constituted contempt punishable by a circuit or superior court. The commission could issue cease and desist orders against persons found to have engaged in discriminatory practices and order them "to take such further affirmative action" as would "effectuate the purposes" of the act. Decisions of the commission were subject to court review, but in the absence of an appeal for judicial review the commission could obtain a court decree for enforcement of its orders if the person charged failed to make efforts to comply. If there was insufficient evidence to support charges of discrimination, the commission was to issue an order dismissing the complaint. The law also authorized the commission "to promote good will and minimize or eliminate discrimination" through the creation of advisory agencies and conciliation councils and through research and publication.[71]

After enactment of the law Governor Welsh issued executive orders to strengthen enforcement of it. He ordered all departments of state government involved in supervising or licensing organizations or persons that operated places of "public accommodation" to take the actions "necessary and appropriate to prevent at all times discrimination because of race, color, creed or national origin" and to implement his order with the "appropriate action permitted by law." This meant that businesses which did not comply with the civil rights law jeopardized the renewal of their licenses. In the case of restaurants, hotels, and bars the Indiana State Board of Health and the Alcoholic Beverages Commission were ordered to assist in the enforcement of the public accommodations provisions of the law.[72]

With the adoption of the 1963 law a major step toward long-sought goals had been taken. The president of the Indianapolis branch of the NAACP said that that organization "was totally satisfied that Indiana had taken another step forward in its drive for equality of opportunities of its citizens."[73] Why did the General Assembly make this major step; why did it give an overwhelming endorsement to a strong bill "with teeth" when it had rejected a similar measure two years earlier? Examination of the membership of the legislature shows that there had been no significant redistribution of political power. In 1961 there were twenty-six

---

[71] Indiana, *Laws* (1963), 216-22. Indiana was the eleventh state to provide for enforcement in a public accommodations law.
[72] Welsh, *View from the State House*, 193-94; Indianapolis *Times*, June 19, 1963.
[73] Indianapolis *Recorder*, March 9, 1963.

Democrats and twenty-four Republicans in the Senate; in 1963 there were twenty-six Republicans and twenty-four Democrats. Republicans held sixty-six of the one hundred seats in the House in 1961; in 1963 they held fifty-seven. There were a few new faces in both houses, but most members of the 1961 session returned in 1963, although some of them had changed their views about civil rights legislation. In 1963 twenty-three of the same House members who had voted down the strong bill sponsored by the Democrats in 1961 voted for the 1963 measure. In the Senate of the eight members who had cast votes against the 1961 bill before it was weakened by amendments, four voted for the 1963 version. Of the two senators who voted against the 1963 bill, one was reported to have explained his vote by saying the measure was hypocritical because it exempted private fraternal and religious organizations, while the other one refused to give a reason except to say it had nothing to do with race. Both were Republicans.[74]

Undoubtedly, one reason that some lawmakers found the 1963 bill more acceptable than the original version of the 1961 bill was that it did not cover discrimination in housing. Another reason, already suggested, was the record of the Civil Rights Commission, which had helped to educate the legislators and the public and to alleviate the fears of both that, if given enforcement powers, it might act in an arbitrary fashion. Also, the experience of other states with strong civil rights laws was demonstrating that all parties preferred administrative enforcement to litigation.

Black civil rights lawyers had framed the successive civil rights bills introduced in the legislature from 1935 to 1963, and most of these bills had been sponsored by black members. The NAACP and its allies had lobbied tirelessly. Democrats had pushed civil rights more vigorously than had the opposing party, but it had been a bipartisan coalition of whites who enacted the laws. Many white legislators were ready to accept in 1963 what they had formerly opposed or evaded. Their own attitudes and what they perceived to be the attitudes of their white constituents had gradually changed.

The attitudes of Hoosiers about civil rights were influenced by the tide of events nationally. The most significant domestic development in the United States in the 1950s and 1960s was the struggle for civil rights. Through television and the press whites witnessed the realities of racial injustice and oppression of which they had been ignorant or which they had chosen to ignore. At the national level the Kennedy administration, compelled to assert the authority of the federal government at Ol' Miss in 1962, was moving toward support for strong federal civil rights legislation. In the

---

[74] Indiana, *House Journal* (1961), 706; *ibid.* (1963), 878; Indiana, *Senate Journal* (1961), 455; *ibid.* (1963), 137; Indianapolis *Recorder*, February 2, 1963.

Breaking Racial Barriers 339

face of an aroused public Indiana lawmakers could not with any consistency oppose equal rights in Indiana while denouncing racism in the South. For many whites racial justice had become a compelling moral issue. At a White House Conference on Civil Rights held in 1963 after the adoption of the Indiana law, Governor Welsh spoke of the part that churches had played "in working with what was essentially a moral question" and asserted that the "forthright role played by the men and women of all faiths" was a major factor in the passage of Indiana's civil rights bill.[75]

Of course all whites did not agree. An indignant owner of a beauty shop in Gary wrote to Welsh to protest the civil rights law and the governor's executive order implementing it.

> I love this country and am writing to you because I am concerned at what you and Mr. Kennedy and others like you are doing to it, and to me personally.
> Why do I feel as I do? Because I see my rights destroyed to please a minority group.

The government, he complained, now said he could not live in an all-white neighborhood and send his children to an all-white school. "The government says we must integrate all public places," and he was unable to run his business as he pleased.[76]

In reply Welsh admitted that some whites might be "inconvenienced" or "displeased" as rights they had formerly enjoyed exclusively were extended to blacks, but he added, the continued denial of these rights to blacks was "a deep cutting insult" that tended to destroy the self-respect and ambition of black citizens. As for himself, the governor said:

> I fail to see how the treatment of Negroes as persons and in accordance with their individual merit or demerits interferes with any legitimate rights of me and my family....
> I hope you will come to feel that the changes that are taking place, instead of limiting your rights, actually make them more secure.[77]

Others recognized that lawmakers, in supporting civil rights, were not motivated solely by moral considerations but were also influenced by what they had come to perceive as the self-interest of all Americans and the position of the United States in world affairs. Assessing the reasons for support of civil rights at the state and national levels, Willard Ransom said that it had come about because "the power structure . . . now recognizes that these things must be done to maintain our image of leadership at home and abroad."[78]

Changing attitudes might result in acceptance of the principle of nondiscriminatory treatment but not necessarily the practice. A

---

[75] Welsh, *View from the State House*, 196 n. 17.
[76] Indianapolis *Times*, July 23, 1963.
[77] *Ibid.*
[78] Indianapolis *News*, August 3, 1964.

NAACP Freedom Rally, August, 1963

Courtesy Indianapolis *Recorder* Collection, Indiana Historical Society, Indianapolis.

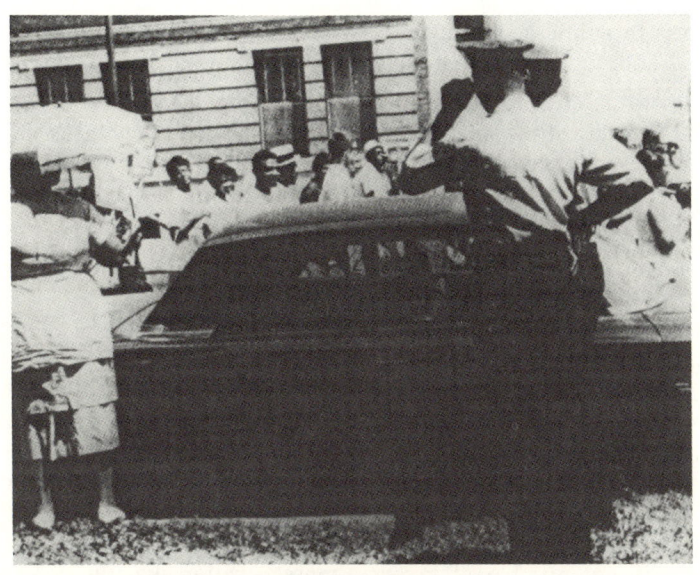

NAACP Freedom Rally, August, 1963

Courtesy Indianapolis *Recorder* Collection, Indiana Historical Society, Indianapolis

survey made by the Civil Rights Commission in 1963 gave the most complete summary at the time of the actual availability of equal access to public accommodations. The survey, conducted by about two hundred volunteers in sixteen cities, showed that blacks might expect to be served in about ninety-nine out of one hundred lunch counters in drug and department stores in the larger cities, and that they could eat in about 80 percent of the restaurants surveyed, although they were less likely to be received in small establishments in all-white neighborhoods. They would probably be turned away from at least three out of five cocktail bars or taverns, exclusive of cocktail bars in major hotels. Black travelers could expect to find lodgings in about 80 percent of major downtown hotels, but in only about two thirds of Indiana's motels. Motels identified with national chains were more likely to accept them than smaller, locally owned ones. Nearly all theaters, public parks, public recreation centers, and bowling alleys in or near larger cities accepted blacks, but only about one fourth of roller skating rinks. Responses to questions about the effect of serving all patrons without regard to race indicated that businesses which complied with the law did not suffer loss of white patronage. The report concluded that, "While a significant number of taverns, motels, roller skating rinks and places of personal service still discriminate, the new enforceable Civil Rights Act and the Governor's Executive Order against discrimination in Public Accommodations ... have greatly accelerated the adoption of equal accommodations policies." It added that "on the basis of present trends, all of Indiana's public accommodations should be available to its citizens regardless of color at an early date."[79]

The report, which was drawn from data collected in larger communities, was not entirely representative of the state as a whole and probably somewhat too optimistic. In many communities blacks would probably have been refused service in spite of the law. Assessing conditions early in 1964, Governor Welsh spoke of the civil rights movement as "a great revolution of the American conscience," adding, "one may not pass a law requiring brotherly love, but one may legislate to insure the basic rights of all citizens in a free land." If gains had not been spectacular, progress had been achieved without strife.[80]

By 1963 Indiana, a state that had before lagged behind other northern states in civil rights matters, had become one of the few states with enforceable laws in the areas of fair employment, public accommodations, and school desegregation. The Indiana laws were adopted before the landmark federal Civil Rights Act of 1964,

---

[79] Indiana Civil Rights Commission, *Civil Rights Bulletin*, I (July, 1963), 8-10.
[80] Indianapolis *Times*, April 11, 1964.

and the public accommodations parts of this federal law were already covered in Indiana by state law. Nevertheless, the existence of the federal law undoubtedly served to reinforce the authority of the state law by outlawing discriminatory treatment nationally.

Complaints over refusal of service in public accommodations steadily declined. The Indiana Civil Rights Commission reported that whereas in 1963, 32 percent of complaints filed with it had been about public accommodations, by 1965 that figure had declined to 15 percent. By 1967 there were only occasional, isolated complaints, which were resolved by negotiation. The general acceptance of the law on public accommodations permitted the commission to direct most of its resources to the areas of employment and housing.[81]

In 1965 the General Assembly passed a measure outlawing discrimination in the sale and rental of private housing and another measure to strengthen the 1949 law so as to assist school desegregation. Finally, at the same session, Indiana, the only state outside the South with an antimiscegenation law, repealed the prohibition against interracial marriage. By the mid-1960s racism was not dead in Indiana, but the more overt manifestations of it were no longer evident. In larger communities, at least, the presence of blacks in restaurants, hotels, and theaters no longer caused comment. Many people had forgotten that it had not always been that way.

---

[81] Indiana Civil Rights Commission, *Report* (1966), 10; *ibid.* (1968), part 1, 6.

PHYLON

THE ATLANTA UNIVERSITY
Review of
RACE AND CULTURE

THIRD QUARTER (Fall), 1965   VOL. XXVI, No. 3

By F. JAMES DAVIS

The Effects of a Freeway Displacement on Racial Housing Segregation in a Northern City

MUCH OF THE RECENT COMMENT about racially segregated housing implies that Northern whites are widely agreed that nonwhites should be denied free access to urban housing.[1] In his final report to the Commission on Race and Housing, Davis McEntire states explicitly that housing discrimination is strongly institutionalized.[2] He presents supporting evidence about popular attitudes, governmental policies, and the various activities of the housing industry; but he also notes certain counter forces.[3] This suggests conflicting values and actions, not a set, monolithic pattern. Whether less than uniform discrimination can produce the marked degree of residential segregation now so common in Northern cities is an important question for sociological theories of race relations.

Any crisis which subjects a city's racial housing pattern to marked strain provides an excellent opportunity to study the processes involved in supporting segregation, those promoting integration, and the consequences. Such a crisis occurred in St. Paul, Minnesota, from 1959 to 1961, when a clearance for freeway construction was made through the most nonwhite part of the city. This paper reports a study of the actions most of the displaced families took, their experiences in the housing market and the pattern of relocation. The fact that both whites and nonwhites were displaced made it possible to test for racial differences.

---

[1] Charles F. Marden and Gladys Meyer, *Minorities in Human Society* (New York, 1962), pp. 310-19.
[2] Davis McEntire, *Residence and Race* (Berkeley and Los Angeles, 1960), p. 5. See Scott Greer, *The Emerging City* (New York, 1962), p. 35, for the view that residential neighborhoods reflect differential rewards in the urban division of labor.
[3] *Ibid.*, pp. 349-50.

THE DISPLACEMENT

By 1950 nearly three-fourths of St. Paul's rapidly increasing nonwhite population lived in the racially mixed Selby-Dale Area, just west and a little north of the central business district. About 93 percent of the nonwhites in the area were in the northeast half of it, so the south and west parts were predominantly white. There were no nonwhites in that small portion of the Selby-Dale Area south of Selby Avenue; so the remainder of the area came to be thought of as the city's "nonwhite area," and it will be so called in this paper.

The city's nonwhite population continued to grow in the 1950's, and to become more concentrated. In 1958 probably over nine-tenths of St. Paul's colored people lived in the nonwhite area.[4] Many of the previously all-white blocks in the southwest part of the area were becoming mixed, and the percentage of whites was declining throughout the area. This trend was accentuated by two redevelopment projects adjacent to (one partly within) the area which compelled most of the 186 colored families involved to seek housing in the nonwhite area. The housing shortage for nonwhites became acute before the freeway clearance.

The St. Anthony-Rondo Freeway demolition went straight west near the north boundary of the area, eliminating 433 household units, 72 percent of them nonwhite. This was about 14 percent of the city's nonwhite housing.[5] It is estimated that about three-fifths of both the white and nonwhite families owned the condemned homes. Most of the families, with limited help from voluntary groups, entered the housing market on their own. The Housing and Redevelopment Authority lent some moral support by keeping an office in the area for over a year to make a survey of the situation, but no public agency received funds for relocation assistance.

THE INTERVIEW SAMPLE

This study became possible when the Hallie Q. Brown Community House made a list of the households in the condemned area just before demolition, and later determined the new address of three-fourths of the relocated households. The other one-fourth had no forwarding address in the local post office, and adequate data for comparing these with the known three-fourths were unavailable. This incomplete and possibly nonrepresentative list was the best available, so it was used for analysis of the pattern of relocation and the sampling for interviewing.

The plan was to make a random sample of half the 328 householders

---

[4] Ernest C. Cooper, "St. Paul's Urban Renewal Program as It Relates to Non-White Citizens," a report to the Sixth Urban League sponsored Urban Renewal Institute at Milwaukee, Wisconsin, May 19-20, 1958.

[5] "Report on Survey of Residents to be Displaced by St. Anthony Expressway," Housing and Redevelopment Authority of the City of Saint Paul, Minnesota, May, 1958, p. 3. It appeared that 485 households would be removed, but 39 were not. This and other corrections produced our final figure of 433.

whose new addresses were known, and to make additional selections to replace those not interviewed. The rate of failure was rather high, so ultimately 310 sampling selections were made, using a table of random numbers. Of these, 177 (57.1 percent) were successfully interviewed.[6] The failure to interview 133 sampled householders, together with the absence of one-fourth of the new addresses on the master list, must be kept in mind in assessing this study.

The interviews were relatively non-directive, but an interview schedule was followed to ensure inclusion of certain questions. The modal interview length was one hour. About half the interviews were done by Negroes, half by whites.

THE PATTERN OF RELOCATION

Hypothesis: As compared with displaced whites, a much smaller proportion of nonwhites were relocated outside the nonwhite area. Table 1 supports this hypothesis. Of the whites with known addresses in mid-1962, 90.5 percent were outside the nonwhite area, but only 15.5 percent of the nonwhites were. This large difference could not be eliminated even if the racial pattern of relocation were completely the opposite for

TABLE 1
RACE OF HOUSEHOLDERS DISPLACED BY 1959-61 ST. ANTHONY-RONDO FREEWAY CLEARANCE BY LOCATION IN 1962

Race	Number Inside Non White Area	Number Outside Non White Area	Number In State Twin Cities Area	Number Out of State	No Information	Total
White	7	67	3	4	37	118
Nonwhite	197	36	2	9	67	311
No Information	2	1	0	0	1	4
Total	206	104	5	13	105	433

the 105 whose new addresses were unknown. The whites were scattered rather widely over the Twin Cities and their suburbs, while most of the 36 Negro families that had succeeded in leaving the nonwhite area were located in small pockets in St. Paul. The clearance contributed to the increase in the nonwhite density in all parts of the (still mixed) nonwhite area.

INTERVIEW FINDINGS

DIFFICULTIES AND SUCCESS IN MOVING OUT OF THE AREA

Of the 177 nonwhite families interviewed, only 12.8 percent had left the nonwhite area. To determine how much discrimination was actually

---
[6] Only 15 percent returned a mailed request for an interview appointment. Despite many telephone and door calls, some were not reached. The majority were cooperative, but some refused to be interviewed.

encountered,[7] one must know how many tried to leave the area, what experiences they had, and the outcome. These matters were discussed in all interviews with whites and nonwhites.

Hypothesis: As compared with displaced white families, a significantly smaller proportion of nonwhites attempted to move outside the nonwhite area. As shown in Table 2, only about one-third of the nonwhites said they attempted to leave the area, while well over two-thirds of the whites did. The racial difference is significant at far better than the desired .05 level. Most of the reasons given for not trying were in terms of satisfaction with the neighborhood, attachment to family and friends, desire to stay close to work or institutional facilities, less expense, etc.; but ten Negroes said they feared discrimination and three implied it. Some of the ten said they should be able to spread out more, but they did not wish to jeopardize family interests by "pioneering."

Hypothesis: As compared with displaced white families, a significantly larger proportion of nonwhites had difficulty when they tried to leave

TABLE 2
RACE OF INTERVIEWEES BY RESPONSE TO
"DID YOU TRY TO GET OUTSIDE THE NONWHITE AREA?"

Race	Yes	No	No Reply *	Indeterminate *	Total
White	25	10	1	1	37
Nonwhite	46	94	0	0	140
Total	71	104	1	1	177

Chi square equals 17.3
p is less than .001
Phi equals .35
*(not included in computations)

the nonwhite area. This hypothesis is supported by Table 3. The three white and five of the nonwhite families specified only financial problems. But 18 nonwhites reported discriminatory experiences, mainly in getting to see a house or in completing the purchase, and half of these mentioned discrimination at two or more points in the home-buying process. Thus almost two-fifths of the Negroes who tried to move out of the nonwhite area said they were discriminated against at least once.

One of the nine Negroes who had difficulty getting an appointment reported that the agent said his company would not sell to Negroes in that neighborhood, but the other reactions from agents and home

---

[7] The proper relating of ecological patterns to social processes is difficult. See Alvin Boskoff, *The Sociology of Urban Regions* (New York, 1962), p. 153; and James M. Beshers, *Urban Social Structure* (New York, 1962), pp. 23-26.

owners were more subtle. The eight nonwhites who reported not being able to see a house after getting an appointment complained mainly that they were shown only poor quality homes when the agent discovered their race. Some were told falsely the house had been sold; others were discouraged by the quoting of a high down payment or selling price, or by having the worst features of a house pointed out.

Four Negroes (and two whites) talked about difficulty in getting a loan, but three of these indicated that they considered other matters than racial discrimination responsible. It appears that most of the pressure to keep nonwhites in the area occurred before the lending stage was reached. Six Negroes related troubles other than with the loan in completing the purchase, three specifying the negative reactions of white neighbors. Most of these difficulties involved attempts to buy outside the nonwhite area, but some concerned previously all-white blocks within it.

TABLE 3
RACE OF INTERVIEWEES WHO TRIED TO LEAVE THE NONWHITE AREA BY RESPONSE TO, "DID YOU HAVE ANY DIFFICULTIES IN THE ATTEMPT?"

Race	Number of Yes Responses	Number of No Responses	Total
White	3	22	25
Nonwhite	23	23	46
Total	26	45	71

Chi square equals 10.14
p is less than .01
Phi equals .24

Those who said they did not have difficulty when attempting to move out of the nonwhite area gave varied explanations. Some Negroes said white real estate agents and neighbors were helpful and accepting, and some emphasized that they had experienced no discrimination of any kind. Some avoided barriers by getting help from friends, voluntary associations, or lawyers. Some did not continue their efforts to leave the area because they wished to avoid troubles.

Since the nonwhites who attempted to leave the area did not encounter a united front, it is important to know how many succeeded. Hypothesis: As compared with displaced white families, a significantly smaller proportion of nonwhites succeeded when they attempted to leave the nonwhite area. This hypothesis is supported by Table 4, which shows a large racial difference, all the whites but only about one-third of the nonwhites being relocated outside the nonwhite area. Even so, it appears that the chances for nonwhites to move out of the area were greater than suggested by the pattern of resettlement shown in Table 1.

SATISFACTION WITH PRESENT HOUSING

Hypothesis: Relocated whites were significantly more satisfied with their new housing than relocated nonwhites were. The interviewees were asked if they were satisfied in general with their new housing, and with nine particular aspects. The responses called for rejection of the hypothesis. About four-fifths of both whites and nonwhites expressed general satisfaction. Three-fourths of the whites as compared with two-thirds of the nonwhites considered their present housing better than what they had prior to displacement, but the difference is not significant

TABLE 4

RACE OF INTERVIEWEES WHO TRIED TO LEAVE THE NON WHITE AREA BY NEW LOCATION

Race	Number Inside Nonwhite Area	Number Outside Nonwhite Area	Number In State Out of Twin Cities Area *	Total
White	0	25	0	25
Nonwhite	29	16	1	46
Total	29	41	1	71

Chi square equals 27.81
.p is less than .001
Phi equals .63
*(not included in computations)

at the .05 level. The whites were significantly less satisfied with present access to work, but no other aspect showed a significant difference.

RESIDENTIAL STATUS

Hypothesis: The freeway clearance reduced white home ownership significantly less than it did for the displaced nonwhites. This hypothesis was rejected. For both races, the percent of home ownership among the interviewees increased roughly from 60 to 70 percent.[8] Perhaps the Negro interviewee was correct when he said that the move was hard on many families, of both races, but that it compelled them to make an effort and that the majority now have better housing than before.

Interpretation

While one-fourth of the 433 displaced families were unaccounted for, the pattern of relocation of the known three-fourths shows a very great racial difference. Thus the freeway clearance, along with the earlier redevelopment projects, increased the density of the nonwhite concentration and extended its boundaries, a trend typical of Northern cities

---

[8] For all 177 interviewees, those who changed from renter to owner status were the most satisfied; next came owner to owner, then renter to renter, with owner to renter the least.

since World War II.⁹ The 177 interviews provided data that help explain the ecological result.

The pattern of the relocation suggests more discrimination than interviewed nonwhites directly encountered. Nearly two-fifths of the interviewed Negroes who attempted to move out of the nonwhite area met discrimination, half of these more than once; and fear of discrimination was one reason why only one-third made the try. But some others received assistance from white agents, friends, or new neighbors, so there were conflicting values and practices rather than a uniform system of housing discrimination. The white resistance might have been stiffer, of course, if much larger numbers of nonwhites had tried to move outward.¹⁰ A definite effort by a nonwhite interviewee to leave the area increased the chances to over one-third, while if one reasoned from the pattern of resettlement alone he would reckon the chances at about one in eight.

The study provided a unique opportunity to study the dynamics of a racial housing pattern subjected to the strain of an imposed community crisis, and to test for racial differences in relocation experiences. A major limitation is the loss of cases, both the one-fourth displaced households not found and the over two-fifths of the sampled families not interviewed. Many characteristics of the families that might be important were not included in the study, such as age, number of children, class level, etc. The economic level of Negroes and whites is believed to have been about the same, an assumption supported by the finding that the percentage of home ownership was about the same for the two groups before the move as well as afterwards.

With these limitations in mind, it would seem that the great racial difference in the (known) pattern of resettlement resulted from an imperfectly institutionalized system of discrimination. Direct discriminatory action does not appear sufficient to account for the increase in racial housing segregation after the freeway clearance.¹¹ Much of the increased concentration of nonwhites was evidently due to fear of discrimination outside of the nonwhite area, and to in-group cohesiveness in the face of potential discrimination.

---

[9] Marden and Meyer, op. cit., pp. 311-12.
[10] Chester Rapkin and William G. Grigsby, *The Demand For Housing In Racially Mixed Areas* (Berkeley and Los Angeles, 1960), pp. 52-72.
[11] Boskoff, op. cit., pp. 123-24, suggests that the persistence of segregated housing is due to more than discrimination.

THE NEGRO VOTE IN PHILADELPHIA ELECTIONS

By William J. McKenna*

BLOC voting[1] has been evident in the pattern of Philadelphia politics for many years. The strength of the Democratic party in Philadelphia has been concentrated in the Italian, Polish, Jewish, and Negro blocs in most of the elections since the election of President Franklin D. Roosevelt in 1932.[2] Religion,[3] economics, and political philosophy[4] have been important factors in the bloc voting pattern of Philadelphia.

The foundation of the strength of the Democratic party in Philadelphia, however, is in the voting behavior of the seventeen so-called Negro wards. This paper will examine this pattern and discuss the factors that have influenced the pattern.

The Negro Population of Philadelphia

Since 1940 the Negro population of Philadelphia has increased by 303,620—from 250,880 in 1940 to an estimated 554,400 in 1963.[5] The Negro population of Philadelphia is largely concen-

---

*William J. McKenna is an associate professor of economics at Temple University.

[1] In 1960 there were approximately 300,000 Jews and 530,000 Negroes in Philadelphia. There were also 700,000 Catholics out of a total population of 2,002,512.

[2] The heavily Jewish wards (49th and 50th) have voted Democratic in all Presidential elections since 1936. They have also voted Democratic in almost all elections since the victory of Joseph S. Clark in the controller election of 1949. This has also been true of the Italian and Polish wards.

[3] In 1928 the nomination of Alfred E. Smith as the Democratic candidate for President resulted in a total Democratic vote in Philadelphia of 276,000. In 1932 the total Democratic vote in Philadelphia decreased to 260,000. In 1960 Senator Kennedy received approximately 75% of the vote of the Catholic Italian wards.

[4] The Jewish wards vote consistently for liberal Democratic candidates even though economically these wards are upper middle class.

[5] This 554,400 estimate is that of the Philadelphia Chamber of Commerce (see the 1964 Edition of *Greater Philadelphia Facts,* Chamber of Commerce of Greater Philadelphia, December, 1963, p. 48). The 1950 Negro population of Philadelphia was 376,041. If the growth of the Negro population of Philadelphia continues, it may reach 40% of the city population by 1980. It is now 27.2%.

406

trated in the areas immediately east and west of the Schuylkill River. This area is one of overcrowded housing, inadequate schools, and industrial plants. It contains many of the families who are on relief and other assistance programs. The rate of unemployment in this area is more than double that of the rest of the city. Public housing has been built in the area but this has not greatly lessened the concentration of Negro population in the region.[6]

THE POLITICAL PATTERN OF PHILADELPHIA

Prior to the election of President Franklin D. Roosevelt in 1932, Philadelphia was definitely a one-party Republican city. As late at 1931 the Democratic candidate for mayor received a total vote of only 30,821 compared to a Republican total of 367,344—a Republican landslide majority of 336,523 or 90.1% of the total vote.[7] In 1932, however, the Republican candidate for President carried the city by only 70,766 votes. The subsequent elections witnessed a further weakening of the strength of the Republican party in Philadelphia for all city, state, and national offices. In Philadelphia the Republican party barely won the elections for United States Senator in 1934 and 1938, and has lost all such elections since 1940 with the exception of the national Republican swing of 1946.[8] Since 1950 the Republican party has lost every election for Governor by substantial margins. Again, since 1932 the Republican party has suffered defeat in all Presidential elections. The climax in the Republican decline in Philadelphia occurred in the Presidential election of 1960, when that party was defeated by 331,544 votes. A similar pattern of Republican decline is evident in all local elections in Philadelphia since 1932. Although the Republican party won the mayoralty elections in 1935-

---

[6] The areas surrounding the University of Pennsylvania and Temple University are areas of heavy Negro population concentration. The redevelopment of these areas is gradually encroaching upon the heavily populated Negro residential areas. These areas have been described as "slum areas" because of the large number of residential dwellings containing from four to six separate apartments.

[7] In the mayoralty election of 1927 the total Democratic vote was approximately 10,000 and the Republican vote 296,551.

[8] The Republicans won the United States Senate race in 1934 by only 3,012 votes and the 1938 election by 17,167 votes. The 1946 election for United States Senator went Republican by 108,853 votes. All such elections since 1946 have been won by the Democratic party by heavy margins.

1947, the majorities were far from impressive,[9] when compared with the pre-1935 majorities.[10] Since 1951 the Democrats have won every mayoralty election.[11]

The principal architects of the rise of the Democratic party in Philadelphia were two unusual men: Joseph S. Clark and Richardson Dilworth. In 1947 these two former Republicans spearheaded the reform movement in Philadelphia. Dilworth ran for mayor in 1947 but was defeated by a Republican ward leader, Bernard Samuel, by 91,622 votes. In 1949 Clark was elected city controller by a Democratic majority of 112,000 votes.[12] The history of the Democratic party since 1947 has largely been the history of these two men. They were reformers. They were both graduates of "Ivy League" colleges (Harvard and Yale), and each was wealthy in his own right. Both men were committed to the elimination of political corruption and political bossism which had characterized Republican politics in Philadelphia for many years. In 1951 Clark was elected mayor by 125,000 votes. Since that date the Democratic party has dominated practically all elections in Philadelphia.[13]

The Negro Vote in Philadelphia

For the purpose of this study the term "Negro Ward" is applied to those wards which in 1960 had a total Negro population of 50% or more. There are sixteen of these wards. The 38th Ward has also been included in this study because in 1960 it had a Negro population of 24,505 (33.3%), and it is contiguous with the other heavily populated Negro wards.

These seventeen wards in 1960 had a total Negro population of 414,864, or 78.4% of the 529,239 Negro population of Philadelphia. Sixteen of these wards had a 1960 Negro population varying from approximately 50.0% to 95.8% (see Table I).

---

[9] The mayoralty Republican majorities were: 1935, 45,478; 1939, 30,006; 1943, 63,465; and 1947, 91,622.

[10] In 1927 the Republican majority was 285,903 (96.4%) and in 1931 the majority was 336,523 (90.1%).

[11] Joseph S. Clark won in 1951 by nearly 125,000, and Richardson Dilworth by 132,000 in 1955. He was reelected in 1959 by 208,000 votes. In 1963, James H. J. Tate was elected mayor by a 68,268-vote majority.

[12] In the same year Dilworth was elected city treasurer. He also ran for Governor in 1950 and, although he carried Philadelphia by 77,000 votes, he was defeated in the state.

[13] In 1953 the Republicans won the city controller election by the narrow margin of 15,579 votes in a very light election of 565,799 total votes.

TABLE I
Negro Population: 17 So-Called Negro Wards, City of Philadelphia, 1950 and 1960.

Ward	Negro Population			
	1950		1960	
	Total	Percent	Total	Percent
4	4,294	42.7	4,055	58.2
13	7,859	59.3	5,070	70.2
14	9,604	67.8	8,560	82.7
20	25,559	58.3	24,110	74.4
24	36,741	58.0	45,666	80.8
28	20,040	39.6	46,230	91.3
29	12,594	41.2	23,095	81.3
30	23,789	87.4	21,587	91.4
32	44,872	73.7	52,191	95.8
36	22,623	43.0	23,542	52.0
37	4,372	20.2	11,284	60.2
38	6,132	8.7	24,505	33.3
44	23,398	56.3	28,598	78.0
46[1]	2,297	2.6	40,171	50.0
47	27,690	76.5	28,173	90.2
52	20,059	35.4	27,975	53.6
17 Wards[1]	291,923	77.6	414,864	78.4
City	376,041		529,239	

[1] In 1961 the 46th ward was divided into the new 46th and 60th wards.
SOURCE: *Greater Philadelphia Facts*, Chamber of Commerce of Greater Philadelphia, 1962 Edition, p. 46. Percentages calculated.

Even before the Democratic party succeeded in winning municipal elections in Philadelphia, these seventeen Negro wards had provided a significant basis of support for the Democratic party. For example, in the Presidential elections of 1940-1948, these wards had provided a Democratic majority that was 44.3%, 52.6%, and 457.5% of the total city-wide Democratic majority.[14] A similar trend prevailed in the elections for the United States Senator and Governor in 1950.[15]

Since 1952 the seventeen Negro wards in Philadelphia have consistently given a still heavier percentage of their votes to the Democratic party. The percentages for each of the seventeen Negro wards for the three Presidential elections since 1952, the

[14] The unusual percentage for 1948 reflects the 30,806 Democratic majority given by these seventeen Negro wards to President Truman in the face of a city-wide majority for Truman of 6,737.
[15] See Table IV.

three Gubernatorial elections since 1954, and the three mayoralty elections since 1955 are shown in Table II.

There is a very high Democratic registration among the Negro population of Philadelphia. It has increased from 170,491 in 1950 to 231,308 in 1962.[16] As is to be expected, there is a large concentration of the Democratic Negro registration in the seventeen Negro wards of the City. The Democratic registration in these seventeen Negro wards has increased from 132,848 in 1950 to 179,013 in 1962, but the percentage of registration has remained constant (see Table III).

As the Democratic margin of victory decreases in city-wide elections, the Democratic majority of the seventeen Negro wards becomes a more significant factor in the Democratic victory. This is evident in the figures presented in Table IV. Thus, in the close election for city controller in 1961, the 61,033 Democratic majority of the seventeen Negro wards accounted for 107.9% of the total Democratic city-wide majority. In the Gubernatorial election of 1962, a Democratic majority in the Negro wards was 68.7% of the city-wide Democratic majority. And in the mayoralty election of 1963 the 85,214 majority of the Negro wards was 123% of the total city-wide Democratic majority of 69,310.[17]

Factors Affecting the Negro Vote in Philadelphia

Many complicated factors influence the voting pattern of any bloc of voters. In Philadelphia there are several factors which seem to have influenced the Negro to vote and to remain Democratic. Among these factors are the following:

(1) The identification of the Democratic party with the Roosevelt policies and philosophy. With the advent of the "New Deal" the Democratic party initiated many programs which have directly benefited the Negro. Social and economic legislation of the 1933-

---

[16] In the 1963 mayoralty election the total Negro registration in the city was estimated at 233,000.

[17] James H. J. Tate, acting mayor of Philadelphia, was the Democratic candidate. He had become acting mayor as a result of the resignation of Mayor Richardson Dilworth, who resigned to run for Governor. The Philadelphia City Charter of 1951 provides that any elected official of the city government must resign from his office in the event he files for another elective office. Tate, as the president of the City Council, became acting mayor in February 1963.

TABLE II

DEMOCRATIC PARTY, PERCENTAGE OF TOTAL VOTE,
17 SO-CALLED NEGRO WARDS OF PHILADELPHIA.
SELECTED ELECTIONS, 1952-1963.
DEMOCRATIC VOTE, PERCENTAGE OF TOTAL VOTE.

Wards	President			Governor			Mayor		
	1952	1956	1960	1954	1958	1962	1955	1959	1963
4	59.4	61.7	72.8	51.4	56.0	57.1	57.0	57.9	76.8
13	44.8	74.5	81.1	46.0	74.1	78.0	57.4	76.0	81.3
14	60.7	71.2	80.3	54.8	73.6	76.1	62.8	77.4	78.5
20	67.8	73.7	83.3	59.2	76.2	77.9	61.6	77.5	79.6
24	71.2	71.1	79.9	63.2	75.8	73.4	73.8	79.2	76.0
28	73.6	73.8	83.6	68.4	78.0	69.4	70.2	79.4	80.3
29	68.3	68.3	79.6	67.3	73.4	74.2	69.2	77.4	77.1
30	74.3	69.0	79.7	65.9	71.5	70.8	70.6	72.9	76.9
32	81.3	78.7	83.1	75.8	79.1	72.9	76.7	78.2	79.7
36	76.8	71.3	83.2	75.4	78.2	74.2	74.4	78.8	74.1
37	58.7	61.2	73.5	58.8	71.1	71.5	63.1	76.4	76.4
38	59.3	57.4	71.8	60.7	63.1	57.0	60.5	66.9	57.8
44	74.8	68.7	80.0	67.6	74.2	70.3	71.4	75.8	78.0
46	55.7	58.7	70.7	59.1	65.8	62.9	61.0	72.1	71.0
47	76.7	74.0	84.0	68.8	76.5	76.6	72.4	78.6	81.6
52	72.1	72.2	76.5	70.1	75.1	70.8	72.9	77.2	72.6
60						67.8			73.7
All 17 Wards	68.3	68.0	78.0	65.2	72.6	69.4	67.9	75.2	73.8
City-Wide	58.5	57.6	68.1	57.7	61.7	56.7	59.3	65.6	54.6

SOURCE: Richard M. Scammon, *America Votes*, Volumes I-IV (Governmental Affairs Institute, New York: Macmillan Company, 1956; Governmental Affairs Institute, Pittsburgh: University of Pittsburgh, 1958-1962). Percentages for mayoralty elections taken from data in City of Philadelphia election returns, *Annual Report of the Registration Commission for the City of Philadelphia*, 1956-1962. Percentages for 1963 calculated from unofficial sources.

TABLE III

NEGRO DEMOCRATIC REGISTRATION IN PHILADELPHIA, CITY-WIDE AND THE 17 SO-CALLED NEGRO WARDS. SELECTED YEARS, 1950-1962.

Year	City-wide	17 Negro Wards	Percentage
1950	170,941	132,848	77.7
1952	178,365	138,196	77.4
1954	173,281	134,200	77.4
1956	195,469	152,278	77.9
1958	210,517	164,618	77.7
1960	219,232	170,569	77.7
1962	231,308	179,013	77.8

SOURCE: *Annual Report of the Registration Commission for the City of Philadelphia*, 1950-1962.

1940 period has laid the basis of much assistance to the Negro, because it was the group which was the most depressed. Although all administrations since Roosevelt have followed to some extent the social welfare policies of President Roosevelt, the Negro in Philadelphia seems to associate these policies with Roosevelt.[18]

(2) Economic factors. The solidity of the Negro vote behind the Democratic party in Philadelphia is largely based upon economic factors. These include jobs, housing, and educational opportunities. The Negro in Philadelphia has in recent years been confronted with an unemployment rate of 10-20%. This is, of course, partly related to the lack of skilled occupations among the Negro group. But it is also affected by the slow rate of hiring of Negro workers by employers and the discrimination against qualified Negroes by certain unions.[19]

The Negro leadership of Philadelphia in the past two years has pursued a determined policy of lessening housing discrimination in Philadelphia. These leaders have felt that the local Democratic

---

[18] Late in the mayoralty campaign of 1963 the Democratic leadership in Philadelphia had James Roosevelt make a campaign appearance in the Negro areas. This was in recognition of the lasting influence of President Roosevelt among the Negroes.

[19] Under the leadership of 400 Negro ministers in Philadelphia there has been a successful drive to place Negroes in jobs in many Philadelphia industries. This result has been attained by a policy of general boycott and picketing of firms which allegedly practiced job discrimination. Cecil B. Moore, the leader of the Philadelphia Chapter of the NAACP, has also aggressively pursued a policy of ending job discrimination.

TABLE IV
Democratic Majorities in Philadelphia, City-Wide and 17 So-Called Negro Wards. Selected Elections, 1940-1963.

Office	Democratic Majority City-Wide	Democratic Majority 17 Negro Wards	Democratic Majority of 17 Negro Wards as Percent of City-wide Majority
President			
1940	177,409	78,656	44.3
1944	149,987	78,983	52.6
1948	6,737	30,826	457.5
1952	160,867	101,694	63.2
1956	123,875	86,366	69.7
1960	331,544	130,233	39.2
U. S. Senator			
1950	63,995	35,018	54.7
1956	170,164	94,033	55.2
1958	133,413	80,809	60.5
1962	180,379	87,071	48.2
Governor			
1950	77,078	42,197	54.7
1954	118,273	63,471	53.6
1958	177,998	87,399	49.1
1962	106,738	73,316	68.7
Mayor			
1951	124,680	43,518	34.3
1955	132,706	68,866	51.9
1959	208,406	85,174	40.9
1963	69,310	85,214	123.0
City Controller			
1949	111,404	33,169	29.8
1957	77,523	50,544	65.2
1961	56,581	61,033	107.9

SOURCE: Compiled from data in *Annual Report of the Registration Commission* for the City of Philadelphia, 1954-1962; also *Pennsylvania Manual*, various years.

leadership has been more sympathetic to this goal than the Republicans.[20]

[20] This drive for integrated housing has met with some opposition in the so-called "white wards," and they have tended to vote Republican in recent elections.

In order to increase the educational opportunities of the Negro population of Philadelphia there has been a concerted drive to transfer Negro pupils to predominantly white schools. This drive has taken the form of transferring Negro pupils to white schools by school buses. The policy has been opposed by the Republican leaders in Philadelphia as the wrong approach to the improvement of educational opportunities for the Negro.[21] At present there seems to be little likelihood that the Negro voter in Philadelphia will end his allegiance to the Democratic party until the Negro feels that the Republican party will offer at least an equal opportunity for the Negro to improve his economic status.

(3) Government jobs. The Democratic administration in Philadelphia has been especially active since 1951 in providing jobs for Negroes in the city government. No published figures are available, but it has been estimated that Negroes hold from 8,000 to 10,000 jobs in the Philadelphia city government.[22] In addition, the Democratic Governors of Pennsylvania from 1954 to 1962 have appointed Negroes to positions in the various state government agencies. Since 1960 a similar policy has been pursued by the Kennedy and Johnson administrations in Washington. The net effect of these policies has been to retain the loyalty of the Negro leaders and their following in Philadelphia.

(4) Public Housing. The Negro housing situation in Philadelphia is one of the blights of the city. Since improved public housing has been initiated under national Democratic administrations, there is a belief among Philadelphia Negroes that the Democratic party is more committed to a policy of improved public housing than is the Republican party. The advances in public housing under the Eisenhower administration did not materially change this attitude among Negroes in Philadelphia.

(5) Civil Rights. Rightly or wrongly, the Negroes in Philadelphia seem to feel that the Democratic party is the best hope for the improvement of civil rights. In recent years this issue has become a very emotional one in Philadelphia. The Negro leaders

---

[21] James T. McDermott, the Republican candidate for mayor in 1963, publicly opposed the policy of "busing" Negro pupils to white schools. He believed it was a sounder policy to improve the Negro schools and their facilities.

[22] An attempt was made by certain Negro leaders to secure an actual census of Negro jobholders in the city government, but such a census was refused on the ground that color is not included in job applications.

of Philadelphia are determined to secure full civil rights in housing, in schools, and in jobs. Until the Republican party in Philadelphia is able to convince the Negro voter on the issue of civil rights, there is little chance that the Republican party can make any headway among the Negro voters.

(6) "Writing off the Negro Vote." There was a definite feeling among the Negro leadership in the mayoralty campaign of 1963 that the Republican party had "written off the Negro vote."[23] This belief, whether it had a logical basis or not, tended to strengthen the Negro support behind the Democrats. The Republican candidate for mayor in 1963, James T. McDermott, vigorously denied the allegation that the Republican party had "written off the Negro vote."[24] He asserted that the issues in the campaign were political bossism and political corruption, and that local economic conditions were dominant in the campaign.

The Future

The issues of political bossism, political corruption, or inept municipal leadership have not been effective in winning the Negro voter to the Republican side in Philadelphia. Nor are they likely to do so in the immediate future unless these issues become far more explosive. The Negro in Philadelphia has a much greater identity with the national Democratic party and its leaders than it does with the local Democratic leaders. The Negro wards will, in my opinion, continue to stick with the Democratic party in Philadelphia until there is a material improvement in the economic position of the Negro; until the Negro feels that equal job opportunities are his; until housing is improved substantially; until educational opportunities and facilities are equal; in other words, until the Negro is convinced that he is guaranteed all his rights by both parties, not by word alone but by performance. Emotions may govern his political behavior, but he is convinced that the Democratic party offers him the realization of his hopes. This, in essence, is the challenge that confronts the Republican party in Philadelphia.

[23] This was one of the reasons given by Cecil B. Moore of the Philadelphia NAACP for his support of the Democratic candidate for mayor in 1963.
[24] It is of interest that a Republican candidate for the state General Assembly from an almost 100% "white ward" in a conversation with me stated that: "When a voter asked him how he should vote, he replied, 'Vote white.'"

BUSINESS THOROUGHFARES AS EXPRESSIONS OF URBAN NEGRO CULTURE

Allan Pred

Mr. Pred, who recently received his doctorate from the University of Chicago, is Assistant Professor of Geography at the University of California, Berkeley.

An engulfing wave of cacophonous sound: from jazz and swinging syncopations blaring-pulsating over loudspeakers recessed in the interiors of bars, liquor stores and record shops; from a shabbily dressed pseudo-blind mendicant, rhythmically shaking his collection box, repeatedly droning out his life song in rasping tones—"I beat the devil runnin' and I'm so glad"; from sidewalk chatterers, the hat-crowned idle and unemployed in front of billiard parlors and barbershops; the shoppers and merchants going about their business; from the agonizing roar of the rapid transit overhead; from the honking, crowded traffic.

A dazzling montage of contrasting colors: melanous folk, ebony, bronze and tan; golden toreador slacks clinging closely to an undulating frame; sport shirts ablaze with fiery versions of every spectral hue; automobiles reflecting their turquoise-crimson-fuchsia tones on sunlit shopwindows; garish signs and window paintings fronting loan banks, fundamentalist churches and unctuous eateries.

A melange of confusing odors emanating from open-doored markets and establishments; smoky-stuffiness from pool rooms and "recreation parlors;" the penetrating fumes of frying oil and "mumbo" sauce from makeshift dining places; alcoholic aromas expiring from beneath bloodshot, hungry-looking eyes.

THUS one may impressionistically describe the commercial complex in Chicago's "Black Belt" on 47th Street, between Cottage Grove Avenue on the east and State Street on the west. Yet to think of this business street, or similar streets in other urban Negro communities, solely in such terms is to fall victim to stereotypes and to ignore features which are common to all commercial areas.

THE NATURE OF THE STUDY

As the "principal business thoroughfare" or "neighborhood business street"[1] is the center of human activity in any residential area its land use patterns of store types provide a telescoped expression of the material features of culture[2] and an ideal basis for comparing such features from community to community.

Contrasts between the commercial land uses of a city's residential areas are likely to be most striking when they are between those of the slum areas and other areas. Whether dealing with the "Black Belt" of Chicago, the Arab quarter of Marseilles, the rocky ridges overlooking Rio de Janeiro's business district, the maze of makeshift structures lying at the periphery of Calcutta, or the slum area of any contemporary

---

[1] Proudfoot defined principal business thoroughfares and neighborhood business streets in terms of store types, vehicular traffic, and customer origins. See Malcolm J. Proudfoot, "City Retail Structure," *Econ. Geog.*, Vol. 13, 1937, p. 427.
Urban commercial concentrations occurring in residential areas are also referred to as "string-streets" or "business ribbons." See Brian J. L. Berry, "Ribbon Developments in the Urban Business Pattern," *Annals Assn. Amer. Geogrs.*, Vol. 49, 1959, p. 149.

[2] The relationship between the distribution of store types in a residential area and the "psychology" of its inhabitants has been considered by French sociologists, amongst others. For example, see P.-H. Chombart de Lauwe, et. al., *Paris et L'Agglomération Parisienne*, Presses Universitaires de France, Paris, 1952, Vol. I, pp. 142–145, and Vol. II, pp. 66–73.

metropolis, one is usually speaking of an area whose population is not completely acculturated, not totally assimilated into the prevailing urban way of life.

Even in those instances where a great proportion of the slum population has been in residence for a considerable period of time, rather than being of recent in-migrant status, the daily pattern of existence in the slum is one which, in varying degrees, normally manifests some vestiges of a sub-culture or way of life which is foreign to the particular city—whether the sub-culture in question be that of a nearby rural area, of another section of the country, or of another land. This being the case, it is to be expected that these sub-cultural differences will find some expression in patterns of consumer behavior and thereby be reflected in the land use structure of the slum's principal business thoroughfare or market.

The main body of this paper is devoted to investigating, comparing, and contrasting the business thoroughfare land use patterns—as external expressions of culture—of a Chicago Negro area and two nearby white areas. The primary objective is to establish those phenomena which distinguish the commercial land uses of the urban Negro sub-culture, and to determine what factors underlie their differences. In a broader sense, the paper may be viewed as a case study of the slum as a mirror of other sub-cultures. Its approach is perhaps also of some importance to the even more general problem of categorizing subjective field observations.

Numerous drawbacks and problems are inherent in the approach and objectives of this study. Previous works on the American Negro written by geographers are strikingly small in number and provide no methodological assistance. Four articles have considered different spatial and temporal variations in the distribution of Negro population in the United States.[3] Hart's note on a Negro resort area in Michigan makes passing references to commercial establishments.[4] An article by Nelson contains a short note on the distribution of Negroes in cities of different service classifications.[5]

The type of data being dealt with, namely store-front characteristics, and the necessity of compartmentalizing this data into a few categories, presents a considerable problem. In striving to capture outward expressions of culture in the urban landscape, one must group and classify data which are essentially subjective, impressionistic, raw, and unrefined. Consequently, in the initial stages of investigation it is difficult to avoid making some highly arbitrary decisions which, in the end, may or may not prove to be inconsistent. Only after considerable field work does it become even remotely possible to establish more precisely defined categories which, though still subjective to some degree, are yet capable of lending themselves to statistical analysis.

An additional obstacle is that of avoiding stereotypes in attempting to explain the presence or absence of given phenomena in Negro areas. Of particular complexity is the problem of distinguishing between phenomena which

---

[3] Wesley Calef and Howard Nelson, "Distribution of Negro Population in the United States," *Geogr. Rev.*, Vol. 46, 1955, pp. 147–168; J. Fraser Hart, "The Changing Distribution of the American Negro," *Annals Assn. of Amer. Geogrs.*, Vol. 50, 1960, pp. 242–266; James F. Woodruff, "Some Characteristics of the Alabama Slave Population in 1850," *Geogr. Rev.*, Vol. 52, 1962, pp. 379–388; and Richard Hartshorne, "Racial Maps of the United States," *Geogr. Rev.*, Vol. 28, 1938, pp. 276–288.

[4] J. Fraser Hart, "A Rural Retreat for Negroes," *Geogr. Rev.*, Vol. 50, 1960, pp. 147–168.

[5] Howard Nelson, "Some Characteristics of the Population of Cities in Similar Service Classifications," *Econ. Geog.*, Vol. 33, 1957, pp. 95–108.

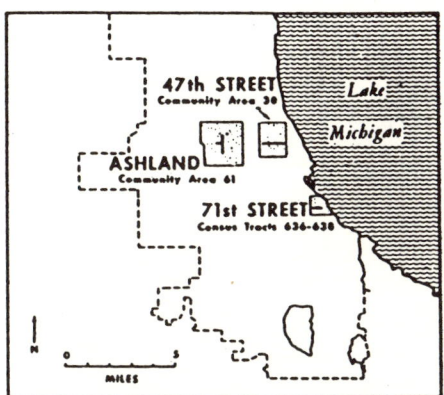

Fig. 1. Location of selected areas of study in Chicago.

are "typical" of Negro areas in general, those which are "typical" of low income Negro areas, and those which are "typical" of all areas that are inhabited by a population of low socio-economic status. However, the desire to avoid stereotypes should not be overdone since, through the research of competent sociologists, many widely held preconceptions have been proven to be reasonably accurate for certain Negro economic classes and personality types.[6]

Areas of Study and Land Use Categories

At one time it could be said that "The present shopping center of the [Chicago] Negro community is 47th Street, having moved south through the years from 35th Street until it is now at the center of density of the 'Black Belt.' On this street is the largest retail business owned and operated by Negroes."[7] A portion of this street, between Cottage Grove on the east and State on the west, serves as the focal point of this study (Fig. 1). Forty-seventh Street is the most important commerical ribbon development in Chicago Community Area 38.[8] That 47th Street still maintains its position of primacy within the "Black Belt" is highly dubious. In 1954, the retail sales volume of the commercial complex on 63rd Street, between Stony Island and Cottage Grove, was at least eight times that of the 47th Street strip.[9] However, the 47th Street ribbon actually extends considerably east of Cottage Grove, meaning that its total retail sales volume is actually larger than that indicated in available sources, and the clientele on 63rd Street is not as overwhelmingly composed of Negroes as that of the 47th Street complex. While 47th Street may not be the most important ribbon development in the entire "Black Belt," there is no disputing that it is the principal business thoroughfare of a community inhabited by well over 100,000 Negroes (Table I).

Two relatively nearby business thoroughfares in white communities were selected for examination and comparison. One of these comprises a segment of Ashland, from 46th Street on the north to 51st Street on the south, as well as another portion of 47th Street which runs from Ashland on the east to Wood on the west (Fig. 1). This is

---

[6] Perhaps the most significant of such works is the dated, but still relevant, investigation made by Warner and his associates: W. Lloyd Warner, Buford H. Junker, and Walter A. Adams, *Color and Human Nature*, Washington, D.C., 1941. This study, based on over 5,000 interviews of Chicago Negroes, delineates behavioral tendencies for 16 "social personality types" of each sex. "Social personality types" were defined in terms of the individual's "degree of Negroidness" and social status within the Negro community.

[7] St. Clair Drake, *Churches and Voluntary Associations in the Chicago Negro Community*, Works Projects Administration No. 3, Chicago, 1940, p. 179. (Mimeographed.)
[8] The selection of business thoroughfares was facilitated through the use of two sources: Paul M. Hauser and Evelyn Kitagawa, *Local Community Fact Book for Chicago*, Chicago Community Inventory, Chicago, 1957; and Evelyn Kitagawa and De Ver Sholes, *Chicagoland's Retail Market*, Chicago Association of Commerce and Industry, and Chicago Community Inventory, Chicago, 1957.
[9] Kitagawa and Sholes, *op. cit.*, pp. 11 and 81.

TABLE I
POPULATION AND INCOME CHARACTERISTICS OF SELECTED AREAS IN 1950[a]

	Community area 38 (47th Street)		Community area 61 (Ashland)		Census tracts 636–638 (71st Street)	
	Number	Per cent	Number	Per cent	Number	Per cent
Total population..................	114,557	100.0	75,917	100.0	18,056	100.0
Native white.....................	892	0.8	62,947	83.0	[b]	.....
Foreign born white................	183	0.2	12,829[c]	16.9	[b]	.....
Negro...........................	113,374	98.9	112	0.1	0	0.0
Median family income (dollars).....	2,527		3,727		6,000	
Land area (sq. miles).............	1.76		5.0		0.5	
Length of business thoroughfare (miles)..	1.0		0.9		0.5	

[a] Sources: *Local Community Fact Book for Chicago, op. cit.*, pp. 158–161, 178–181, and 250–253; and *Chicagoland's Retail Market, op. cit.*, pp. 55, 81 and 125.
[b] Not available.
[c] Of which 5416 were Poles, and nearly 3000 of other Slavic nationalities.

the largest commercial development in Chicago Community Area 61—an area which is dominated by Poles and other Slavic groups.[10] This business development serves as an almost ideal basis for comparison, since the income level of the community area which it dominates is extremely low for a white residential area.

The other white community business thoroughfare is located in a middle-class neighborhood on 71st Street, between Jeffrey on the west and South Shore Drive on the east (Fig. 1). This is the most important business thoroughfare in census tracts 636–638, which are in Chicago Community Area 43. Because of the much higher income level in this Community Area, the contrasts between it and the Negro area are much more glaring than those between the low-income Ashland complex and the Negro area.

Preliminary mapping of land uses on each of the thoroughfares was carried out by using the personal service, business service, and retail categories set forth in the Census of Business. The result was a land use map showing no less than 65 commercial and professional

[10] Hauser and Kitagawa, *op. cit.*, p. 205.

uses; it is of little value because of its complexity and consequent inability adequately to show the areal differences which were so apparent in the field. After some hesitation and deliberation the diverse uses were subjectively classified into four major categories: (A) those uses which appeared to be more characteristic of, although not necessarily unique to, the Negro area; (B) those uses which appeared to be most characteristic of low-income area business thoroughfares; (C) those uses which were common to all three areas; and (D) those uses which appeared to be more characteristic of, although not necessarily unique to, white areas. A not inconsiderable number of uses were left uncategorized because of their rare occurrence or other complicating factors. In no case was there any possibility that the unclassified use was one unique to 47th Street.

The difficulties in distinguishing between the four major categories, and particularly between the first two, were often quite intricate and involved. It is no mean task to distinguish that which is "typical" of a Negro area and its culture from that which is "typical" of low socio-economic areas; consequently the decisions made are to some degree at variance with one another. The following two examples may be given:—(1) Bars were found to be of approximately the same relative frequency on both 47th Street and in the Ashland complex, and were consequently classified in the second category, namely most characteristic of low income area business thoroughfares. This was done despite the fact that the bars in the two neighborhoods present a totally different appearance to the observer in the field. Bars in the white area have, more often than not, a very unimposing

FIG. 2. A Negro bar on 47th Street.

exterior which tends to give an impression that very little is going on inside. In contrast, those in the Negro area tend to exude a character which is distinctly their own—music blasting from an open doorway, an off-beat name, and a window cluttered with colors and advertisements (Fig. 2). (2) Dry cleaning and other "valet" services are striking in their number and unimpressive appearance on 47th Street, and for this reason were classified as more "typical" of the Negro area. However, it is questionable whether this land use reflects an aspect of urban Negro culture (something inherent to the Negro's self-directed pattern of existence) or an aspect of the limited economic horizons of a large proportion of the urban Negro population (an externally imposed characteristic). On the one hand, there is some evidence that certain Negro personality types are quite concerned with personal appearance,[11] whereas, on the other hand, it has been shown that this business type attracts Negro investors because it does not require a large capital outlay.[12]

MORE CHARACTERISTICALLY NEGRO LAND USES

The land uses in this category (which are summarized in Table II and Figures 3 and 4), presumably distinguish the low-income Negro area business thoroughfare from all other residential area business thoroughfares in Chicago. In addition, it may be anticipated that these land uses occur frequently in low-income Negro communities in other American cities.

Beauty parlors and barbershops are the most frequently occurring store-front phenomena on 47th Street, between Cottage Grove and State. The beauty shops (which are twice as common as the barbershops) are generally drab in appearance though they are occasionally distinguished by their exotic names, such as "Tropical Beauty Nook," "The Treasure Chest," "Sarah's Beauty Box." The barbershops are typified by a somewhat neater appearance, by small groups of men idling outside, and by the presence of additional functions such as bail bonding and shoeshining. If undocumented sources are correct, these shops also serve as "fronts" for the negotiation of various illegal activities. The high rate of occurrence of beauty parlors and barbershops seems to be attributable to at least two factors.

[11] Warner, et. al., op. cit., pp. 65–66.
[12] E. Franklin Frazier, "Negro Harlem: An Ecological Study," Amer. Journ. Sociology, Vol. 43, 1937, p. 87.

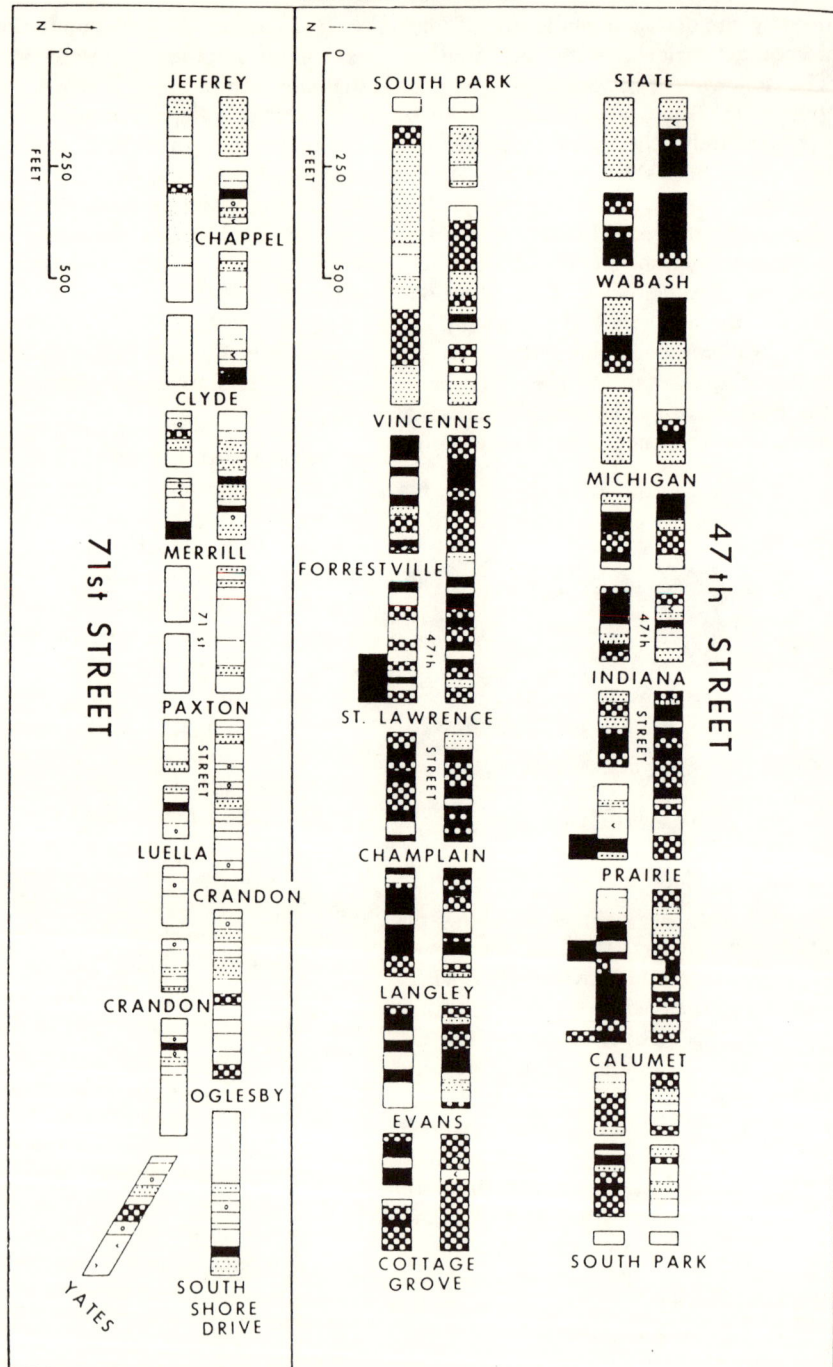

Fig. 3. Commercial land uses on 47th Street (low-income Negro) and 71st Street (middle-class white). The key to the land uses is given in Figure 4.

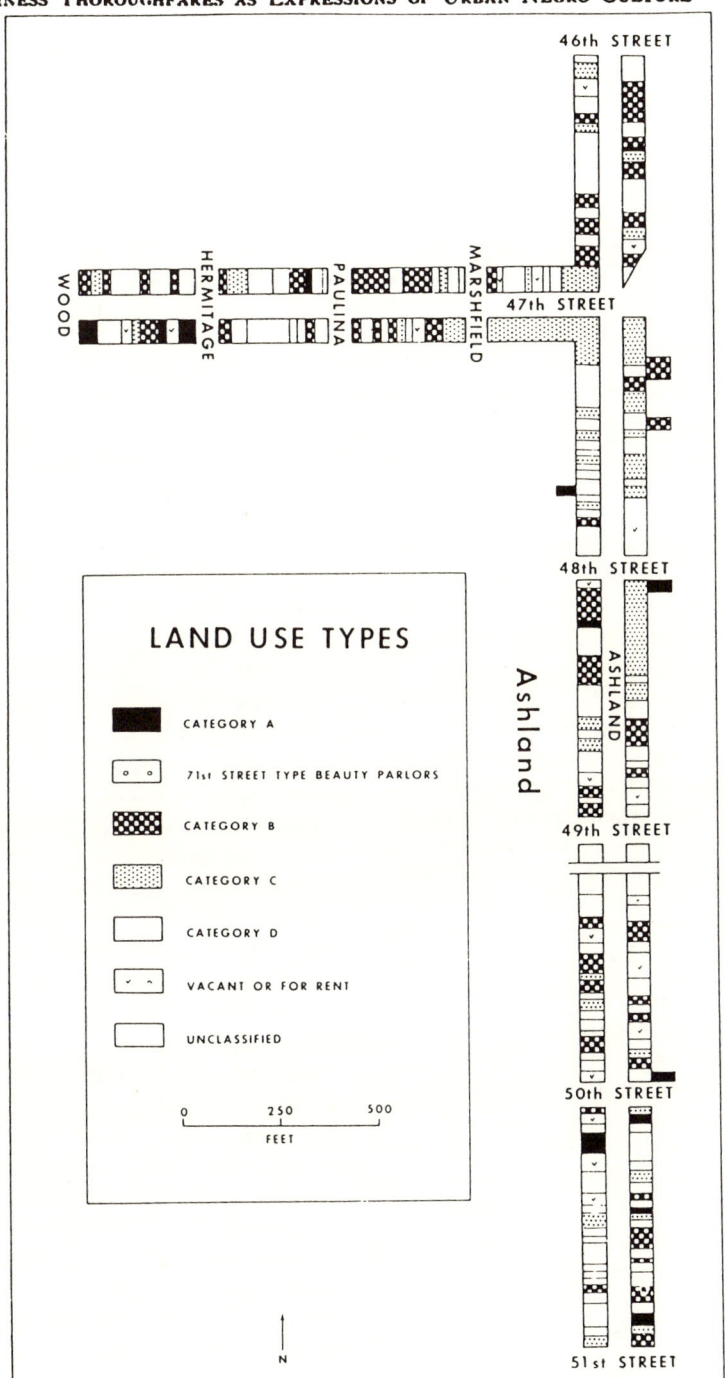

FIG. 4. Commercial land uses in the Ashland complex (low-income white).

TABLE II
DISTRIBUTION OF LAND USES IN CATEGORY A: MORE CHARACTERISTIC OF 47TH STREET

	47th Street		Ashland		71st Street	
	Number	Per cent	Number	Per cent	Number	Per cent
Total store-fronts....................	343	100.0	250	100.0	165	100.0
Total in Category A...................	132	38.7	17	6.8	31	18.8
Beauty parlors and barbershops.........	37	10.8	4	1.6	14	8.5
Dry cleaners and other "valet" services...	31	9.1	4	1.6	12	7.3
Tailor-made men's clothing	6	1.7	0	0.0	0	0.0
Disassociated uses	16	4.7	1	0.4	0	0.0
Independent groceries..................	17	5.0	5	2.0	4	2.4
Billiard parlors.......................	9	2.7	0	0.0	0	0.0
Record stores.........................	7	2.0	2	0.8	1	0.6
Store-front churches and spiritual consultants................................	9	2.7	1	0.4	0	0.0

First, the stereotype of the Negro's concern about the woolly or "kinky" quality of his hair is apparently true for certain Negro economic groups and personality types.[13] This is substantiated by advertisements for "hair processing" which appear in the majority of establishments, and by the fact that expenditure for barbershop and beauty parlor services, at given income levels, have been found to be "somewhat higher for Negro than white families in urban areas."[14] Second, these businesses fall into Frazier's category of "personal services" which attract Negro investors because of the absence of any need to make large capital outlays.[15] However, because of the first factor this commercial land-use type may be considered a reflection of a segment of urban Negro culture.

It is evident, from Table II, that beauty parlors and barbershops have a relatively high rate of incidence on the middle-class white business thoroughfare (71st Street). There is, however, such a distinct contrast in physical appearance between the shops on 47th

[13] Warner, et. al., op. cit., passim; and J. T. Johnson, The Potential Negro Market, New York, 1952, pp. 37 and 158.
[14] Richard Steiner, The Negro's Share, New York, 1943, p. 142.
[15] Ibid.

Street and 71st Street that there is no need to question the misleading nature of the comparative percentages shown in the table for this phenomenon. Beauty parlors on both the white commercial streets present a very aseptic exterior, whereas those on 47th Street are usually located in obviously decrepit quarters (Fig. 5).

The frequency of dry-cleaning and associated valet service establishments on 47th Street has already been mentioned. In addition to a more frequent occurrence, particularly in comparison with the low-income white Ashland complex, dry cleaning establishments on 47th Street have an external aspect which clearly sets them apart from their counterparts on 71st Street and on Ashland. These establishments are generally unimposing, often to the point of being rundown, and perform additional valet functions, usually hat blocking (Fig. 6). As previously indicated, the number of valet services on 47th Street may or may not be a reflection of the concern for personal appearance held by certain Negro personality types. To the extent that this concern for personal appearance may be held responsible, the frequent occurrence of valet services may be considered as a component of urban Negro culture.

Stores selling tailor-made men's clothing were found to be unique to 47th Street. An explanation for this stems partly from the fact that Negroes "may attach more importance than whites to clothing,"[16] and from the fact that some male Negroes, particularly those of darker skin in the lower income classes, are inclined to be "flashy" in dress.[17] Because of this factor, custom-made men's clothing stores may be considered along with beauty parlors, barbershops, and valet service establishments as a single sub-category—all three uses being, to some extent, a response to the needs of different Negro personality types who are in one way or another concerned with personal appearance.

The next two land uses which are more characteristic of 47th Street may also be grouped into a sub-category, insofar as they both mirror extremely low economic conditions. The first is the not uncommonly occurring group of disassociated uses within one store possessing a single entrance. The following are but a few examples of the combinations which are to be encountered on 47th Street: record shop and beauty parlor, radio-TV repairs and

[16] Sterner, *op. cit.*, pp. 137–138.
[17] Warner, *et. al.*, *op. cit.*, pp. 65–66.

FIG. 6. A dry cleaning establishment with additional valet services on 47th Street.

shoe repairs, barbershop, and insurance agent, and barbershop and billiard hall. On the side streets off 47th Street, the juxtaposed uses are sometimes even more bizarre: a "restaurant" and coal-hauling service, a sandwich shop and extermination service, for example. These combinations are apparently related to the marginal character of some of the businesses and the inability of most of the businessmen involved to bring in enough revenue to pay rentals by themselves.

The second store-type in this sub-category is that run by the independent grocer or food merchant. The profusion of these stores (which often stay open 24 hours per day) is presumably a reflection of the willingness of many Negroes to pay high prices on credit, rather than lower prices in cash at large chain stores. Independent groceries on 47th Street, and their less numerous Ashland counterparts, may be distinguished by certain items which they carry. Neck bones or chicken necks are the most conspicuously-advertised items to be found in 47th Street groceries or butcher shops; they contrast starkly with the choice meats, poultry and sea food displayed in 71st Street butcher-shop windows. Other food consumption patterns of low-income urban Negroes also determine the merchandise

FIG. 5. A billiard parlor and beauty parlor (right, partially obscured) on 47th Street.

carried by independent grocers (for example, turnip greens and other leafy, green, and yellow vegetables).[18] However, as such commodities are not prominently advertised or arranged in store windows, they do not make an impact upon the urban landscape and are not, therefore, of such interest as the more obviously displayed items. In speaking of such "interesting differences" in food consumption, Myrdal points out that: "One may call these . . . differences 'cultural,' but that does not mean that they have nothing to do with economics. In part they may depend on traditions from a time when the Negro's economic conditions were different. In part they may depend on circumstances inherent in the Negro's present economic status."[19]

The remaining land uses which are more characteristic of 47th Street all conform in some way to stereotypes commonly held by various segments of the American white population. Although Table II shows billiard parlors to be unique to 47th Street, such establishments are occasionally encountered in white communities. However, 47th Street's preponderance of these "recreation centers" (and the groups of milling men in their interiors) would, at first sight, seem to confirm the stereotype of the Negro as idle and "shiftless." Obviously, if the stereotype is accurate in any way it does not apply to Negroes as a group, but only to poolroom "hangabouts" and other unemployed types. Once again we are confronted by the question of whether a particular land use reflects an aspect of urban Negro culture (something inherent in the Negro's self-directed pattern of existence) or an aspect of the limited economic horizons of the urban Negro population (an externally imposed characteristic). More specifically, the question to be answered in this instance is whether or not the relatively high frequency of billiard parlors is attributable to the inherent "shiftlessness" of the Negro or to the high rate of unemployment amongst Negro males, the latter being a condition often externally imposed directly via the color line in some firms and occupations, and indirectly by restricted educational opportunities.

The record shop is not an unusual sight on 47th Street (Fig. 7), whereas its infrequent occurrence on Ashland

FIG. 7. A record shop on 47th Street.

or 71st Street is rarely if ever characterized by jazz music blaring from an open doorway. Because of their numbers, these shops could conceivably serve as a prop for the popular image of the Negro as a happy-go-lucky, carefree, music-loving individual. Yet the greater frequency of such stores on 47th Street would give little credence to this stereotype, even if it could be shown that the per capita dollar sales significantly exceed those of the smaller number of shops in the less densely-populated white areas.[20] If any explanation is to

---

[18] See the discussion of Negro food consumption patterns in Sterner, *op. cit.*, pp. 102–127.
[19] Gunnar Myrdal, *An American Dilemma*, New York, 1942, Vol. I, p. 372.

[20] It has been established that certain racial differences in phonograph ownership exist, with a higher percentage of Negroes in comparable income groups owning such appliances. Sterner, *op. cit.*, p. 159.

be found for this phenomenon it probably lies within the subtle and complex intricacies of the Negro's cultural heritage,[21] and not within the stereotyped happy-go-lucky, carefree personality. Regardless of the underlying explanation, the noisy record shop is one of the most singular characteristics of the low-income urban Negro business thoroughfare.

The presence of store-front churches and spiritual consultants on 47th Street may be interpreted by some as an affirmation of the Negro's basically simple, if somewhat "primitive," spiritual needs. Again this is a generalization which lacks validity because it looks at Negroes as a single group rather than as a vast complex of personality types. As a rule, the store-front churches cater to first-generation migrants from the South. "The denominational churches do not always offer to the migrant the satisfaction which he found in the Church of the South. The store-front church comes into existence as a result of an effort to maintain the face-to-face relationships of the South."[22] The store-front church is not as common on 47th Street as it is on less intensely-developed business thoroughfares, since the distribution of such churches is intimately related to the availability of cheap rentals.[23] In accordance with this fact, several of these fundamentalist churches were to be seen on the unmapped side streets, off 47th Street, where rents are naturally somewhat cheaper.

LAND USES MORE CHARACTERISTIC OF LOW-INCOME AREA BUSINESS THOROUGHFARES

In some respects, these uses are of greater interest than those in the previous category, in that their near-equal rate of occurrence on the low-income Negro and low-income white thoroughfares aids in dispelling certain widely-held and preconceived notions of Negro behavior. On the other hand, similar frequencies of given land uses are sometimes misleading because their form and function are far from being coincident on the two thoroughfares. Therefore, it may be argued that some of these uses, once they had been more rigorously defined, could be placed in the previous category, because they reflect certain aspects of urban Negro culture and because they create a singular sense impression to the field observer.

The dingy-looking restaurant or eating place, often referred to in the vernacular as a "greasy spoon," is a commonplace on 47th Street and in the Ashland complex. Though establishments on both streets specialize in cheap foods, there are some important distinctions to be noted. Stores on Ashland have a pronounced tendency to deal in such items as hamburgers, fountain orders, and frankfurters. A few of the more decrepit-looking places on Ashland sell pizza. The menu listings on 47th Street are more often characterized by such items as fried or barbecued chicken (the acrid-odored barbecue sauce is often referred to as "mumbo" sauce in window advertisements), pigs' ears, and frog legs. It is to be recalled that Myrdal pointed out that such dietary discrepancies may be thought of as "cultural," although this does not mean that they are divorced from economic factors. In the light of these differences, as well as of the dismal aura of most of the Negro eating places, it should be recognized that a stricter definition of terms can permit the reclassification,

[21] See Melville J. Hershkovits' discussion in *The Myth of the Negro Past*, New York, 1941, pp. 261–269.
[22] E. Franklin Frazier, *The Negro Family in Chicago*, Chicago, 1932, p. 113.
[23] Drake, *op. cit.*, p. 300.

TABLE III

DISTRIBUTION OF LAND USES IN CATEGORY B: MORE CHARACTERISTIC
OF LOW-INCOME AREA BUSINESS THOROUGHFARES

	47th Street		Ashland		71st Street	
	Number	Per cent	Number	Per cent	Number	Per cent
Total store-fronts..................	343	100.0	250	100.0	165	100.0
Total in Category B................	86	25.0	53	21.2	6	3.6
Cheap restaurants..................	20	5.8	13	5.2	2	1.2
Bars...............................	19	5.5	14	5.6	2	1.2
Liquor stores......................	13	3.8	5	2.0	2	1.2
Loan and pawn establishments.......	8	2.3	7	2.8	0	0.0
Shops advertising credit............	26	7.6	14	5.6	0	0.0

into Category A, of most of the dining establishments on 47th Street.

The large number of bars and liquor stores on 47th Street might be offered as a substantiation of the argument that a high percentage of Negroes are large consumers of alcohol. However, Table III shows that there is approximately the same percentage of bars on the commercial streets of the low-income Slavic neighborhood. Of course, one bar on Ashland is not necessarily the equivalent of one bar on 47th Street, though in fact, the numbers in attendance at 47th Street drinking places might serve to reinforce arguments concerning Negro alcoholism. In any case, the obvious differences in external appearance between bars on 47th Street and those on Ashland have already been brought to light (Fig. 2). The sedate appearance of the two 71st Street drinking places offers an even more striking contrast. These visual differences once again demonstrate that a more precise definition, which would distinguish between bar types, could allow for the reclassification of most of the drinking establishments on 47th Street into Category A.

Loan offices or loan "banks," and pawnshops are scattered along both low-income area business thoroughfares at about the same frequency. Loan establishments on Ashland are usually operated on a cash on interest basis, whereas stores on 47th Street are usually of the variety which exchange cash for material articles. Here it might prove rather difficult to reclassify establishment types in order to identify those which are more typical of 47th Street, since both varieties (pawnshops and loan offices) are present on each of the low-income area streets. However, it is likely that a detailed inventory of the items pawned on 47th Street would differ significantly from one for those pawned on Ashland. Regardless of the outcome of such an inventory, the fact to be re-emphasized is that a profusion of loan and pawn establishments is not peculiar to Negro areas.

Likewise, the credit sign is by no means unique to Negro business thoroughfares. If establishments, regardless of type, offering credit do not form as high a proportion of the total number of store-fronts on Ashland as on 47th Street, they still make a very noticeable impression. On Ashland, credit signs most often appear in stores selling higher-priced items, such as jewelry shops and appliance stores. On 47th Street, credit signs are apt to be in the windows of stores selling items in all price ranges, though they appear with the greatest consistency in shops which sell clothing. Without drawing any further conclusions concerning the relative occurrence of credit signs on the two business thoroughfares, it is to be observed that, in a business development which caters to neighborhood clientele, there is no reason to conclude that the absence of a credit sign in a given establishment means that there is no credit offered there. Similarly, the total absence of credit signs on 71st Street does not mean that none of the establishments there offers credit.

No attempt was made to quantify another characteristic which is common to both low-income area business thoroughfares, namely, shops which are in various states of delapidation. The feeling here was that impulse rather than reason was likely to reign in making decisions with regard to such a highly-subjective question.

LAND USES COMMON TO ALL THREE BUSINESS THOROUGHFARES

The land uses in this category (which are summarized in Table IV and Figures 3 and 4), were found to be ubiquitous in business thoroughfares located in all community areas, regardless of racial composition or socio-economic level. They thereby presumably support the contention that there are features which are commonplace to all urban commercial areas. Yet, even in this category, there are establishment types for which there exists a distinct possibility that a redefinition of terms would result in their reclassification into one of the first two categories.

Some independent corner drug stores tend to differ in appearance from one business thoroughfare to the next, whereas the chain drug stores have a fairly uniform appearance regardless of location. Drug stores situated on 47th Street are sometimes in a more run-down state (Fig. 8), and are often a little more blatant in conveying the fact that they carry alcoholic beverages. Therefore, if drug stores are differentiated into subtypes a few additions could be made to Category A. Whether these distinctive drug stores are a result of external economic forces, of traits inherent in urban Negro culture, or of some other factors is not easily established.

Shoe stores, on both 47th Street and Ashland, on occasion advertise extremely cheap merchandise with such signs as "2 Pair for $5." Clearly, such shops could have been reclassified into Category B. In addition, some of the styles displayed in 47th Street shoe

TABLE IV
DISTRIBUTION OF LAND USES IN CATEGORY C: COMMON TO ALL THREE BUSINESS THOROUGHFARES

	47th Street		Ashland		71st Street	
	Number	Per cent	Number	Per cent	Number	Per cent
Total store-fronts....................	343	100.0	250	100.0	165	100.0
Total in Category C..................	58	17.3	46	18.4	26	15.6
Miscellaneous business services[a].........	12	3.5	11	4.4	8	4.8
Jewelers and optometrists[b].............	15	4.4	15	6.0	5	3.0
Shoe stores........................	15	4.4	14	5.6	6	3.6
Corner drug stores...................	9	2.7	2	0.8	4	2.4
Automatic laundromats................	4	1.2	3	1.2	2	1.2
Gas stations........................	3	0.9	1	0.4	1	0.6

[a] Currency exchanges, realtors, insurance agencies, etc.
[b] Often found in conjunction.

store windows are quite distinctive. Once again they may be interpreted as being demonstrative of the inclination which some Negro personality types have to be "flashy" in dress.

At least two other major features were found to be common to all three commercial thoroughfares. One such feature was the second-story professional office of doctors, dentists, and lawyers. The second phenomenon was a decrease in the intensity of use of space toward the periphery of each business thoroughfare. General concepts of land economics would point to the

FIG. 8. A drug store on 47th Street.

expectation of this second feature; consequently there is no necessity for considering the deterioration of use on the margin of the 47th Street complex as a possible concomitant of urban Negro culture. The remaining land uses in Table IV appear to show no significant variations from one business street to the next and, therefore, require no interpretation.

LAND USES MORE CHARACTERISTIC OF BUSINESS THOROUGHFARES IN WHITE AREAS

The land uses in this category (which are summarized in Table V and Figures 3 and 4), are presumably more representative of Ashland and 71st Street, that is, of white areas regardless of socio-economic composition.

A relatively low percentage, or total absence, of women's apparel shops, which are neither run-down nor display credit signs in their shop windows, could probably be pointed to as another singular characteristic of the low-income urban Negro business thoroughfare, but the origin of this phenomenon appears to be economic rather than cultural. The better women's shops on 47th Street are not unlike those on 71st Street and Ashland, save for the frequent occurrence of credit signs in their windows. Such signs are certainly not manifestations of sub-cultural traits; and, as already mentioned, the absence of a credit sign in a white neighborhood shop does not preclude the possibility that credit is given.

The small number of confectionaries, cigar stores, florists, gift shops, and miscellaneous specialized-retail establishments on 47th Street could also be interpreted as being peculiar to the low-income urban Negro shopping street. In this instance, the peculiarity may be, at least in part, attributable to sub-cultural differences, especially since there are some noticeable differences between the merchandise lines carried in the few shops on 47th Street and those on the two white thoroughfares. Differences in general appearance, however, would suggest that economic factors, including consumer buying power, are also at work. Clearly, if such establishments are to be used for describing differences in the urban landscape then there again arises the problem of reclassifying land uses on the basis of more precisely-defined terms.

The total absence of stores selling fresh-baked goods on 47th Street is in accord with the observation that Negro homes in general have smaller expenditures for baked goods than "white homes of the corresponding income class."[24] Therefore, assuming that this dearth of bakeries on 47th Street is characteristic of other Negro low-income business thoroughfares, this dietary difference may be thought of as something "cultural."

Although, in all probability, there is some cultural factor underlying the rarity of "presentable" restaurants (or restaurants which have an attractive exterior and serve moderately to expensively priced dinners) on 47th Street, the number of such establishments on all three thoroughfares was so small that it would be foolhardy to draw any conclusions.

It is more than likely that the less intense development of Ashland and 71st Street, as indicated in Table V by the greater preponderance of storefronts which are either vacant or for rent, is not due to any cultural factor, but is instead a result of the fact that these two thoroughfares serve communities which are less-densely populated than 47th Street.

Although they do not belong to this category, unclassified land uses (shown as blank spaces in Figures 3 and 4), merit some discussion. Several of them were arbitrarily left uncategorized; others may well have been placed in Category C; whereas the remainder of omitted uses have little or no bearing on the over-all theme of this paper. Some of the unclassified uses include governmental functions (post offices, military recruiting stations, and police stations), hardware and building materials stores, and furniture and appliance stores which were neither run-down nor outwardly offered credit.

OBSERVATIONS ON A HARLEM STREET

The distinctive character of the low-income Negro business thoroughfare is apparently derived from both the economic and cultural attributes of its customers, that is, the over-all impression created by 47th Street is caused not only by the fact that it is used by Negroes, but also by the fact that it caters to a low-income population. In several instances, it has been rather difficult to choose between the economic and cultural bases of features singular to 47th Street. Therefore, in checking to see whether or not the atmosphere created by the land uses on 47th Street is similar to that of other low-income Negro business thoroughfares in northern cities it is necessary to compare

[24] Sterner, *op. cit.*, p. 105.

TABLE V
DISTRIBUTION OF LAND USES IN CATEGORY D: MORE CHARACTERISTIC OF WHITE AREA BUSINESS THOROUGHFARES

	47th Street		Ashland		71st Street	
	Number	Per cent	Number	Per cent	Number	Per cent
Total store-fronts	343	100.0	250	100.0	165	100.0
Total in Category D	31	9.0	69	27.6	64	38.8
Women's clothing stores (neither run-down nor advertising credit)	14	4.1	22	8.8	31	18.8
Confectionaries, gift shops, florists, cigar stores and related misc. shops	8	2.3	19	7.6	15	9.1
"Presentable" restaurants	1	0.3	2	0.8	6	3.6
Bakeries	0	0.0	6	2.4	3	1.8
Vacant or for rent	8	2.3	20	8.0	9	5.5

TABLE VI
COMPARISON OF LAND USES IN CATEGORIES A AND B ON 47TH STREET (CHICAGO) AND 8TH AVENUE (NEW YORK)

	47th Street		8th Avenue	
	Number	Per cent	Number	Per cent
Total of store-fronts....................	343	100.0	284	100.0
Total in Category A....................	132	38.7	102	35.9
Beauty parlors and barbershops........	37	10.8	34	12.0
Dry cleaners and other "valet" services..	31	9.1	18	6.3
Tailor-made men's clothing............	6	1.7	0	0.0
Disassociated uses....................	16	4.7	12	4.2
Independent groceries.................	17	5.0	26	9.2
Billiard parlors.....................	9	2.7	3	1.1
Record stores.......................	7	2.0	2	0.7
Store-front churches and spiritual consultants........	9	2.7	7	2.5
Total in Category B....................	86	25.0	51	18.3
Cheap restaurants....................	20	5.8	19	6.7
Bars...............................	19	5.5	16	5.6
Liquor stores.......................	13	3.8	6	2.1
Loan and pawn establishments........	8	2.3	5	1.8
Shops advertising credit..............	26	7.6	5	1.8

the frequency of land uses in Category B, as well as in Category A.

Land uses on 8th Avenue (between 125th Street on the south and 135th Street on the north),[25] in the Harlem area of Manhattan were examined and found generally to conform with those on 47th Street (Table VI). Beauty parlors and barbershops, almost without exception, displayed "hair processing" advertisements, were in general somewhat more dilapidated than their "Black Belt" counterparts, and were sometimes found in almost staggering numbers on certain side streets off 8th Avenue (not included in Table VI). Cheap restaurants and bars also had a higher rate of occurrence; and again important distinctions (based on appearance and foods sold) could be made between these establishments and those with similar functions in low-income white neighborhoods. The highly peculiar incidence of store-front churches, as well as of disassociated uses within a single establishment, was nearly equal on the low-income Negro thoroughfares of both Chicago and New York. Tailor-made men's clothing stores did not occur on 8th Avenue, and record stores, liquor stores, and loan and pawn establishments occurred somewhat less frequently there than on 47th Street. As it might be expected that little difference in the frequency of these store types would occur from one low-income Negro business thoroughfare to another (particularly since the rate of occurrence of record shops and tailor-made men's clothing stores on 47th Street was considered to be in some way reflective of urban Negro culture), it should be mentioned that all four of these establishment types are clustered in numbers on 125th Street, and near that street's intersection with 8th Avenue. Billiard parlors and "valet" services also appear less often on 8th Avenue than on 47th Street. No adequate explanation for these differences appears available in either case, although it must be emphasized that a good number

---

[25] The ribbon development along 8th Avenue was selected in preference to that of 125th Street, which is clearly the busiest thoroughfare in Harlem, because the latter has so many uses which are characteristic of an entertainment center.

of the "valet" services on 8th Avenue had the same characteristics as those on 47th Street; that is, they were generally run-down and performing more than one "valet" function, such as, shoe repairing and hat blocking. A noteworthy discrepancy exists between the occurrence of shops advertising credit on the two Negro business thoroughfares, and this may or may not be totally explained by the fact that on 47th Street such shops usually dealt in new (as opposed to secondhand) women's clothing. Stores selling previously-unused women's clothing are again to be found in greater numbers on 125th Street rather than on 8th Avenue.

Conclusion

Many of the observations and interpretations in this study have been presented in a most tenuous terminology. To some degree this has been done intentionally. The singular atmosphere imparted to the low-income Negro business thoroughfare by its shopkeepers and clientele is more than a result of cultural characteristics and externally-imposed economic conditions. It is also a consequence of the aggregate behavior and needs of a particular group of individuals. When interpreting a landscape whose impact is to some extent determined by the unique behavior of individuals one cannot employ ultimates, absolutes, or incontrovertible arguments.

Nevertheless, the distinctive (but *not* necessarily unique) land uses of the "Black Belt's" 47th Street, Harlem's 8th Avenue, and other low-income Negro business thoroughfares, may be grouped into four categories. First, there are those land uses which to some extent are a response to the needs of certain Negro personality types which are in one way or another concerned with personal appearance; beauty parlors and barbershops, dry cleaners and associated "valet" services, and stores specializing in tailor-made men's apparel may be included in this category. Second, there are those land-use types whose very preponderance mirrors extremely low standards of living; independent groceries and stores with disassociated uses are included in this category. Third, there are those uses whose rate of occurrence in some way tends to confirm stereotypes of the Negro held by various segments of the white population; this group comprises billiard parlors, record shops, and storefront churches, and, in each case, there is evidence to suggest that the explanation does not necessarily lie within the framework of stereotyped personality traits. Finally, there are those land uses which have the same relative frequency on business thoroughfares located in both low-income white and low-income Negro areas, but whose exterior appearance differs considerably between areas; bars, cheap restaurants, and possibly loan and pawn establishments fall into this classification.

Acknowledgment

The photographs were taken by Robert Tennant and James Simmons.

SOCIAL CLASS SEGREGATION AMONG NONWHITES IN METROPOLITAN CENTERS

LEO F. SCHNORE
University of Wisconsin

RESUMEN

Es bien conocido que en las ciudades de Estados Unidos ha habido segregación residencial entre la población blanca y negra. Este estudio trata de determinar el grado de esta segregación dentro de áreas habitadas por negros, de acuerdo a diferentes estratos socio-económicos. En 24 ciudades seleccionadas, se calculó para la población de color, la composicion educacional, de ingreso y ocupación en zonas sucesivas fuera de los límites de la ciudad central. Esto se hizo usando areas censales, agrupándolas en zonas de acuerdo a la distancia. En las ciudades industriales del norte se encontró que el status socio-económico de las comunidades de color era mas alto, mientras mas alejadas estuvieran del centro de la ciudad. Este mismo fenómeno sucede en las ciudades que quedan en el límite del norte y sur. En el sur existe este tipo de segregación pero no sigue el comportamiento zonal. Lo mismo sucede en las ciudades del oeste. Las razones de esta diferencia no son fáciles de enunciar se necesita mayor investigación, incluyendo un análisis histórico.

A rather clear-cut segregation of color groups is a "fact of life" within large cities in all parts of the United States. Whites and nonwhites are residentially segregated from each other.[1] We also know that urban populations are residentially segregated according to social class. The wealthy do not ordinarily live side by side with the poor in the community at large. In part, of course, the residential segregation of *color* groups is a *class* phenomenon. Despite recent advances in income, for example, most Negroes simply cannot afford life in "suburbia," no matter how much they might like to move out of the crowded ghettos of the metropolitan centers.

These facts lead to some interesting questions: (1) Does residential segregation according to social class exist *within* color groups? (2) More particularly, are the social classes segregated within the nonwhite ghetto? In other words, does the force of color segregation today operate to oblige nonwhites of widely different social status to live side by side?

Such questions have been raised repeatedly by social scientists; studies have been carried out again and again, in the North and in the South, in small towns and in large cities. For example, small southern towns in the thirties were usually characterized by social scientists as so rigidly segregated according to color that class segregation could not be expressed. Speaking of one such town she had studied, the anthropologist Hortense Powdermaker referred to the area "Across the tracks, where side by side live the respectable and the disreputable, the moderately well-to-do and the very poor, the pious and the unsaved, the college graduates and the illiterates ... all thrown together because all are Negroes."[2] Given the sweeping social changes since that time, in the South and elsewhere, it may be worth our while to consider some of these questions again.

RESIDENTIAL SEGREGATION BY SOCIAL CLASS WITHIN THE NONWHITE GHETTO

The framework for this study was supplied some forty years ago by a group of sociologists working at the University of Chicago. One of these men—Professor Ernest W. Burgess—set out an account of urban community development that came to be known as the concentric-zonal hypothesis. His hypothesis represented an attempt to describe some consequences of growth and radial expansion for changing land uses, residential and nonresidential,

---

[1] See Karl E. Taeuber, "Negro Residential Segregation: Trends and Measurement," *Social Problems*, XII (Summer, 1964), pp. 42–50.

[2] Hortense Powdermaker, *After Freedom* (New York: Viking Press, 1939), p. 13.

126

and his stylized map of Chicago has been frequently reproduced, appearing again and again in social science textbooks.

For our purposes, the most interesting portion of the Burgess hypothesis concerns the changing residential distribution of "social classes." Stated most succinctly, his idea was that growth of the city core and extension of the urban periphery set off "waves of succession." New groups of in-migrants, low in income, education, and occupational standing, settled in and around the central business district; as these groups worked their way *up* in the social class structure, they worked their way *out* toward the periphery, only to be "succeeded" by other more recent arrivals. As long as this process continued, then, one would expect to find people with higher income, education, and occupational standing living farther out from the center. As one examines a map of the city, and moves his eye from the center toward the edge in any direction, progressively higher status groups should be found.[3]

Does the Burgess pattern appear within subcommunities? Sometimes it does. One of the earliest uses of census statistics in *testing* the Burgess hypothesis was made by one of his students at the University of Chicago, and it happens to have been concerned with the Negro ghetto. In a doctoral dissertation on *The Negro Family in Chicago*, the late E. Franklin Frazier examined 1920 census statistics and other materials for the "Black Belt" that stretched southward from the Loop.[4] Some years later, and in another book dealing with the American Negro, Frazier summed up his earlier findings on Chicago in this way:

> The expansion of the Negro community was similar, on the whole, to that of other racial and cultural groups. The Negroes had gained a foothold in and near the center of the city and as the city expanded, the segregation of the Negro population was part of the general process of segregation of different racial, economic, and cultural groups. Moreover, as the Negro community moved southward [toward the edge of Chicago] there was a process of selection and segregation of various elements in the Negro community on the basis of occupation, intelligence, and ambition. ... It was possible to measure the process of selection and segregation in the Negro community in 1920 by dividing the community into zones coinciding more or less with the expansion of the city as a whole.[5]

Tables and maps prepared by Frazier suggest a rather regular progression upward in various measures of socio-economic status with increasing distance from the Loop.[6]

One might ask, however, whether or not this pattern has been observed within Chicago's "Black Belt" *since* 1920. It has. Subsequent studies, using somewhat different methods, have confirmed the fact that it has persisted in a general way as the "Black Belt" has expanded. Two of these studies are reported in *Black Metropolis*, by St. Clair Drake and Horace R. Cayton, and in *The Negro Population of Chicago*, by Otis Dudley Duncan and Beverly Duncan, and they make use of 1930 and 1950 census materials, respectively.[7]

A more critical question, however, concerns the extent to which we can generalize about this matter in American cities

[3] Ernest W. Burgess, "The Growth of the City: An Introduction to a Research Project," *Publications of the American Sociological Society,* XVIII (1924), pp. 85–97; reprinted in Robert E. Park, Ernest W. Burgess, and Roderick D. McKenzie, *The City* (Chicago: University of Chicago Press, 1925), pp. 47–62.

[4] *The Negro Family in Chicago* (Chicago: University of Chicago Press, 1932).

[5] *The Negro in the United States* (New York: Macmillan, 1949), pp. 257–58.

[6] Some of these materials have been reproduced in a posthumously published essay; see Frazier, "The Negro Family in Chicago," in Ernest W. Burgess and Donald J. Bogue (eds.), *Contributions to Urban Sociology* (Chicago: University of Chicago Press, 1964), esp. Table 1, p. 407.

[7] St. Clair Drake and Horace R. Cayton, *Black Metropolis; A Study of Negro Life in a Northern City* (New York: Harcourt, Brace & Co., 1945); Otis Dudley Duncan and Beverly Duncan, *The Negro Population of Chicago: A Study of Residential Succession* (Chicago: University of Chicago Press, 1957), esp. pp. 278–98.

128 DEMOGRAPHY

other than Chicago. Frazier himself examined this question in later years, setting out some brief accounts, mostly impressionistic, of color *and* class segregation in northern and southern cities in the twenties, thirites and forties.[8] A solidly based inquiry, confined to ten large cities and looking at a number of other ethnic minority groups as well as Negroes, was published more recently by Lieberson. In this study, Lieberson examined long-term trends, as revealed in census statistics, up to and including 1950.[9]

But what is the situation in nonwhite ghettos *today?* As we all know, the fifties comprised a decade of remarkable changes in relations between white and nonwhites in all parts of the country. Moreover, Lieberson and Frazier and others have shown us that such patterns as can be observed with census statistics do not "hold still" for us; equally important, they have shown that there are variations from one city to another at any one point in time.

METHODS AND LIMITATIONS OF THIS STUDY

Unfortunately, not many cities can be subjected to a comparable mode of analysis with published census tract statistics. Census tract statistics have distinct limitations for this type of study. Census tracts, of course, are small areas into which large cities and adjacent areas have been divided for statistical purposes. They vary in size and shape; they are not easily arranged into neat distance zones. Although census tract publications give considerable detail on such matters as income, education, and occupation, there are inevitable problems stemming from nonresponse, deliberate distortion, and so forth. The use of self-enumeration, sampling, and electronic computer processing in the 1960 census did not solve all these problems. In some of the very areas we are considering—nonwhite ghettos—the mobility of the population, lower-than-average levels of literacy, and technical problems involved in field enumeration and mechanical allocation of nonresponse combined to yield new difficulties. There is published evidence of such problems having arisen in certain parts of Chicago's "Black Belt," for example.[10] This fact makes comparisons with earlier studies of Chicago less than perfectly precise, and it gives us another reason for wanting to look at more than just one large city.

In any case, we have examined 1960 census tract statistics in the areas of heaviest nonwhite concentration within a number of large metropolitan centers. We selected only those tracts which (1) contained at least 400 nonwhites *and* (2) were contiguous to the main areas of nonwhite concentration, that is, the major ghettos. We then eliminated those tracts with unusual population characteristics, such as those containing large institutional populations.[11] Finally, we tabulated the data—for nonwhites only—by combining tracts within radial distance zones, based on a one-mile interval, and (except in

[8] Frazier, *The Negro in the United States*, pp. 229–72.

[9] Stanley Lieberson, *Ethnic Patterns in American Cities* (New York: Free Press of Glencoe, 1963).

[10] See U.S. Bureau of the Census, *U.S. Censuses of Population and Housing: 1960, Census Tracts*, Final Report PHC (1)-26 (Washington: Government Printing Office, 1962), Appendix Table A, "Percent of Persons in Sample and Percent of Persons with Sample Information, for Census Tracts in Chicago City: 1960," pp. 675–78. Chicago was the only city for which such a tabulation was published.

The extent of the under-reporting of sample information can be seen in some of the "Black Belt" tracts:

Census Tract Number	Percent of Persons with Sample Information
357	55.4
368	63.8
369	59.6
372	51.4
516	65.0
573	66.2
574	68.4
579	61.2
880	61.8
898	63.1

[11] Tracts eliminated included those with majorities of the nonwhite population living in group quarters—people living in "rooming houses, college dormitories, military barracks, or institutions" (*ibid.*, p. 3).

New York City) centered on the heart of each central business district.[12] The results are presented in the form of averages for the nonwhite populations of the various distance zones.

The three measures of socio-economic status used in this study comprise a familiar set—income, education, and occupation. *Income* here means family income rather than individual income. *Education* refers to the number of school years completed by persons aged 25 years and over. Only the *occupation* of employed males aged 14 and over was considered. The three tables accompanying this paper report simple proportions for each zone of each named metropolitan center. As noted, these proportions are averages for each distance zone, and each of them conceals

[12] Census tracts identified as part of the "central business district" in each city are listed in U.S. Bureau of the Census, *U.S. Census of Business*, Vol. VII, *Central District Report*, Summary Report BC58-CBD 98, Revised (Washington: Government Printing Office, 1961), Appendix 3.

a certain amount of intra-zonal variation, that is, there are differences from tract to tract within each zone. Moreover, each of the three measures comes from sample statistics rather than" complete-count" data, and this fact introduces another element of variability.

FINDINGS

The entries in Table 1 show the percentage of all nonwhite families in each zone reporting an aggregate income of $7,000 or more in the calendar year preceding the 1960 census. Similarly, the entries in Table 2 show for each zone the percentage of all nonwhite persons aged 25 or over who reported that they had completed twelve or more years of formal schooling. Finally, Table 3 shows for each zone the percentage of all employed nonwhite males aged 14 or over who reported that they worked in occupations classified by the census as (a) professional; (b) owners, managers, and officials; (c) cleri-

Table 1.—PERCENT WITH FAMILY INCOME OF $7,000 OR MORE IN 1959, BY DISTANCE FROM CENTRAL BUSINESS DISTRICT, NONWHITE FAMILIES, TWENTY-FOUR SELECTED CITIES, 1960

Miles	NORTH								SOUTHWEST		WEST	
	New York	Chicago	Detroit	Philadelphia	Cleveland	Indianapolis	Newark	Buffalo	Dallas	Houston	San Francisco	Los Angeles
0-1	}9.3	}12.2	3.3	8.2	11.8	11.4	13.5	7.9	}5.5	4.2	24.3	}14.8
1-2			6.7	12.4	10.8	15.2	17.5	12.5		8.2	20.4	
2-3	12.8	11.8	10.7	15.4	19.1	16.1	33.8	22.1	7.9	19.6	28.7	19.3
3-4	13.6	16.2	15.7	26.1	29.3	25.9	37.4	32.3	5.5	7.2	27.0	21.8
4-5	18.8	20.4	21.2	26.2	36.0	46.0			5.0	8.6	34.2	29.6
5-6	18.8	27.9	23.7	29.8	46.1					10.8	44.2	34.3
6-7	22.5	26.8	27.3	37.5							27.1	35.6
7-8	15.0	27.7	30.8									34.1
8-9	11.3	41.2										16.3
9-10	---	50.4										29.5
10-11	25.6	45.6										
11-12	40.0	54.6										
12-13	46.9											

Miles	BORDER						SOUTH				
	Washington	St. Louis	Kansas City	Baltimore	Cincinnati	Louisville	Atlanta	Richmond	New Orleans	Birmingham	Memphis
0-1	12.6	1.8	4.1	7.0	4.7	4.0	5.1	4.0	5.8	2.3	1.9
1-2	19.1	4.1	7.9	11.2	9.6	8.3	8.0	10.9	6.5	8.2	4.2
2-3	24.4	9.4	17.4	21.2	15.1	12.7	10.6	10.4	10.3	10.5	5.4
3-4	35.1	15.7	17.3	27.5	29.1	16.1	14.9	10.4	8.7	5.0	8.0
4-5	41.0	21.4	28.7							7.0	34.3
5-6	28.0									8.2	4.0

339

cal; or (*d*) sales. In sociological parlance, these are "white-collar" as opposed to "blue-collar" occupations.

The various metropolitan centers have been grouped according to the broader regions in which they are located. It will be seen immediately that these are *not* the "regions" traditionally recognized in census publications over the years. Note that a "border" region is designated in the tables. The "border" cities are those which have been repeatedly identified as "way stations" in the literature dealing with the northward migration of southern Negroes over the years or as cities "caught between North and South" as far as social and cultural influences are concerned.[13] The four main quadrants of each table have been arranged in a way that permits a quick grasp of the major findings. In each column of figures—zonal percentages for each named metropolitan center—the highest percentages have been italicized.

As expected, the Burgess pattern was found to be quite general as far as Northern metropolitan centers were concerned. The upper-left quadrant in each table shows that the highest value occurs in the outermost zone in twenty-two out of twenty-four instances. In general, there is an upward-sloping gradient with increasing distance from the center. If we ignore minor deviations, it is safe to say that the nonwhite ghettos in large northern cities still tend to display the pattern observed earlier in considering Chicago. That is, *as distance increases from the center of the city, the socio-economic status of nonwhite neighborhoods goes up. Nonwhite family income is higher, nonwhite educational levels mount, and the relative number of nonwhite males in "white-collar" employment increases.*

Some of the deviations just characterized as "minor" are quite interesting, for example, the obvious tendency in a number of cities for the first or innermost zone to exhibit higher values than the next. Some of these departures from a "perfect" pattern are apparently attributable to urban renewal programs focused on the "blighted cores" in and around central business districts. In other cases, deviations stem from the fact that nonwhites other than Negroes are included in the study.

The exception to be stressed in this group of eight northern cities concerns the case of New York City. Tables 2 and 3 suggest a rather marked departure from a perfect pattern. When graphed, the data on education and occupation approximate a U-shaped pattern rather than an upward-sloping gradient with distance from the center. This is mainly attributable to the fact that tracts throughout the entire city were classified according to distance from a *single* point—the midpoint of the southern border of Central Park in Manhattan. Actually, substantial concentrations of nonwhites are now found in four of the five boroughs of the city of New York—not just in Harlem and the Lower East Side of Manhattan, as in the past.[14]

If we turn now to the data for the "border" cities—represented in the lower-left quadrant—we see the Burgess pattern manifested again. In five out of the six cities, the highest values appear in the outermost distance zones. Again, there is generally an upward-sloping gradient. Washington, D.C., is a clear-cut exception, showing three out of three deviations from the pattern found in the other five border cities. In general, however, *nonwhite ghettos in large border cities tend to resemble those in cities of the North, insofar as internal "class segregation" is concerned.*

As for Washington itself, the widely noted influx of nonwhites into the city, especially since World War II, is apparently the main cause of the deviation from a perfect zonal pattern. Nonwhites have

---

[13] Frazier, *The Negro in the United States*; see also T. J. Woofter, Jr. (ed.), *Negro Problems in Cities* (Garden City, N.Y.: Doubleday, Doran and Co., 1928); Charles S. Johnson, *Patterns of Negro Segregation* (New York: Harper & Bros., 1943); Robert C. Weaver, *The Negro Ghetto* (New York: Harcourt, Brace & Co., 1948).

[14] Oscar Handlin, *The Newcomers: Negroes and Puerto Ricans in a Changing Metropolis* (Cambridge, Mass.: Harvard University Press, 1959).

Table 2.—PERCENT COMPLETING HIGH SCHOOL, BY DISTANCE FROM CENTRAL BUSINESS DISTRICT, NONWHITE POPULATION AGED 25 AND OVER, TWENTY-FOUR SELECTED CITIES, 1960

Miles	NORTH								SOUTHWEST		WEST	
	New York	Chicago	Detroit	Philadelphia	Cleveland	Indianapolis	Newark	Buffalo	Dallas	Houston	San Francisco	Los Angeles
0-1	}37.0	}17.1	12.5	12.4	16.9	14.2	16.4	16.2	}23.6	22.2	27.3	}28.6
1-2			15.0	16.4	16.3	20.9	21.1	17.7		26.7	34.6	
2-3	27.2	16.9	16.4	21.1	26.2	26.0	32.0	26.5	25.4	45.1	37.8	37.1
3-4	24.9	22.1	23.2	35.6	35.0	32.2	42.3	36.7	25.5	31.6	36.5	37.6
4-5	30.0	21.7	30.5	30.6	39.1	52.2			19.7	21.3	49.1	44.7
5-6	26.7	28.2	34.1	35.1	46.9					22.8	50.5	52.3
6-7	32.1	30.0	35.2	47.8							36.0	52.7
7-8	25.2	33.1	38.2									38.7
8-9	23.5	41.1										30.0
9-10	---	52.5										37.7
10-11	34.3	46.6										
11-12	45.9	50.5										
12-13	51.4											

Miles	BORDER						SOUTH				
	Washington	St. Louis	Kansas City	Baltimore	Cincinnati	Louisville	Atlanta	Richmond	New Orleans	Birmingham	Memphis
0-1	18.1	11.5	16.8	8.4	6.1	12.6	10.4	16.8	11.2	11.5	11.0
1-2	25.7	11.0	23.5	12.9	11.9	17.7	20.1	17.3	13.5	21.5	13.1
2-3	27.6	16.6	33.1	22.1	26.8	32.2	29.3	22.2	17.7	23.4	14.9
3-4	42.3	25.5	36.2	32.0	36.3	32.4	29.1	17.9	15.0	18.4	16.7
4-5	50.7	32.5	46.2							19.0	17.3
5-6	35.8									19.6	14.0

Table 3.—PERCENT EMPLOYED IN WHITE-COLLAR OCCUPATIONS, BY DISTANCE FROM CENTRAL BUSINESS DISTRICT, EMPLOYED NONWHITE MALES AGED 14 AND OVER, TWENTY-FOUR SELECTED CITIES, 1960

Miles	NORTH								SOUTHWEST		WEST	
	New York	Chicago	Detroit	Philadelphia	Cleveland	Indianapolis	Newark	Buffalo	Dallas	Houston	San Francisco	Los Angeles
0-1	}35.0	}11.2	7.6	13.2	10.1	6.4	11.0	6.6	}8.6	7.3	26.5	}21.7
1-2			9.7	12.4	8.0	9.4	9.6	6.0		12.4	22.4	
2-3	24.1	11.8	8.9	14.5	13.4	13.9	14.9	11.5	12.3	22.4	22.0	26.5
3-4	21.8	15.1	10.8	23.5	16.2	15.1	26.1	25.0	10.3	9.4	20.0	22.6
4-5	24.3	13.1	14.6	24.8	20.5	32.0			7.7	8.9	30.9	27.9
5-6	18.3	16.2	15.4	23.3	25.5					10.6	31.5	30.4
6-7	21.5	16.7	18.6	32.8							17.5	39.1
7-8	17.4	17.0	18.6									17.9
8-9	16.5	22.2										12.0
9-10	---	33.0										17.3
10-11	22.2	30.2										
11-12	27.0	33.2										
12-13	32.4											

Miles	BORDER						SOUTH				
	Washington	St. Louis	Kansas City	Baltimore	Cincinnati	Louisville	Atlanta	Richmond	New Orleans	Birmingham	Memphis
0-1	16.2	11.5	7.8	11.7	6.7	6.9	6.2	9.5	8.5	5.7	7.7
1-2	18.7	8.4	10.5	11.1	9.6	7.6	10.3	13.5	12.4	11.3	9.3
2-3	19.6	11.7	15.1	13.5	15.7	14.5	15.9	14.4	12.8	11.5	9.1
3-4	32.1	17.4	18.2	21.8	19.5	17.3	20.2	11.3	11.9	7.5	11.2
4-5	39.4	17.7	23.0							6.7	11.7
5-6	25.7									9.5	4.4

spread from "traditional Negro neighborhoods" into formerly white neighborhoods throughout much of the city. The changes that have occurred there do not represent a steady progression away from the center and toward the periphery in only one or two directions, as in most other northern and border cities.

When we turn to the large cities of the South, where most nonwhites are Negroes, quite a different pattern appears. Examination of the lower-right quadrants in the three tables reveals that four out of five cities display a certain consistency: *moving away from the center of the city, nonwhite areas show a rise in socio-economic status, followed by a decline.*

Atlanta constitutes a clear-cut exception; the values are highest in the outermost zone in two out of three instances, and in the case of education (Table 2) the difference between the third and the fourth zone is trivial. In short, Atlanta resembles the northern and border cities in the study more than it resembles the other four southern cities.

There is no ready explanation for *either* (1) the "southern pattern," or lack of pattern, revealed in these four cities *or* (2) Atlanta's departure from the regional configuration. In any case, the writer is not sufficiently familiar with southern cities to hazard any *ad hoc* "explanations" of the differences. An examination of the literature dealing with nonwhite areas in southern cities, supplemented by conversations with knowledgeable people from the South, has produced quite a long list of factors that *may* explain the similarities and the differences. Most of these seem to involve "history" over the short or long run; they include such factors as changing patterns of migration and residential mobility on the part of both whites and nonwhites, the impact of urban renewal and slum clearance, and the location of Negro colleges and universities.

Up to this point, we have talked only about "southern" *versus* "northern" patterns of class segregation within nonwhite subcommunities, noting that "border" cities tend to resemble cities in the North. We should probably be surprised if clear-cut differences *did not* exist between North and South. But some of the dangers attending easy and casual "explanations" of such materials as these are suggested by the remaining quadrant in the tables.

The upper-right quadrant shows data for four metropolitan centers. The first two are in the "Southwest"—Dallas and Houston. In both cases, the patterns of class segregation within nonwhite areas are clearly more similar to comparable areas in southern cities than to northern nonwhite ghettos. Perhaps this will come as no surprise to those who are familiar with these two cities, but the results do tend to contradict assertions to the effect that developments of the forties and fifties had made both Dallas and Houston much less "southern" and more "northern" and/or "western."

As for the metropolitan centers of the Far West, the same upper-right quadrant gives a summary characterization of Los Angeles and the San Francisco–Oakland "Bay Area." Superficially, they would appear to resemble the southwestern and southern cities as far as class segregation within major nonwhite areas is concerned. Actually, the data are not unequivocal. In the case of Los Angeles, there are a number of problems of interpretation because of the many peculiarities in the legal city limits. A long series of annexations of territory, and the persistence of enclaves like Beverly Hills, would make an analysis of city tracts alone very difficult, and the results would not be very meaningful. But ignoring the city's legal boundaries, as in this study, requires the use of many odd-shaped census tracts.[16] In the Bay

[16] For a detailed study of this area, see Dorothy Slade Williams, *Ecology of Negro Communities in Los Angeles County: 1940–1959* (unpublished doctoral dissertation, Department of Sociology, University of Southern California, 1961). Williams examined data for 1940 and 1950 and found that "Educational attainment of communities showed no progressive rate of increase or decrease with greater distance from the city center outward" (p. 148).

Area, we have given separate consideration to San Francisco and Oakland. In any case, the situation can be summed up very briefly: (1) San Francisco reveals the "northern" pattern in only one out of three instances. (2) Oakland's three "deviations" from the same pattern seem almost entirely due to the influence of the University of California at Berkeley, Oakland's "neighbor." The Berkeley ghetto is included in the data for Oakland, and even though tracts with large numbers of students were eliminated, the impact of the university's presence is still quite evident.

One last point: the "nonwhite areas" in metropolitan centers of the Far West are not at all like the "Negro ghettos" in some other parts of the country. The same thing can be said for Dallas and Houston. For one thing, ethnic minority groups other than Negroes are present in large numbers. In Dallas and Houston, there are substantial numbers of Mexican-Americans, most of whom are white according to census terminology. The areas most heavily occupied by persons of Mexican descent in these two cities happen to overlap the nonwhite areas of concentration rather considerably. The same thing can be said for Los Angeles, with the added qualification that nonwhite persons of Oriental descent are also present in large numbers; this complicates the question of "class segregation" considerably. Finally, all these groups are well represented in the San Francisco–Oakland Bay Area. This caveat is inserted to prevent possible misunderstandings concerning the implications of the observed patterns in these cities.

CONCLUSIONS

We found a pattern of class segregation *within* a number of nonwhite areas that is very familiar to all students of the American city; it can be summed up as, "The higher up the social ladder, the farther out you live." Perhaps even more important, however, is the fact that we found variations. The *regional* variations stressed in this paper are perhaps the most interesting of all the differences from city to city so evident in the data presented here.

A number of scholars have diligently pursued the quite diverse historical forces that lie behind these gross differences in pattern, forces which deserve continuing attention in research on the American city. There is no quick and easy substitute for detailed historical study—and in as much "depth" as our data permit. It is hoped that the comparative materials presented here will provide a framework within which detailed historical studies of individual cities will become more meaningful.[16]

[16] See Williams, *ibid.*, and Karl E. Taeuber and Alma F. Taeuber, "The Negro as an Immigrant Group: Recent Trends in Racial and Ethnic Segregation in Chicago," *American Journal of Sociology*, LXIX (January, 1964), pp. 383–94.